POLICY-MAKERS
AND CRITICS

Conflicting Theories of
American Foreign Policy
Second Edition

Cecil V. Crabb, Jr.

New York
Westport, Connecticut
London

Library of Congress Cataloging-in-Publication Data

Crabb, Cecil Van Meter, 1924–
  Policy-makers and critics.

  Includes index.
  1. United States — Foreign relations — 1945–
I. Title.
JX1417.C7 1986   327.73   86-16901
ISBN 0-275-92209-X (alk. paper)
ISBN 0-275-92210-3 (pbk. : alk. paper)

Library of Congress Catalog Card Number: 86-16901
ISBN: 0-275-92209-X
ISBN: 0-275-92210-3

First published in 1986 (pbk.)

Praeger Publishers, 521 Fifth Avenue, New York, NY 10175
A division of Greenwood Press, Inc.

Printed in the United States of America

∞

The paper used in this book complies with the Permanent
Paper Standard issued by the National Information Standards
Organization (Z39.48-1984).

10 9 8 7 6 5 4 3 2 1

Contents

Introduction

What principles ought to guide the foreign policy of the United States in responding to an increasingly turbulent, unstable, and violence-prone world?

This fundamental question provides the central focus of our study. If anything, the question has become more urgent and — in the light of the traumatic Vietnam War episode — more difficult for U.S. citizens today than when the first edition of *Policy-Makers and Critics* was published in 1976.

The informed student of the nation's diplomatic history would be hardpressed to recall a period in which public and official opinion appeared to be as uncertain and confused about the proper diplomatic role of the United States as in the post-Vietnam War era. Studies of U.S. public opinion, for example, use terms like "self-doubt" and "disarray" and "dissensus" to describe national attitudes toward foreign policy questions. By the mid 1980s, on almost every major issue facing the United States abroad, President Ronald Reagan confronted disunity among his own executive advisers, between the White House and Congress, and among the people of the United States concerning the nation's correct diplomatic course.

In turn, these doubts usually revolved around two specific questions. What goals should the United States seek to achieve beyond its own borders? What means should national leaders employ to attain these goals? On the latter issue, the role of military force in implementing U.S. diplomatic goals was more than ordinarily controversial after the Vietnam War.

Stated differently, in the post-Vietnam War era, most informed citizens and their leaders had a reasonably clear idea about what they wanted the United States to avoid in foreign affairs. A majority of U.S. citizens thought the ship of state must steer a diplomatic course between two hazards. One of these is exemplified by the determination to avoid "another Munich" or "another Pearl Harbor" abroad — dangers that were uppermost in the minds of successive presidents from World War II until the end of the Vietnam War. For a generation, the nation's diplomatic "mistakes" before World War II served as indelible lessons influencing U.S. attitudes and behavior toward foreign affairs in the postwar period.

The traumatic and internally divisive Vietnam War episode, however, focused attention upon a different set of diplomatic dangers for the United States. These dangers included the risk of becoming "overcommitted" and "overextended" abroad, of basing the nation's conduct overseas upon "the illusion of U.S. 'omnipotence,'" and of allowing the "national interests" of the United States to become steadily inflated, without reference to those interests that were truly vital and to those that were quite clearly less important.

After Vietnam, for millions of Americans the transcendent lesson, perhaps, was that the United States must become more discriminating and selective in assuming overseas obligations. Yet if doubt existed about the matter during most of the 1970s, by the end of the decade a majority of Americans also believed that, despite the Vietnam episode, the United States remained a superpower. More specifically, this meant that the United States had vital strategic and diplomatic interests abroad that sometimes had to be protected by military force, that expansionism by the Soviet Union and its clients still must be contained, that the diplomatic credibility of the United States needed to be restored and maintained, and that Washington must possess the power required for achieving these and other objectives.

Broad national recognition that the United States must avoid these two diplomatic hazards, however, leaves wide latitude for debate concerning the principles that should govern the nation's diplomatic activity. Toward particular problems, such as ongoing political upheaval in Central America, public and official attitudes in recent years have been clearly ambivalent and confused. On the one hand, relatively few Americans believed that the United States could ignore such problems as political instability, economic backwardness, poverty, Communist machinations, and other challenges existing throughout Central America. On the other hand, recalling the recent reverse in Southeast Asia, Americans also demanded that national leaders avoid another Vietnam in Latin America. Citizens were clearly apprehensive about large-scale military intervention by the United States in other countries; implicitly, they conceded that Washington could not single-handedly solve Central America's pervasive and deep-seated problems. Not untypically perhaps, the people and their representatives in Congress were considerably clearer about what they did not want executive officials to do abroad than about the specific actions they wanted the president and his advisers to take to achieve U.S. diplomatic objectives. Without knowing quite how, Americans expected national leaders to avoid another Munich and another Vietnam concurrently.

Our analysis of alternative approaches to U.S. foreign policy begins with an examination in Chapter 1 of the "isolationist" mentality in the nation's diplomatic tradition. Even today, better understanding of isolationist thought offers useful insights into U.S. diplomatic behavior. It is essential to recall, for example, that the isolationist mentality dominated the U.S. approach toward the Old World for more than 150 years, approximately four times longer than the U.S. society has operated upon an "internationalist" approach to foreign relations.

In the next two chapters, and again in the final chapter, contemporary varieties of isolationist (or neo-isolationist) thinking are identified and examined in detail. In Chapter 2, the main tenets of the conservative version of neo-isolationism are specified and evaluated. A different species of neo-isolationism — advocated by liberally oriented individuals and groups — is analyzed in Chapter 3. Then in Chapter 6, brief attention is directed to the revival of neo-isolationist thinking witnessed in the period immediately following the Vietnam War.

Chapter 4 deals with the concept of *Realpolitik* and its application to recent U.S. foreign policy. The leading principles of political realism are identified; then the pros and cons of basing U.S. diplomacy upon *Realpolitik* teachings are assessed.

The liberal-humanitarian impulse to interventionist behavior by the United States is the theme of Chapter 5. As the evidence makes clear, both before and after World War II political liberals within the U.S. society have time and again called upon national leaders to engage in interventionist behavior abroad.

In a new Chapter 6, considerable attention is devoted to a transcendent question confronting U.S. foreign policy in the post-Vietnam War era. This is the problem of formulating a rationale for using the nation's military force in behalf of foreign policy objectives.

Most U.S. citizens would agree with the abstract proposition that in foreign affairs the United States must avoid another Vietnam. Concurrently, however, the people of the United States also believe that it is essential for the United States to pursue other goals — such as containing Soviet expansionism, preserving Western access to the Persian Gulf area, and endeavoring to achieve some minimal degree of political stability in Central America — that involve major U.S. commitments abroad.

After the Vietnam conflict, what principles ought to govern the application of U.S. power abroad? How should the national interest of the United States be redefined in order to avoid the kind of overextension of national power that led to the Vietnam quagmire? In the post-Vietnam War era, what sense of geographical or regional priorities ought to influence the foreign policy of the United States? These and other fundamental questions concerning U.S. foreign policy are considered fully in Chapter 6.

Intentionally, this book offers no answers or ready-made solutions for the difficult problems and dilemmas confronting the United States in foreign affairs. As the reader will discover, the choices confronting policy-makers are almost never clearcut or easy. Any proposed course of action abroad poses moral-ethical dilemmas, and all available alternatives will entail undesirable consequences. As an experienced State Department official, Charles B. Marshall, observed several years ago, defining the national interest in a particular case usually involves choosing a course of action that meets a twofold test. It entails the least damage to the nation, and it offers at least a reasonable prospect of achieving some positive results.

As is emphasized in Chapter 6, perhaps the term that best describes the U.S. approach to foreign affairs is "pragmatic." On the basis of the nation's diplomatic experience since World War II, it is a safe prediction that the foreign policy of any incumbent administration will consist of some combination or synthesis of the approaches to U.S. diplomacy examined in these pages.

1

The Isolationist Heritage

On June 12, 1783, the Congress of the United States resolved that "the true interests of these states [i.e., the United States] require that they should be as little as possible entangled in the politics and controversies of European nations."[1]

Thirteen years later, in one of the most celebrated state papers in the nation's history, President George Washington's Farewell Address, Americans were solemnly warned against "permanent antipathies against particular nations and passionate attachments for others"; instead, the new Republic should cultivate "just and amicable feelings toward all" nations. Then, in what came to be referred to widely in later years as "Washington's rules," the president declared:

> The great rule of conduct for us in regard to foreign nations is, in extending our commercial relations to have with them [the nations of Europe] as little political connection as possible. . . . Europe has a set of primary interests which to us have none or a very remote relation. Hence she must be engaged in frequent controversies, the causes of which are essentially foreign to our corners. Hence, therefore, it must be unwise in us to implicate ourselves by artificial ties in the ordinary vicissitudes of her politics or the ordinary combinations and collisions of her friendships or enmities. . . . It is our true policy to steer clear of permanent alliances with any portion of the foreign world. . . . Taking care always to keep ourselves by suitable establishments on a respectable posture, we may safely trust to temporary alliances for extraordinary emergencies.*

---

*For a detailed excerpt from President Washington's Farewell Address, see Appendix 1.

1

Referring to the existence of warfare in Europe, President Washington reaffirmed the "neutral position" of the United States toward the conflict. A neutral stance would "gain time to our country to settle and mature its yet recent institutions, and to progress without interruption to that degree of strength and consistency which is necessary to give it . . . the command of its own fortunes."

Later presidents and statesmen amplified the meaning of "Washington's rule," applying it to concrete issues that arose in U.S. foreign relations and adapting it to new conditions confronting the United States abroad. Despite a popular tendency to attribute the phrase to Washington, for example, it was President Thomas Jefferson who in 1801 admonished Americans to shun "entangling alliances" with other nations.[2] In a message to Congress on December 2, 1823, President James Monroe reaffirmed and amplified these principles, applying them specifically to the twofold threat of intervention by the Holy Alliance in the Western Hemisphere and Czarist Russia's territorial ambitions in the Pacific Northwest.* In what came to be known in the years thereafter as the Monroe Doctrine, Monroe stated that "the American continents, by the free and independent condition which they have assumed and maintain, are henceforth not to be considered as subjects for future colonization by any European powers." At the same time Monroe pledged, "In the wars of the European powers in matters relating to themselves we have never taken any part, nor does it comport with our policy to do so." He observed that "the political system of the allied [i.e., European] powers is essentially different . . . from that of America." Accordingly, the United States would "consider any attempt on their part to extend their system to any portion of this hemisphere as dangerous to our peace and safety." Yet with Europe's "existing colonies" in the New World, Monroe added, "we have not interfered and shall not interfere."

For more than a century and a half — from the time it declared its independence in 1776 until the outbreak of World War II — the United States was devoted to an "isolationist" position in world affairs.[3] As we shall see, isolationism is not an easy or simple concept to define. Throughout the course of U.S. history, the doctrine acquired numerous implications and tenets, some of which were not always mutually consistent or compatible. From the time of Washington's Farewell Address onward, isolationism was in reality a cluster of attitudes and

---

*The portions of President Monroe's message of December 2, 1823, setting forth the Monroe Doctrine are included in Appendix 2.

assumptions about the proper relationship of the United States with the outside world. Isolationism had several components from the beginning, and every age tended to modify its content as the concept was applied to specific conditions prevailing at home and abroad.

We shall examine the main components or facets of isolationism at a later stage. Meanwhile, two points about the doctrine require emphasis at the outset. The first is that, for approximately 150 years after the United States became an independent nation, a foreign policy of isolationism was viewed by most citizens as an indispensable condition for their national security, the continued success of their democratic experiment, their political stability, and their economic prosperity — in brief, for all the benefits conferred by successful pursuit of the "American way of life." However much they often disagreed upon domestic issues, most Americans subscribed to the view that the "timeless principles" enunciated by Presidents Washington, Jefferson, and Monroe must be adhered to diligently in foreign relations. Continued devotion to them would enable the society to realize the promises implicit in the U.S. society's unique way of life. Conversely, departure from them risked a host of evils: foreign intervention in the political and economic affairs of the nation; the growth of militarism and escalating armaments expenditures; the loss of freedoms guaranteed by the Bill of Rights and other liberties; the emergence of presidential dictatorship and the consequent decline of Congress; a steadily mounting national debt; internal divisiveness and acute political factionalism; economic retrogression, precipitated by the loss of foreign markets — to mention but a few of the dangers that proponents of an isolationist position sought to avoid. As time passed, prominent U.S. historians discerned a direct causal relationship between stability and progress at home and steadfast adherence to a policy of isolationism abroad. Thus one of the nation's most eminent historians in the pre-World War II period, Charles A. Beard, was convinced that an isolationist policy had "enabled the American people to go ahead under the principles of 1776, conquering a continent and building a civilization which, with all its faults, has precious merits for us and is, at all events, our own." Under the shelter provided by this doctrine, Beard was convinced that "human beings were set free to see what they could do on this continent, when emancipated from the privilege-encrusted institutions of Europe and from entanglement in the endless revolutions and wars of that continent."[4]

Some 50 years earlier, the perceptive British observer Lord Bryce had said much the same thing about the United States: "America lives in a world of her own. . . . Safe from attack, safe even from menace, she hears from afar the warring cries of European races and faiths. . . . But for the present at least — it may not always be so — she sails upon a summer sea."[5]

A second point requires emphasis at the outset of our study of the isolationist approach to U.S. foreign relations. Pervasive and deeply rooted as it was until World War II, today isolationism, per se, no longer commands the allegiance of the U.S. society. Following the most destructive global conflict in the history of the world, the Americans and their leaders overwhelmingly rejected an isolationist stance for the United States in the postwar period.[6] One of the most vocal and influential spokesmen for pre-World War II isolationism, Senator Robert A. Taft (Republican of Ohio), said in 1950: "I don't know what they mean by isolationism, nobody is an isolationist today."[7]

The transformation witnessed in the viewpoints of Senator Taft and other political leaders about foreign affairs may be taken as representative of the fundamental shift in U.S. opinion toward the outside world as a result of World War II. A substantial majority of Americans now accepted the fact that after World War II isolationism no longer served as a viable foreign policy posture for the most influential nation on the world scene. Indeed, by the end of World War II, the concept of isolationism not only had few overt adherents; the very term had rapidly fallen into disrepute and had become something of an epithet, signifying myopia toward the course of world events and an unwillingness to accept the most elementary realities about the United States' involvement in them. Thus one of the most tireless champions of the doctrine before World War II, Senator Gerald P. Nye (Republican of North Dakota), said in 1944 that isolationism had become identified with "everything that was bad, terrible, un-American, and indecent."[8]

Admittedly, therefore, it is difficult for the contemporary student of U.S. foreign policy to evaluate the traditional isolationist point of view sympathetically and with due regard for its more positive and beneficial features. Isolationism often seems as relevant for the successful conduct of foreign policy in the modern period as mercantilism for the operation of the economic system or an understanding of pre-Copernican astronomy for insight into the problems of the space age. Yet it is an assumption of this chapter that — even though very few Americans subscribe to an avowedly isolationist position — the nation's more or less consistent adherence to an isolationist stance for more than a century and a half profoundly affected the U.S. approach to foreign relations after World War II, as well as before it.

Even though relatively few Americans regard themselves as isolationists today, the isolationist mode of thought continues to exert a potent influence upon the nation's approach to foreign affairs. In Chapters 2 and 3, we shall examine certain recent manifestations of neo-isolationist attitudes toward foreign relations. Meanwhile, even while they reluctantly acknowledge the necessity for the United States to play an international role commensurate with its position as a superpower, Americans frequently exhibit evidence of isolationist thinking in their approach to international issues. The continued lack of interest of the people of the United States in most international questions and their immersion in domestic affairs; their limited knowledge of most developments beyond the borders of the United States and their disinclination to acquire understanding about them; their ongoing suspicion (reinforced by the results of the Vietnam War) of Washington's reliance upon military force to achieve diplomatic objectives; their according relatively low priority to the State Department in terms of budgetary allocations to federal agencies and programs; their lingering distrust of diplomacy and of those involved in it; their conviction that, in the last analysis, the nation's solution of urgent domestic problems is the most useful contribution that the United States can make to the improvement of the human condition; their continuing deemphasis upon the study of foreign languages in the nation's educational program (including even graduate-level programs) — these are merely a few examples illustrating the persistence of old isolationist habits of mind and thought within the United States. While they acknowledge the practical impossibility of doing so, psychologically and emotionally, even in the late twentieth century, many Americans would unquestionably like to return to the comfortable and carefree era of isolationism, when the nation was largely spared the frustrations and costs inherent in trying to solve the problems of a crisis-ridden world.

THE MANY FACETS OF ISOLATIONISM

A remarkable quality of the concept of isolationism — and a characteristic that was crucial in enabling it to serve as the basis for the nation's foreign policy for more than a century and a half — was the richness and adaptability of the doctrine. During no era of U.S. history did isolationism comprise a coherent, internally consistent body of foreign policy principles. Instead, the exact content of isolationism tended to vary from era to era; even within any given historical period, no two proponents of the doctrine were likely to define it identically. The isolationism of the late eighteenth century Jeffersonian was likely to differ in several important respects from the isolationism espoused by the agrarian radicals a century later, and the foreign policy viewpoints of this latter group in turn could be contrasted at several points with the isolationism of the America First Committee and other groups that attacked the Roosevelt administration's foreign policies during the 1930s. From the time of Washington's Farewell Address onward, there has always been a tendency for isolationism to be defined by reference to concrete policy issues confronting the United States in its foreign and domestic affairs.

Moreover, as Riseselbach has emphasized, isolationist thought could and did exist on several levels. The concept might emphasize the geographic separation of the United States from other continents, particularly Europe. It might stress mainly the U.S. spiritual and philosophical separation from Europe, underscoring the contrast between the progressive "American way of life" versus Europe's stagnant social and economic systems. It might call attention primarily to fundamental political and ideological distinctions between the democracy of the New World and the authoritarian or despotic political systems and ideologies of the Old World. By the twentieth century, isolationism might also have reference to the relative economic self-sufficiency of the United States and its ability to prosper, if need be, without access to the markets of the world. After 1900 isolationism might denote the nation's relative military security and invincibility in the Western Hemisphere. Many of the isolationists of the 1930s, for example, were convinced that an Axis victory in Europe, or even worldwide, posed no serious military consequences for the security of the United States. Isolationism could also convey the inherent apathy and antipathy toward foreign affairs generally vis-à-vis domestic affairs of the Americans. The former was a realm abounding in problems, frustrations, unwanted burdens, and dangers for the U.S. Republic, whereas the latter was a sphere in which the promises and benefits implicit in the "American way of life" could be, and were being, rapidly realized. The isolationism expressed by a particular individual or school of thought might embody an almost infinite combination of these and other elements, or it might give almost exclusive attention to one of the above dimensions of the idea, while largely ignoring other dimensions.

Within these general limitations, let us take note of several specific facets or connotations of the term isolationism, recognizing at all times that the concept never comprised a universally accepted or internally consistent set of foreign policy guidelines. Throughout the course of U.S. history, perhaps the most widely accepted definition for isolationism — the idea viewed by many authorities as its core or most intrinsic meaning — was the idea of diplomatic and military nonentanglement, as illustrated by President Jefferson's admonition in 1801 against "entangling alliances."[9] The variant phrase, "no entangling alliances," in time became the watchword of isolationism and a keynote of the U.S. national credo. After 1800 nearly every U.S. president was compelled to reassure the nation that his policies were designed to avoid entangling alliances with other countries, in conformity with principles enunciated by the Founding Fathers.

Jefferson was merely giving authoritative and forceful expression to a principle, foreshadowed in Washington's Farewell Address, that had already found wide acceptance among Americans and their leaders. Adherence to the principle of no entangling alliances was designed to safeguard the new Republic against a specific danger: involvement in the upheavals that gripped Europe during the period of the French Revolution and the Napoleonic era. French assistance during the American Revolution had been of inestimable importance — some historians have regarded it as absolutely essential — for a U.S. victory and the achievement of independence from England. On February 6, 1778, the United States and France signed a treaty of alliance; according to its terms, the United States was obligated to assist France "forever" in retaining possession of its New World colonies, like the French West Indies.[10] Even before the pact was signed, and even more so while it was in force, French officials had repeatedly intervened in the internal affairs of the United States (vigorous French efforts designed to prevent ratification of the Jay Treaty, signed with England on November 19, 1794, was a case in point). As new conflicts erupted among the European powers at the end of the eighteenth century, there was the real danger that the United States might find itself involved in another war with England to fulfill its obligations under the alliance with France. As had occurred many times in the past, the risk existed that Americans would find themselves entangled once more in a European struggle, in which their interests were secondary to those of the more powerful belligerents and in which their capacity to affect the outcome was minimal. This was the specific danger against which Jefferson's admonition against entangling alliances was directed.

As was not unusual with later principles of U.S. foreign policy (such as those associated with the Monroe Doctrine in 1823), the injunction against entangling alliances, in time, came to be universalized and sanctified into a kind of law. The tendency was to interpret and apply it far more rigidly and indiscriminately than its early advocates had intended. The principle was enunciated, we need to be reminded, in response to a particular set of circumstances that appeared to threaten the security and well-being of the young and vulnerable democracy of the United States. The threat arose from the machinations of European powers. As with nearly all other tenets of isolationism, it was at prevention of U.S. involvement in European conflicts that the maxim was aimed. The specific danger identified was entangling alliances. Neither Washington nor Jefferson, nor any other early statesman had urged the United States to avoid involvement in foreign (and certainly not in foreign economic and commercial) affairs; the injunction of Washington and Jefferson contained no suggestion that the United States could be indifferent to events outside its own borders, take its precarious security for granted, or pretend that its destiny was otherwise unaffected by the behavior of other countries.

A closely related connotation of isolationism from the infancy of the Republic to the period of World War II was preservation of national sovereignty and independence in decision making. Why should the United States avoid entangling alliances with more powerful European states? It should do so primarily because, as a weak and vulnerable country, its independence might be jeoparidzed by close diplomatic and military association with more powerful nations. For example, Secretary of State Timothy Pickering believed that the government of France had aided the colonial cause during the American Revolution chiefly to promote its own interests — a leading French objective being to keep the United States dependent upon France for an indefinite period thereafter.[11]

President Monroe's famous message to Congress (December 2, 1823), laying the foundation for what came to be called the Monroe Doctrine, was directed against two (real or imaginary) dangers: a threatened intervention by the Holy Alliance in Latin America and expansionism by Czarist Russia in the Pacific Northwest. Although the principles enunciated by President Monroe became well known in the years to follow, his paramount concern was the security and independence of the United States.[12] Invited to join with Great Britain in asserting the concepts contained in his doctrine, President Monroe refused. A joint declaration with the vastly more powerful England, Secretary of State John Quincy Adams wrote, would have reduced the United States to "a cock-boat in the wake of the British man-of-war."[13]

Another facet of the doctrine of isolationism was unilateralism; during the 20 years that followed World War I, this was perhaps the doctrine's dominant connotation. According to Paul Seabury, the term signified the United States' "preference for autonomous action in world politics and a disinclination to be bound by alliances or by any supranational agreements committing the nation in advance to policies which might involve the use of force or war."[14] In 1924, Secretary of State Charles Evans Hughes declared that, although the United States was willing to participate in certain forms of international collaboration (like arms reduction), it "would not tolerate the submission of such questions which pertain to our own policy to the determination of any group of Powers. . . . We should not be willing to enter any organization through which a group of Powers would be in a position to intervene to attempt to determine our policies for us."[15] Called the "perfect isolationist," Senator William E. Borah once declared: "What I have opposed from the beginning is any commitment of this nation to a given line of procedure in a future exigency, the facts as to which could not be known before the event."[16]

As war clouds gathered in Europe (and more specifically after Italy invaded Ethiopia in 1935), the Roosevelt administration tried to take limited steps to prevent further aggression. In this process, one commentator has written, Secretary of State Cordell Hull "was careful to avoid any appearance of being led by the League [of Nations]."[17] Irrespective of what the particular U.S. response to Axis expansionism might be — and there was a considerable range of opinion, even among isolationists, on this issue — the United States was required to act unilaterally. It was precluded by the isolationist heritage from using its military, economic, and frequently even its moral influence abroad in concert with other nations.

Still another component or facet of the isolationist credo was its insistence upon the nonparticipation of the United States in foreign wars. In the Monroe Doctrine, President Monroe had declared: "In the wars of the European powers in matters relating to themselves we have never taken any part, nor does it comport with our policy to do so. It is only when our rights are invaded or seriously menaced that we resent injuries or make preparation for our defense."

As with other aspects of the isolationist mentality, the desire of the United States to escape involvement in foreign wars was no abstract principle formulated by the fathers of the Republic. To the contrary, it was a determination that had evolved out of the U.S. society's experience during the colonial period and the early years under the Constitution. The diplomatic historian, Thomas A. Bailey, has noted that between 1689 and 1815 England and France fought each other seven times, engaging in conflict for 60 out of 126 years. Americans had been involved in every one of these major and minor wars, irrespective of their own wishes in the matter.[18] The benefits accruing to Americans from avoidance in Europe's wars had been one of the main advantages of separation from England, as advocated by Thomas Paine in *Common Sense* and by other pre-Revolutionary leaders.[19]

Something of the dominant U.S. attitude on this point is conveyed by President Woodrow Wilson's mental anguish during World War I, after he had prepared his "war message" (presented to Congress on February 26, 1917). According to one historian, Wilson feared that U.S. entry into World War I would "overturn the world we had known."

Until World War II, the connection between staunch adherence to a policy of isolationism and nonparticipation in war was twofold. First, if the U.S. society could successfully avoid becoming embroiled in foreign conflicts, it could escape such evils as infringement upon its independent decision making by more powerful states, a tendency toward militarism at home, the possible loss of such liberties as those incorporated in the Bill of Rights, higher taxes, and distraction from more important and promising domestic pursuits. Second, the evident success of their isolationist stance, in enabling the United States to avoid involvement in major foreign conflicts for more than a century after the War of 1812, tended to confirm Americans in the wisdom of their behavior toward other countries. (As Sheldon Appleton has noted, Americans tended to overlook the fact that for nearly 100 years after the defeat of Napoleon in 1815, there was no general European war!)[20]

Yet, fundamental as it was to the concept of isolationism, we should not imagine that the principle of avoiding war was unqualified or free of ambiguities and limitations. The Monroe Doctrine's provisions, for example, were more heavily qualified than most Americans realized. President Monroe had pledged the United States to abstain from participation in Europe's wars; as with certain other dimensions of the isolationist viewpoint, the restrictions envisioned upon U.S. diplomatic behavior were directed primarily at entanglement in Europe's rivalries and conflicts. But President Monroe had gone even further: he affirmed that the United States would not participate in the "wars of the European powers *in matters relating to themselves* [italics added]." Moreover, he had emphatically warned the European powers that "when our rights are invaded or seriously menaced" the United States would "make preparation for our defense." Despite the mythology that came to surround it, the Monroe Doctrine, in other words, contained no blanket prohibition against U.S. participation in foreign wars. The United States proposed to be a nonbelligerent — or adopt a position of neutrality — (1) toward wars involving the major powers of continental Europe, (2) with regard to disputes that were of concern to these states, (3) so long as the security of the United States was not jeopardized. This is quite literally what President Monroe announced to the world. As time passed, the Americans (not excluding sometimes their leaders) lost sight of the qualifications surrounding the nonbelligerency principle. Thus, President Franklin D. Roosevelt informed the Australian prime minister, Joseph A. Lyons, in 1935 that the United States would never again be drawn into a European war for any reason.[21]

Although the nonbelligerency concept became associated with the isolationist credo, we must not imagine that isolationism was synonymous with pacificism or total indifference toward the problem of national defense and security. As with other specific connotations of the isolationist doctrine, the meaning and relative importance of the nonbelligerency idea tended to vary, depending upon circumstances at home and abroad. Those Americans who opposed interventionism in Europe's conflicts during the 1930s, for example, were convinced that isolationism was a viable diplomatic strategy that would enable the United States to defend its interests and security successfully. For many isolationists, a salient feature of their approach to foreign policy, for example, was the premise that within the Western Hemisphere, the power of the United States was supreme, and it must continue to be supreme. As long as this was the case, U.S. security was not endangered by the Axis powers.[22] Robert E. Sherwood has emphasized that most pre-World War II isolationists were in no sense pacifists. Their attitude toward Japan and Soviet Russia, for example, was sometimes very belligerent. More generally, they favored reliance upon armed force to achieve national policy goals under two conditions: all battles must be waged on so-called home ground of the United States in the Western Hemisphere, and the United States must fight its military engagements alone, without allies, thereby presumably avoiding the mistakes of World War I.[23]

Isolationists of an earlier era had sometimes taken a different view of the proper use of military force for the achievement of U.S. foreign policy objectives. Thus, in the period from the end of the nineteenth century to World War I, one school of thought, typified by Senator Henry Cabot Lodge (Republican of Massachusetts), advocated a large U.S. policy, involving expansionism and territorial annexations. Lodge entered political life at a time when the advantages accruing from U.S. geographic isolation were being undermined by modern means of communication and transportation. In this period the United States was coming of age, emerging as one of the most powerful nations on the globe. A disciple of Admiral Alfred Mahan, foremost U.S. advocate of seapower and of control over sea lanes and bases upon which its effective exercise depended, Lodge called for an energetic and expansionist foreign policy for the United States, entailing a rapid buildup in naval strength, particularly in the Pacific region.[24] Thus, Lodge favored U.S. annexation of Hawaii on strategic-military grounds: possession of these islands gave the United States mastery of the Pacific sea lanes, and the United States had to deny ownership of them to any foreign power.[25] Similarly, on the eve of World War I, Senator William E. Borah urged the Republican party to "make our position strong for America first, for the protection of American rights here and abroad." Responding to President Wilson's assertion (May 10, 1915) that "there is such a thing as a man [or nation] being too proud to fight," Borah stated: "A nation which declares itself too proud to fight will soon be regarded by the nations of the earth as too cowardly to live." In Borah's view, "weakness is a source of war." Borah was the author of the phrase (from which the "America First" movement, one of the most influential organizations during the 1930s, took its name): "America first, let it cost what it may."[26]

In connection with a controversy with Great Britain, on January 21, 1821, Secretary of State John Quincy Adams had informed London: "Keep what is yours, but leave the rest of the [American] Continent to us."[27] This highlights another component of isolationist thought: the idea of continentalism. After independence, one of the goals served by an isolationist stance was filling out the U.S. boundaries westward and extending the hegemony of the United States up to its natural frontiers on the Pacific Ocean, the Canadian border, and the Gulf of Mexico. (Some Americans, of course, believed that eventually Canada, and perhaps Cuba, were destined to form part of the Union.) This aspiration was unquestionably implicit in the noncolonization principle of the Monroe Doctrine and reiterated many times after 1823. As expressed in President James K. Polk's celebrated corollary to the Monroe Doctrine (December 2, 1845), the United States was dedicated to the "settled policy that no future European colony or dominion shall with our consent be planted or established on any part of the North American continent." Polk continued that the United States was committed to

> the principle that the people of this continent alone have the right to decide their own destiny. Should any portion of them, constituting an independent state, propose to unite themselves with our Confederacy, this will be a question for them and us to determine without any foreign interposition.[28]

A generation earlier, Congress had forcefully asserted another concept, the no-transfer principle, in connection with Spanish possessions in Florida. On January 15, 1811, a Congressional resolution announced that the United States could not, "without serious inquietude, see any part of the said territory [East and West Florida] pass into the hands of any foreign Power." Proponents of the no-transfer injunction were unquestionably aware that ultimately the United States might wish to annex Florida and other European colonial possessions in North America.[29] When the Monroe Doctrine and the no-transfer principle were invoked against outside powers, therefore, this was done in some degree on the premise that it was the destiny of the United States to incorporate foreign territorial possessions on the North American continent.

To the U.S. mind, such expansionist impulses had little in common with the hegemonial tendencies of nations in the Old World. Pursuit of continentalism not only would benefit the United States but ultimately would uplift human society at large, not excluding the conduct of international affairs. This mentality perhaps reached its culmination in the approach of Wilsonian idealists to foreign policy questions. Compelled by events to abandon the preferred U.S. position of neutrality toward the belligerents in World War I, President Wilson was determined that, as a result of U.S. entry into the war, the basic pattern of international relations would thereafter be fundamentally changed. For Wilsonians, this conflict became "the war to end wars" and to "make the world safe for democracy." As Walter Lippmann expressed the idea, "The Wilsonian doctrine was the adaptation of the American tradition to an unexpected necessity — that of returning to Europe, of fighting on the soil of Europe, and of reuniting politically with the European nations." In order to achieve these Wilsonian ends, "the principles of democracy would have to be made universal throughout the world. The Wilsonian ideology is American fundamentalism made into universal doctrine."[30]

ISOLATIONISM: A BALANCE SHEET

With all its variegated, complex, and sometimes ambiguous connotations, isolationism was the foreign policy credo of the United States for a century and a half after the adoption of the Constitution. How well did this doctrine serve the nation's diplomatic and security interests? What relevance does an understanding of the concept have for the student of U.S. foreign relations in the modern period? Let us try to answer such questions by focusing initially on the benefits and advantages that isolationism conferred upon the United States.

That isolationism remained the avowed foreign policy position of the United States throughout the greater part of its experience as an independent nation provides strong prima-facie evidence that it served the country's needs in external affairs. Many parallels have been drawn in the post-World War II period between the traditional isolationist stance of the United States and the policy of neutralism or nonalignment professed by the vast majority of newly independent nations throughout Africa, the Middle East, and Asia.[31] These countries often found themselves in the same position as the United States did in the eighteenth and nineteenth centuries.

Three points of similarity seem especially pertinent. First, these new nations were weak and militarily vulnerable for a prolonged period of time. Second, they risked being "drawn into" conflicts between the great powers, which they believed extraneous to their interests and detrimental to their security. They were especially concerned about participation in great power alliance systems, in which they risked losing their own independent decision-making capacity (a fear heightened by the fact that, for many years before independence, they had been pawns in great power contests). Third, after achieving their independence, for an indefinite period they were massively preoccupied with internal concerns. Their leaders and informed citizens were convinced that, in the last analysis, the destiny of the country depended upon the successful solution of internal problems.

Both for the Afro-Asian nations in the contemporary period and for the United States during much of its history, therefore, a position of isolationism or nonalignment was a natural — if not perhaps an inevitable — stance.[32] Better than any conceivable alternative, nonalignment or isolationism met the internal and external requirements of the societies involved extremely well. Indeed, in most respects it is difficult to see how any other diplomatic position could have served this purpose.

Let us examine some of the more specific advantages that isolationism conferred upon the United States. Perhaps the principal attraction of the isolationist policy for Americans was that it was phenomenally successful. As the historian C. Vann Woodward has said, for a century or so after the War of 1812 the United States was "blessed with a security so complete and so free that it was able virtually to do without an army and for the greater part of the period without a navy as well."[33] Other benefits that Americans attributed to the isolationist policy included a very low level of military expenditures (approximately 1 percent of the gross national product); the ability to dispense with expensive fortifications along the Canadian and Mexican frontiers; and, with foreign threats eliminated, the ability to use the armed forces for internal purposes (such as pacification of the Indians). Justifiably or not (and we shall discuss that point more fully below), millions of Americans unquestionably did believe that the isolationist policy was the cause of a century or more of remarkable security and other advantages that accorded with the U.S. ethos.

As is true of the policy of diplomatic nonalignment espoused by the Afro-Asian nations today, isolationism was also a kind of strength-through-weakness approach to foreign relations. It enabled the United States to derive maximum benefit from several advantages it possessed as a new nation, such as the fact of geographical separation from the great powers of Europe and opportunities to develop the resources of the extraordinarily rich North American continent. Countless leaders of the United States and diplomatic historians have emphasized that, for well over a century after 1776, the security of the United States depended upon the existence of the European balance of power; as long as this balance was maintained — as long as there were several great powers in Europe and they remained intensely suspicious of each other — expansionist nations were unable to concert their policies at U.S. expense.[34] Fortuitously, with regard to many issues in the New World, the interests of one of the strongest European powers, Great Britain, increasingly coincided with those of the United States. Much as the idea might be overtly rejected by Americans (and Anglophobia remained deeply embedded in some segments of U.S. thought until World War II), this basic identity of interests was detectable as early as the issuance of the Monroe Doctrine in 1823; for several decades thereafter, such enforcement as the doctrine received was provided by the Royal Navy to safeguard British interests in the New World. This same underlying similarity of interest led to a series of treaties and understandings whereby, with British cooperation, the United States finally acquired the rights to construct and operate the Panama Canal.[35]

Isolationism was an attractive posture for the U.S. mind also because it rested upon a widely accepted premise that, however much its validity has come to be questioned in the contemporary period, was accepted with little question during the isolationist heyday. This was the assumed existence of an American community comprising the nations of North and South America. These nations formed the New World, united in opposition to the Old World. As the Monroe Doctrine asserted, a different set of principles guided the behavior of nations in the New World vis-à-vis those outside it. As newly independent republics, the nations of the New World were concerned above all with maintaining their independence in the face of foreign threats; if they could succeed in doing so, they would ultimately create new and distinctive political, economic, and social systems that would benefit not only their own citizens but those in the Old World as well.

Although until around 1900 the United States was relatively weak in contrast to the great powers of Europe, it quickly became powerful within its limited and natural geographic orbit, the Western Hemisphere. Until well into the twentieth century, the United States was unable to influence developments on the European continent or determine the outcome of disputes among the European powers over colonial issues in Asia or Africa. Increasingly, however, it could and did influence the course of events decisively in the Western Hemisphere (with vital assistance from time to time provided by Great Britain and, inadvertently, by the favorable European balance of power). Accordingly, proponents of isolationism often differentiated sharply between the capacity of the United States to use its power within the Western Hemisphere and outside it. Before World War II, for example, the historian Charles A. Beard was convinced that "in the rest of the world, outside this hemisphere, our interests are remote and our power to enforce our will is relatively slight."[36] The implication of Beard's judgment was that, marginal as its power might be toward Europe, the United States had crucial diplomatic interests within the Western Hemisphere, and that inside this zone its power was decisive. It was not by coincidence, for example, that the most ominous confrontation between the United States and the Soviet Union, the Cuban missile crisis of 1962, occurred in the Western Hemisphere. Similarly, when he wanted to demonstrate forcefully that (in the wake of a number of diplomatic reverses) the United States remained a superpower, determined to preserve its diplomatic vital interests, President Ronald Reagan successfully applied U.S. power to Grenada, in a successful effort to avert Communist control over that Caribbean nation.

The opposite side of this coin was the idea that, with very limited power to start with, the United States should not squander its influence or resources by intervening in the affairs of Europe, where its ability to affect the outcome of events was minimal and perhaps nonexistent. During the 1930s, for example, Senator Borah and other isolationists steadfastly opposed U.S. intervention in European politics, because "for the United States to become a part of European affairs . . . would be in the end to ruin our own country, while we would not save Europe." Another tireless champion of isolationism, Senator Gerald P. Nye, believed that U.S. power was "localized sharply in this hemisphere, where there is a job big enough for us to do." Secure in the Western Hemisphere, the United States could be "self-sufficient and live within ourselves without regard to what happens in the outside world."[37]

This mentality accounted in no small measure for isolationism's being the guiding precept of U.S. foreign policy toward European affairs, much less so toward Asia, and less still toward Latin America. Norman A. Graebner and other commentators have noted, for example, that even during the 1920s and 1930s both official and public opinion in the United States was more inclined to depart from traditional principles in trying to halt Japanese aggression than in restraining expansionist impulses of the European Axis Powers.[38]

As in the developing nations today, during the isolationist era the attitudes of Americans toward domestic issues directly and often crucially influenced their attitudes toward the outside world. As an example, the isolationist mentality displayed by partisans of the Progressive movement and by advocates of Wilsonian democracy in the early 1900s illustrates the point. Determined above all to achieve economic and social justice at home, spokesmen for Progressivism were usually proponents of an isolationist foreign policy as well. They believed that the United States' "unique mission was to purify and offer herself to decadent Europe, as an example of democracy triumphant over social and economic injustice. This self-purification involved also an end to America's experiment in imperialism and a weakening of American naval power." To the minds of most Progressives, international conflicts had primarily an economic origin: they arose out of the machinations of bankers, industrialists, munitions makers and other groups seeking to profit from war and violence among nations. Accordingly, many Progressives of that era opposed military preparedness on the grounds that it would tend to convert the United States into an armed camp and would jeopardize domestic reform programs.[39]

This same connection between attitudes toward domestic and foreign questions was discernible during the period of the Great Depression. Confronted with pervasive economic and financial dislocations within the United States, business interests during the late 1920s and the 1930s favored an isolationist approach to the outside world. They believed such an approach would result in lower taxes, a smaller national debt, reduced expenditures on armaments, and other essential steps enabling the United States to surmount the Depression and to enter a new era of plenty and prosperity.[40] During this economic crisis at home, as William L. Langer and S. Everett Gleason concluded, most Americans appeared convinced that the United States should "concentrate all efforts on the solution of national social and economic problems, so as to preserve intact the great stronghold of democracy."[41]

After the unhappy experience of the U.S. society under the Articles of Confederation, Samuel F. Bemis observed, President Washington became convinced that it was imperative for the new Republic to maintain a "united front in the face of foreign nations."[42] Bemis's observation underscores one of the most valuable contributions that an isolationist foreign policy made for the people of the United States. Again, an analogy can be drawn between its usefulness to the U.S. society and one of the noteworthy contributions that a policy of nonalignment makes to Afro-Asian societies today. Until World War II, for Americans an isolationist approach to foreign relations — especially to U.S. relations with the European powers — was vital for the preservation of internal unity, social cohesiveness, and domestic political stability. It is difficult to think of any other foreign policy orientation that could have made a similar contribution.

Even before the American Revolution, the U.S. society had become an ethnic melting pot.[43] After independence the United States was a nation of immigrants, and the mass immigration process continued until after World War I. From the 1880s to the 1920s, for example, some 40 million foreigners settled in the United States.[44] The significance of the diverse ethnic origins of the U.S. society for the nation's behavior in foreign affairs can hardly be exaggerated. The relationship was at once complex and vitally important for U.S. policy-makers. It was complex, because the melting-pot characteristic of the U.S. society generated multiple, and often intense and conflicting, pressures upon national leaders as they attempted to formulate policies toward particular countries. Because the vast majority of immigrants to the United States had come from European nations, this problem was especially acute in U.S. relations with the countries of Europe. First-generation immigrants particularly were apt to have strong familial and sentimental ties with the old country; although they had left it to come to the United States, they remained concerned about its welfare and tended to oppose any U.S. policy deemed inimical to its interests. In some instances ethnic minorities favored policies that, however much they might depart from the nation's isolationist credo, were designed to benefit the country of their origin. A particularly noteworthy example of this phenomenon was afforded by the influence of Polish-Americans upon U.S. foreign policy during and after World War II. During the war and for at least 40 years thereafter, this ethnic minority could be counted upon to champion the rights of Poland in its ongoing efforts to gain freedom from Soviet control. Similarly, throughout the postwar period, Greek-Americans have been outspoken, and sometimes highly influential in shaping attitudes on Capitol Hill, in behalf of the Greek government's position on issues like the Cyprus controversy with Turkey.

As we have already observed, throughout the nineteenth and early twentieth centuries, suspicions, quarrels, and conflicts tended to divide the nations of Europe. While this situation was salutary for the preservation of U.S. national security, in that it prevented the European powers from uniting to the detriment of the United States, it also made it extremely difficult for an incumbent U.S. administration to formulate policies toward European affairs that commanded a high degree of national unity. The only policy likely to gain widespread support among all (or most) major ethnic minorities within the United States was isolationism, by whose canons the nation refrained altogether from intervening in European political controversies, leaving it to the European states themselves to work out their destinies, while Americans concentrated upon domestic pursuits (and, in the process, immigrant groups became largely assimilated into the U.S. way of life).

Yet U.S. policy-makers were also required to deal with a contrary tendency. In time, some immigrants' groups became politically very powerful in certain regions of the United States and used their political influence in behalf of causes that bore directly upon U.S. relations with other countries. The classic case in this regard was, of course, the Irish-Americans. Their political leverage in pivotal states like Massachusetts, New York, and Illinois often gave them an ability to influence national policies vastly out of proportion to their relative size within the population. The intensity with which Irish-Americans expressed their views (coupled with the relative apathy of other Americans toward issues like the Irish question) added to their impact upon policy-makers in Washington. Deeply concerned about the wrongs inflicted upon Ireland throughout modern history, the Irish-Americans exhibited what one commentator has called "an all-consuming Anglophobia," making them congenitally suspicious of Great Britain and hostile to the idea of Anglo-American collaboration. As late as World War I, for example, in Irish-American eyes England remained "perfidious Albion"; a de facto alliance united the Irish-Americans and the German-Americans in their enmity toward the Allied side.[45] Irish-Americans accused President Wilson of trying to make the United States a vassal state of England; opposition to the Wilson administration by this ethnic minority was a significant force responsible for the defeat of the Democratic party in 1920 and for U.S. rejection of the League of Nations.[46]

Even though it did not prevent all partisan or internal discords over foreign policy questions, the isolationist principle served remarkably well as a broad platform upon which ethnic minorities and other interest groups in the United States could stand. Although such groups might agree upon little else, they approved (or at least most were not adamantly opposed to) a U.S. policy that treated the countries of Europe impartially and equally, as symbolized by U.S. neutrality toward European wars. By contrast, a departure from the isolationist stance was almost certain to arouse powerful ethnic and other interest group opposition.

As every informed citizen in the postwar period is aware, the historic U.S. policy of isolationism also had certain defects and major disadvantages, which became pronounced after the United States emerged as a great power in the twentieth century. Let us take note of its principal shortcomings, recognizing at the outset that many of the criticisms of isolationism which follow ought properly to be directed against distorted or uninformed interpretations of isolationist sources like Washington's Farewell Address or the Monroe Doctrine. (Many vocal apostles of isolationism before World War II probably never read these state papers in their entirety; still less did they make an effort to understand the historical context in which such statements were issued.)

This qualification leads to the first criticism of the isolationist credo as an adequate basis for U.S. foreign policy, especially after 1900. As we have emphasized, in the infancy of the Republic, the principles and maxims that came to be associated with an isolationist approach to foreign relations were enunciated in response to a particular combination of forces deemed by the country's leaders to be inimical to national security. To their minds, isolationism was thus a means for achieving goals, like preservation of independence and continental expansion, under a prevailing set of conditions facing the United States in its early history. Yet as the years passed the principles and diplomatic strategies identified with Presidents Washington, Jefferson, Monroe, and other chief executives tended to become timeless and universalized formulas, reiterated without qualification; for millions of citizens they became an integral part of the "American way of life" and of their constitutional system. Phrases like "no entangling alliances" or "nonintervention in European affairs" were elevated to incantations, which, it was imagined, by their very repetition, somehow kept hostile external forces at bay or otherwise warded off tendencies abroad that might harm U.S. security. Because it had formed part of the collective wisdom of the Founding Fathers, the isolationist tradition tended to be placed beyond debate or objective analysis. Even those national leaders who were convinced that conditions in the external environment had changed fundamentally — beginning with President Theodore Roosevelt around 1900 and continuing with Woodrow Wilson and Franklin D. Roosevelt — were seldom able to convince others to accept that reality. It required Japan's surprise attack against Pearl Harbor late in 1941 to convince a majority of the people of the United States and Congress that a foreign policy of isolationism no longer coincided with the facts of international life.

The apparent success of the isolationist policy also perhaps confirmed Americans in a tendency that has been lamented by innumerable commentators and diplomatic historians: uncritical faith in the efficacy of words, of presidential pronouncements, in Congressional resolutions, in signed documents and the like to achieve diplomatic purposes. Having convinced themselves, for example, that it was the solemn issuance of the Monroe Doctrine by a U.S. president — rather than the willingness of Great Britain to enforce it in the years that followed or the inability of the European powers to collaborate at the young nation's expense — it was easy for Americans thereafter to believe that the assertion of a policy or the mere expression of good intentions was tantamount to their achievement. This tendency is illustrated by the isolationism espoused by Senator Borah. Although no pacifist, Borah was passionately devoted to the cause of world peace. After playing a leading role in defeating U.S. entry into the League of Nations, during the 1920s Borah became an equally energetic proponent of the Kellogg-Briand pact (or the Pact of Paris, signed on August 27, 1928) to "outlaw" war.[47] Borah regarded his sponsorship of this proposal as a singular contribution to international stability and security.

Yet the Kellogg-Briand pact epitomized the tendency we are describing. Its terms carried no enforcement provisions, and Borah was adamantly opposed to the use of U.S. power in concert with other nations for that purpose. The pact was the kind of moralistic-legalistic gesture that was, in many crucial respects, worse than futile. Not only did aggressive nations violate its terms with impunity, but its ratification contributed to a basic confusion in the U.S. mind about the steps required to achieve genuine security and the costs to the nation involved in doing so. The Kellogg-Briand pact thus symbolized one of isolationism's gravest defects. As Raymond L. Buell assessed U.S. "neutrality legislation" several years later: "Now the difficulty with present American policy is that it is belated, unconscious, and ineffectual. We try to satisfy our consciences without taking risks. We want to do good in the world, provided it does not cost anything."[48] Or, as England's Prime Minister Neville Chamberlain declared in a comment on President Roosevelt's Quarantine Speech in 1937: "It is always best and safest to count on nothing from the Americans but words."[49]

Belief in the efficacy of isolationism thus tended to mislead Americans with regard to the true bases of their national security and the steps required to maintain it. Thus Samuel F. Bemis notes that, as a result of pervasive confidence in the isolationist credo, the United States seriously neglected its national defense requirements. During the 1920s and 1930s, the United States was "hopelessly unprepared." The U.S. Army was "smaller than that of third-rate European powers." By 1942, as a result of a series of arms-reduction agreements made during the previous 20 years, the United States was still trying to reach the limits of military forces allowed under these treaties; rival powers had long since violated their terms.

After the Japanese attacked Pearl Harbor on December 7, 1941, one of the foremost advocates of isolationism, Senator Arthur H.

Vandenberg, declared: "That day ended isolationism for any realist."[50] Yet there were many realists who had become aware of the inadequacies of isolationism a half-century or more earlier. In the late eighteenth century, for example, England's Prime Minister Benjamin Disraeli observed that it would likely be the U.S. democracy that would "ultimately decide the fate of the two Americas and of Europe."[51] In his last address before leaving the White House (on September 5, 1901), President William McKinley had warned that "isolationism is no longer possible or desirable. . . . The period of exclusiveness is past." In the same period, former Secretary of State Richard Olney cautioned against the tendency to invoke the foreign policy principles of 1776 a century later. An isolationism that amounted to nothing more than "a shirking of the responsibilities of high place and great power is simply ignominious." The time had arrived for the United States to "come out of its shell" and to cease trying to be a "hermit among nations."[52]

Despite such prophetic insights, the isolationist mentality persisted — and became in some respects even more deeply entrenched after World War I. Perhaps more than any other era in U.S. history, the interwar period was characterized by the existence of pervasive and deeply embedded misconceptions concerning the bases of U.S. security in a rapidly changing global environment. Within a few years after their participation in World War I made an Allied victory possible, for example, Americans had become deeply disillusioned about the course of world events, particularly developments in Europe. As time passed, countless Americans became convinced that the nation's entry into World War I had been a tragic mistake. Influential writers, historians, and political leaders disseminated the view that a diplomatically inexperienced United States had been misled, duped, and manipulated by selfish groups at home and by skilled propagandists overseas into abandoning genuine neutrality in favor of the Allied cause. In doing so, the U.S. society endured frightful human and financial losses; and, as isolationists had long maintained, events in the two decades after 1918 indicated that its intervention into European affairs had apparently done nothing fundamentally to alter the ingrained pattern of Old World enmity and conflict, which threatened once again to plunge the world into war.

Revulsion against the horrors of war and disillusionment with its apparent lack of constructive results made a majority of Americans determined never again to take part in it. Instead of reliance upon armed force or participation in the League of Nations to maintain international peace, prominent isolationists assured the country that moral force, global public opinion, and the supposedly pacific instincts and wise judgments of the common people throughout the world would guarantee the maintenance of a benign global order.[53] Many Americans also believed that, because of the injustices incorporated into the Treaty of Versailles (particularly its provision requiring Germany to acknowledge sole responsibility for instigating World War I), the United States had to refrain from any action showing favoritism for Britain or France over Germany.

Then in the 1934–37 period came the widely publicized Nye Committee investigations into the reasons for U.S. participation in World War I.[54] The committee's operating premise was that a combination of powerful and self-serving forces — such as industrialists, munitions makers, and Eastern financiers who sought to profit from armed conflict, along with pro-British elements and Allied propagandists — had been responsible for the United States' lamentable departure from its historic isolationist principles. By the 1930s these same groups, now in alliance with the New Deal of President Roosevelt, were seeking once more to implicate the United States in a new global conflict extraneous to its interests. The Nye Committee's activities lent seemingly authoritative credence to a highly distorted impression of why the United States had entered World War I, and it reinforced the prevailing public disillusionment about the course of world events since that time. In the words of Secretary of State Cordell Hull, the committee's investigations plunged the country "into deepest isolationism at the very moment when our influence was so vitally needed to help ward off the approaching threats of war abroad."[55]

Closely akin to these shortcomings of isolationism was its deficiency as a sound defense strategy. On purely eclectic and pragmatic grounds, isolationism had to be abandoned because it failed to protect national security and the nation's vital diplomatic interests during periods of global crisis. With some exceptions, isolationists were seldom pacifists. The majority believed in what the America First Committee called "an impregnable defense" for the United States.[56] Before World War II, isolationists in Congress frequently voted for higher military appropriations designed to keep "America first" and to strengthen its position as the "arsenal of democracy." Yet they consistently miscalculated in their predictions concerning the likelihood of global war, in their assessments of Axis intentions toward the United States, in their evaluations of the consequences for U.S. security of an Axis victory, and, perhaps most crucially, in their failure to comprehend the necessity of allies in an increasingly interdependent world, whose natural geographical barriers were being overcome by modern methods of communication and transportation.

Very few isolationists favored a policy of national military weakness and unpreparedness, even though the early months of World War II proved these conditions to exist in the United States. Instead, the keynotes of isolationism had been unilateralism and national (or possibly hemispheric) self-sufficiency. In the words of one commentator, some isolationists were even "evangelical" in their apparent devotion to the cause of global peace, justice, and respect for international law.[57] Yet they demanded that the United States defend its independence and diplomatic interests alone. The basic defect in such reasoning, of course, is highlighted by the question: if the United States were truly committed to upholding the principles of international law and justice, and if it were genuinely concerned about the cause of world peace, why then should the United States not act in collaboration with other like-minded nations to achieve these goals, thereby confronting international lawbreakers with a united force they dared not ignore?

Eventually, in 1941, after its own vital interests had been gravely imperiled, the United States was compelled to follow this course, joining the Allies in common opposition to Axis expansionism. Would it not have been elementary prudence to have done so much earlier, before the enemy had completed one conquest after another and had constructed a power base that, in the early years of World War II, gave it an extremely formidable military position? Why not, in other words, endeavor to prevent the conquest of Western Europe, rather than resorting to its liberation following one of the bloodiest and most devastating military engagements in the history of warfare? If isolationists were never able to answer such questions satisfactorily, few Americans (not excluding most former isolationists) were in doubt about the answers after the experience of World War II. A fundamental weakness in isolationist reasoning was thus its failure to realize that, as in medicine or fire-fighting, prevention is almost invariably preferable to cure — especially when the treatment risks worldwide destruction, chaos, political and social disorganization, bankruptcy, and other evils whose existence may in turn pose new threats to the security and well-being of the United States. The necessity for preventive diplomatic action by the United States and other nations becomes more than ordinarily imperative in the nuclear age, when the threat of an atomic war between the superpowers — or between less powerful nuclear-armed nations — risks nothing less than the future of human civilization.

One final deficiency of the isolationist mentality remains to be noted. For the U.S. society the War of Independence was of course a decisive act of political separation from Europe. But to many citizens, it was no less a spiritual and philosophical divorce as well. Americans tended to view the values of the New World and the Old World as antithetical. The dedication of the United States to equality and democratic principles of government stood in sharp contrast to European autocracy and despotism. Americans sought peace, justice, and social harmony, while European societies remained addicted to dynastic quarrels, territorial rivalries, and class conflicts. Ultimately, Thomas Jefferson once wrote, "we may formally require a meridian of partition" through the Atlantic Ocean demarcating the boundary between the Old World and the New, separating what Jefferson described as these "two hemispheres."[58] A century later, Senator George W. Norris echoed this attitude. According to one biographer, Norris's isolationist outlook derived in some measure from his revulsion at "mutual distrust among the nations which still permeated the framework of the whole European culture. But in the New World these conditions did not prevail."[59]

Studies of the isolationist mentality in the twentieth century have confirmed that a profound suspicion of foreign societies — sometimes manifesting itself in xenophobia and ultranationalism — sustained U.S. isolationist viewpoints. In this philosophical rejection of Old World values and principles, Americans were prone to classify diplomacy as a European concept, which was incompatible with the values supposedly actuating the U.S. society. To the U.S. mind, diplomacy was intimately associated with autocracy; it was the pastime of an aristocratic elite practiced to the detriment of the common people in both the Old World and the New World; success in diplomacy required skills — deceit, dishonesty, immorality, and dissimulation — that Americans believed conflicted directly with their own unique value system.[60] It was but a step from this conviction to the attitude that foreign affairs generally were suspect: extensive involvement in events abroad was inherently detrimental to the U.S. way of life. If the United States could not avoid all contact with the outside world (and most isolationists conceded that this was impossible), then the nation's diplomatic activities ought to be confined mainly to observing and reporting developments (U.S. diplomats were sometimes referred to as the government's "eyes and ears abroad"), rather than taking any part in them. Even in the post-World War II period, experienced diplomats often still regarded their principal responsibility as reporting accurately on events overseas. The frontier tradition — the idea that the American was a man of action who got things done (in contrast with effete and idle European intellectuals and aristocrats) — also contributed to U.S. denigration of diplomacy. The United States did not establish a professional diplomatic corps until the passage of the Rogers Act in 1924. A half-century later, Congress still refused to provide many U.S. ambassadors with salary levels and expense accounts enabling them to represent the United States adequately abroad. As the United States approached the end of its second century as an independent nation, the State Department still lacked the kind of domestic constituency or base of popular support that other departments (Labor, Commerce, Agriculture) commanded; even among U.S. presidents, criticisms and suspicions of the State Department were intense.[61] Studies of public attitudes revealed that, even after the United States had emerged as a superpower, public interest in foreign affairs remained low; with rare exceptions, foreign policy issues still did not have the salience for Americans of domestic questions.

NOTES

1. Quoted in Richard W. Leopold, *The Growth of American Foreign Policy: A History* (New York: Alfred A. Knopf, 1962), p. 18.

2. See Jefferson's First Inaugural Address (March 4, 1801), in House of Representatives, *Miscellaneous Documents.* 53d Congress, 2d Session, 1893–94 (Washington: Government Printing Office, 1895), pp. 321–24.

3. When the United States abandoned isolationism is a debatable question that elicits diverse answers from commentators. Some believe that President Franklin D. Roosevelt's Quarantine Speech of October 5, 1937, in which he likened Axis aggression to a disease and called on the nations of the world to quarantine it, marked the end of U.S. isolationist posture. See William L. Langer and S. Everett Gleason, *The Challenge to Isolation: 1937–1940* (New York: Harper and Row, 1952), p. 11.

4. Quoted form Charles A. Beard, *Giddy Minds and Foreign Quarrels* (New York: Macmillan 1939), reprinted in Robert A. Goldwin, ed., *Readings in American Foreign Policy,* 2d ed. (New York: Oxford University Press, 1971), pp. 131–33.

5. Quoted in Norman A. Graebner, "Isolationism," *International Encyclopedia of the Social Sciences* (New York: Crowell Collier and Macmillan, 1968), 8:218.

6. After analyzing the results of public opinion polls in the early postwar period, one commentator concluded that no more than 10 percent of the people of the United States could accurately be described as isolationists. See Alfred O. Hero, *Americans in World Affairs* (Boston: World Peace Foundation, 1959), pp. 10–11.

7. Quoted in Graebner, "Isolationism," p. 219.

8. Quoted in Wayne S. Cole, *Senator Gerald P. Nye and American Foreign Relations* (Minneapolis: University of Minnesota Press, 1962), p. 216.

9. Although Jefferson did not use the term isolationism, in time the phrase "no entangling alliances" became synonymous with it. See Samuel F. Bemis, *A Diplomatic History of the United States*, 2d ed. (New York: Henry Holt, 1942), pp. 202–3; and Leopold, *The Growth of American Foreign Policy*, pp. 22–23.

10. Despite the in perpetuo agreement, on July 7, 1798, Congress declared the French alliance void on the grounds that the French government had violated its terms. Thomas A. Bailey, *A Diplomatic History of the American People*, 8th ed. (New York: Appleton-Century-Crofts, 1969), p. 95.

11. Henry J. Ford, "Timothy Pickering," in Bemis, ed., *The American Secretaries of State*, pp. 205–6. Pickering served as Secretary of State during the period 1795–1800.

12. Frank Donovan, *Mr. Monroe's Message: The Story of the Monroe Doctrine* (New York: Dodd, Mead, 1963), p. 9.

13. Quoted in Bailey, *A Diplomatic History of the American People*, p. 182, citing C. F. Adams, *Memoirs*, 6:179 (November 7, 1823).

14. Paul Seabury, *Power, Freedom, and Diplomacy: The Foreign Policy of the United States of America* (New York: Random House, 1963), p. 38.

15. Quoted in Charles C. Hyde, "Charles Evans Hughes," in Bemis, ed., *The American Secretaries of State*, p. 356.

16. John C. Vinson, *William E. Borah and the Outlawry of War* (Athens: University of Georgia Press, 1957), p. 1.

17. Quoted in Pratt, "Cordell Hull," 1:199.

18. See the views of Thomas A. Bailey, as cited in Sheldon Appleton, *United States Foreign Policy: An Introduction with Cases* (Boston: Little, Brown, 1968), p. 39.

19. Bemis, *A Diplomatic History of the United States*, p. 12.

20. Appleton, *United States Foreign Policy*, p. 56.

21. For Roosevelt's views, see Robert H. Ferrell, *American Diplomacy: A History* (New York: Norton, 1959), p. 367.

22. See Burton K. Wheeler, *Yankee from the West* (Garden City, N.Y.: Doubleday, 1962), p. 22; and Pratt, "Cordell Hull," 1:251.

23. See Robert E. Sherwood, *Roosevelt and Hopkins* (New York: Bantam Books, 1950), 1:161.

24. Admiral Alfred Mahan (1840–1914) exercised a profound influence upon U.S. military strategy for perhaps a half-century or more after 1900. He was a prolific author and well-known lecturer; his most famous book was *The Influence of Seapower Upon History* (1918). For a succinct discussion of Mahan's views, see Margaret T. Sprout, "Mahan: Evangelist of Sea Power," in Edward M. Earle, ed., *Makers of Modern Strategy* (New York: Atheneum, 1966), pp. 415–46.

25. John A. Garraty, *Henry Cabot Lodge: A Biography* (New York: Alfred A. Knopf, 1953), pp. 150–55.

26. Marian C. McKenna, *Borah* (Ann Arbor: University of Michigan Press, 1961), pp. 138–43.

27.   See Adams's views as quoted in Leopold, *The Growth of American Foreign Policy*, p. 42.

28.   Julius W. Pratt, *A History of United States Foreign Policy* (Englewood Cliffs, N.J.: Prentice-Hall, 1955), pp. 243–44.

29.   See ibid., pp. 129, 165.

30.   See Walter Lippmann, *Isolation and Alliances: An American Speaks to the British* (Boston: Little, Brown, 1952), pp. 21–22.

31.   For more detailed discussion of the postwar doctrine of diplomatic nonalignment, see Cecil V. Crabb, Jr., *The Elephants and the Grass: A Study of Non-alignment* (New York: Praeger, 1965).

32.   The author is aware, and the reader should be cognizant, that although nonalignment and isolationism have many points in common, advocates of the former in the contemporary era uniformly deny that nonalignment is equivalent to isolationism, insofar as the latter designates a withdrawal from world affairs, lack of interest in international decision making, or indifference to the course of events outside their own borders. In its most essential meaning, nonalignment denotes primarily diplomatic freedom of action or what, in our discussion of isolationism, we have called unilateralism. For further discussion of this point, see Crabb, *The Elephants and the Grass*, pp. 3–14.

33.   Quoted in Ekirch, *Ideas, Ideals, and American Diplomacy*, p. 103.

34.   Thus Seabury asserts that the United States was "a passive beneficiary of the European balance of power for nearly a century" after 1815. See Seabury, *Power, Freedom, and Diplomacy*, p. 41.

35.   Following a prolonged series of negotiations on the construction of a canal in Central America, in the second Hay-Pauncefote Treaty (November 19, 1901), Britain accepted the United States' evident determination to construct a canal alone in Panama. See Pratt, *A History of United States Foreign Policy*, pp. 286–90, 329–30, 395–400.

36.   Quoted in Goldwin, ed., *Readings in American Foreign Policy*, p. 133.

37.   For the views of Senator Borah, see Vinson, *William E. Borah and the Outlawry of War*, p. 51. For Nye's attitudes, see Cole, *Senator Gerald P. Nye and American Foreign Relations*, pp. 168–69.

38.   Graebner, "Isolationism," p. 218.

39.   Arthur S. Link, *Woodrow Wilson and the Progressive Era, 1910–1917* (New York: Harper and Row, 1954), pp. 180–82.

40.   See the views of R. N. Stromberg on the attitudes of U.S. business groups toward foreign affairs, as cited in Ekirch, *Ideas, Ideals, and American Diplomacy*, pp. 131–32.

41.   Langer and Gleason, *The Challenge to Isolation*, p. 13.

42.   Bemis, *A Diplomatic History of the United States*, p. 85.

43.   See J. Joseph Huthmacher, *A Nation of Newcomers: Ethnic Minority Groups in American History* (New York: Dell, 1967), p. 7.

44.   Ibid., p. 11.

45.   Carl Wittke, *The Irish in America* (Baton Rouge: Louisiana State University Press, 1956), pp. 273–74.

46.   See ibid., pp. 279–85; and William V. Shannon, *The American Irish* (New York: Macmillan, 1963), pp. 328–30.

47. The Kellogg-Briand pact was initially adhered to by the United States and 14 other countries, with most of the nations of the world eventually joining it. The treaty permitted the signatories to engage in "defensive war"; but otherwise, it prohibited war as "an instrument of national policy." For more detailed treatment, see R. H. Ferrell, *Peace in Their Time: The Origins of the Kellogg-Briand Pact* (New Haven: Yale University Press, 1952). For Senator Borah's views, see McKenna, *Borah,* pp. 237–50.

48. Raymond L. Buell, *Isolated America* (New York: Alfred A. Knopf, 1940), p. 331.

49. Quoted in Arthur C. Turner, *The Unique Partnership: Britain and the United States* (New York: Bobbs-Merrill, 1971), p. 65.

50. Vandenberg, ed., *The Private Papers of Senator Vandenberg,* p. 1.

51. Disraeli's views are cited in Allan Nevins, ed., *America Through British Eyes* (New York: Oxford University Press, 1948), p. 500.

52. The views of McKinley and Olney are quoted in Leopold, *The Growth of American Foreign Policy,* pp. 204–5.

53. For example, Senator Borah was persuaded that "the power of public opinion in international affairs is stupendously greater than the power of force." Quoted in Vinson, *William E. Borah and the Outlawry of War,* p. 120.

54. The Nye Committee's investigations were contained in a voluminous compilation of information. See United States Senate, *Hearings before the Special Committee Investigating the Munitions Industry.* 73d Congress, 2d Session (Washington, D.C.: 1934–1937), Parts 1–39.

55. Hull's views are cited in Pratt, "Cordell Hull," 1:193.

56. The America First Committee was formed on September 4, 1940. Consisting of 450 local chapters, and more than 800,000 members, including some of the most prominent individuals in U.S. life, the committee was a highly influential medium for the isolationist point of view. See Wayne S. Cole, *America First* (Madison: University of Wisconsin Press, 1953), esp. pp. 89–104.

57. See McKenna, *Borah,* p. 152.

58. Jefferson's views are cited in Ekirch, *Ideas, Ideals, and American Diplomacy,* p. 17.

59. Norman L. Zucker, *George W. Norris: Gentle Knight of American Democracy* (Urbana: University of Illinois Press, 1966), p. 136.

60. Thus President Washington cautioned one of his early ministers to Europe to develop a "horror of finess and chicane [chicanery]," the hallmarks of Old World diplomacy. John Adams was convinced that Americans could "never be a match" for European diplomats, who would resort to any device to achieve their ends. The views of Washington and Adams are cited in Ilchman, *Professional Diplomacy in the United States,* p. 25.

61. See, for example, the criticisms made of the State Department by President John F. Kennedy, cited in Arthur M. Schlesinger, Jr., *A Thousand Days* (Boston: Houghton Mifflin, 1965), pp. 406–47.

2

Contemporary Neo-Isolationism: Conservative Conceptions

In this and the next chapter we shall assess contemporary manifestations of the old isolationist mentality — viewpoints toward U.S. foreign policy that became prominent during and after the Vietnam War and that are likely to remain influential. This frame of mind has been labeled "neo-isolationism," which has at least two reasonably distinct versions, conservative and liberal.

The use of the term neo-isolationism presents two problems. One is that it is frequently used pejoratively, indiscriminately, and as a deliberate political epithet. As emphasized in Chapter 1, the historic concept of isolationism became widely discredited after the Japanese attack against Pearl Harbor, and it has never fully regained respectability since that traumatic event.[1] In our discussion, however, the term neo-isolationism is not employed as a value judgment or derisive label. It is intended to describe a particular approach to U.S. foreign policy that seeks to limit the involvement of the United States in global affairs according to principles and criteria we shall identify more fully below.

The second problem relates to the difficulty of formulating a meaningful definition of neo-isolationism. The term is conditional and relative; its precise meaning is always affected by time and circumstances; and as is true of other aspects of life in the United States, the concept of neo-isolationism evolves in the light of internal and external developments.

Neo-isolationism, on the one hand, unlike isolationism, recognizes that the United States is a superpower with many important global responsibilities and commitments. Since World War II, that has been the central reality of U.S. foreign relations. On the other hand, neo-isolationism may be contrasted with globalism or indiscriminate internationalism, whose basic premise is that the interests of the United States are directly involved in every significant international development, from Latin America to East Asia. This latter approach, for example, led to the policeman-of-the-world mentality, which was largely responsible for prolonged U.S. involvement in the Vietnam War.

The neo-isolationist believes that, although the United States remains a superpower, after the Vietnam conflict it must be more discriminating or selective in assuming international commitments, especially those requiring the application of military force in behalf of diplomatic objectives. Or in different terms, in the light of the Vietnam War experience, the United States must thereafter define its diplomatic vital interests more clearly, more intelligently, and with better understanding of the consequences to be expected from assuming them. It must be reiterated that no unanimity exists — even among neo-isolationists themselves — concerning the principles that ought to guide the United States in assuming and protecting diplomatic commitments in the post-Vietnam War era. (Chapter 6, for example, calls attention to a wide variety of approaches to the problem of U.S. interventionism in the period following the Vietnam War.)

TENETS OF CONSERVATIVE NEO-ISOLATIONISM

In the contemporary period what does conservative neo-isolationism mean? Our discussion begins by identifying several basic principles or tenets that are common to this approach to U.S. foreign policy. Conservative neo-isolationists broadly share the following body of principles, which influences their attitudes and activities in foreign policy:

The external environment is viewed as hostile, intractable, and uncongenial for the achievement of U.S. foreign policy goals — especially for the promotion of democracy, liberty, and individual freedom abroad.

The United States is, and for an indefinite period will likely remain, a superpower; the power of the United States is vital both for its own security and for the peace and stability of the international system.

Since World War II, Soviet communism has been — and it still poses — the most dangerous threat to the security of the United States and other freedom-loving nations; the Communist threat has not diminished; the Kremlin will still seek to exploit U.S. weakness to its advantage; and whenever possible, Moscow will intervene in global trouble-spots in pursuit of its expansionist objectives.

Two prerequisites are essential for the preservation of U.S. security and for diplomatic success: a powerful and modern military establishment second to none; and allies and friends who share the U.S. interest in maintaining global peace and security, especially against Communist adversaries.

The United States cannot serve as the policeman of the world; it must choose its international commitments carefully, particularly those that may require the application of U.S. military power for their protection.

After exercising discrimination in assuming global commitments, it is essential that the United States honor its commitments abroad; it must defend those countries it has pledged to protect; and it must otherwise maintain the nation's diplomatic credibility; Americans must not lose their nerve during periods of external crisis; and they must stay the course when their vital interests are at stake.

Yet U.S policy-makers must also define the nation's diplomatic goals clearly and unambiguously; the application of U.S. military power abroad must always be related to some clearly defined objective, which is acceptable to, and understood by, the people of the United States; national officials must give high priority to creating and maintaining a solid public consensus in using military force overseas.

With John Quincy Adams, the conservative neo-isolationist believes that the United States "goes not abroad in search of monsters to destroy"; the United States cannot single-handedly eliminate poverty, promote successful modernization, guarantee the future of democracy, or protect the human rights of individuals in over 160 independent nations throughout the contemporary world; more often than not, efforts to do so will dissipate U.S. resources and influence, create ill will for the United States abroad, and in the end fail to accomplish their objective.

Progress throughout regions like the Third World will result to the extent that developing societies engage in maximum self-help, with limited U.S. assistance; in their efforts to modernize, such societies will find in time that a market or free enterprise economic system is essential in achieving the goal; by contrast, collectivist approaches to national development will impede the quest for modernization.

Communist-led and other revolutionary methods for effecting political change should be resisted by the United States; on the basis of experience, such revolutionary programs usually fail to achieve their announced and idealistic goals; they often result in the imposition of totalitarian, authoritarian, or other oppressive political systems; and in many cases, they lead to a global expansion of Soviet power and influence, to the detriment of the security of the United States and its allies.

THE CONSERVATIVE POLITICAL TRADITION

No understanding of contemporary conservative neo-isolationism is possible without brief reference to the conservative political tradition.

One of the most articulate spokesmen for modern U.S. conservatism, William F. Buckley, Jr., has observed: "There is no commonly acknowledged conservative position today."[2] Traditionally, as Edmund Burke believed, conservatism has taken the view that the existence of ideological blueprints for the reconstruction of society was "one sure symptom of an ill-conducted state." Or, as British Prime Minister Benjamin Disraeli once asserted, conservatives professed "no program," nor did they have a Conservative Manifesto.[3] Such observations possess special cogency for the U.S. society. Many commentators believe the United States lacks a genuine conservative tradition. Political ideas central to "the American way of life" — belief in progress, democracy, and equality of opportunity — are dominant motifs of political liberalism.[4]

Nevertheless, we may identify certain general principles that have been integral to modern conservative ideology. Thus, one definition holds that a conservative is "a defender of the status quo who, when change becomes necessary in tested institutions or practices, prefers that it come slowly, and in moderation."[5] In terms of more specific tenets, the conservative political mentality is characterized by belief in the existence of a universal moral order sanctioned by organized religions; belief in the inherent fallibility of man, who is actuated by a mixture of rational and irrational, humanitarian and egocentric impulses; belief in the reality of mental and physical inequality of people, which gives rise to social classes and elites; devotion to the concept of private property and opposition to governmental regulation of it; a conviction that political power ought to be decentralized, diffused, and balanced, leading to the

Let us begin ou
foreign policy issue
global environment i
its external objectives
that setting tends to b
the achievement of l
student of international

Foreign politics are th
themselves in the area o
state is the potential ene
either seeking to increa
Failing, they are gobbled
inevitably will — be tomo

This set of conditions —
effective supranational poli
ultimate dependence upor
security."9

After World War II, the i
hostile and uncongenial for th
because of one transcenden
expansive Communist move
global Marxist system control
between the United States and
mind, the pivotal fact about po
grasp the significance of this fa
power since World War II. The
international position, Senator Go
simply: "Our enemies have under
have not. They are determined to
as President Ronald Reagan obse
Union remains the "locus of ev
ambitious and expansionist policies
like Cuba, Nicaragua, and Ethiopi
danger to global peace and security.
were also candid in their denunciatio
Iran and Libya), which relied upon a

conviction that the trend toward "Big Government" ought to be resisted; a preference for order over freedom, or for liberty over equality; and support of the idea that the standard of the prudent (or reasonable) man provides the only reliable criterion for solving national policy questions.[6]

Toward foreign policy issues, an authentically conservative viewpoint is difficult to define and articulate — more so after World War II perhaps than in any previous era of U.S. history. The point needs to be reiterated that studies of public opinion reveal little significant correlation between the attitudes of citizens toward domestic questions and toward foreign policy issues. In the latter realm, since World War II conservative attitudes have been characterized by a conviction that the global environment is relatively hostile to the achievement of U.S. foreign policy goals and impervious to successful manipulation by the United States; by an evident preoccupation with the expansive ambitions and policies of international communism, centered in Moscow, and the continuing threat it poses to the security of the United States and its allies; by a tendency to visualize this threat very largely in military terms and to rely heavily upon military and paramilitary responses to it; by a related insistence upon the maintenance of U.S. military superiority over (or, at the very least, stable parity with) possible enemies like the Soviet Union and Communist China, accompanied by the necessity for civilian policy-makers to heed the advice of their professional military advisers; by support for the United Nations and continued U.S. membership in it, provided the United States avoids overreliance upon the organization and recognizes the U.N.'s defects as an effective peace-keeping agency; and by ingrained skepticism concerning the ability of the United States to modernize the Third World, successfully implant the principles of political democracy in it, instill the Puritan work ethic in non-Western cultures, and, even less, to buy reliable friends and allies overseas by furnishing them military and economic assistance. Also, down to the period of the Nixon administration, conservatives remained at best skeptical about what diplomatic summit conferences, negotiations, trade agreements, cultural exchange programs, and other efforts to relax international tensions really achieved that counterbalanced the deleterious consequences often inherent in such undertakings.

In the sphere of foreign relations, as in other areas of national life, conservatives seldom served as policy and program innovators. More often than not, they played the role of critic of established policies, insisting that their value be assessed carefully and realistically by reference to their cost and their actual contribution to national policy

goals. In the co
many existing p
eliminated.

One distinctiv
special mention. T
as the "radical rig
some of its detra
Individuals and grou
Senator Joseph R.
Chairman of the Se
Permanent Subcomm
of the supporters of
Korean War; writers li
the publishers of *Huma*
the Minutemen; Christ
groups active in conten
organizations of merc
communism and who
activities at home and abr

A legitimate question
right deserves to be called
example, that it appears
constitutional tradition g
association, and other libe
liberal and left-wing groups)
often jeopardize social and
and they sometimes lead t
opposing political views.

Yet for several reasons,
discussion of conservative n
conservative opinion has alw
opinion, ultraright-wing groups
expressing their viewpoints; the
great intensity; and during som
early 1950s), they have exerted
proportion to their limited mem
instances the radical right has ex
perplexities felt by many America
foreign affairs.

achieve their objectives.[11] In the conservative assessment, and in marked contrast to the idealistic expectations of the Roosevelt administration during World War II, the world of the late twentieth century remained a volatile and dangerous environment, which was in many respects uncongenial for the realization of U.S. diplomatic goals. Moreover, according to some criteria (such as the number of political conflicts existing throughout the Third World) the external milieu was becoming less receptive than ever to U.S. influence and the achievement of national diplomatic objectives. These realities convinced most conservatives to support record-level expenditures for national defense.

Conservative opinion about the nature of the Communist challenge and its implications for U.S. foreign policy can be divided into two schools of thought, with the distinction between them often more of degree than of principle. The mainstream conservative viewpoint is that, during and immediately after World War II, U.S. policy-makers exhibited a sentimental or naive view of the outside world, especially with regard to the nature and goals of communism. Officials of the Roosevelt administration displayed chronic optimism toward Soviet and Chinese communism; they chose to ignore communism's more repressive features and to overlook the obstacles Stalin was placing in the path of a peaceful and durable postwar order; officials in Washington were emotional, rather than objective, in their appraisals of the Soviet system, believing that, in Edgar A. Mowrer's words, communism was "good gone wrong" and that, despite its often harsh methods, the basic aim of Marxism was "improvement of man's lot on earth." Accordingly, U.S. policy-makers erroneously tried to reach an accommodation with Stalin's government and to convince Russians that Americans were their friends. However admirable their intentions, until 1947 (when President Truman belatedly launched the Greek-Turkish Aid Program, designed to contain Communist expansionism), Democratic leaders totally and routinely misconstrued Moscow's wartime and postwar objectives; they pursued polices that strengthened the position of communism vis-à-vis the free world; and they thereby placed the security of the United States in grave jeopardy.[12]

The ultraright-wing conservative view adds other counts to this indictment. During the 1950s, Senator Joe McCarthy and his followers frequently accused Democratic policy-makers of "twenty years of treason." To their minds, since the 1930s, under Democratic presidents Communist and pro-Communist elements had infiltrated the highest levels of the U.S. government; and in some instances, the influence of such groups upon the nation's diplomacy had been crucial. Because of such pro-Communist influence, concessions had repeatedly been made to the Kremlin, to the detriment of the United States' own diplomatic well-being and security. For example, the loss of China to communism was attributed in this explanation to the undue influence exercised upon the State Department and White House by pro-Marxist groups under the Roosevelt and Truman administrations.[13] In more recent years, ultraright-wing groups have repeatedly complained about Washington's unwillingness to oppose Soviet behavior in Poland, Afghanistan, Latin America, and other settings decisively and successfully.

Comparable doubts have been expressed by leading conservatives in more recent years about the value of détente between the United States and the Soviet Union. For many conservatives, détente is a diplomatic trap for the United States, laid by the Kremlin for the explicit purpose of beguiling Americans into a false sense of security that will facilitate Moscow's achievement of its foreign policy objectives. Yet many conservatives are convinced that the Kremlin advocates détente primarily because of Soviet weakness and realization by the Communist heirarchy that the Soviet Union is unable to compete economically, scientifically, and in other respects with the United States and its free world allies. As President Ronald Reagan emphasized time and again, Soviet interest in arms control agreements with the United States was a direct function of U.S. military strength — the most influential factor convincing Communist leaders to act peacefully outside their own borders.[14]

A logical corollary to the conservative assessment of the hostility of the external environment and to the danger posed to the United States by expansionist communism is the emphasis placed upon military prepared-ness and superiority as a paramount requirement of U.S. foreign policy. The cornerstone of national policy, Senator Barry Goldwater has asserted, must be the conviction that "we would rather die than lose our freedom." Accordingly, the United States must achieve and maintain military superiority over the Soviet Union and other potential enemies.[15]

During the mid 1980s, President Ronald Reagan said that he knew of no political or diplomatic contests that the United States had lost because it was too strong. Accordingly, the Reagan administration was determined to maintain a military establishment second to none; and the Reagan White House was convinced that only record-level defense expenditures by the United States could maintain stability in Soviet-U.S. relations. Conservatives were virtually unanimous in their conviction that the U.S. society could afford whatever defense expenditures were necessary to preserve national security and global peace. Both implicitly and explicitly, they rejected the contrary viewpoint — that eliminating poverty at home or increased spending on educational programs could be a substitute for a strong and modern defense establishment.[16] In effect, contemporary conservatives reiterated the old "peace through strength" adage, which had guided most administrations in Washington since the end of World War II. Adequate national defense was what Senator Vandenberg once called a form of "peace insurance."

Several related ideas follow from the conservative emphasis upon the necessity of national military preparedness. Unlike the pre-World War II isolationists, modern conservatives are convinced that to promote its own security the United States needs military allies and alliance systems. After witnessing the Soviet occupation of Eastern Europe during and after World War II, the Communist attempt to take over Greece, Moscow's determination to drive the West out of Berlin, and the Soviet occupation of Czechoslovakia in 1948, Republican Senator Arthur H. Vandenberg took the initiative in preparing a Senate resolution paving the way for formation of the North Atlantic Treaty Organization (NATO), the first U.S. peacetime military alliance system outside the Western Hemisphere, and still its most important defense pact. The resolution was approved by a Republican-dominated Senate on June 11, 1948, by a vote of 64–6.[17] Similarly, under the Eisenhower administration the United States sponsored and joined the Southeast Asia Treaty Organization (SEATO). One of President Eisenhower's firm convictions was that the defense of Southeast Asia from communism ought to be a collective responsibility of the United States, Britain, France, and Asian nations.[18] It is interesting to note that, much as the United Nations soon became a prime target of criticism by ultraright-wing political groups, most of these critics did not favor a go-it-alone policy by the United States after World War II. In lieu of a Communist-dominated U.N. many of them called for an alliance of free nations dedicated to winning the battle against communism; the U.N. would be converted into a kind of "enlarged NATO."[19]

By the 1950s, the United States had created a network of regional military pacts encompassing more than 40 military allies. The tendency reached its zenith under the Eisenhower administration, when Secretary of State John Foster Dulles was widely accused of being addicted to "pactitis." By the end of the 1960s, however, it had become evident that some of these alliances were of dubious value to the United States. The outstanding example was the Southeast Asia Treaty Organization (SEATO), which in effect fell into disuse after the Vietnam War. Under the provisions of the Nixon Doctrine (one of whose primary goals was to reduce U.S. global commitments), the Nixon administration declared that the United States would undertake no new formal treaty obligations to defend other nations — and successive administrations in Washington have followed that principle in their diplomacy. Despite the history of SEATO, most conservatives remain convinced that defense alliances, such as NATO and the Rio Treaty of hemispheric defense, are crucial to the preservation of national security. It was noteworthy, for example, that the Reagan administration continually emphasized the importance of these military pacts and, in several key respects, endeavored to strengthen them.

To conservative minds, the existence of the nation's alliance system entails another fundamental obligation — highlighted by the Vietnam War. It is essential that the United States honor its treaty commitments, thereby maintaining its diplomatic credibility. In the conservative assessment, the real tragedy of Vietnam was that the United States failed to carry out its treaty obligations; and as conservatives predicted, this fact did encourage subsequent Communist expansionism in Southeast Asia and other settings, such as Afghanistan, black Africa, and Latin America.[20] Conservatives are convinced that the United States must be more selective than was true before the Vietnam War in assuming obligations to defend other countries; having accepted that commitment, however, then the United States must scrupulously and decisively honor this commitment when it is challenged by the Soviet Union or other diplomatic adversaries. Conservatives like ex-President Richard Nixon have been outspoken in their belief that Congress is especially prone (as during the Vietnam War) to abandon such national commitments when they are challenged by other countries or when the cost of honoring them is higher than originally anticipated.[21] This tendency led conservative spokesmen, like Secretary of Defense Caspar Weinburger under the Reagan administration, to urge Americans to calculate the costs of external interventionism very carefully before undertaking military commitments abroad. (Secretary Weinburger's views on U.S. interventionism are examined more fully in Chapter 6.)

In contrast to the classical isolationist mode of thought, in the post-World War II period most conservatives value the nation's main military alliances, viewing them as essential for U.S. security and for the preservation of global peace. At the same time, conservative minds do not believe that such alliances exhaust the external military obligations of the United States. For example, the United States has no formal treaty ties with the State of Israel. Yet (along with most liberals) conservatives believe that the United States has a clear and compelling interest in preserving the security of Israel — a defense obligation reiterated by every chief executive since the Truman administration. Similarly, as formally expressed in the Carter Doctrine (1980), the United States also has a vital strategic interest in maintaining access to, and the security of, the Persian Gulf area. This commitment was emphasized several times by the pronouncements and actions of the Reagan administration, which was determined that the United States would possess the military capability to carry out this commitment.[22]

A noteworthy strain in conservative thought since World War II has been its emphasis upon achieving victory when U.S. forces are committed abroad. Many conservatives during the 1950s and afterward, for example, repeated General Douglas MacArthur's dictum that, "in war there is no substitute for victory." Consistent with this belief, conservatives were widely dissatisfied with the results of both the Korean and the Vietnam Wars, neither of which resulted in a clearcut victory by the United States. A long-standing conservative lament about the containment policy has been that it is a "no win" strategy for the United States and that it leaves the initiative to the Soviet Union. (As explained more fully in Chapter 4, the containment policy was initially — and it remains — a defensive reaction by the United States to the challenge of Soviet expansionism.) In more general terms, throughout the postwar era, conservatives have complained about the reactive quality of U.S. diplomacy; and they have urged officials in Washington to "go on the offensive" against Soviet and other varieties of Communist expansionism.

Yet a majority of U.S. conservatives, in contrast to members of the radical right, are also aware of the realities of the nuclear age. They are cognizant of the dangers — not only to the United States, but to human civilization as well — of a nuclear confrontation between the superpowers; and they realize that the nuclear age has created a new set of rules for conducting international politics. More specifically, they are mindful that in the nuclear era, the traditional concept of a diplomatic or military victory risks worldwide devastation. In the light of this reality, a number of conservatives have been at the forefront of those calling for the United States to formulate an effective limited war strategy adapted to the realities of the nuclear age.

Former President Richard Nixon has pointed out, for example, that most wars throughout history have in fact been limited wars.[23] An inescapable corollary of this idea is that in military encounters abroad, the United States cannot realistically expect to achieve the unconditional surrender of the enemy, the dismantling of foreign political regimes, and the total imposition of the will of the United States upon the enemy (as occurred in dealing with Germany and Japan at the end of World War II). In the contemporary era, wars may be limited in several senses — not least, in the *objectives* which Americans have when they commit their armed forces overseas. In contrast to earlier conservative verdicts, for example, from this perspective ex-President Nixon believes that the United States won the Korean War, in the sense that it accomplished its goal of preserving the independence of South Korea.

Psychologically and emotionally, many conservatives concede, this is not a viewpoint congenial to large numbers of Americans, whose attitudes toward war were decisively shaped by experiences like the First and Second World War. As the diplomatic experiences of the Reagan administration in Lebanon and Central America amply illustrated, Americans continue to be impatient in expecting quick and decisive results from the commitment of their forces abroad; and they become easily frustrated and apprehensive when that does not occur. As Chapter 6 emphasizes, formulating an effective limited war or interventionist strategy abroad remains both a high priority item on the agenda of U.S. foreign policy and an issue that elicits highly divergent responses from informed citizens.

Throughout the post-World War II period also, conservatives as a rule have favored the extension of U.S. arms-aid to other countries, especially those facing actual or potential Communist expansionism. During the Truman and Eisenhower administrations, even Senator Joseph McCarthy and his followers approved of the Greek-Turkish Aid Program and other efforts to provide military assistance to the nation's friends and allies abroad. For some 40 years after enactment of the Greek-Turkish Aid Program, foreign military aid has been a major component of U.S. foreign policy. In contrast to their liberal counterparts, conservatives do not usually invoke a test of ideological purity in providing arms-aid to foreign countries; they are not unduly troubled by the fact that military assistance has frequently been provided to nondemocratic governments abroad or the fact that such aid has frequently been used by incumbent governments against internal political opposition groups.

In the conservative view the dominant criterion for supplying military aid to foreign nations is that doing so promotes the diplomatic and security interests of the United States, especially in Washington's efforts to contain expansive Communism. President Dwight D. Eisenhower, after all, is identified with the principle of letting "Asians fight Asians" or, in more general terms, of seeking to gain the collaboration of other countries in the worldwide effort to contain Communist expansionist tendencies.[24] During the 1970s, in the Nixon Doctrine the same basic idea was reiterated: in the post-Vietnam War era, the United States would seek to furnish the resources and arms-aid required, while endeavoring to get other countries to supply the manpower needed, to implement the containment policy. Successful application of this strategy would thereby avoid one of the primary mistakes of the Vietnam War; in effect, it accepted General MacArthur's earlier warning to the United States not to become "bogged down" in a land war on the Asian continent.[25]

Many of the ideas and principles we have identified with the conservative approach to national defense policy were embodied in the concept of "Fortress America," identified with ex-President Herbert Hoover during the early 1950s. At the outset, it should be emphasized that the Fortress America concept did not enjoy widespread support within the United States, even among Republicans and other conservatives. In fact, a number of Hoover's Republican colleagues vocally opposed his strategy. Hoover's proposal involved a synthesis of a very old strategic concept with a more recent one. As we noted in Chapter 1, classical U.S. isolationist thought had emphasized the notion of hemispheric self-sufficiency and the uniqueness of the New World. Since World War II, conservative thought has called for U.S. air and naval superiority over possible enemies. Combining these ideas, on January 27, 1952, Hoover asserted that "the first national purpose of this republic must be defense of this final Gibraltar of freedom — that is, the Western Hemisphere." In a series of speeches on this theme, Hoover demanded that U.S. defense policy take account of the following realities: communism controlled most of the great Eurasian land mass; Moscow and Peking possessed overwhelming strength in ground forces, but they were weak in air and naval power, which were the United States' most potent military components; any attempt to defeat the Communist nations in a land war would, therefore, be "sheer folly"; by contrast, by relying upon dominant air and sea power, the United States along with a limited number of allies could prevent any hostile force from threatening the Western Hemisphere via the Atlantic or Pacific oceans; implementing this strategy would require the United States to maintain a defense line, with one end anchored in Great Britain and the other in Japan, Formosa, and the Philippines; successfully defending Fortress America demanded that the United States "arm our air and naval forces to the teeth"; the defense of Western Europe (and presumably any other area outside Hoover's indicated defense perimeter) would be left mainly to the non-Communist states of Europe themselves.[26]

Hoover's Fortress America concept is perhaps largely of historic interest today. Yet it merits brief attention for several reasons. Hoover's proposal represented one of the earliest efforts in the postwar era to limit U.S. military commitments abroad, in recognition of the fact that the United States could not, and should not, attempt to serve as a global policeman. The Fortress America strategy also highlighted the historic and continuing interest of the United States in preserving the security of the Western Hemisphere. As exemplified by the Monroe Doctrine in 1823, this was one of the oldest and most consistent goals in U.S. diplomacy; hemispheric security was at stake in the Cuban missile crisis of 1962 — the most dangerous Soviet-U.S. encounter since World War II; and as was evident from the Reagan administration's extensive involvement in Central America, preserving the security of the Western Hemisphere still ranks high on the list of Washington's diplomatic priorities.

Ex-President Hoover's concept was also noteworthy because of its relative lack of concern about the need for allies. Only four countries (Great Britain, Japan, Formosa or Taiwan, and the Philippines) were mentioned specifically as playing a significant role in Hoover's defense strategy; and during the 1950s, three of these were very weak nations, while British power was declining, and has continued to decline, throughout the postwar period. In effect, former President Hoover declared, the United States will defend the Western Hemisphere alone if necessary! On the basis of its actions (if not necessarily its foreign policy pronouncements), this was the same position taken by the Reagan administration during the 1980s.

Perhaps no single issue in postwar U.S. foreign policy highlights the differences in outlook between the radical right and more moderate or orthodox U.S. conservative thought than the question of U.S. membership in, and support for, the United Nations. During and immediately after World War II, the vast majority of conservative spokesmen approved of the creation of the U.N. and of the U.S. assumption of a leadership role in it. Influential conservatives like John Foster Dulles and Senator Arthur H. Vandenberg were instrumental in establishing and maintaining bipartisan cooperation between the Democrats and Republicans in behalf of this goal. Indicative of the nearly universal support for the nascent United Nations was the fact that on July 28, 1945, the Senate ratified the U.N. Charter by a vote of 89 to 2.

By the early 1950s, however, conservatives had begun to express genuine apprehension about the United Nations and its role in U.S. foreign policy. During the "McCarthy era," the United Nations quickly became a prime target of criticism from ultrarightist spokesmen. In time, most of them agreed with the demand expressed by leaders of the John Birch Society: "Get the U.S. out of the U.N. and the U.N. out of the U.S." For this group, the U.N. had become anathema. As Robert Welch assessed the organization: "The U.N. was conceived by Communists. The U.N. was created by Communists. The U.N. is controlled by Communists and the U.N. has constantly furthered the objectives of Communism."[27] Numerous counts are included in the indictment of the U.N. brought by members of the radical right. The U.N. was established initially as the result of "Kremlin planning," with pro-Soviet U.S. officials (like Alger Hiss) playing a key role; the very existence of the U.N. is contrary to the idea of U.S. nationalism and sovereignty; a world government, and perhaps a world dictator, will someday emerge from the United Nations; by belonging to the U.N., the United States has yoked itself with ungodly states, which seek its destruction; the U.N. is controlled by Communist and pro-Communist nations that are congenitally opposed to the goals of U.S. foreign policy; the U.N. fosters international "do-goodism," the equalization of wealth and other ideas at variance with the U.S. credo: by belonging to the U.N., the United States is unavoidably engaged in an attempt to conciliate and appease communism; the U.N. has become merely a sounding board for Communist and anti-U.S. propaganda.[28] With the passage of time, another count was added to the ultraconservative indictment of the United Nations: in the U.N. General Assembly particularly, its decisions were controlled by an anti-U.S. majority of Third World nations. If this group's deliberations were not dictated by the Soviet Union, at a minimum they reflected a consistent anti-Western orientation and reliance upon a double standard in judging Soviet and U.S. conduct.

While moderate conservatives usually reject such conspiratorial evaluations of the United Nations, it is clear that conservative opinion toward the U.N. has become increasingly critical in recent years, contributing significantly to the crisis of confidence that has characterized U.S. opinion toward the organization. The early hopes that Americans entertained for the U.N. quickly dimmed. The expectation that a new community of nations was in the process of being created — or the hope that the U.N. could assume the primary responsibility for international peace keeping — proved illusory. Instead, to the U.S. mind the U.N. was, at best, an increasingly irresponsible body, in which Third World nations endeavored to make decisions they were unable to carry out; at worst, the U.N. had become an instrument used by the Soviet Union and other diplomatic adversaries to achieve their foreign policy goals. President Ronald Reagan's decision to withdraw U.S. membership in the United Nations Educational, Scientific, and Cultural Organization (UNESCO) symbolized growing conservative disaffection with the United Nations. Under the Reagan administration also, U.N. Ambassador Jeane Kirkpatrick was frequently outspoken in identifying the organization's faults and in demanding that Third World nations be more objective in their evaluations of Soviet and U.S. behavior. By the mid 1980s, U.S. disenchantment with the United Nations was at its highest level in the postwar period.[29]

Late in 1971, in an unexpected move, the Senate of the United States voted 41–27 to terminate the foreign aid program, thereby reversing a major trend in U.S. foreign policy that began in the late 1940s. This setback for the foreign aid program was largely symbolic and temporary. The adverse Senate vote came about as the result of opposition by a curious antiforeign aid coalition, which found political liberals and conservatives alike opposed to the continuation of the program.[30] (We shall examine liberal objections to foreign aid more fully in Chapter 3.) As time passed, Congress reverted to its predictable practice of approving an annual foreign aid appropriation, and military and economic assistance to other countries remained a major instrument of U.S. diplomacy under the Reagan administration. For fiscal year 1986, the Reagan administration's foreign aid program amounted to $16 billion.[31]

Yet ever since the beginning of the foreign aid program under the Truman administration, conservatives have expressed doubts and concerns about the extension of military and economic assistance abroad. Time and again, for example, conservatives have insisted that the foreign aid program be administered according to sound business principles, by officials outside the State Department. They have repeatedly cautioned the president and his advisers against operating an international welfare program at the expense of the U.S. taxpayers; and they have warned Americans against a tendency to believe that the United States can buy friends abroad. Under the Reagan administration, U.S. officials placed unprecedented emphasis upon the idea that the financial needs of the developing nations would have to be met primarily by private investment;

and Third World nations were likely to attract such foreign capital only by creating and maintaining the required investment climate needed to achieve it. In practice, however, it must also be noted that the Reagan administration extended a loan that saved Communist-ruled Poland from bankruptcy; and it encouraged U.S. banks to reschedule the massive debts owed by a number of Latin American nations.

Ever since the late 1940s, conservatives (much more than liberals) have viewed foreign aid as an essential component of U.S. containment strategy. To conservative minds, the anti-Communist rationale of the foreign aid program has been (or ought to be) clear and central: during the 1980s, no less than the 1950s, a leading purpose of military and economic assistance to other countries is to enhance their ability to resist communism, internally and externally. In even broader terms, conservatives believe that foreign aid must be viewed candidly as an instrument of U.S. foreign policy; it is designed primarily to promote the interests of the United States abroad. By contrast, other countries do not have a right to U.S. foreign aid, and Washington is under no obligation to assist foreign nations in meeting their financial and security needs.

A corollary of this idea is that, in judging foreign aid requests (always collectively greater than the budgetary allocation for this purpose), Washington should make its foreign aid allocations selectively; it should consider the attitudes and actions of nations requesting U.S. assistance, in terms of their attitudes toward the United States; and it should, without apology, use foreign aid to achieve the nation's foreign policy objectives. As our earlier discussion emphasized, conservatives are considerably less inclined than liberals to impose a test of democratic purity for the recipients of U.S. foreign assistance. The former are more likely to rely upon a strategic test, for example, in providing military aid to countries facing an urgent Communist threat to their security. Regarding economic assistance, conservatives are prone to insist that foreign societies engage in a maximum degree of self-help in meeting their internal needs and that they engage in the domestic reforms needed to make the use of U.S. aid effective.

Another significant implication of conservative attitudes toward foreign aid deserves brief mention. Conservatives are dubious, for example, about the idea that by supplying large amounts of external assistance to other countries, the United States is somehow directly promoting global peace, stability, and security. In the opinion of many conservatives, hunger, poverty, and human misery were not the primary causes of violence among nations (if they were, then India, China, and

Egypt would be among the most violence-prone nations on the globe). In Mowrer's view, the wars and conflicts of modern history stemmed from a "sickness" that was "in the soul, not in the belly." Soviet Russia posed the most serious danger to global peace after it had embarked upon the path of industrialization and modernization. In addition, conservative spokesmen objected to foreign aid because it reflected a Utopian or "millennial tendency" in the U.S. mind to believe that the United States could remake the world and that officials in Washington could solve problems (like poverty and economic backwardness in other countries) that had long eluded solution by officials of other nations. When such goals were not achieved, only disillusionment would be the result.[32]

During the late 1970s, many conservative doubts about the results to be expected from foreign aid were confirmed by developments in Iran. According to a number of criteria, under the monarchy Iran had achieved one of the best records of national development to be found within the Third World. The Kennedy administration had encouraged the Shah of Iran to undertake a "White Revolution" (or government-sponsored revolution) designed to make the benefits of the country's growing prosperity available broadly to all sectors of Iranian society; and, with the notable exception of the political realm, the Shah's government was carrying out a series of reform measures in nearly all spheres of national life. Yet early in 1979, the Iranian monarchy was overthrown by a revolutionary movement eventually dominated by the Shi'ite clergy. The new government quickly became one of the most outspokenly anti-U.S. nations in the Third World. In the Persian Gulf area, and in the Middle East generally, the Ayatollah Khomeini's regime was determined to oppose the "Great Satan" in Washington — as, for example, in Iran's complicity in terrorist attacks against U.S. forces and officials in Lebanon.[33] From the Iranian experience, conservatives were prone to draw lessons such as efforts to buy friends abroad seldom succeed, the results of U.S. foreign aid and proffered friendship often have unforeseen (and sometimes highly adverse) consequences, and the United States must be extremely careful about encouraging radical changes in foreign societies.

In the conservative assessment, the Iran case is merely a particularly dramatic example of a larger phenomenon. Experience has amply demonstrated that whatever its intended objective (and the persistent lack of clarity about the goals of the foreign aid program has always troubled conservatives), providing aid to other countries does not automatically win friends abroad for the United States. To the contrary, the reverse is frequently true: the foreign aid process inherently generates tensions between donor and recipient. In both foreign and domestic affairs, the creditor-debtor relationship is seldom marked by friendship and good will. If the U.S. foreign aid program is quite clearly not the sole (or even the principal) cause, conservatives are convinced that there has been an overall decline in U.S. global influence since the early postwar era, not least among countries that have been primary beneficiaries of U.S. foreign aid. Two prominent examples of this phenomenon are France and India, where in both cases U.S. influence has sometimes appeared to be negligible. As one commentator has said, foreign aid inevitably appears to societies overseas as "manipulative interference in other people's business." Or, as Senator Goldwater expressed the idea, the result of foreign aid has been to create a "vast reservoir of anti-Americanism" among peoples who resent "dependence on a foreign dole."[34] If a major objective of U.S. foreign assistance has been to create politically stable, democratic, and more prosperous nations throughout the Third World, by the mid 1980s it was evident to most conservatives that, with very rare exceptions, the foreign aid program has not achieved its purpose.

A particularly sensitive point about foreign aid for conservatives has been the provision of external assistance to neutralist or nonaligned nations and, in a few instances, to those with Marxist or quasi-Marxist regimes. For conservatives, the distinction between these two categories of nations has always been tenuous. Time and again, conservatives have complained about the pro-Communist bias that characterized neutralist attitudes toward the United States and the West generally. During the Reagan administration, U.N. Ambassador Jeane Kirkpatrick's denunciations of neutralist attitudes and actions won widespread conservative commendation. To the conservative mind, little evidence existed that the provision of U.S. aid to neutralist countries altered their viewpoints toward the United States. Naive expectations that gratitude for U.S. assistance would be expressed tangibly, in the form of greater military or diplomatic support for Washington's foreign policy objectives, have almost never materialized. Instead, for reasons already discussed, the extension of U.S. foreign aid to other countries was likely to introduce new sources of misunderstanding and disagreement between them. Despite the Alliance for Progress launched by the Kennedy administration, for example, by some criteria U.S.-Latin American relations appeared to be at a lower ebb in the 1980s than in the 1960s. Little evidence existed that the long hoped-for "American community" was in the process of emerging in the near future.

Despite such conservative reservations about foreign aid, it remains true that the Nixon, Ford, and Reagan administrations supported the principle of external military and economic assistance to other countries. They did so perhaps for one transcendent reason: on balance, the foreign aid program seemed to these conservative administrations to possess more advantages than disadvantages for the United States. Or to express the idea differently: the adverse consequences of not providing U.S. aid to selected nations abroad were greater than the defects of the foreign aid program. An example is provided by the Reagan administration's provision of large-scale foreign assistance to Egypt during the 1980s; by the mid 1980s Egypt had become the second largest (next to Israel) recipient of U.S. foreign aid. Conservatives and liberals alike often criticized U.S. aid to Egypt on several grounds, such as Arab unwillingness to make peace with Israel, the growing severity of Egypt's internal problems, the growth of "Islamic Fundamentalism" within the country, and the deteriorating state of Egyptian-Israeli relations. In the end, however, President Reagan and his advisers concluded that the provision of massive foreign assistance to Egypt was in the interest of the United States. The official hope was that by doing so the United States would prevent Egypt's massive reliance upon the Soviet Union to meet its internal and external security needs, that it would encourage moderate political regimes within Egypt and the Arab world generally, that it would provide tangible evidence of the United States' continuing interest in a resolution of the Arab-Israeli conflict, and that it would provide the United States with at least limited influence with one of the most influential Arab states. In brief, U.S. assistance to Egypt was viewed by U.S. officials as a more desirable alternative than Egyptian reliance upon the Soviet Union exclusively.[35]

THE CONSERVATIVE CONTRIBUTION TO FOREIGN AFFAIRS

Conservative viewpoints toward postwar U.S. foreign relations deserve serious study for a number of reasons. Let us analyze their contribution further by focusing upon their positive and negative features, recognizing that the latter often tend to receive more attention from serious students of foreign policy than the former.

A clearly beneficial contribution of conservative thought in promoting more intelligent understanding of foreign relations is its role as a corrective for one of the most troublesome and recurrent problems confronting foreign policy decision makers in the United States. This is the all-too-familiar cycle of idealistic and unqualified expectations, followed by a prolonged mood of popular disillusionment when ambitious and often imaginative programs fail to achieve their avowed goals.[36]

A recent example of this phenomenon was provided by the Vietnam War syndrome, which influenced U.S. attitudes and actions in foreign affairs during most of the 1970s. For some citizens (perhaps always a minority), that the United States had failed to achieve its goals in Southeast Asia meant that it was incapable of accomplishing any worthwhile purpose in foreign affairs. Pervasive apprehensions about another Vietnam created widespread doubts that the nation could employ its armed forces successfully in any foreign setting to achieve diplomatic objectives. As in the period following World War I, an era of unlimited diplomatic expectations was soon followed by an era of profound public disillusionment and withdrawal from the world after the nation's high hopes were not realized. This is an all-too-familiar cycle in U.S. diplomatic experience.

In the conservative view, the key to its prevention is continual recognition that, vast as it is, U.S. power is limited, that the external environment is usually intractable and unreceptive for the achievement of U.S. goals, and that basing the nation's foreign policy upon illusions about what the United States is able to accomplish abroad will result in popular disillusionment with the diplomatic outcome. In the case of the Vietnam War, many conservatives are convinced that there was always a fundamental lack of clarity in Washington, and among the people of the United States, about whether the security of South Vietnam was a vital diplomatic interest of the United States. Avoiding that kind of confusion, therefore, is one of the transcendent lessons of Vietnam for the future.[37] By the same token, conservatives — whose expectations concerning the United Nations were always modest — have not been particularly surprised that the U.N. has failed to fulfill the expectations of many of its supporters.

Similarly, by the late 1960s the U.S. society manifested an attitude of foreign aid weariness. As a percentage of its gross national product, the level of aid provided other countries by the United States has steadily declined. According to this standard, the United States now ranked among the lowest foreign aid contributors among the industrialized nations. This phenomenon also no doubt had manifold causes. A major one, however, unquestionably was that, as with the case of the United Nations, the benefits both for the United States and for recipient countries to be expected from foreign aid had been exaggerated to Congress and the public by successive administrations in Washington and by friends of the foreign aid program. After witnessing the phenomenally successful example of European recovery, facilitated by the Marshall Plan during the 1950s, devotees of foreign aid tended to apply this model rather indiscriminately to the Third World, where similar results were anticipated within a relatively brief period. A noteworthy example was the Alliance for Progress for promoting Latin American modernization. Many of the president's advisers were convinced that the rapid modernization of this region was a feasible undertaking; that substantial aid provided by the United States, coupled with Latin America's own efforts, would make achievement of the goal possible; and that, as economic conditions improved throughout the area, political extremism would be inhibited, while the prospects for genuine democracy would be greatly enhanced.

Experience with foreign aid in Latin America and other economically backward regions since World War II has shown that for the most part such expectations were highly unrealistic, if not totally illusory. For example, significant progress toward modernization has occurred in only a handful of societies throughout the Third World. For the vast majority of Third World nations either little perceptible progress has been achieved, or else they have actually retrogressed (in spheres like per capita food production) since the 1950s. Moreover, within the Third World violence and political turmoil have escalated; various species of authoritarian governments are the rule (with the dominant type being the military junta); there is no evidence that regional stability has been appreciably enhanced in Latin America or the Afro-Asian world. On balance, it must be conceded that experience with foreign aid has tended in the main to confirm the conservative estimates of what it would achieve, vis-à-vis the more uncritical and romanticized expectations entertained by pro-foreign aid spokesmen.

These are merely selected examples illustrating a more general point. Conservatives tend to be congenitally dubious about the likelihood of beneficial social, economic, and political changes, and more so in the realm of foreign affairs than in domestic affairs. They do not regard the external environment as highly malleable and susceptible to successful manipulation by officials in Washington. As a rule, conservatives are inclined to regard governmental intervention in the social and economic affairs of other countries as unwise and unproductive. In the

military-controlled regimes in black Africa, or other nondemocratic governments. Few conservatives believe that a comprehensive antipoverty program — or a new effort to reconstruct the U.S. educational system — is really an answer to growing Soviet naval power or to Cuba's interventionist policies in Africa and Latin America. In the traditional competition between guns and butter, it does not exaggerate to say that conservatives give the higher priority to preserving national security in the face of external threats. Accordingly, the Reagan administration could simultaneously urge the reduction of overall federal spending and the expansion of the national defense budget to record peacetime levels. Implicitly, the conservative position accepts President Abraham Lincoln's assertion during the Civil War that "the Union must be preserved!" Efforts to achieve the good life within the United States presuppose the continued existence of the U.S. Republic as a democratic and independent nation.

True conservatives, as distinct from reactionaries, we need to be reminded, do not reject the idea of change, but they do insist that such changes be made gradually and that innovations represent genuine improvements over the status quo. Insofar as the lack of needed domestic reforms might ultimately create internal divisiveness and generate rising political instability within the United States, this fact might detract from the ability of policy-makers to achieve national purposes abroad. Yet in the conservative view domestic programs to eliminate poverty, unemployment, illiteracy, and the like in the United States are not substitutes for measures like an adequate defense program. The conservative thus rejects the dichotomy that liberals often postulate: governmental expenditures for a modernized air force, for example, are not to be regarded as spending at the expense of society's welfare.

In both the Korean and the Vietnam Wars, conservatives often emerged as defenders of the nation's military leaders against their detractors. During the Vietnam War it became highly fashionable in some circles to attribute the blame for U.S. involvement in the conflict, or the failure to achieve national objectives, upon a supposedly all-powerful "military-industrial complex." Conservatives regard this tendency as a compound error. While few of them deny the existence of waste and mismanagement in the military establishment (a condition from which no military organization in history has entirely been free), they look upon such indiscriminate accusations as highly deleterious to military morale at a time when the armed forces are more hard pressed than ever to compete with civilian sectors for manpower and when the role of military force in promoting national policy goals is more complex and ambiguous than ever. Polemical denunciations of the military-industrial complex tend to obscure the real problem involved: improving civilian leadership, to assure that it exercises wisely and effectively the authority it possesses under the Constitution. Placing the blame for the Vietnam War upon the military-industrial complex also tends to imply an absurdity: if the United States did not possess a powerful military establishment, it would somehow escape traumatic and costly experiences like the prolonged involvement in Southeast Asia! In a different geographical setting, what would it cost the United States to liberate Europe a third time, rather than to prevent its subordination to a hostile power? Or in the context of the ongoing political crisis in Central America, conservatives ask critics of the Reagan administration's diplomacy, "If the United States is not prepared to take a stand against Communist attempts to subvert El Salvador and Soviet efforts to gain a foothold in the region, where is a better place to resist communism in Latin America more successfully? In Panama, in Guatemala, in Mexico, or perhaps along the Rio Grande border?" (In all these cases, as critics complained about El Salvador, none of the governments concerned satisfied most Americans' conception of democracy or otherwise presented a more favorable environment for contesting Communist gains.) In contrast to his liberal counterpart, the conservative believes that the applicable lesson for U.S. policymakers is avoidance of another Cuba in the Western Hemisphere. Or if there is analogy with the Vietnam War, to conservative minds it lies in avoiding the kind of defeat which the United States experienced in Southeast Asia.

Conservatives are often more aware than political liberals that national security and foreign policy are opposite sides of the same coin; one relates to, and impinges directly upon, the other. As in the Korean and Vietnam conflicts, and the Reagan administration's intervention in Lebanon and Central America, if the nation has experienced difficulty in achieving its diplomatic objectives, a major reason is that Americans have not understood this vital relationship clearly and based their diplomatic behavior upon it.

In its application to U.S. diplomacy, conservative thought also, of course, has been characterized by the existence of certain lacunae, blind spots, and inadequacies. Let us take note initially of certain defects nearly always present in ultrarightist attitudes and behavior in the foreign policy field.

During the late 1940s and 1950s, even critics of "McCarthyism" and other manifestations of the extreme right sometimes justified the phenomenon on the grounds that indiscriminate anti-Communist crusades awakened the nation to the dangers posed by communism at home and abroad. In reality, of course, national policy-makers were mindful of the Communist challenge some five years or so before Senator McCarthy embarked upon his well-publicized and free-wheeling exposure of Communist influences in the U.S. government and other segments of national life. President Franklin D. Roosevelt, for example, had become openly critical of Stalin's behavior before the end of World War II. Under President Truman, the United States inaugurated the policy of containment, tangibly expressed in such undertakings as the Greek-Turkish Aid Program, the Marshall Plan, NATO, and the Mutual Defense Assistance Program; the determination of policy-makers to defend the nation's rights during the first Berlin crisis in 1948 also afforded graphic evidence that they were alert to the implications of Communist expansionism.

Whatever contributions ultrarightist individuals and groups may have made in familiarizing the U.S. society with the Communist threats, therefore, seem more than counterbalanced by the negative features of extreme right-wing thought and conduct. Insofar as communism or other forms of political extremism are actually fostered by the polarization of society, by the growth of suspicion among citizens, by popular distrust of leaders, and by lack of consensus among the population, the ultraright has facilitated the growth of political movements that are largely alien to the U.S. tradition.

From the perspective of bold and imaginative decision making, involving the dispassionate consideration of policy alternatives, the impact of the radical right has been considerably more destructive than constructive. Aside from impairing the morale of countless officials in agencies like the State Department and the U.S. Information Agency (USIA), the activities of ultrarightist critics of U.S. foreign policy often made it all but impossible for citizens and their leaders to comprehend objectively why communism triumphed in China or why Eastern Europe emerged from World War II under Soviet domination. Unquestionably, it was easier for some Americans to understand the idea that China had been sold out to communism by subversive influences in the State Department than to comprehend the manifold and complex origins of the Chinese civil war, to grasp the effects of World War II upon the internal power struggle within China, and to assess the factors ultimately favoring victory by Mao Tse-tung's Marxist movement over the Nationalist government. Explanations of U.S. foreign policy in this vein, offered by the radical right, can seriously impede the diplomatic efforts of the United States. They encourage the people to believe that they were sabotaged by pro-Communist elements within the U.S. government, instead of believing that in most cases their diplomatic setbacks have stemmed from widespread public apathy toward, and pervasive ignorance about, crucial international issues.

Moreover, the radical right's conception of communism has always been and remains primitive, simplistic, and often highly misleading. If the concept of international communism as a monolithic movement controlled from Moscow ever possessed validity, after Stalin's death it became increasingly inaccurate and deceptive. The radical right never conceded the possibility that the Soviet system was capable of change, nor was it prepared to recognize that fissures like the Sino-Soviet dispute could destroy the unity of the Communist bloc. Thanks in no small measure to the implacable opposition of ultrarightist groups like the "China Lobby," it was not until the 1970s that U.S. policy-makers were able to recognize Chinese independence of Soviet control, to arrive at a limited détente with Peking, and to resolve a number of major issues engendering Cold War tensions with the Soviet Union.

Another characteristic of the radical right's approach to foreign affairs was exemplified by the attitudes of certain fundamentalist religious groups during the 1980s. This was the tendency to equate their own (often highly primitive and emotionally colored) view of international questions with Christian morality and ethics, as though there is a Christian position on most controversial political issues. If they were certainly not alone in doing so, such groups frequently failed to understand that, on a complex issue like Soviet-U.S. relations, the really salient question usually was how to oppose communism most effectively. Or on the issue of U.S. relations with Israel, the really difficult problem was how to assure the security of Israel, and of the Middle East generally, in the long run. Or on U.S. relations with Latin America, as often as not, the fundamental problem was how to counter Communist influence within the region without providing new sources of resentment toward the United States for the people and leaders of Latin America. Almost never did literal reiteration of biblical passages or other religious authorities shed light upon these complex and difficult questions.

With regard to more orthodox or middle-of-the-road conservative thought, the same criticisms may appropriately be made of its approach to foreign policy issues that are often made of it as a political philosophy. Conservatives can seldom be counted upon to furnish alternatives to existing policies. In the postwar period moderate conservatives have often served as incisive and timely critics of developments in foreign relations. Many of their reservations about foreign aid programs and their skepticisms about tendencies within the United Nations have been substantiated by experience. Although they did not employ the phrase, in effect conservatives have frequently cautioned policy-makers about the "arrogance of American power," by which was meant a presumption by officialdom in Washington that problems like the existence of poverty throughout the Third World, or the population explosion, or recurrent political instability within Afro-Asian and Latin American societies were susceptible to a U.S. solution.

It is equally true, however, that in its preference for the status quo or relatively modest changes, conservative thought exhibits certain shortcomings as a guide to foreign policy. For example, conservatives show genuine reluctance to recognize that cherished U.S. concepts like capitalism, free enterprise, and even Western-style democracy are often unpalatable for less advanced societies. To the Afro-Asian or Latin American mind, these concepts are often tainted because of their association with the colonial era; they are synonymous with exploitation by foreign corporations; and they evoke images of absentee landlords and usurious moneylenders at home.

Conversely, conservatives seem no less oblivious to the appeal of socialist programs for such societies. In the popular mind, socialism is often equated with human betterment, modernization, and progress. Despite the presumed willingness of moderate conservatives to accept gradual change, which enjoys wide popular support, their thought is often characterized by what might be called a "semantic lag." While they have largely accepted the major programs identified with the New Deal and the Fair Deal within the United States, they continue to react emotionally and negatively to terms like socialism or collectivism or governmental intervention in economic and social affairs. As the legislative programs sponsored by the Eisenhower, Nixon, Ford, and Reagan administrations clearly indicated, mainstream conservatism not only has come to terms with the Social Security program, MEDICARE, unemployment compensation, and other components of the welfare state in contemporary America. Republican administrations have also extended and improved the benefits of such programs, sought to administer them more efficiently, and accepted them as a permanent feature of modern

U.S. life. Yet it remains difficult for moderate conservatives in the United States to admit that they have sponsored such changes or to accept the idea that in other societies, the case for government intervention in social and political affairs may be even more compelling.

From the Eisenhower to the Reagan administrations, mainstream conservative opinion has from time to time also exhibited an obsession with "the Communist problem," which sometimes blinded it to the existence of other challenges to the nation's diplomatic interests and well-being. Under the Eisenhower administration, for example, Secretary of State John Foster Dulles was extraordinarily preoccupied with international communism (and even in the 1950s, that movement exhibited evidence of widening fissures and schisms, leading in time to several varieties of "national communism"). Again in the 1980s, the Reagan administration exhibited a comparable tendency, as illustrated by Reagan's belief that the Soviet Union was "the locus of evil" in the modern world. Yet it was also President Reagan who saved the Communist-governed Polish regime from bankruptcy and who continued the policy (begun by President Nixon and expanded by President Carter) of seeking closer ties with the People's Republic of China.

Conservative thought has often had difficulty distinguishing between communism as a cause or agent of revolutionary upheaval and violence and as a force that exploits and uses conditions favorable to the Communist cause. Even if communism did not exist in the Soviet Union, China, North Vietnam, Cuba and other settings, for example, the United States would still confront difficult and frustrating challenges abroad, posed by such forces as Afro-Asian nationalism, the desire of primitive societies to modernize rapidly, jealousy and resentment toward the United States, and Arab animosity toward Israel. The Kremlin did not create widespread suspicion toward the "North American Colossus" throughout Latin America, much as it seeks to exploit such sentiment for its own diplomatic purposes. Nor would the independent nations of black Africa be politically stable and democratic today if there were no Communist parties, or no Soviet and Cuban agents, on the African continent. Fervent U.S. denunciations of communism, or pledges by conservative political leaders to stand firm against Communist encroachments, usually do little to equip the United States to respond to these global challenges effectively.

Noteworthy also has been the conservative tendency since World War II to identify, and to respond to, the Communist challenge abroad very largely in military terms. Perhaps because it became a serious and graphic threat to U.S. security during World War II and its aftermath, communism has been visualized by conservatives primarily as a military danger, to be countered by U.S. reliance chiefly upon military and paramilitary strategies. While they are congenitally skeptical about how economic or technical assistance programs to other countries promote U.S. security and diplomatic interests, conservatives normally exhibit no such hesitancy or doubt about the necessity of costly national defense budgets, military alliance systems, and overseas arms-aid programs. The diversion of increasingly scarce raw materials and other national resources by the United States and other countries to military expenditures, the evident waste that has characterized the U.S. (and all other) defense programs, the steadily escalating cost of modern armaments, the dangers to humanity posed by an uninterrupted arms race between the two superpowers and smaller countries possessing nuclear weapons, the rising level of military expenditures — such problems seldom trouble conservatives deeply.

This deficiency in conservative thought as related to global problems was highlighted by the dilemma of the Reagan administration. On the one hand, perhaps more than any other chief executive since World War II, President Reagan was determined to improve the defense position of the United States and to maintain a military establishment second to none. (Yet it must also be recalled that, following the Iranian hostage crisis and the Soviet invasion of Afghanistan, the Carter administration had initially proposed a substantial increase in national defense spending.) In the main, the Reagan White House was able to resist the demands by its critics that significant reductions be made in defense expenditures in the effort to reduce the federal deficit.

On the other hand, from the day he entered the Oval Office, President Reagan had difficulty explaining how his administration proposed to use growing U.S. military power to achieve its diplomatic objectives. Some applications of U.S. military force were perhaps obvious, as in the Reagan administration's successful attempt to prevent a Communist takeover of the Caribbean nation of Grenada. Yet what would the effect of the augmention of U.S. military power be upon the Soviet Union? Would it (as the Reagan administration confidently expected) compel the Kremlin to arrive at new arms control agreements and other accords with the United States? Or would it in fact trigger a new round of higher defense spending by Soviet officials in order to preserve a position of military parity with the United States? Would the net result be something that President Reagan and his supporters decried — a new and costly arms race between the superpowers?

On a different level, conservative policy-makers faced no less troublesome problems in applying military force in regional and local conflicts. For example, the Reagan White House had little or no success when it relied upon military intervention to create and maintain political stability in Lebanon. After considerable loss of U.S. life, the policy not only failed; but in the view of many informed commentators, U.S. intervention in Lebanon compounded the problem of Middle Eastern violence and led to such results as the enhancement of Syrian influence within the region. Similarly, by the early months of Reagan's second term, it was difficult to see how the nation's overwhelming military power was relevant to the ongoing political crisis in Central America. It was clear that Congress and the people of the United States were extremely apprehensive about the possibility of military interventionism by the United States in Latin America; and even Washington's friends south of the border repeatedly warned the Reagan administration against that course of action. Once again, conservative policy-makers were experiencing difficulty in demonstrating how the nation's armed strength could be applied effectively to a diplomatic problem in a way that elicited the broad support of the people of the United States.

These quandaries produced an ongoing debate among President Reagan's diplomatic advisers concerning the circumstances under which the United States ought to rely upon the armed forces to achieve foreign policy goals. That continuing debate will be analyzed more fully in Chapter 6.

NOTES

1. See Lloyd A. Free and Hadley Cantril, *The Political Beliefs of Americans: A Study of Public Opinion* (New Brunswick, N.J.: Rutgers University Press, 1967), pp. 61–68; Alfred O. Hero, *Americans in World Affairs* (Boston: World Peace Foundation, 1959), pp. 6–14; and Barry Goldwater, *The Conscience of a Majority* (New York: Macfadden, 1970), p. 76.

2. William F. Buckley, Jr., *Up from Liberalism* (New York: McDowell, Oblensky, 1959), pp. xv, 59.

3. The views of Burke and of Disraeli are quoted in Clinton Rossiter, *Conservatism in America* (New York: Random House, 1962), p. 20.

4. For a detailed statement of the idea that U.S. society has never been congenial to a conservative position, along with contrary views, see John H. Redekop, *The American Far Right: A Case Study of Billy James Hargis and Christian Crusade* (Grand Rapids, Mich.: W. B. Eerdmans, 1968), pp. 155–61. See also the discussion of U.S. conservatism in Edward Cain, *They'd Rather Be Right: Youth and the*

Conservative Movement (New York: Macmillan, 1963), pp. 11–36.

5. William Safire, *The New Language of Politics* (New York: Random House, 1968), p. 89.

6. For a more detailed discussion of the major elements in conservative thought, see Clinton Rossiter, "Conservatism," in David L. Sills, ed., *International Encyclopaedia of the Social Sciences* (New York: Macmillan, 1968), pp. 292–93.

7. For a detailed description of these and other organizations belonging to the radical right in the United States, see Ferdinand V. Solara, *Key Influences in the American Right* (Denver, Colo.: Polifax Press, 1972); Seymour M. Lipset, "The Sources of the 'Radical' Right," in Daniel Bell, ed., *The New American Right* (New York: Criterion Books, 1955), pp. 186–219; and James Rorty and Moshe Decter, *McCarthy and the Communists* (Boston: Beacon Press, 1954).

8. Edgar Ansel Mowrer, *The Nightmare of American Foreign Policy* (New York: Alfred A. Knopf, 1948), pp. 4–5.

9. Ibid., pp. 12–13.

10. Barry Goldwater, *The Conscience of a Conservative* (New York: Macfadden, 1963), pp. 90–91.

11. See Strobe Talbott, *The Russians and Reagan* (New York: Random House, 1984); Bernard Weisberger, *Cold War, Cold Peace: The United States and Russia since 1945* (New York: American Heritage Foundation, 1984); and Alexander Haig, *Caveat: Realism, Reagan, and Foreign Policy* (New York: Macmillan, 1984), pp. 95–116.

12. See Mowrer, *The Nightmare of American Foreign Policy*, pp. 129–65; and Thomas J. Dodd, *Freedom and Foreign Policy* (New York: Bookmailer, 1962), pp. 276–81.

13. Senator Joseph McCarthy's views concerning the nature and influence of the "Communist conspiracy" operating in the United States during and after World War II are succinctly set forth in his book, *America's Retreat from Victory: The Story of George Catlett Marshall* (New York: Devin-Adair, 1951). For a detailed series of excerpts from McCarthy's speeches and writings highlighting this theme, see Morris H. Rubin, ed., *The McCarthy Record* (New York: Anglobooks, 1952).

14. Conservative views on détente are discussed in Talbott, *The Russians and Reagan*; in several of the essays in Norman Podhoretz, *The Present Danger* (New York: Simon and Schuster, 1980); in Richard Nixon, *The Real War* (New York: Warner Books, 1981); and in Haig, *Caveat*, pp. 100–10.

15. Goldwater, *The Conscience of a Conservative*, pp. 93, 113, 122; and his *The Conscience of a Majority*, pp. 105, 109; and Arthur H. Vandenberg, Jr., ed., *The Private Papers of Senator Vandenberg* (Boston: Houghton Mifflin, 1952), p. 510.

16. See the analysis in Christopher Coker, *U.S. Military Power in the 1980s* (Salem, Mass.: Salem House, 1983); *U.S. Defense Policy*, 3d ed. (Washington, D.C.: Congressional Quarterly, 1983); Kenneth A. Adelman, "SDI: Setting the Record Straight," Department of State, Current Policy No. 730 (August 7, 1985), pp. 1–4.

17. See Vandenberg, ed., *The Private Papers of Senator Vandenberg*, pp. 399–420.

18. See Dwight D. Eisenhower, *Mandate for Change: The White House Years, 1953–1956* (Garden City, N.Y.: Doubleday, 1963), pp. 368–75.

19. Redekop, *The American Far Right*, p. 73.

20. See Nixon, *The Real War*, pp. 250–69; several of the essays in Podhoretz, *The Present Danger*; Richard Nixon, *No More Vietnams* (New York: Arbor House, 1985); and Haig, *Caveat*, pp. 29–31, 96–97.

21. Nixon, *No More Vietnams*, pp. 165–212; and the views of former Senator James L. Buckley (Republican of New York) in his *If Men Were Angels: A View from the Senate* (New York: G. P. Putnam's Sons, 1975), pp. 117–51.

22. The Carter Doctrine (1980) — subsequently accepted by the Reagan administration — is discussed more fully in Cecil V. Crabb, Jr., *The Doctrines of American Foreign Policy: Their Meaning, Role, and Future* (Baton Rouge: Louisiana State University Press, 1982), pp. 325–71; and in Jimmy Carter, *Keeping Faith: Memoirs of a President* (New York: Bantam Books, 1982), pp. 479–89.

23. Nixon, *No More Vietnams*, pp. 210–37.

24. See, for example, the views of President Eisenhower, that the defense of Southwest Asia against communism had to be "the concern of all nations outside the Iron Curtain." Dwight D. Eisenhower, *Mandate for Change: 1953–1956* (Garden City, N.Y.: Doubleday, 1963), pp. 336, 347.

25. The Nixon Doctrine is analyzed in greater detail in Crabb, *The Doctrines of American Foreign Policy*, pp. 278–325; and in the White House publications, *U.S. Foreign Policy for the 1970's: Building for Peace* (Washington, D.C.: 1971) and *U.S. Foreign Policy for the 1970's: The Emerging Structure of Peace* (Washington, D.C.: 1972).

26. For the text of Hoover's speech on January 27, 1952, see his *Addresses Upon the American Road, 1950–1955* (Stanford, California: Stanford University Press, 1955), pp. 3–11; for later speeches advocating the Fortress America concept, see pp. 23–45.

27. For statements by leaders of the John Birch Society on the U.N., see Benjamin R. Epstein and Arnold Forster, *The Radical Right: Report on the John Birch Society and Its Allies* (New York: Random House, 1967), pp. 156–57. In the quotation from Robert Welch, italics are in the original.

28. Redekop, *The American Far Right*, pp. 65–73.

29. See Gregory J. Newell, "The New U.S. Observer Role in UNESCO," Department of State, Current Policy No. 649 (January 15, 1985), pp. 1–3; Kurt Waldheim, "The United Nations: The Tarnished Image," *Foreign Affairs* 63 (Fall 1984):93–108; Seymour M. Finger, "Jeane Kirkpatrick at the United Nations," *Foreign Affairs* 62 (Winter 1983/84):436–58; and Edward C. Luck, "The U.N. at 40: A Supporter's Lament," *Foreign Policy* 57 (Winter 1984/85):143–60.

30. For an analysis of antiforeign aid sentiment on Capitol Hill in this period, see the New York *Times*, October 30, 1971, dispatch by Felix Belair, Jr. A more detailed discussion of legislative sentiment toward foreign aid may be found in the *Congressional Quarterly Almanac*, 27 (1971):387–407.

31. For fiscal year 1986, the Reagan administration proposed a total of some $16 billion in foreign aid — $9.4 billion in economic assistance and $6.6 billion in military aid — to other countries. A detailed description of the foreign aid program may be found in Department of State, *Foreign Assistance Program: FY 1986 Budget and 1985 Supplemental Request*, Special Report No. 128 (May 1985).

32. Mowrer, *The Nightmare of American Foreign Policy*, p. 36; Edward C.

Banfield, "American Foreign Aid Doctrine," in Robert A. Goldwin, ed., *Why Foreign Aid?* (Chicago: Rand McNally, 1968), pp. 17, 29–31.

33.　U.S. relations with Iran in the post-World War II era are analyzed fully in Barry Rubin, *Paved with Good Intentions: The American Experience and Iran* (New York: Penguin Books, 1981). See also Mohammed Heikal, *Iran: The Untold Story* (New York: Pantheon Books, 1982); and Cyrus Vance, *Hard Choices: Critical Years in America's Foreign Policy* (New York: Simon and Schuster, 1983), pp. 314–49, 368–84.

34.　John F. Campbell, *The Foreign Affairs Fudge Factory* (New York: Basic Books, 1971), p. 29; and Goldwater, *The Conscience of a Conservative*, p. 97.

35.　See Dankwart A. Rustow, "Realignments in the Middle East," *Foreign Affairs* 63 (Special Issue 1984):599–601; and Henry Grunewald, "Foreign Policy under Reagan II," *Foreign Affairs* 63 (Winter 1984/85):231–33.

36.　For an illuminating discussion of the existence of cycles of public attitudes toward foreign affairs throughout U.S. diplomatic experience, see F. L. Klingberg, "The Historical Alternation of Moods in American Foreign Policy," *World Politics* 4 (January 1952):239–73. See also Dexter Perkins, *The American Approach to Foreign Policy* (Cambridge, Mass.: Harvard University Press, 1952), pp. 114–28.

37.　See Podhoretz, *The Present Danger*, pp. 79–89; Haig, *Caveat*, pp. 117–41; James H. Michel, "Soviet Activities in Latin America and the Caribbean," Department of State, Current Policy No. 669 (February 28, 1985), pp. 1–6; and Langhorne A. Motley, "The Need for Continuity in U.S. Latin American Policy," Department of State, Current Policy No. 655 (January 29, 1985), pp. 1–8.

3

Contemporary Neo-Isolationism: Liberal Versions

In this chapter we turn to a consideration of a different and more recent species of neo-isolationist thought advocated by individuals and groups, most of whom approach foreign policy issues from a liberal political orientation. This version of neo-isolationism gained wide currency during and after the period of peak U.S. involvement in the Vietnam War. During the 1970s especially, spokesmen for this point of view were vocal in criticizing U.S. overinvolvement in the affairs of other countries and its tendency to serve as the policeman of the world.[1] Although the Vietnam conflict unquestionably provided an impetus for such criticisms, it should not be imagined that the liberal neo-isolationist mentality was solely an outgrowth of that frustrating encounter. As our treatment will show, many of the neo-isolationist propensities exhibited by liberal groups in the modern period have their origins in causes antedating the Vietnam War. Some of them can be traced far back into U.S. diplomatic history, and others date at least from the promulgation of the Truman Doctrine in 1947. By the 1980s, liberal neo-isolationists were often at the forefront in criticizing the Reagan administration's diplomatic interventionism in Lebanon, Central America, and other regions. Ironically, however, many left-wing and liberal groups advocated more active interventionism by the United States against the white-ruled government of South Africa and other regimes (such as the Philippines and South Korea) that consistently violated the rights of their own citizens.

Perhaps to a greater degree even than its conservative counterpart, liberal neo-isolationism entails a wide spectrum of diverse opinion concerning the proper U.S. role in global affairs. At one extreme, there is the pacificistic tradition, whose devotees believe that any reliance upon military force to achieve external goals is immoral, unethical, and usually ineffectual. In the contemporary period, advocates of this viewpoint have been prominent in the "Better Red Than Dead," "Ban the Bomb," and "Nuclear Freeze" movements, whose objectives have been to convince U.S. policy-makers to eliminate (or drastically curtail) the nation's nuclear arsenal.

At the other extreme, there is a species of liberal neo-isolationism that advocates a highly selective use of military force to achieve diplomatic goals. As our later discussion will show, even this group is far from unified in its policy recommendations. Yet perhaps the common idea broadly shared by its members is the twofold belief that the United States must not be hegemonial, imperialistic, and arrogant in the use of its own power abroad; but it should use its power selectively in behalf of liberally approved or democratic ends, such as promoting democracy, human rights, and religious freedoms and comparable causes in other countries.

MAJOR TENETS OF LIBERAL NEO-ISOLATIONISM

While recognizing the diversity that characterizes liberal neo-isolationist thought today, it is possible without undue distortion to identify a number of fundamental ideas that its adherents share. Major tenets of the liberal neo-isolationist viewpoint include the following:

The welfare of the U.S. society is directly and crucially affected by social, economic, and political developments beyond the nation's borders; constructive interaction with other peoples is essential for the United States' own survival and well-being; and it should be equally beneficial for the welfare of foreign societies.

As the world's oldest functioning democracy, the United States is inescapably identified with the future of political freedom and democracy throughout the world; the Wilsonian ideal of making "the world safe for democracy" remains a central goal of U.S. foreign policy.

A "large" or overtly interventionist foreign policy — especially one that relies heavily upon military force — poses both an internal and an external danger for the United States; internally, it risks undue military influence upon national policy, a steadily escalating defense budget, and ongoing political divisiveness within the U.S. body politic; externally, it risks another Vietnam abroad, the dissipation of national power and resources in unsuccessful diplomatic ventures, and the loss of U.S. influence and credibility overseas.

Even though the United States must maintain an adequate defense establishment, Americans must rely upon military forces sparingly and selectively to achieve foreign policy objectives; they must avoid the temptation to seek military solutions for the Communist challenge, political instability throughout the Third World, anti-Americanism in other countries, and most other contemporary global problems.

In nearly all cases, particularly when it relies upon military force abroad, the United States must seek and maintain the cooperation of other countries in pursuing its diplomatic objectives; Washington will almost never be able to realize its external goals by acting unilaterally; U.S. officials must at all times demonstrate what Thomas Jefferson called a "decent respect for the opinions of mankind."

In exercising their power abroad, Americans must be mindful of the harmful and unintended effects of an interventionist policy; almost always, overt interventionism in the affairs of other countries creates resentment toward the United States, gives aid and comfort to Communists and other political adversaries, divides the United States from its friends and allies abroad, strengthens the powers of the "imperial presidency" vis-à-vis Congress and public opinion, and creates new sources of internal political discord.

The success of a nation's foreign policy is heavily conditioned by the effectiveness of its efforts to solve pressing domestic problems; as much today as ever, U.S. diplomacy must be guided by the old adage that, "foreign policy begins at home"; ultimately national security depends as much upon the nation's ability to eliminate poverty, promote better medical care, and improve education, as it does upon acquiring a military arsenal second to none.

A precept central to traditional isolationism — that the example of the United States is a crucial element in its international influence — remains a valid principle today; while it seeks to promote democracy abroad, the United States must concurrently endeavor to strengthen and expand it at home; while it seeks racial justice on the African continent, the United States must make certain that it is creating a society free of discrimination within its own borders.

The United States must take risks for peace; it must continue to take the lead in efforts to achieve global disarmament, in codifying and strengthening international law, in achieving a more just international economic order, and in strengthening regional and multinational institutions; successfully doing so will of course involve restrictions upon U.S. sovereignty and freedom of diplomatic action.

An enduring and still dominant goal of U.S. foreign policy must be creating and strengthening an emerging sense of global community; in the final analysis, this is the surest guarantor of national security in the nuclear age; and it has always been — and it remains — the ultimate objective of the Judeo-Christian and Western humanistic tradition.

LIBERALISM AND THE U.S. POLITICAL ENVIRONMENT

Any intelligent comprehension of liberally-motivated neo-isolationism must be grounded in an understanding of the main tenets of liberal political ideology and of certain unique characteristics of the U.S. ethos and political system. Rooted in the Judeo-Christian religious heritage, in Renaissance humanism, and in the principles of Enlightenment philosophy as exemplified by thinkers like John Locke, Jean-Jacques Rousseau, and Thomas Jefferson, liberalism is dedicated to the achievement of such fundamental goals as individual freedom, equality, the maximum realization of human potential, and the expansion of community ties among individuals and groups at home and abroad. In contrast to conservatives, liberals have traditionally believed that moral-ethical precepts do apply to the behavior of states, no less than to individuals and groups within them. Liberals reject the view that "reason of state" or "national interest" can legitimately justify any action the United States engages in abroad. For liberals, the United States' national interest is indistinguishable from the welfare of individuals inside and outside the nation's borders.[2]

Moreover, as Wilsonians were convinced, the liberal mind believes there is an intrinsic connection between the existence of democracy in other countries and the prospects for global peace and stability. An axiom of liberal thought is that democratic political systems are less prone to engage in aggression, expansionism, and hegemonial behavior abroad; to the extent, therefore, that the world is made safe for democracy, the prospects for peaceful relationships among nations are maximized. (As the informed student of contemporary international politics is aware, this assumption stands in some opposition to the contention of many liberal neo-isolationists that the activities of the United States — the world's oldest functioning democracy — constitute the primary danger to global peace and stability.) Accordingly, a leading diplomatic goal of the Carter administration — promoting human rights abroad — must remain a high-ranking objective of U.S. foreign policy.[3]

Liberals are likely to be extremely sensitive to infringements upon such basic rights as freedom of speech, of the press, and of assembly. During and after the Vietnam War, they repeatedly complained about the "wall of secrecy" surrounding decision making by the Johnson and Nixon administrations. They championed the right of — and in some cases, the necessity for — dissent from official explanations of national policy; they called upon national leaders to listen to critics of prevailing policy; and they nearly always opposed covert interventionism by the Central Intelligence Agency or other instruments of the government to achieve foreign policy goals.

To the liberal mind, freedom is essential for the maximum realization of human potential. Liberals believe that the organic unit of human society is the individual: the welfare of the individual serves as the yardstick whereby the legitimacy of the state's actions and policies must always be measured. Hand in hand with the concept of freedom, liberals also cherish and seek to promote the principle of equality among the members of human society. The idea of "equality of opportunity" (or the judicial concept of "equality before the law") best expresses the essence of the principle: individuals must be free to realize their fullest potential on the basis of merit and talent.

Given its deep attachment to these goals, liberalism naturally and logically favors democracy as the system of government best designed to achieve them — a conviction dramatically highlighted during World War I by President Wilson's expressed determination to "make the world safe for democracy." To the liberal mind, the existence of freedom and of a democratic political order are inseparable phenomena. On international issues, liberal attitudes usually reflect the Wilsonian conviction (evident in President Wilson's policy toward Imperial Germany) that ordinary people throughout the world are devoted to peace and the pursuit of the good life. In this conception, wars, tensions, and conflicts among nations arise out of the antisocial propensities of governments (or in modern political nomenclature, political establishments), which are often controlled and manipulated by self-serving political elites. It follows that an enduring goal of U.S. diplomacy must be to influence the thought and behavior of the Soviet, the Chinese, the Cuban, or other people, who will in turn presumably bring pressure to bear upon their leaders to moderate their diplomatic ambitions and to resolve international disputes peaceably.

Implicit in this mentality, of course, is the liberal's conviction that public opinion ought to constitute a major input in the formulation of national policy. Conversely, the liberal rejects an elitist conception of government, whereby policy making is the province of a small group of public officials (and in the realm of U.S. foreign relations, the prototypical group is the Foreign Service of the United States), which is indifferent to public sentiment. As an admirer of the principles of Jacksonian democracy, the U.S. liberal has always exhibited great confidence in the judgments of the plain people.

In terms of its direct applicability to our subject — U.S. postwar foreign policy — modern liberalism emphasizes two ideas. As a kind of philosophical first principle, the liberal credo believes that human society is, or can be made to be, harmonious and cooperative. Thus the liberal rejects any doctrine postulating conflict and alienation as the natural and inevitable lot of mankind. According to one of its influential spokesmen, the "social ideal" of liberalism has always been to create an "ethical harmony" in human affairs, to be achieved "partly by discipline" and "partly by the improvement of the conditions of life" for the members of society.[4]

In the realm of external affairs, a belief in the possibility of a harmonious political order has led liberals to take a leading role in efforts designed to make the conduct of international relations more benign, to eliminate coercion and violence from relationships among nations, and to make the conduct of international politics more directly consonant with the promotion of human well-being. Rejecting the *Realpolitik* idea that international politics inherently entails an endless power struggle among nations leading to large or small wars or that its essence is an endless process of conflict resolution among major and minor international actors, since 1900 liberals have been energetic champions of innovative and reformist measures. Disarmament conferences and arms control agreements; the establishment of the League of Nations and its successor, the United Nations; attempts to outlaw war as an instrument of national policy and other efforts to strengthen the authority, and broaden the compass, of international law; sponsorship of various methods for improving communication and understanding among societies, such as student and scientific exchange programs and people-to-people movements, on the theory that, as the members of human society get to know each other better, conflicts among them will diminish; concerted attacks upon the long-range causes of war and political instability, such as programs designed to eliminate global poverty and to promote the modernization of primitive societies; a preference for employing the methods of persuasion, negotiation, and diplomacy instead of armed force in the conduct of foreign affairs — during the twentieth century, these have been among the more prominent steps advocated by liberals as effective measures for reducing global tensions and for bringing about a more harmonious and socially constructive international system.

A second conspicuous and closely related tenet of liberal thought applicable to international relations is a deeply ingrained belief in the necessity of growth and progress, and the perfectability of human institutions. It would be a distortion of the liberal credo to assert (as conservatives are sometimes prone to do) that devotees of liberalism believe in automatic or inevitable progress in human affairs. Yet the bias in liberal thought is nearly always in favor of change vis-à-vis the status quo in human affairs. Furthermore, liberals are convinced that change is inevitable in all aspects of human society. Because change cannot be prevented, attempts by conservatives or other partisans of the status quo to avert or stifle it will nearly always result in even more disruptive and violent upheavals. More specifically, liberals tend to believe that the desire for revolutionary change is pervasive throughout the Third World today. U.S. efforts to oppose this tendency are both unrealistic and bound to fail. Moreover, U.S. opposition to radical change in foreign societies greatly enhances the appeal of communism and other extremist movements for peoples living in disadvantaged societies. A favorite maxim of liberal groups is the demand that the United States remember its own revolutionary heritage and that it be guided by its own revolutionary principles in its relations with other countries.

As an ideology favorably disposed toward change, liberalism itself is a constantly evolving credo. Ever since the eighteenth century, two reasonably distinct varieties of liberal thought may be identified: a classical version and a modern version.[5] (By the second half of the twentieth century, devotees of the former were apt to be classified as political conservatives.) It would not be germane to our purpose to distinguish these two approaches in detail. Suffice it to say that their most crucial distinction perhaps lay in their respective viewpoints concerning the proper role of the government in economic affairs — the classical liberal favoring a laissez-faire attitude discouraging governmental intervention in this realm, while the modern liberal demanded extensive and continuing intervention by government in the operation of the economic system.

More directly relevant for our study of foreign affairs perhaps is the difference between these two schools of thought regarding the role of executive power in the U.S. system of government. As reflected in the views of Thomas Jefferson and other Enlightenment philosophers, the classical liberal position was extremely suspicious of executive power; for this group, Congress was the true voice of the people and the repository of liberty. By the period of World War I and continuing through the New Deal, however, liberal opinion became vocal in demanding vigorous executive leadership in solving the nation's urgent problems; Congress and the Supreme Court were frequently viewed as impediments to this process. Then by the 1960s, largely as an outgrowth of the nation's prolonged involvement in the Vietnam War, modern political liberals tended to revert to the views of the classical school.

Executive power was regarded as inherently dangerous and suspect, as exemplified by the concept of the imperial presidency. In the liberal view, the tendency toward unrestrained executive power was a direct outgrowth of an interventionist foreign policy, leading to massive U.S. involvement in the Vietnam War, to the Johnson administration's intervention in the Dominican Republic, and to the Reagan administration's interventionism in Lebanon, Grenada, and Central America. Liberals, therefore, often led the way in calling for a more active and decisive role by Congress in the foreign policy process. An implicit assumption of Congressional activism in foreign affairs in the post-Vietnam War era was the idea that it would avoid another Vietnam and, more generally, it would make U.S. foreign policy more pacifically inclined and more successful. (Interestingly enough, liberal opinion still demands dynamic White House leadership in dealing with internal problems, like unemployment, school integration, and the elimination of poverty.)[6]

Two distinctive characteristics of the U.S. political milieu affect the role of liberal opinion in foreign affairs. The first is that liberalism and the "American way of life" are closely related (if not synonymous) concepts. Much more than conservatism, liberal thought has influenced the U.S. democratic tradition and the behavior of the U.S. government.[7]

The second, and perhaps somewhat contradictory, reality is that Americans are remarkably nonideological people; it would not be an exaggeration to say that they are anti-ideological and repulsed by rigid philosophical systems. If it can accurately be called a philosophy, pragmatism is the U.S. credo.[8] As one commentator has expressed it, "We are not doctrinaire, we have no dogmas to exalt; we are empiricists. . . . We leave ourselves free to act as seems rationally requisite or emotionally satisfying in any present situation."[9] In the light of this fact, it is not surprising that studies have shown little or no correlation between a liberal or conservative political orientation and a predetermined attitude (for example, isolationist or internationalist) in foreign affairs. While this chapter is concerned with liberal neo-isolationism, we must continually remember that liberalism is far from a monolithic ideology and that (as with conservatism) incongruities and contradictions frequently characterize the attitudes of individual citizens with regard to specific questions in internal and foreign policy.[10]

THE LIBERAL CRITIQUE OF POSTWAR U.S. DIPLOMACY

For a wide circle of liberal commentators, the starting point of their analysis of recent U.S. foreign relations — and the basis of their conviction that the nation is overextended abroad — is a critical evaluation of the basic rationale of, and the results achieved by, what is variously labeled the United States' "internationalist" or "globalist" or "universalist" approach to foreign relations since World War II. To most such observers, by whatever term it is described, the postwar foreign policy of the United States has become increasingly egocentric and interventionist, heavily involving the nation in the affairs of other countries throughout the world, to the detriment both of the United States' own true diplomatic interests and of its domestic institutions and values. Thus, Paul Seabury observed that for many years the United States held and acted upon a Ptolemaic conception of foreign affairs — that is, the idea "that a desirable system of international politics should be an American-centered one."[11]

Another student of U.S. postwar diplomatic record conceives of its foreign policy as having embodied three mutually dependent elements: (1) it is characterized by a "worldwide reach," involving the United States in the affairs of a multitude of nations far and near, great and small; (2) it is a policy of "messianic globalism," reflecting a deeply embedded U.S. conviction that the United States can and should "save" other societies from a variety of problems and evils; and (3) at base, despite its idealistic gloss, U.S. globalist policy is calculated to promote and protect the nation's own self-interest, particularly its foreign investments, access to markets, and raw material supplies throughout the world. Routinely since World War II, presidents have equated the purposes of the United States with those of humanity at large, as when President Lyndon B. Johnson declared in 1966 that the only interests the United States had in world affairs were "those we regard as inseparable from our moral duties to mankind."[12]

Liberal disenchantment with the course of U.S. postwar diplomacy, of course, reached its zenith in the late 1960s, after the United States became deeply embroiled in the Vietnam War. As much as any other episode in recent U.S. diplomatic history, the Vietnam conflict highlighted the defects of the nation's foreign policy since World War II. The liberal indictment of the U.S. role in this conflict constituted a long and varied bill of particulars, too lengthy and detailed to reproduce here. Our interest must be confined to emphasizing the idea that, to many critics of the nation's internationalist foreign policy, the Vietnam imbroglio was no accident or aberration in the nation's diplomatic experience. It was the logical and inevitable result of hegemonial impulses evident in U.S. foreign relations perhaps since the early nineteenth century, but certainly since World War II. Typical of this viewpoint is Stephen Ambrose's judgment that massive U.S. involvement in Vietnam was "the logical extension of a policy of military containment of communism."[13]

For what reasons did U.S. foreign policy after World War II inevitably become interventionist and hegemonial? On this question liberal critics provide a variety of answers. One group calls attention to the expansionist urge that has been present in U.S. history since the founding of the Republic. As we emphasized in Chapter 1, a posture of isolationism toward other countries was never deemed incompatible with a policy of continental expansionism and annexation of certain external territories like Alaska, the Philippines, and islands in the Caribbean. Indeed, in the view of some historians one of the principal benefits of an isolationist foreign policy was that it facilitated this expansionist process by enabling Americans to devote primary attention to their "Manifest Destiny." Since U.S. history has been synonymous with expansionism, there was no reason to expect this process to come to an end when the United States became a superpower.

A variant explanation is provided by William Appleman Williams and other revisionist commentators. This group agrees that the U.S. imperialistic urge has deep historical roots, going back at least to the end of the nineteenth century, when the United States came of age as a nation and, within a few brief years thereafter, joined the ranks of the great powers. Following the Industrial Revolution and the emergence of finance capitalism in the post-Civil War period, the United States began in effect to pursue an "Open Door" policy abroad. The Open Door concept was specifically enunciated toward China at the end of the century, and it was viewed by many Americans as the epitome of an idealistic and humanitarian approach to foreign affairs.[14] Yet Williams contends that after 1900 in reality the United States became committed to a worldwide Open Door policy. Disguised by a façade of isolationism and by Wilsonian and Rooseveltian idealism, in Williams's view, the U.S. global Open Door policy was pursued consistently until World War II. After the war the nation's adoption of globalism as its foreign policy strategy was merely a natural and inevitable extension of the diplomatic strategy it had been pursuing for more than 50 years. The fundamental objective of the Open Door principles, to Williams's mind, was acquiring and maintaining unlimited U.S. access to the markets and raw materials of other countries in order to maintain prosperity and a rising standard of living at home.[15] According to Williams and those who subscribe to this school of thought, the Open Door impulse continues to motivate U.S. foreign policy toward, for example, the relations of the United States with the Third World.

The central idea of Williams's explanation — that U.S. diplomacy has been dominated by an expansionist urge, ultimately deriving from internal economic forces — has been expressed in different forms by other commentators (not excluding, of course, Marxist ones). A recent analysis, for example, accounts for the emergence of "America's Empire" in these terms. Despairing of U.S. ability to shed its hegemonial impulses, and to use its vast wealth for the betterment of mankind, the author contends that on the contrary, for the United States "to maintain its prosperity and satisfy six percent of the world's population, it must preserve access to the whole world's immense resources. America does not realize that the American dream is dead. It could be resuscitated only through abandonment of the empire."[16]

The conviction that U.S. foreign policy has been motivated by economically derived pressures impelling it toward imperial domination was of course a conspicuous theme in the viewpoints expressed by critics of the nation's involvement in the Vietnam War. Among these critics, some believed that the Vietnam conflict was merely an outgrowth of the U.S. traditional urge to exploit Asia economically and commercially, keeping it dependent upon the United States for an indefinite period in the future. To other commentators, the prospect that significant oil deposits existed off the coast of Southeast Asia provided the lure for the United States' massive intervention in the region. A variation on basically the same theme was that defense industries within the United States, which formed part of a larger military-industrial complex, required continuing escalation of the U.S. presence in Vietnam in order to maintain overseas markets and access to raw materials, to maintain a high level of production and employment, and to reap excessive profits.[17]

A variant, although complementary, explanation of U.S. will to dominate other countries is offered by those critics who underscore the U.S. society's deeply embedded belief in the superiority of its own way of life and the conviction that the U.S. system is destined to become universal. According to this interpretation, a powerful thrust toward what might be called cultural or ideological imperialism has formed part of the U.S. ethos since the Republic was founded. As one student of U.S. diplomacy has expressed it: "We engaged in a kind of *welfare imperialism,* empire-building for noble ends rather than for such base motives as profit and influence." Referring specifically to the Vietnam War and other recent instances of U.S. interventionism, this commentator concluded: "It is this desire to translate American ideals into a universal political system [modeled after America's own] that lies at the core of the current crisis in American diplomacy."[18]

In Chapter 1 we called attention to the fact that belief in the superiority of the U.S. system formed an integral part of the isolationist credo: The United States ought to refrain from involvement in foreign political conflicts so that it could be left free to redeem the world by the power of its own example. After World War II, something closely akin to this old idea reappeared, particularly in certain analyses of Soviet-U.S. conflict throughout the Third World. In this arena of Cold War competition, the crucial issue was: which model of national development would the countries of Black Africa or East Asia choose? (As events revealed, in reality most Third World societies wanted to be carbon copies of neither the U.S. nor the Soviet model, preferring their own unique systems, in keeping with their traditions, and perhaps combining elements of several foreign models available.)[19]

Whether this was a correct and realistic evaluation of superpower conflict in the Third World is not a relevant inquiry for us at this stage. Here, our interest is confined to emphasizing several points about this view. Considerable continuity exists between what the devotee of traditional isolationism was to call the "power of example" and what the modern internationalist refers to as the attraction of the "American model." Whether it was the New World versus the Old World in an earlier era or U.S. welfare capitalism versus Soviet (or Chinese) communism after World War II, Americans continue to believe in the superiority of their system; and they still anticipate that, sooner or later, other societies will recognize its virtues, preferring it in time over rival models.

How would this process of exporting the U.S. system occur? On this point, two interpretations have been advanced. With some exceptions, perhaps, proponents of isolationism believed that the eventual Americanization of the world would be a peaceful and gradual process, coming about as a result of a decision by other societies that — largely because of its outstanding record in solving its domestic problems — the U.S. system was worthy of emulation. At worst — and this is one of the most frequently expressed indictments that liberal commentators have brought against postwar U.S. diplomacy — a belief in the moral superiority of the U.S. system supplied a powerful and irresistible incentive toward creation of a worldwide *Pax Americana*. Isolationists may have believed in the superiority of the U.S. way of life, but for the most part they lacked the power and inclination to impose it on other societies. Modern internationalists tend to share this view, but after World War II the crucial difference was that the United States now possessed the power to carry out its self-appointed mission; and, according to many liberal observers, policy-makers in Washington have not hesitated to use their power to achieve this goal.

A second major theme in the liberal indictment of the U.S. postwar diplomatic record is associated specifically with former Senator J. William Fulbright (Democrat of Arkansas), who was chairman of the Senate Foreign Relations Committee during the Vietnam War. Among liberal critics, Senator Fulbright's viewpoints have been widely quoted and accepted as authoritative (indeed, in some circles it would not be too much to say that they have been venerated). As an individual of considerable intellectual attainment and experience in dealing with complex foreign policy questions, Fulbright clearly ranks among the ablest and most prestigious critics of the recent U.S. diplomatic record.[20]

At the risk of some oversimplification, the title of one of Senator Fulbright's books — *The Arrogance of Power* — may be taken as the pivotal concept around which much of his criticism of recent U.S. diplomacy revolves. Likening the U.S. rise to the status of, and conduct as, a superpower to the behavior of earlier empires like ancient Greece and Rome, Napoleonic France, and Hitler's Third Reich, Fulbright argues that all such empires sooner or later "overextended their commitments and they came to grief." In time, all empires exhibited the "arrogance of power," failing to understand that "power tends to confuse itself with virtue and a great nation is peculiarly susceptible to the idea that its power is a sign of God's favor, conferring upon it a special responsibility for other nations — to make them richer and happier and wiser, to remake them, that is, in its own shining image." In common with other influential nations known to history, in the years since World War II the United States has tended to "confuse great power with unlimited power" and to mistake "great responsibility with total responsibility" for the destiny of the world.[21]

Fulbright of course has not been alone in bringing this indictment against postwar U.S. foreign policy. In the early postwar period, for example, the Scotsman D. W. Brogan identified the "illusion of American omnipotence" — the idea that Americans were capable of solving any problem in foreign affairs, no matter how intractable or impervious to solution by other countries — as a behavior trait characteristic of the United States in global affairs.[22] Similarly, President John F. Kennedy once urged his countrymen to remember that "the United States is neither omnipotent nor omniscient . . . we cannot impose our will upon the other 94 per cent of mankind . . . we cannot right every wrong or reverse each adversity . . . there cannot be an American solution to every world problem."[23]

Yet many liberal neo-isolationist critics believe that such admonitions have too often been forgotten. One commentator has said that since World War II no nation has "talked so much, and so ambitiously, of its duty and its power to direct the destiny of the world" as has the United States.[24] Senator Fulbright believed that the United States was imbued with its own sense of power, forgetting that power "is a narcotic, a potent intoxicant," with the result that in its foreign relations "America has been on a 'trip'"— a propensity Fulbright hoped would be abandoned once the massive U.S. commitment in Southeast Asia was liquidated.[25]

In judging the impact of U.S. power upon many weaker societies overseas, Senator Fulbright cites the verdict of Captain Cook, an early explorer of the western Pacific, about the experiences of the Polynesians: "It would have been better for these people never to have known us."[26] Unintentionally, perhaps, but nonetheless crucially, the extension of U.S. power abroad has had a "shattering effect" upon less advanced societies. In Fulbright's words, it has "shattered traditional societies, disrupted fragile economies and undermined people's self-confidence by the invidious example of their [the United States'] own power and efficiency." This phenomenon raises a problem that we shall deal with more fully at a later stage: U.S. response to revolutionary conditions in other countries. On this point, the liberal indictment of postwar U.S. foreign policy is twofold: policy-makers in Washington have been oblivious to the extent to which the extension of U.S. power overseas has triggered revolutionary ferment in other societies, and their response to revolutionary movements abroad has been negative and ineffectual.

Several differences may be identified briefly between Senator Fulbright's lament about the arrogance of U.S. power and the viewpoint, examined earlier, that U.S. foreign policy is inherently expansionist and interventionist. While the effect of U.S. behavior on other countries may be substantially the same whatever its motivation, Fulbright does not believe that the United States is innately and inescapably an imperialistic nation. The burden of his analysis of U.S. foreign policy is that there is no inherent necessity for the behavior of a superpower to be arrogant or why the exercise of U.S. power should have mainly inimical consequences for other countries. For the most part, the process occurred without conscious design; it was indeliberate, unintentional, and thoughtless, coming about mainly as the result of failure by officials to consider the consequences of U.S. actions (like intervention in Cuba during the Bay of Pigs episode or initial U.S. commitments to the government of South Vietnam).

It is not so much with the objectives of postwar U.S. foreign policy that fault may legitimately be found — Fulbright concedes that many of these goals have been laudable — but with the means employed by policy-makers in Washington to achieve them. In far too many instances the methods used conflicted with, and in the end defeated achievement of, the declared goal. Expressed differently, one of Fulbright's recurrent complaints is that officials in Washington have tended to be indifferent to the actual results achieved by the extension of U.S. power overseas vis-à-vis the desired results. By the 1980s, liberal critics of U.S. diplomacy were making comparable indictments of the Reagan administration's policies toward Lebanon and Central America. In both cases, overt interventionism by the United States signified attempts to impose a U.S. solution upon foreign societies; it stemmed from pervasive ignorance by U.S. policy-makers of the underlying causes of political instability in the Middle East and Latin America; it indicated Washington's tendency to rely upon military solutions for complex social, economic, and political problems in other countries; and it was bound to produce another Vietnam or another spectacular failure of U.S. diplomacy.[27]

A third idea prominent in liberal assessments of postwar U.S. foreign relations, and a factor viewed as crucial in producing the overextension of U.S. power abroad, is a deeply held and durable antipathy toward communism. Soviet and other varieties of communism, Senator George McGovern said, have challenged "a variety of deeply felt American dreams and values at their core." Since World War II Americans have tended to make "an almost irresistible identification of any event related to Communism as a crisis, a dire and fundamental threat to basic values."[28] Bernard Morris says that "the myth of an expansive and imperialistic Soviet Union" has dominated postwar U.S. foreign policy, while Fred W. Neal observes, "The key factor in American policy since the war is the obsession that we have faced the constant and pressing danger of Soviet military aggression." Sometimes this fear has become a "national paranoia."[29] Early in his administration, President Jimmy Carter warned Americans against an anti-Communist obsession, or what he called an "inordinate fear" of communism, which he believed strongly colored their worldview.[30]

In the liberal indictment, official U.S. belief in the existence of what was often called "an international Communist conspiracy" has been repeatedly invoked to justify U.S. interventionism abroad. Ever since the enunciation of the Truman Doctrine in 1947, national leaders have cited the necessity to contain Communist expansionism in order to rationalize interventionist moves from South Korea and Southeast Asia to the Persian Gulf area and Central America. In turn, an interventionist foreign policy requires the existence of a constantly expanding and ever more costly military arsenal, highly questionable activities by the Central Intelligence Agency (CIA) and other federal agencies, attempts by executive officials to maintain a wall of secrecy around their diplomatic machinations, the exercise of largely unrestrained presidential power, and the continuing neglect of the nation's internal needs.

The existence of a deeply ingrained antipathy toward communism as a major motivation of U.S. foreign policy is the pivotal concept in the "re-examinist" approaches of liberal commentators like D. F. Fleming, Frederick L. Schuman, and others to account for global tension and instability since World War II. U.S. animosity toward communism can be traced to the period of World War I and to Western refusal to accept the results of the Bolshevik Revolution. After 1917 the United States and other Western countries displayed hostility toward the new Bolshevik government, going so far as to attempt its overthrow during the period of the "White Invasions" that followed Lenin's seizure of power. [31] Failing in that objective, Western policy-makers — whose attitudes toward communism were heavily influenced by business groups and other right-wing elements in the West opposing revolutionary change — ostracized Soviet Russia from the family of nations, refused to cooperate with it during the 1930s to contain Axis expansionism, and in many cases expressed their preference for Nazism over communism (or, at a minimum, their hope that these two totalitarian systems would eliminate each other).

During World War II and in the early postwar period, opposition to communism increasingly dominated U.S. diplomatic behavior. Washington's reluctance to open the long-awaited "second front" against Hitler's European empire suggested U.S. indifference to Soviet military needs (perhaps implying to Stalin that the United States was actually encouraging a war of exhaustion between Germany and Russia). Even before the war had ended the United States and other Western governments intruded themselves into the affairs of Poland and other Eastern European countries, a zone that traditionally lay within Russia's sphere of influence. Yet the West showed no disposition to grant Moscow a voice in the affairs of occupied Italy or Japan, or in the Western Hemisphere. In the closing months of the war, the United States abruptly canceled Lend Lease aid to Moscow. Both the act and the unilateral manner in which it was done indicated U.S. indifference toward Russia's wartime contribution and its postwar needs.

To members of this school of thought, as much as any other single factor, the U.S. nuclear monopoly poisoned the atmosphere of postwar Soviet-U.S. relations and guaranteed the onset of the Cold War. Supported by an overwhelming Congressional majority and by a public opinion that had already become highly suspicious of Moscow's intentions, the Truman administration refused to share the United States' atomic secrets with other countries, least of all with Communist Russia. Washington's offer to place the atomic bomb under international control (embodied in the Baruch Plan for disarmament presented in 1946) contained provisions unacceptable to the Kremlin, and many liberal critics were convinced that this result was intentional, leaving the United States with its nuclear advantage. Some liberal commentators are persuaded that, for several years after 1945, U.S. policy-makers engaged in "atomic diplomacy," relying upon their superior nuclear arsenal to exact political concessions from the Soviet Union. [32]

The proclamation of the Truman Doctrine (March 12, 1947) was, to the minds of many liberal commentators, the United States' official declaration of Cold War against the Communist enemy. Thereafter, from the Truman through the Reagan administrations, the avowedly anti-Communist character of U.S. foreign policy remained fundamentally unchanged; and although it might have appeared otherwise for a few years after the Vietnam War, public and official U.S. opposition to communism was perhaps the most constant element in the consensus supporting the nation's foreign policy. Intemperate as his language might have been, when President Ronald Reagan identified communism as "the locus of evil" in the modern world, he was expressing an idea which continued to enjoy widespread U.S. support.[33] Public and Congressional approval of substantial increases in the national defense budget under Presidents Carter and Reagan indicated convincingly that opposition to communism remained a dominant conviction of the people of the United States. (As always on foreign policy issues, public opinion on this question was anomalous and contradictory. Americans could and did continue to remain apprehensive about the Soviet Union's intentions abroad, while simultaneously calling for renewed progress in efforts by the superpowers to reduce the level of global armaments, while favoring a new Soviet-U.S. summit conference, and while urging national leaders to resolve major international issues by negotiations. Similarly, Americans could endorse the general principle of Soviet-U.S. détente, while remaining highly suspicious and critical of Moscow's behavior in Poland, Afghanistan, and Latin America.[34])

The anti-Communist mentality that dominated U.S. foreign policy after World War II had multiple origins. Some commentators have attributed it to the fundamental ideological incompatibility between Marxism and capitalism. Believing firmly in the superiority of their free enterprise system, Americans felt increasingly threatened by communism, all the more so after World War II, when the Soviet Union emerged as an expansionist, nuclear-armed superpower. Understandably, corporate interests and business groups in the United States felt most directly jeopardized by Communist gains. And since, to the minds of many liberals, this was the most influential group affecting the governmental decision-making process, it was natural and inevitable that its views would dictate national policy.[35]

A related idea is that the United States' antipathy toward communism, and the interventionist policies stemming from this aversion, were an outgrowth of the natural ideological predispositions of the elite that has controlled the foreign policy process in the United States since World War II. Sometimes referred to as the "national security managers," this select group has comprised high-level presidential advisers in agencies like the State and Defense Departments, along with other advisers drawn from outside the government. As a rule, its members have represented upper-middle-class and upper-class backgrounds; they have been graduates of Ivy League or other prestigious universities; they have come predominantly from the business, financial, legal, and educational professions (with lawyers frequently disproportionately represented); and they have belonged to influential organizations like the Council on Foreign Relations.

Personified by individuals like Secretaries of State Dean Acheson and John Foster Dulles, by the Soviet specialist George F. Kennan, and presidential advisers like Averell Harriman and Clark Clifford, this group has formed a closely knit foreign policy establishment, whose viewpoints have usually been decisive in determining national policy. Almost to a man (its membership has been almost exclusively male), its viewpoints have been characterized by a consensus manifesting uncompromising hostility to communism and a determination to take any step required for the United States to win the Cold War. According to the rules of the game observed by the national security managers, global problems are never solved, only managed to maximize U.S. power and influence.[36]

Still another impetus toward the maintenance of a rigid anti-Communist stance, according to other liberal and left-wing commentators, was supplied by the military-industrial complex in the United States. Consisting of high-level military officers (including those subsequently employed by private industry); large corporations engaged in defense production (and encompassing thousands of smaller business firms serving as subcontractors in defense industries); labor unions and workers whose livelihoods depend upon maintaining a high level of defense production; scientists, educators, and employees of "think tanks" (like the Rand Corporation and the Hudson Institute) who benefited from contracts and subsidies provided by the Pentagon and defense-related industries; officials of the Central Intelligence Agency, over which the president and his principal advisers have found it difficult to exercise effective control as the agency has arrogated to itself the right to intervene in the affairs of other countries in order to save them from communism; and influential legislators, particularly those belonging to the powerful House Armed Services Committee, whose members maintain a close rapport with the Pentagon and who are nearly always receptive to pleas for higher military appropriations — the military-industrial complex has acquired a potent vested interest in waging a global anti-Communist campaign, requiring maintenance of a high level of U.S. armed forces and a readiness to intervene in other countries. Thus, John Swomley has concluded that, since World War II, "[the] cold war and the military-industrial complex have created and sustained each other. Their impact on the domestic scene is overwhelming but on the international scene they perpetuate the arms race and heighten international tensions."[37]

Among liberal critics of U.S. involvement in the Vietnam War, a frequently heard argument was that the withdrawal of U.S. troops from Southeast Asia would result in a peace bonus or a substantial savings in the military budget that could be used for constructive purposes within the United States, such as education, the improvement of health services, and antipoverty programs. For several years during the 1970s, U.S. defense spending did decline; but by the end of the Carter administration (largely as a result of the Soviet incursion into Afghanistan), it increased sharply. Then under the Reagan administration, the national defense reached unprecedented levels; and the prospect was that it would remain at these (or higher) levels in the years ahead. As merely one illustration of the phenomenon, President Reagan's Strategic Defense Initiative (SDI or "Star Wars" proposal) was an extraordinarily costly undertaking, estimated to cost more than $95 billion to the year 2000, before the United States would possess the ability to destroy most Soviet strategic missiles in outer space before they could hit North America. Liberal critics viewed Star Wars as a conspicuous example of official preoccupation with extremely expensive military "gadgetry," whose feasibility remained highly questionable and whose contribution to national security was, at best, debatable. To the minds of many critics, in fact, Star Wars was worse than a waste of national resources: it actually weakened the security of the United States, in that it would almost certainly trigger countermeasures by the Soviet Union and provide momentum for a renewed arms race between the superpowers.[38] The Reagan administration's determination to proceed with the project simply confirmed the existence of the military-industrial complex and its pervasive influence upon national policy making.

For many liberal critics of U.S. diplomacy, Americans have consistently failed to understand the Soviet society's fixation (some commentators would call it a phobia) with security; and too often, U.S. diplomatic moves have aggravated these Soviet fears. From the period of the Mongol invasions of Russia, through Napoleon's Russian campaign, to Hitler's surprise attack against the Soviet Union in 1941, the Russians have suffered countless foreign invasions and suffered untold damage, in lives lost and property destroyed, as a result of them. Accordingly, security remains a dominant concern of the Soviet Union; and according to this interpretation, a number of the Kremlin's diplomatic moves in the recent period must be understood as an effort by the Communist hierarchy to protect the security of the Soviet state from real or imagined external threats. Certain U.S. diplomatic moves — such as the Reagan administration's efforts to install a new offensive missile system in Western Europe, or its Star Wars proposal, or providing increased U.S. arms-aid to the Afghan rebels and Pakistan — exacerbate these age-old Russian fears and lead to new efforts by the Kremlin to strengthen national security.[39]

A related idea, emphasized by liberal critics of recent U.S. diplomacy, is that in contrast to prevailing conceptions, the Soviet Union is in reality a weak nation, which continues to face severe internal economic problems, widening social and ethnic divisions, and ongoing political dissidence. Increasingly, as many liberal commentators see it, Soviet leaders have become conservative and devoted to the status quo; they have lost their earlier messianic compulsion to engage in world revolution or otherwise save the world; and they are increasingly preoccupied with a broad range of acute domestic problems to which they are required to devote attention. As a result, with each passing year the gravity of the Soviet threat to U.S. security declines, as Communist leaders are severely challenged to solve urgent problems at home. In effect, many liberal critics believe that George F. Kennan's prediction in the late 1940s has in fact come true: with the passage of time, the Soviet state has mellowed, has steadily lost its expansionist urge, and has presented a steadily decreasing danger to the security of the United States and other non-Communist nations. Yet offical and public thinking within the United States has not accepted this reality and adapted U.S. diplomacy to it.[40] This is a noteworthy example of the kind of pervasive misperception that has too often guided U.S. diplomacy in the past and that continues to perpetuate the Cold War today.[41]

Other studies assign a pivotal role in precipitating and perpetuating the Cold War to the mass media in the United States. By uncritically accepting the prevailing myth of a monolithic Communist bloc determined to enslave the world, and by repeatedly indoctrinating the public with a "disease theory of Communism," the U.S. mass media played a crucial part in exacerbating Soviet-U.S. tensions.[42] Even if they did not instigate the Cold War and the interventionist urge in postwar U.S. foreign policy, another study has found, the U.S. mass media have become "a pillar of the emergent imperial society," serving as "the ganglia of national power and expansion."

This is one of the most persistent ideas in liberal neo-isolationist thought: that since World War II, the United States has consistently opposed revolutionary movements abroad, has become identified as a defender of the status quo in other countries, and in doing so, has abandoned its own revolutionary heritage in foreign affairs. In turn, this behavior pattern has contributed to repeated U.S. diplomatic failures and has strengthened the appeal of communism and other extremist political movements for disadvantaged peoples throughout the world. From early postwar efforts to prevent a Communist victory in the Chinese civil war, to the Eisenhower administration's intervention in Guatemala in 1954, to President Kennedy's efforts to overthrow Castro's regime in Cuba in 1961, to the United States' massive involvement in the Vietnam War, to the Reagan administration's intervention in Lebanon and Central America — in these and other cases, liberals are widely convinced, the dominant goal of U.S. diplomacy was to prevent revolutionary change abroad. In most cases, not only did the effort fail, but in the process the global influence and diplomatic credibility of the United States was severely impaired. An enduring result, for example, was to permit Communists to become identified as the agents of radical change, and this fact in turn greatly enhanced the popular appeal of communism for discontented masses overseas.[43]

What factors are responsible for the image of the United States as a country that opposes revolutions and is aligned with the existing order? Among liberal commentators there is wider agreement on the existence of this phenomenon than on its basic causes. A number of different (although often interrelated) explanations have been advanced to account for this defect in postwar foreign policy. Some liberal spokesmen believe, for example, that very few policy-makers in Washington really understand and empathize with the revolutionary process in other countries. The most charitable explanation is that U.S. officials are incapable of understanding foreign revolutionary movements adequately and sympathetically, since such experiences are alien to the U.S. society's own traditions and needs. Other liberal observers are convinced that policy-makers in the United States did not really want to understand the revolutionary process abroad intelligently and dispassionately, being ideologically and psychologically repelled by radical movements, largely uninterested in the destiny of countries outside Western Europe and Latin America, and preoccupied with other issues, like nuclear competition and the space race with the Soviet Union.[44]

Yet, even if U.S. officials were prepared to concede the necessity of changes in primitive societies throughout the world, they often misjudged the nature of the changes likely to occur, deceiving themselves in the view that a majority of Third World countries could achieve modernization and progress by adopting gradual and peaceful reform programs, formulated in cooperation with the United States. As in the case of the Alliance for Progress inaugurated by the Kennedy administration, policy-makers believed that social and economic modernization throughout Latin America could be accomplished by a process of controlled revolution (or, as the Alliance for Progress was sometimes called, a "revolution in freedom"). As the Alliance's listed goals indicated, officials in Washington were convinced that rapid progress in economic and social modernization would lead to Western-style democratic governments and growing political stability throughout Latin America.

Similarly, in the face of mounting opposition to its diplomacy, the Reagan administration adhered to a policy of "constructive engagement" with the white-dominated government of South Africa. The basic premise of this policy was that gradual and evolutionary change in South Africa's apartheid system was both possible and desirable; it was preferable either to supporting the status quo within South African society or to encouraging revolutionary transformations in its social, economic, and political affairs. Yet liberal critics believed that by the mid 1980s, constructive engagement was a diplomatically bankrupt position for the United States. To their minds, neither the government of South Africa nor the disfranchised black majority within the country really supported the policy. Consistent opposition of the United States to "the African revolution" in South Africa and other settings, critics were convinced, was responsible for a continued decline in the influence of the United States on the African continent.[45]

Policy-makers in the United States have also been frequently prone to confuse the commitment of the Third World societies to revolutionary change with Communist expansionism, entailing a diplomatic victory for the Soviet Union. Moscow and Peking, of course, have sought to win universal acceptance of their respective claims as the fountainhead and guardian of revolutionary movements throughout the world. Many critics assert that, intentionally or not, officials in Washington have accepted this important tenet of Marxism uncritically. By the late 1950s the United States and the Soviet Union had reached a level of nuclear parity with each other. This fact induced restraint by the superpowers in their relations with each other and in time transferred the arena of most active Soviet-U.S. competition to the Third World. Soviet Premier Nikita Khrushchev spoke publicly about the dangers inherent in a superpower nuclear confrontation. At the same time, he identified "wars of national liberation" as a permissible form of struggle between Marxism and capitalism in the nuclear age. Khrushchev left no doubt that the Soviet Union intended to support and to win these contests. Accordingly, to U.S. leaders the decisive battleground of the Cold War had shifted to the Third World, where Communist groups subservient to Moscow were committed to fomenting revolutions, insurrections, and subversion against established governments. In the light of this shift in the locale of Cold War competition, policy-makers in the United States were prone to confuse indigenous revolutionary movements abroad with efforts by Moscow to expand its hegemony. U.S. officials, Stephen Ambrose has asserted, tended to see "Communist involvement in every attack on the status quo anywhere and convinced themselves that the Kremlin was at the center of a master-plot to conquer the world."[46]

This leads to another reason why, according to liberal neo-isolationists, the United States has opposed revolutionary changes abroad and in time adopted a counterrevolutionary posture. U.S. officials were driven by the logic of their position to prefer military dictatorships and other right-wing regimes identified with the status quo over alternative, more popularly based, political systems attuned to the needs of the society, especially its disadvantaged elements. After the United States promulgated the Truman Doctrine, Ambrose has contended, "All the Greek government, or any dictatorship, had to do to get American aid was to claim that its opponents were Communist." Despite his liberal professions, Richard J. Walton has concluded, even President John F. Kennedy's "definition of progress and self-determination was limited to regimes found acceptable by Washington — almost always not on the basis of their service to their own people but on the basis of their anti-Communism." Senator Fulbright has similarly expressed his bewilderment at the United States' "gratuitous tender-heartedness toward right-wing dictators" throughout the postwar period.[47]

During some periods — and the short-lived Kennedy administration was perhaps the outstanding example — officials in Washington opposed revolutionary tendencies abroad for another reason: their confidence that the United States was able to devise and carry out an effective strategy of counterinsurgency, capable of winning the Cold War against Communist-led revolutionary movements throughout the Third World. Believing that the Third World had become the decisive arena of Soviet-U.S. competition, President Kennedy and his advisers gave high priority to developing U.S. skill in counterinsurgency and "nation building" — concepts that became increasingly prominent during the period of maximum U.S. involvement in the Vietnam War. U.S. defeat in that conflict tended of course to discredit such concepts.[48] For many liberal critics the outcome in Vietnam provided additional evidence that the United States neither understood the process of revolutionary political change, nor was it able to formulate a diplomatic strategy capable of opposing it successfully. Liberal neo-isolationists believed that during the 1980s, the Reagan administration's interventionism in Central America reflected a failure in Washington to understand, and learn from, these earlier diplomatic failures.

Another reason why U.S. efforts to engage in nation building and to promote revolutionary changes abroad often fail was highlighted by the collapse of the Iranian monarchy in 1979. Any incumbent government cooperating with Washington to carry out sweeping internal reforms is likely to encounter popular disaffection because of its subservience to a foreign power; and with the passage of time, political opposition groups will be able to use this association with telling effectiveness against the established government. Considerable popular disaffection, for example, has been directed against the United States by Latin Americans because of the former's insistence upon the reforms needed to make the Alliance for Progress a success. (The fact that incumbent regimes in Latin America often had agreed to such changes made these reforms more politically unpalatable than ever!) In Iran, the Kennedy administration had insisted that the monarchy undertake a comprehensive set of internal reforms (collectively known as the White Revolution). Yet in the end, the net effect of these revolutionary currents was to create growing popular disaffection with the monarchy and its U.S. sponsor. Even more recently, several Third World nations (and Mexico was a prominent example) expressed widespread resentment toward demands by the International Monetary Fund (IMF), viewed as under decisive U.S. influence, that effective reforms be undertaken before new loans and credits were made available to needy societies.[49]

An additional reason why the United States became increasingly identified as an opponent of revolution was an outgrowth of its historical experience and ideological orientation as a nation. Popular mythology and Fourth of July oratory extolling the American Revolution to the contrary, the reality was that historically Americans have exhibited no real sympathy for revolutionary ideologies or programs at home; their support for revolutionary movements abroad has usually been little more than symbolic. Preferring gradual and evolutionary changes, the people of the United States have never advocated or carried out the kind of sweeping and perhaps violent restructuring of society demanded throughout much of the Third World. Down to the postwar period their own unequaled progress in elevating living standards and solving many of the social problems that had baffled the Old World confirmed Americans in their preference for gradual and orderly methods, all the more so after World War II, when revolutionary movements were nearly always viewed as emanating from Moscow or Peking. As what the historian David Potter has described as the "people of plenty," Americans never really understood that the stability of their cherished democratic political system, their economic productivity, their belief in progress, and many other ideas intimately associated with the U.S. way of life, derived primarily from the fact of the material abundance with which the North American continent was blessed. In less fortunately endowed societies, however, such ideas and values might possess little appeal or utility.[50] By contrast, in less-developed societies, what John Gerassi has called "negative violence," produced by conditions of pervasive poverty and disease, along with food shortages and little or no improvement in the standard of living, is often inherent in the situation. For poverty-stricken masses, the violence accompanying a revolutionary transformation of society may well be preferable to the negative violence inherent in a hopeless existing order.[51]

Yet another group of critics is convinced that the real reason why the United States opposes revolutionary movements abroad is very simple: even more today than in the past, the prosperity and political stability of the United States demands maintenance of the status quo in other countries, particularly those closely associated with the United States economically. Thus, Ambrose accounts for U.S. opposition to revolutionary causes by the contention that the nation has made

> continuous and consistent efforts to incorporate (by both liberal and conservative means) the now underdeveloped countries into a single mercantile and industrial capitalist system. The economic surplus (raw materials, cheap labor, etc.) of the underdeveloped countries has been and

continues to be appropriated for the benefit of the capitalist structure, i.e., the United States.

U.S. postwar foreign aid programs, according to Ambrose's assessment, had the perpetuation of this essentially colonialist system as their paramount goal.[52] Similarly, Taubman believes that recent U.S. foreign policy toward the Third World has been motivated chiefly by a desire to protect its own private investments abroad, to provide continued access to critical raw materials, and to maintain pro-U.S. regimes in power.[53]

At the conclusion of *The Crippled Giant,* a book analyzing the principal reasons why U.S. power and influence in global affairs had declined sharply, Senator Fulbright underscored a fifth idea prominent in the assessment of other liberal neo-isolationist critics, of the nation's recent diplomatic record. The contemporary world, Fulbright asserted, does not need "a new imperial power, but there is a great need of the leadership of example." In Fulbright's judgment, Americans have not sufficiently grasped the consequences for their own internal society of pursuing an interventionist foreign policy: "The price of empire is America's soul and the price is too high."[54] It will be recalled from Chapter 1 that Fulbright's concern was one of the more prominent ideas in isolationist thought before World War I. In the isolationist mentality, one of the most compelling reasons why the United States should avoid foreign entanglements was fear that an interventionist foreign policy would jeopardize the U.S. way of life.[55] One of the most outspoken isolationists of the interwar period, Senator Gerald P. Nye, said in 1939 that the United States' place in the world "is in a very definite and large way dependent upon her own strength of mind and body." Instead of trying to remedy the problems of other societies, Nye advised the nation to concentrate upon "correcting our own ills . . . saving our own democracy rather than soliciting trouble to come from any move to police and doctor the world."[56]

After World War II many other liberal commentators joined Senator Fulbright in deploring U.S. overextension abroad because of its adverse effects at home. For example, in their detailed and often highly critical assessment of U.S. postwar diplomacy, Edmund Stillman and William Pfaff emphasize that national greatness "does not lie in foreign policy." Diplomatic success serves primarily as a means for enhancing (or, more accurately, provides an opportunity for enhancing) domestic policy. "A skillful foreign policy will ensure the external peace within which the conditions of a private national excellence may be achieved." After their country became a superpower, Americans forgot that a "society's true greatness lies within itself — in the condition of its intellectual life, the quality of its arts, the justice with which it treats its citizens and enables them to deal with one another."[57]

The general point made by liberal critics concerning U.S. readiness to intervene in the affairs of other countries is that it neglects the organic interrelationship between foreign and domestic policy. Within this general criticism, liberal commentators tend to emphasize four corollary ideas. In the first place, national leaders, and many U.S. citizens, have overlooked the crucial fact that the primary objective of foreign policy is to make possible conditions in the outside world conducive to promoting domestic well-being. As Senator Fulbright has expressed it, the United States' "vital interests are essentially domestic in character."[58]

In the second place, liberal critics believe that an interventionist foreign policy, pursued at the expense of domestic well-being, inevitably projects a hypocritical image of the United States abroad, weakening the nation's influence and subjecting it to derision and ridicule from other countries. How can the United States presume to act as the policeman of the world when it is increasingly unable to police its own cities adequately? Or how can officials in Washington formulate programs for eliminating poverty throughout the Third World when they cannot eliminate it in the most affluent society known to history? Or, as Steel has remarked, Americans ought to "set our own house in order before we declare ourselves responsible for the welfare of the entire world."[59]

In the third place, an increasingly interventionist foreign policy can be — and many liberals are persuaded that it has been — destructive of the United States' own values and its highest ethical and constitutional traditions. The United States cannot indefinitely preserve its democratic institutions and adhere to its highest ethical principles at home while relying upon authoritarian and police-state methods, like counter-insurgency programs, to achieve its foreign policy goals.

In the fourth place, as Stillman and Pfaff expressed the idea, for many years the United States has used the Cold War "as a means of avoiding self-confrontation" at home — that is, as a convenient excuse for failing to come to grips with progressively more serious domestic problems.[60] For Americans, in other words, the Cold War plays the same role which Communist China's "Hate America!" campaign played during the 1950s, or which the U.S. "Great Satan" plays in the diplomacy of revolutionary Iran today. As innumerable nations throughout history have discovered, nothing is better designed to unite the country, and to divert the people's minds from internal problems, than a foreign threat. For liberal neo-isolationists, it is infinitely easier for the Reagan administration to identify the Soviet Union almost daily as the locus of evil in the contemporary world, than it is to formulate and carry out effective antipoverty programs or to improve the nation's health and educational systems or to eliminate hazards to the environment. Moreover, a strong or interventionist foreign policy provides justification for record-level spending on national defense, for the space program (which often has military application), for foreign military aid programs and other projects ostensibly designed to contain expansive communism. Without this external danger, political leaders would be hard pressed to maintain popular support. In this sense, political elites often have a strong vested interest in maintaining a high level of Soviet-U.S. (or perhaps Cuban- or Nicaraguan-U.S.) tensions, that justify interventionist behavior by the United States.

LIBERAL NEO-ISOLATION: A CRITIQUE

Let us begin our assessment of the liberal neo-isolationist viewpoint by taking note of four constructive contributions that this school of thought has made to the recent and future conduct of U.S. foreign relations. Initially — and this unquestionably ranks among the most useful services rendered by this school of thought — they remind Americans of a basic but too often forgotten truth: in the democratic ideology, the foreign policy of any nation ought always to be organically related to, and ought to promote, the fundamental purposes for which the state exists — namely, the enhancement of human well-being. This is one of the recurrent and most valuable themes evident in liberal neo-isolationist thought. The ultimate criterion for measuring the utility or success of any given policy in foreign relations is this: how well does it contribute to the welfare of Americans and (insofar as many liberals also tend to believe in the concept of global community) of individuals broadly throughout the world?

Foreign policy, many liberal critics insist, is not the exclusive province of a policy-making elite; it is not (as devotees of *Realpolitik* sometimes assume) the sport of kings or a realm removed from the application of democratic and humanitarian values. According to liberal tenets, the ordinary citizen has a right to expect two things from foreign policy decision-makers: that the public's views and aspirations will constitute a major input in formulating national policy and that some kind of reasonably clear correlation will exist and be maintained between the implementation of a particular foreign policy and the well-being of individuals at home and abroad. A familiar indictment of postwar U.S. foreign relations by liberal interventionist critics is that the conduct of the United States overseas failed to meet one or both of these tests.

For the past quarter-century or so, liberal neo-isolationism has also been better attuned to the *Zeitgeist* (spirit of the age) than many alternative approaches to U.S. foreign relations. Despite the fact that governments and political groups abroad often solicit various forms of U.S. interventionism in other countries, ostensibly the nations of the Third World are opposed to U.S., Soviet, and other forms of outside interference in their affairs. Wedded to a policy of diplomatic nonalignment, most Third World nations resent efforts by the superpowers to align them with rival Cold War power blocs or otherwise to make them pawns in contests for the regional or global hegemony of more powerful nations. The dominant concern of these nations tends to be national development. Perhaps even more than in advanced societies, citizens of these countries tend to judge the behavior of their own and of foreign governments by the test of how well it improves the lot of the common people. On the basis of that test, as liberal neo-isolationists have frequently insisted, the performance of the United States in global affairs since World War II has often fallen considerably short of expectations. To cite but a single example: U.S.-sponsored alliances and arms-aid programs to a host of countries have unquestionably encouraged the Third World nations to divert already scarce domestic resources for military use, with the result that military expenditures were often escalating more rapidly among the poorer countries of the world than among the advanced nations. Meanwhile, the prospects facing most Third World societies in terms of successful national development and internal progress were unpromising.

Another useful contribution of liberal neo-isolationist thought lies in repeated admonitions expressed concerning the dangers of bureaucratic inertia and ossification in the foreign policy process. As a political credo, liberalism is inherently favorably disposed toward change. (Conversely, as we shall see, one of the weaknesses of this political credo is a tendency to be almost totally uncritical in its assumption that any change constitutes an improvement over existing policy.) With this orientation, liberal critics have naturally been at the forefront in urging national decision makers to reexamine established policies and to make the changes required to adapt U.S. foreign policy to contemporary and emerging conditions in the external environment. As early as the end of the 1950s, for example, it had become apparent that (in the light of Yugoslavia's defection and of the Sino-Soviet split) the concept of international communism had largely outlived its usefulness. Similarly with regard to foreign aid programs, liberal neo-isolationists have unquestionably been correct in asserting that an approach that was effective for achieving the reconstruction of Western Europe had little relevance for the problem of modernizing Latin America or raising productivity in Asia.

In these and other respects, foreign policy officials in the United States have been slow to make needed modifications in the nation's approach to a rapidly changing external milieu. As in the sphere of foreign economic assistance, basically the same programs have been recommended to, and approved by, Congress year after year, long after experience had raised major questions about their effectiveness. If one of the objectives of foreign aid — along with foreign military spending, propaganda programs, political intervention, and other techniques utilized by the United States since World War II — is to enhance U.S. influence abroad and to create a global environment more receptive to the realization of U.S. external policy goals, then liberal neo-isolationists are not infrequently correct in the contention that these techniques have in fact had the opposite effects.

Another noteworthy contribution of liberal neo-isolationist thought lies in calling attention to the domestic costs of what in an earlier age was referred to as a strong foreign policy and in the postwar period is known as a policy of globalism or internationalism. Experience since World War II leaves little doubt that a dynamic and expansive foreign policy exacts a high price from the United States internally. The consequences for the U.S. society of the nation's global involvement have been manifold. Untold billions of dollars have been expended on foreign economic and military aid programs, many of them of dubious value for either the recipients or the United States. A significant portion of these funds might more usefully have been spent on worthwhile domestic projects within the United States. U.S. interventionism on a global scale has also unquestionably enhanced the powers of the president vis-à-vis Congress, strengthening the tendency toward executive dominance in national decision making and leading to the further erosion of the legislative role in foreign relations. "Crisis diplomacy" — which appears to have become the established pattern during much of the postwar era — augments the prerogatives of the president and accelerates the trend toward centralization of national authority in the White House. Since World War II, there has also been an evident tendency toward greater secrecy surrounding governmental decision making. An interventionist foreign policy and covert governmental activities perhaps inevitably go hand in hand.

A number of serious criticisms of liberal viewpoints applied to the realm of foreign affairs have been treated in earlier chapters. These include the tacit premise on which liberal neo-isolationist attitudes are often established: the idea that the U.S. model of democracy (or, at any rate, some Western liberal system of democracy) is normative for other countries. A logical corollary of this view is that, stated positively, the United States should support democracy abroad and that, stated negatively, it should cease supporting dictatorships. Sometimes liberal neo-isolationist thought also exhibits a massive naiveté concerning the existence of rivalry and conflict among nations. As a credo denigrating the Christian idea of original sin or the egocentric propensities of individuals, groups, and states, liberalism retains an uncritical faith in the natural harmony and sense of community characteristic of the international political system. A prescription frequently expressed by devotees of this viewpoint is that international understanding is a universal solvent for conflicts among the nations of the world. This simplistic idea tends to overlook the fact that during the 1930s the more the West "understood" Hitler, the more certain it became that his expansionist moves menaced the security of other nations. During and after World War II, the more the outside world learned about Stalin's personality, the more it became convinced that the Soviet dictator suffered from paranoia and other forms of mental aberration that influenced Russian decision making.

To cite a more recent example: the outside world may understand many of the reasons why members of the Palestine Liberation Organization (PLO) and other guerrilla organizations engage in terroristic acts against the governments of Israel, the United States, and other targets. Individuals and groups utilizing terroristic methods may (and usually are) alienated politically; they are (or believe that they are) excluded from established channels of political participation; not infrequently, they are motivated by religious principles or belief in a cause, requiring them to eliminate their enemies; in many cases also, they are unquestionably seeking worldwide publicity; in some instances, terrorists are actively seeking martyrdom. For these and other reasons, by the 1980s international terrorism threatened to assume epidemic proportions.[61] Yet understanding the reasons for this phenomenon did not, of course, make it more endurable or legitimate for governments and individuals who were subject to terroristic acts.

Moreover, liberal neo-isolationist thought largely ignores the fact that the overextension of U.S. policy abroad since World War II has come about in no small measure as a result of applying liberal ideas and extending liberal-approved programs to the sphere of external affairs. Such goals as the modernization and democratization of the developing nations; or the idea that political stability is a function of economic and social progress; or the notion that the U.S. revolutionary experience is broadly applicable to societies outside the West; or great confidence in the ability of U.S. policy-makers to resolve problems (like the Arab-Israeli dispute) whose solutions have defied the efforts of other nations — these ideas often animating the U.S. interventionist urge abroad owe much to liberal sources. To a significant degree (seldom acknowledged by liberal spokesmen), the disillusionment characteristic of liberal neo-isolationist thought after the Vietnam War with the nation's role in external affairs stemmed from disenchantment with U.S. attempts to achieve liberal goals in foreign settings.

Still another vulnerable point in many liberal neo-isolationist assessments of recent U.S. diplomatic experience is the tendency to explain foreign policy ventures that fail or otherwise do not promote the nation's interests overseas by invoking a conspiracy theory — which can sometimes compound the already difficult problems confronting national policy-makers and citizens in the realm of foreign relations. It is ironic that liberal commentators, many of whom have been extremely vocal in condemning the tendency of other groups to blame adverse conditions at home and abroad upon the "Communist global conspiracy," not infrequently offer a conspiratorial explanation of their own to account for conditions inside and outside the United States that they lament.

The liberal equivalent to the international Communist conspiracy is the machinations of the foreign policy elite (alternatively, the national-security managers or the military-industrial complex), whose decisions have allegedly involved the United States in a series of major and minor misadventures abroad since World War II. Numerous parallels can be drawn between the right-wing and left-wing (or liberal) conspiratorial explanations given to explain postwar diplomatic failures. In both versions, for example, a supposedly all-powerful group is actually in control of the national decision-making process; the president and other executive officials, together with key committees of Congress and influential legislators, are manipulated by this group to achieve its ends; the true extent of this group's covert influence upon the policy process is unknown (and perhaps unknowable), but it is assumed to be pervasive and decisive; the group's goals and methods are concealed from the public and the press; and its decisions are assumed to be contrary to the desires of the U.S. people and inimical to the democratic values of the society.

The effect of accepting either theory is also basically identical: it is to convince the credulous not that factors like widespread public ignorance and indifference with respect to important foreign policy issues, or misinformation and miscalculation by public officials were responsible for errors, but that the correct and wise impulses of the U.S. people and their leaders were somehow counteracted by the activities of a subterranean group bent on achieving its own antidemocratic ends.

A number of legitimate questions and objections can be raised regarding the dependency of liberal neo-isolationist critics upon their own unique conspiracy theory of U.S. foreign policy inadequacies. No two commentators, for example, agree upon the precise composition of the foreign policy elite that presumably dominates the decision-making process. Nor is this theory able to explain how or why successive presidents, their principal advisers, and members of Congress permit themselves to become the captive of this elite without successful resistance and without even being aware that the process has occurred. Such critics also tend to disregard innumerable instances in the diplomatic record since World War II in which chief executives have rejected the advice of their military advisers or other members of the so-called foreign policy elite and have refused to engage in the kind of interventionist behavior that it nearly always advocates.

Proponents of such conspiracy theories also routinely fail to differentiate clearly between foreign policy failures produced by faulty information or mistaken judgments by decision makers, on the one hand, and those made as a result of successful pressure exerted by this elite in behalf of a predetermined goal. Nor do liberal neo-isolationist critics holding this view evince awareness of the fact that in contexts like the Korean or Vietnam Wars, or U.S. relations with Cuba in the early 1960s, or in responding to the threatened renewal of a boycott imposed upon the West by the oil-producing states of the Middle East, the U.S. people may in fact be even more in favor of interventionist moves abroad than their leaders in the White House and Congress. During certain stages of the

Vietnam War, for example, the public was unquestionably more "hawkish" than President Johnson and most of his advisers.

Again, by the late 1970s the people of the United States had become extremely apprehensive and impatient about the global decline of U.S. power and about the seeming inability of their elected officials to reverse that tendency. This popular anxiety contributed significantly to President Carter's political defeat in the election of 1980 by Ronald Reagan. Four years later, the Reagan administration once more successfully appealed to the people of the United States to support a foreign policy of "standing tall" abroad. Toward Poland, toward Afghanistan, toward the Persian Gulf area, toward Central America, and toward other settings in which U.S. diplomatic interests were threatened, citizens clearly indicated their desire that the president and his advisers protect U.S. lives and interests abroad. By contrast, the results of the presidential election of 1984 indicated that the Americans had little desire to return to the diplomatic indecisiveness associated with the Carter administration or the mood of national guilt and self-doubt identified with the "Vietnam War syndrome."[62] As always, of course, public opinion on international questions was characterized by the existence of contradictions and paradoxes. Under the Reagan administration, the people wanted the White House to protect the nation's security and diplomatic interests abroad, without becoming involved in another Vietnam; the people broadly approved massive increases in defense spending, and yet they remained apprehensive about how the armed forces would be used for diplomatic ends; they opposed South Africa's apartheid system, although little public sentiment existed in behalf of overtly interventionist or coercive measures by the United States in relations with the South African government.

Many of the ideas and principles we have identified with the liberal neo-isolationist viewpoint, in other words, attracted considerable support among the people of the United States in the post-Vietnam War era. A number of commentators called attention to the lack of consensus in U.S. public opinion concerning foreign policy questions.[63] After the Vietnam War, public attitudes in the United States were more than ordinarily marked by dichotomies, evident contradictions, and incongruities. If considerable doubt existed concerning what the people of the United States wanted their national leaders to do abroad, two assertions could be made about what they wanted officials in Washington to avoid diplomatically. In the late twentieth century, the people of the United States rejected both a foreign policy of isolationism, comparable to the nation's position toward foreign conflicts during the 1930s; and they no less opposed the kind of policeman-of-the-world mentality that had led the nation into the Vietnam quagmire. If they were less certain about what they wanted positively in foreign affairs, it seemed clear that — reflecting the U.S. society's historic association with liberal political values — they wanted their leaders to be guided by many of the axioms of liberal neo-isolationism.

In addition to the weaknesses of the liberal neo-isolationist mentality we have already identified, four others may be alluded to briefly. One is the often uncritical liberal assessment of revolutionary movements throughout the contemporary world. More often than not, the liberal bias is sympathetic to any political movement that claims the label, "revolutionary." The liberal mind is nearly always prone to give such movements the benefit of the doubt, to equate revolutionary programs with beneficial change, and to assume that individuals and groups advocating radical (usually highly idealistic) goals are both able and willing to achieve them successfully. Conversely, the liberal neo-isolationist is seldom prepared to be as charitable in judging the motives and capacities of those forces that oppose revolutionary change (including the U.S. government). Yet on the basis of recent history, in regions like Latin America and black Africa, the evidence seldom supports such uncritical assessments of revolutionary movements. More often than not perhaps, they have resulted in new political orders as internally repressive and exploitive, and as dangerous to regional and global peace, as the regimes they replaced. Yet relatively few liberal neo-isolationists exhibit awareness of this reality.

A related defect of this mode of thought is its traditional bias in favor of left-wing regimes abroad and its congenital suspicion of right-wing (particularly military-dominated) governments overseas. Liberal minds consistently condemn Washington's association with and support of military dictatorships in other countries — often at the very time they call for détente with the Soviet Union, closer relations with the People's Republic of China, a "thaw" in Cuban-U.S. relations, and normalization of relations with North Vietnam. Yet ever since the Axis defeat in World War II, in the overwhelming majority of instances, it has been the expansionist policies and behavior of left-wing governments throughout the world that have posed the most critical danger to international peace and security and to the diplomatic interests of the United States.

Finally, liberal neo-isolationists continue to exhibit the same blind spot today that characterized the reaction of many isolationists to events like the Spanish civil war, and the Japanese invasion of China, during the 1930s. This is a failure to confront squarely, and to evaluate objectively, the consequences of a policy of nonintervention by the United States and its friends abroad. In the Spanish case, for example, the outcome of a noninterventionist position was a result that few liberals were prepared to accept and defend: the defeat of the Spanish Republic and a prolonged period of pro-Axis rule by the regime headed by the dictator, General Francisco Franco.

Or consider another example of the same phenomenon: the U.S. failure (along, of course, with other Western nations) to prevent Nazi Germany's effort to exterminate the Jewish population of Europe. Time and again since World War II, for example, the government of Israel and its supporters have reminded Americans of their "moral failure" in allowing the Holocaust to occur and of the indescribable toll it exacted upon Jewish lives and property. Avoiding another Holocaust, therefore, ranks high on the list of Isarel's foreign policy objectives. In this and other cases, the U.S. failure to act or to intervene beyond its own borders has been viewed as both a major diplomatic setback and as an affront to the U.S. society's highest moral-ethical principles.

This leads to a final observation about liberal neo-isolationism as an approach to U.S. foreign policy. Not infrequently, devotees of this point of view advocate a form of diplomatic "bloodless surgery" or "painless dentistry" for the United States. The liberal neo-isolationist rejects the traditional policy of isolationism, but he wants the U.S. society to enjoy many of the benefits associated with that diplomatic orientation in responding to contemporary problems. For example, national policy is expected to support revolutionary movements and modernization in the developing nations — but without intervening in their internal affairs. Washington ought to strengthen the observance of human rights abroad and promote the cause of racial justice in Africa — but it should avoid reliance upon military force in resolving these and external problems. More so than their conservative counterparts, liberal neo-isolationists are often prone to disregard the costs of pursuing their foreign policy goals in what is often a highly adverse environment abroad. As in the United States' long-standing commitment to the creation and security of the State of Israel, when that cost proves to be high — and when the commitment must sometimes be carried out by reliance upon military force — liberal neo-isolationists are often among the most vocal critics of national policy.

NOTES

1. See Walter Laqueur, *Neo-Isolationism and the World of the Seventies* (Washington, D.C.: Center for Strategic and International Studies, Georgetown University, 1972); H. Schuyler Foster, *Activism Replaces Isolationism: 1940–1975* (Washington, D.C.: Foxhall Press, 1983); Robert W. Tucker, *The Purposes of American Power: An Essay on National Security* (New York: Praeger Publishers, 1981); Aaron Wildavsky, ed., *Beyond Containment: Alternative American Policies toward the Soviet Union* (San Francisco: Institute for Contemporary Studies, 1983); Seyom Brown, *The Faces of Power: Constancy and Change in United States Foreign Policy from Truman to Reagan* (New York: Columbia University Press, 1983); Lloyd C. Gardner, *A Covenant with Power: America and World Order from Wilson to Reagan* (New York: Oxford University Press, 1984); and Donald E. Neuchterlein, *America Overcommitted: United States National Interests in the 1980s* (Lexington, Ky.: University of Kentucky Press, 1985).

2. Our summary of liberal political thought relies heavily upon Max Mark, *Modern Ideologies* (New York: St. Martin's Press, 1973); L. T. Hobhouse, *Liberalism* (London: Oxford University Press, 1964); Robert A. Goldwin, ed., *Left, Right and Center: Essays on Liberalism and Conservatism in the United States* (Chicago: Rand McNally, 1967); Gerald F. Gaus, *The Modern Liberal Theory of Man* (New York: St. Martin's Press, 1983); Douglas MacLean and Claudia Mills, *Liberalism Reconsidered* (Totowa, N.J.: Rowman and Allanheld, 1983); and (n. a.), *The Relevance of Liberalism* (Boulder, Colo.: Westview Press, 1978).

3. Hobhouse, *Liberalism,* p. 7.

4. Ibid., pp. 7–9.

5. More detailed discussion of divisions within, and subspecies of, liberalism may be found in Theodore J. Lowi, *The End of Liberalism: The Second Republic of the United States* (New York: W. W. Norton, 1979), pp. 127–63; and in MacLean and Mills, *Liberalism Reconsidered,* pp. 67–87.

6. Congressional activism in the foreign policy, especially since the end of the Vietnam War, is examined in greater detail in Cecil V. Crabb, Jr. and Pat Holt, *Invitation to Struggle: Congress, the President, and Foreign Policy,* 2d ed. (Washington, D.C.: Congressional Quarterly Press, 1984); Thomas Franck and Edward Weisband, *Foreign Policy by Congress* (New York: Oxford University Press, 1979); and Steven P. Soper, ed., *Congress, the President, and Foreign Policy* (Chicago: American Bar Association, 1985).

7. See Louis Hartz, *The Liberal Tradition in America: An Interpretation of American Political Thought since the Revolution* (New York: Harcourt, Brace, 1955).

8. The impact of pragmatic thought upon U.S. diplomatic behavior is treated more fully in Cecil V. Crabb, Jr., *The American Approach to Foreign Policy: A Pragmatic Perspective* (Lanham, Md.: University Press of America, 1985); and in a more detailed exposition of the same subject by the author in *A Pragmatic Worldview: American Diplomacy and the Pragmatic Tradition* (forthcoming).

9. Lewis Galantiére, "America Today: A Free-Hand Sketch," *Foreign Affairs* 28 (July 1950):532.

10. For a fuller discussion of the relationship between overall ideological attitudes and opinions on foreign policy issues, see V. O. Key, *Public Opinion and American*

Democracy (New York: Alfred A. Knopf, 1961), pp. 154–63; and Lloyd A. Free and Hadley Cantril, *The Political Beliefs of Americans: A Study of Public Opinion* (New York: Simon and Schuster, 1968), pp. 73–76.

11.   Paul Seabury, *Power, Freedom, and Diplomacy: The Foreign Policy of the United States of America* (New York: Random House, 1963), p. 357.

12.   William Taubman, ed., *Globalism and Its Critics: The American Foreign Policy Debate of the 1960's* (Lexington, Mass.: D. C. Heath, 1973), p. viii. The quotation from President Johnson apears on p. ix.

13.   Stephen E. Ambrose, *Rise to Globalism: American Foreign Policy, 1938–1970* (Baltimore, Penguin Books, 1971), pp. 302–31.

14.   America's Open Door policy toward China, enunciated in a note from Secretary of State John Hay to the European powers late in 1899, endeavored to prevent any one country from gaining a privileged commercial and economic position in China, thus preserving equality of opportunity for U.S. trade. As the years passed, the Open Door principle became broadened into a U.S. commitment in behalf of Chinese territorial integrity. See Julius W. Pratt, *A History of United States Foreign Policy* (Englewood Cliffs, N.J.: Prentice-Hall, 1955), pp. 434–41; see also the discussion of the Open Door policy in John K. Fairbank, *The United States and China* (New York: Viking Press, 1958), pp. 254–62.

15.   See William A. Williams, *The Tragedy of American Diplomacy* (Cleveland and New York: World Publishing Co., 1959); and Claude Julien, *America's Empire* (New York: Random House, 1971).

16.   See Julien, *America's Empire,* passim, but specifically pp. 407–8.

17.   Explanations of the U.S. role in Southeast Asia emphasizing such themes may be found in Richard J. Barnet, *Roots of War: The Men and Institutions behind U.S. Foreign Policy* (Baltimore: Penguin Books, 1972), pp. 137–75; Julien, *America's Empire,* pp. 223–67; and John W. Swomley, Jr., *American Empire: The Political Ethics of Twentieth-Century Conquest* (New York: Macmillan, 1970), pp. 197–229.

18.   Ronald Steel, *Pax Americana* (New York: Viking Press, 1970), pp. 17, 308.

19.   In their critique of U.S. postwar diplomacy, Stillman and Pfaff contend that policy-makers in Washington viewed the national development of Third World societies as "development toward us"; they thought in terms of an "idealized America" abroad. See Edmund Stillman and William Pfaff, *Power and Impotence: The Failure of America's Foreign Policy* (New York: Random House, 1966), p. 135. For a comparable view, see Steel, *Pax Americana,* p. 341.

20.   Fulbright's evaluation of U.S. foreign policy in the modern period is substantially set forth in three books that would repay careful study by the interested student. See his *Old Myths and New Realities* (New York: Random House, 1964); *The Arrogance of Power* (New York: Random House, 1966); and *The Crippled Giant: American Foreign Policy and Its Domestic Consequences* (New York: Random House, 1972).

21.   Fulbright, *The Arrogance of Power,* pp. 3, 22.

22.   See D. W. Brogan, "The Illusion of American Omnipotence," *Harper's Magazine* 205 (December 1952):21–28.

23.   Quoted in Theodore Sorensen, *Kennedy* (New York: Harper and Row, 1965), p. 511.

24.   See Neal D. Houghton, ed., *Struggle against History: United States Foreign Policy in an Age of Revolution* (New York: Simon and Schuster, 1968), p. xxiii.

25.   Fulbright, *The Crippled Giant*, p. 100.

26.   Quoted in Fulbright, *The Arrogance of Power*, pp. 11–12.

27.   See the criticisms of recent U.S. diplomatic undertakings in Tom Hayden, *The American Future: New Visions beyond Old Frontiers* (Boston: South End Press, 1980); Noam Chomsky, *Towards a New Cold War* (New York: Pantheon, 1982); T. D. Allman, *Unmanifest Destiny* (New York: Dial Press, 1984); Jonathan Kwitny, *Endless Enemies: The Making of an Unfriendly World* (New York: Congdon and Weed, 1984); and Stephen E. Ambrose, *Rise to Globalism*, 4th ed. (New York: Penguin Books, 1985).

28.   George McGovern, *A Time of War — A Time of Peace* (New York: Random House, 1968), pp. 179–80.

29.   Fred W. Neal, "The Cold War in Europe, 1945–1967," in Houghton, *Struggle against History*, p. 22.

30.   The diplomacy of the Carter administration is dealt with more fully in Jimmy Carter, *Keeping Faith: Memoirs of a President* (New York: Bantam Books, 1982); Cyrus Vance, *Hard Choices: Critical Years in America's Foreign Policy* (New York: Simon and Schuster, 1983); and Hamilton Jordan, *Crisis: The Last Year of the Carter Presidency* (New York: G. P. Putnam's Sons, 1982).

31.   See D. F. Fleming, *The Cold War and Its Origins: 1917–1950*, Vol. 1, and *The Cold War and Its Origins: 1950–1960*, Vol. 2 (Garden City, N.Y.: Doubleday, 1961). For briefer treatments in the same vein, see Frederick L. Schuman, *The Cold War: Retrospect and Prospect* (Baton Rouge: Louisiana State University Press, 1967).

32.   The United States' reliance upon its nuclear arsenal to gain diplomatic advantages in the early postwar period is the theme of Gar Alperovitz, *Atomic Diplomacy — Hiroshima and Potsdam: The Use of the Atomic Bomb and the American Confrontation with Soviet Power* (New York: Simon and Schuster, 1965); for a briefer discussion, see David Horowitz, *The Free World Colossus: A Critique of American Foreign Policy in the Cold War* (New York: Hill and Wang, 1971), pp. 265–79.

33.   See Strobe Talbott, *The Russians and Reagan* (New York: Random House, 1984); Rowland Evans and Robert Novak, *The Reagan Revolution* (New York: E. P. Dutton, 1981), pp. 157–85; and Norman Podheretz, "The Reagan Road to Détente," *Foreign Affairs* 63 (Special Issue 1984), pp. 447–64.

34.   The dichotomous and complex nature of U.S. public opinion on foreign policy questions in the post-Vietnam War era is highlighted in Foster, *Activism Replaces Isolationism*, pp. 329–75; Ralph B. Levering, *The Public and American Foreign Policy: 1918–1978* (New York: William Morrow, 1978); Bernard C. Cohen, *The Public's Impact on Foreign Policy* (Boston: Little, Brown, 1973); and Daniel Yankelovich and John Doble, "The Public Mood," *Foreign Affairs* 63 (Fall 1984):33–47.

35.   Thus Parenti believes that the so-called national policies of countries are "actually reflections of the interests of the country's dominant socioeconomic classes"— which, in the case of postwar America, was the business-commercial class. See Michael Parenti, "The Basis of American Interventionism," in Michael Parenti,

ed., *Trends and Tragedies in American Foreign Policy* (Boston: Little, Brown, 1971), pp. 119–72, 216; see also the views of Barnet in *Roots of War*, pp. 176–205.

36.   This is the thesis of Gabriel Kolko's study, *The Roots of American Foreign Policy* (Boston: Beacon Press, 1969).

37.   John M. Swomley, Jr., "The Military-Industrial Alliance," in Houghton, *Struggle against History*, p. 58.

38.   See the symposium on "Star Wars: Pros and Cons," *Foreign Affairs* 62 (Spring 1984):820–57; and the symposium, "The President's Choice: Star Wars or Arms Control," ibid. 63 (Winter 1984/85):240–79.

39.   The Soviet Union's preoccupation with security is a dominant theme of "revisionist" interpretations of the Cold War. In this view, since World War II, U.S. officials have been insufficiently cognizant of, and sensitive to, this deep-seated Soviet concern. George F. Kennan, for example, believed that this was a dominant motivation in the Soviet Union's invasion of Afghanistan in 1979. For a detailed interpretation of Soviet diplomacy emphasizing this idea, see Fleming, *The Cold War and Its Origins*, passim. Critics of this view emphasize the degree to which Soviet policy poses a threat to the security of other nations. See, for example, Richard Pipes, "Can the Soviet Union Reform?" *Foreign Affairs* 63 (Fall 1984):47–62.

40.   The idea that in reality the Soviet Union is a weak nation — and becoming weaker every year — leads some commentators to believe that the Soviet Empire is in the process of disintegration. See, for example, Emmanuel Todd, *The Final Fall: An Essay on the Decomposition of the Soviet Sphere* (New York: Harz, 1979). See also, Robert Wesson, *The Aging of Communism* (New York: Praeger, 1980); Alexandr Solzhenitsyn, *The Mortal Danger: How Misconceptions about Russia Imperil America* (New York: Harper and Row, 1980); Robert Wesson, ed., *The Soviet Union: Looking to the 1980s* (Stanford, Calif.: Hoover Institution Press, 1980); and Grayson Kirk and Nils H. Wessell, eds., *The Soviet Threat: Myths and Realities* (New York: Praeger, 1978).

41.   The impact of misperceptions on the diplomatic behavior of the United States, the Soviet Union, and Communist China is the major theme of the study by John G. Stoessinger, *Nations in Darkness: China, Russia, and America,* 3d ed. (New York: Random House, 1981). See also Morton Schwartz, *Soviet Perceptions of the United States* (Berkeley, Calif.: University of California Press, 1980); and Solzhenitsyn, *The Mortal Danger.*

42.   See D. W. Smythe and H. K. Wilson, "Cold-War-Mindedness and the Mass Media," in Houghton, *Struggle against History,* pp. 59–78.

43.   The idea that post-World War II U.S. foreign policy has been inherently and consistently opposed to revolutionary movements abroad is a basic theme of Richard J. Barnet, *Intervention and Revolution: America's Confrontation with Insurgent Movements around the World* (Chicago: World Publishing Co., 1968); and of Melvin Gurtov, *The United States against the Third World: Antinationalism and intervention* (New York: Praeger, 1974).

44.   See Houghton's "Foreword," in his *Struggle against History,* p. xii; Walton, *Cold War and Counter-Revolution,* p. 35; and Fulbright, *Old Myths and New Realities,* p. 35.

45.   Background on postwar U.S. diplomacy toward South Africa is provided in Julian W. Witherell, comp., *The United States and Africa: 1785–1975* (Washington,

D.C.: Library of Congress, 1978); Walter Goldschmidt, ed., *The United States and Africa* (New York: Praeger, 1963); and Rupert Emerson, *Africa and the United States* (Englewood Cliffs, N.J.: Prentice-Hall, 1967). More recent discussions focusing upon the Reagan administration's policy of constructive engagement are Carol Lancaster, "United States Policy in Sub-Saharan Africa," *Current History* 81 (March 1982):97–101; J. Gus Liebenow, "American Policy in Africa: The Reagan Years," ibid. 82 (March 1983):97–102; Michael Clough, "United States Policy in Southern Africa," ibid. 83 (March 1984):97–101; Thomas G. Karis, "Black Politics in South Africa," *Foreign Affairs* 62 (Winter 1983/84):378–407; and David Martin and Phyllis Johnson, "Africa: The Old and the Unexpected," ibid. 63 (Special Issue 1984):602–31.

    46.   Ambrose, *Rise to Globalism*, p. 139.

    47.   See Ambrose, *Rise to Globalism*, p. 150; Walton, *Cold War and Counter-Revolution*, p. 208; and Fulbright, *The Crippled Giant*, pp. 81–82.

    48.   For an authoritative discussion of the Kennedy administration's strategy of counterinsurgency in Southeast Asia, see Roger Hilsman, *To Move a Nation: The Politics of Foreign Policy in the Administration of John F. Kennedy* (Garden City, N.Y.: Doubleday, 1967), pp. 91–159, 413–541. A highly critical assessment is Richard J. Walton, *Cold War and Counter-Revolution: The Foreign Policy of John F. Kennedy* (Baltimore: Penguin Books, 1972).

    49.   An informed and balanced analysis of recent U.S.-Iranian relations is Barry Rubin, *Paved with Good Intentions: The American Experience in Iran* (New York: Penguin Books, 1981). See also Mohammed Heikal, *Iran: The Untold Story* (New York: Pantheon Books, 1982); and Yonah Alexander and Allan Nanes, eds., *The United States and Iran: A Documentary History* (Lanham, Md.: University Press of America, 1980).

    50.   See David M. Potter, *People of Plenty: Economic Abundance and the American Character* (Chicago: University of Chicago Press, 1954).

    51.   Gerassi, "The United States and Revolution in Latin America," p. 180.

    52.   See Ambrose's discussion of President Truman's Point Four program in *Rise to Globalism*, pp. 174–75.

    53.   Taubman, *Globalism and Its Critics*, pp. 187–88; see also N. B. Miller, "Underdevelopment and U.S. Foreign Policy," in Houghton, *Struggle against History*, pp. 136–44.

    54.   Fulbright, *The Crippled Giant*, pp. 256, 278–79; and his *The Arrogance of Power*, pp. 131, 217.

    55.   See William L. Langer and S. Everett Gleason, *The Challenge to Isolation: 1937–1940* (New York: Harper and Row, 1952), p. 13; and John C. Vinson, *William E. Borah and the Outlawry of War* (Athens: University of Georgia Press, 1957), pp. 10–11.

    56.   Quoted in Wayne S. Cole, *Senator Gerald P. Nye and American Foreign Relations* (Minneapolis: University of Minnesota Press, 1962), p. 158.

    57.   Stillman and Pfaff, *Power and Impotence*, p. 186.

    58.   Fulbright, *The Crippled Giant*, p. 155.

    59.   Steel, *Pax Americana*, p. 347.

    60.   Stillman and Pfaff, *Power and Impotence*, p. 189.

    61.   For fuller discussion of international terrorism, see Yonah Alexander, *Terrorism: Theory and Practice* (Boulder, Colo.: Westview Press, 1980); Edward F.

Micholus, *Transnational Terrorism: A Chronology of Events, 1968–1979* (Westport, Conn.: Greenwood Press, 1980); Clair Sterling, *The Terror Network: The Secret War of International Terrorism* (London: Weidenfeld and Nicolson, 1981); William P. Lineberry, *The Struggle against Terrorism* (New York: H. W. Wilson, 1977); Michael Stohl and George A. Lopez, eds., *The State as Terrorist* (Westport, Conn.: Greenwood Press, 1984); and Melvin Small and J. David Singer, *Resort to Arms: International and Civil Wars, 1816–1980* (Beverly Hills, Calif.: Sage Publications, 1982).

62.   The foreign policy implications of the 1980 and 1984 elections are analyzed more fully in Ellis Sandoz and Cecil V. Crabb, Jr., eds., *A Tide of Discontent: The 1980 Elections and Their Meaning* (Washington, D.C.: Congressional Quarterly Press, 1981), pp. 157–91; and the same authors', *Election '84: Landslide without a Mandate?* (New York: New American Library, 1985), pp. 179–204. See also George Shultz, "New Realities and New Ways of Thinking," *Foreign Affairs* 63 (Spring 1985):705–22; and Henry Grunwald, "After the Election: Foreign Policy under Reagan II," ibid. 63 (Winter 1984/85):219–40.

63.   See Yankelovich and Doble, "The Public Mood," pp. 33–47; Foster, *Activism Replaces Isolationism*, pp. 347–93; George H. Quester, *American Foreign Policy: The Lost Consensus* (New York: Praeger, 1982); and Samuel P. Huntington, *American Politics: The Promise of Disharmony* (Cambridge, Mass.: Harvard University Press, 1981).

4

Realpolitik and the Containment Strategy

In the nineteenth century Lord Palmerston (1784–1865) succinctly stated the principle that, in his view, had guided and should continue to guide British foreign policy: "We have no eternal allies and we have no perpetual enemies. Our interests are eternal and perpetual, and those interests it is our duty to follow."[1] More than a century later, one of the United States' most experienced diplomats agreed with French President Charles de Gaulle's dictum that nations are "cold monsters devoid of sentiment . . . and guided by their own material interests."[2] Thus, India's Prime Minister Nehru once observed that

> the art of foreign affairs of a country lies in finding out what is most advantageous to the country. . . . In the ultimate analysis, a government functions for the good of the country it governs, and no government dare do anything which in the short or long run is manifestly to the disadvantage of that country.[3]

These are merely three examples illustrative of an approach to foreign policy often characterized by the German term *Realpolitik* — a concept associated most conspicuously perhaps with Germany's skillful Chancellor Otto von Bismarck (1815–1898). Since World War II prominent students of U.S. foreign policy, such as Walter Lippmann, George F. Kennan, Hans J. Morgenthau, and Henry A. Kissinger, have led the way in a rediscovery of classical *Realpolitik* principles. The late Professor Morgenthau was at the forefront of this movement.[4] Similarly, George F. Kennan, while he has warned about Soviet Russia's hegemonial tendencies, has nonetheless asserted that a peaceful and stable postwar political settlement was possible: "All that was really required to assure stability among the great powers was 'the preservation of a realistic balance of strength between them and a realistic understanding of the mutual zones of vital interest.'"[5] In more recent years, among his prescriptions for a new U.S. foreign policy in the light of the traumatic Vietnam experience, Professor Morgenthau reiterated the idea that "the United States has one primary national interest in its relations with other nations: the security of its territory and institutions."[6]

Our analysis of the *Realpolitik* approach to postwar U.S. foreign policy will proceed within a frame of reference that emphasizes three pivotal and interrelated concepts integral to this point of view: national interest, balance of power, and spheres of influence.

THE CONCEPT OF NATIONAL INTEREST

No idea is more central to the *Realpolitik* approach to foreign policy than the concept of national interest. In his Farewell Address,* President Washington asserted that "Europe has a set of primary interests, which to us have none, or a very remote relation." Twentieth-century spokesmen have echoed the same idea. Foreign policies, said Secretary of State Charles Evans Hughes "are not built upon abstractions. They are the result of practical conceptions of national interest arising from some immediate exigency or standing out vividly in historical perspective." Writing on the eve of World War II, one of the United States' most eminent historians, Charles A. Beard, called the principle of national interest "an inescapable rule for the nation — a rule written in the nature of things."[7]

The task of diplomacy, George F. Kennan has observed, is to take "the awkward conflicts of national interest" and to deal with them "on their merits with a view to finding solutions least unsettling to the stability of international life."[8] Shortly before his death, in a speech at American University on June 10, 1963, President John F. Kennedy delivered a major foreign policy address in which he urged détente between the United States and the Soviet Union. The existence of common interests between the superpowers was a conspicuous theme of his message. The prospects for peace were not likely to be enhanced "because of a sudden revolution in human nature," but they could be substantially improved "as

---

*See Appendix 1.

the result of concrete actions and effective agreements which are in the interest of all concerned."[9] Again, in 1971 President Nixon declared that the nation's overseas objective "is to support our interests over the long run with a sound foreign policy." The United States' "interests must shape our commitments, rather than the other way around."[10]

As idealists and other critics of *Realpolitik* often point out, the concept of national interest is vague, inexplicit, and often highly ambiguous. (In some usages, the concept tends to be circular, as in the idea that the interests of the United States in foreign affairs are what Americans are interested in.) As our later discussion will emphasize, the concept of national interest also poses certain troublesome moral-ethical questions for the conduct of U.S. diplomacy. Some informed students of contemporary international politics are convinced that the term, national interest, should be abandoned altogether. Yet despite its defects, the concept of national interest has established itself as part of the lexicon of diplomacy; and it continues to be used widely by officials of the United States and other governments today as a term that collectively describes the nation's highest-ranking diplomatic goals, especially as these relate to the protection of national security. The durability of the doctrine may be accounted for by reference to several positive contributions it makes to the conduct of foreign relations by the United States, as well as other states.[11]

First, the term national interest calls attention to the essentially competitive and sometimes violent nature of the international environment within which external policy operates. Implicit in the doctrine is the idea that all states have interests to whose protection and promotion they are devoted — if necessary, by reliance upon armed force. Sometimes, of course, the interests of states may be convergent and basically harmonious. An evident mutuality of interests has emerged in recent years between the United States and the Soviet Union in avoiding nuclear war and in inhibiting the proliferation of nuclear weapons throughout the international community. Yet, such examples to the contrary, as Walter Lippmann and other commentators have emphasized, the "rivalry of nations" is the dominant feature of the international environment. Americans especially need to be reminded that a greater or lesser degree of conflict among nations is not an exceptional or transitory phenomenon. Rather, it is a recurrent and ubiquitous characteristic of the international system.[12]

Second, the doctrine of national interest underscores an obvious and commonplace, although often overlooked, fact about U.S. foreign policy. As a member of the international state system, the United States has interests to which it is devoted. Some of these, frequently designated its "vital interests," are so intimately related to the preservation of its independence and well-being as to require protection by reliance upon armed force when necessary.

From the isolationist era, many Americans may have gained the impression that, as a society exemplifying the New World, the United States lacked identifiable interests abroad; or they may have imagined that U.S. diplomatic interests were synonymous with those of humanity at large or with "world public opinion." *Realpolitik* regards such notions as dangerously illusory and as politically naive. In this perspective, no less than other nations the United States has a set of external interests; and the dominant purpose of U.S. diplomacy is to promote and safeguard them. Only confusion at home and abroad — and the danger of a global conflict because of miscalculation — can result from believing otherwise. Some of these interests — usually designated its vital interests — are so intimately related to the preservation of national security that the United States is prepared to use military force to protect them. By the 1980s, specific interests in the latter category include maintaining the security of the NATO area; preserving continued Western access to the Persian Gulf region; preventing the Soviet Union or other hostile powers from establishing a position of strength in the Western Hemisphere; and averting threats to the security and independence of Japan, South Korea, the Philippines, and other countries in East Asia.

A third function served by the doctrine of the national interest lies in contributing to an ordering process whereby policy-makers in the United States and other countries establish and adhere to a scale of priorities among the various goals and objectives to which the nation is committed overseas. No nation, not even a superpower, is omnipotent. Maintaining relations with more than 160 independent nations today, the United States is compelled, so to speak, to ration its power, allocating the preponderance of it to those diplomatic goals deemed most urgent and compelling. A major implication of the complaint that during the 1960s the United States became overcommitted abroad is the idea that for many years Americans lacked a sense of diplomatic priority. During some periods, leaders and citizens alike imagined that U.S. interests were directly involved in virtually anything that happened abroad; and the logical extension of that idea was that the power of the United States must be used to produce an outcome favorable to Americans. Among the lessons of the Vietnam War, in the *Realpolitik* view, one surely is that this kind of indiscriminate approach to foreign policy is misguided and is a certain recipe for diplomatic failures.

A fourth, and closely related, contribution that the concept of national interest makes to the conduct of U.S. foreign policy is that it provides guidance to policy-makers in other countries concerning those overseas objectives to which the United States is deeply committed because they are centrally related to its security and welfare. As we shall see, although the national interest of the United States may embrace many diverse concerns and goals, its quintessential meaning perhaps is the idea of national security. In the terminology of today, the political realist believes in "telling it like it is," on the theory that candor and understanding among nations are essential for avoiding war and conflict among them. On that assumption, Americans must continually recognize — and they must repeatedly make clear to other nations — that the United States is willing and able to use all means necessary, including military force, to protect its national security. In the post-World War II era of U.S. internationalism, following this axiom, of course, means that the nation will be required from time to time to use force beyond its own borders to promote its highest diplomatic and security goals.

Facilitating the search for common interests among the members of the international system and enhancing the prospects for durable agreements among them is a fifth function of the concept of national interest. Along with many experienced foreign policy officials, George Ball believes that sound foreign policy entails "a disciplined search for common interests" among the nations of the world. A leading function of diplomacy, most students of international politics agree, is to reconcile and harmonize the disparate interests to which the countries of the world are devoted. For diplomacy to operate successfully, a reasonably distinct conception of each nation's interests seems indispensable.

A sixth value of the doctrine of national interest to the conduct of U.S. foreign policy is underscored by Charles E. Bohlen's observation that, in the eyes of other countries, the diplomatic behavior of the United States often suffers from "naïve sentimentality."[13] Or, as Walter Lippmann commented during World War II, the allies and other nations would "greatly prefer an American foreign policy founded on an enlightened conception of our own national interest to the ambiguous platitudes with which we have regaled them for the past fifty years."[14] To such commentators, a foreign policy avowedly based upon the principle of national interest has the virtue of honesty and candor. To that extent, it commands the respect and understanding, if not always the support, of other countries, whose leaders and citizens are often more prepared than Americans to believe that every nation's foreign policy is designed to defend and promote its interests. When Americans attempt to deny that their behavior abroad is heavily influenced by considerations of national interest, they engender confusion in the minds of foreigners about the true aims of the United States in world affairs and raise questions about the adequacy and constancy of its diplomatic leadership.[15]

The concept of national interest has utility for the diplomacy of the United States in a seventh respect, with regard to a problem that besets democracies uniquely in the conduct of their foreign affairs. The doctrine enhances what Henry Kissinger has called the nation's "staying power" in maintaining its overseas commitments, often in the face of widespread public apathy or indifference. When the United States denies that its national interests are directly involved in a particular obligation or crisis abroad, Kissinger is convinced, this "diminishes our staying power when we try to carry out these commitments." Conversely, a frank admission by policy-makers that certain foreign commitments or policies are essential to the national interest communicates forcefully their importance to the citizenry and enhances continuing public support for them.[16]

How is the national interest of the United States to be defined? What are its principal components or elements? These are difficult and complex questions, yielding diverse and often highly dissimilar answers, no less among exponents of *Realpolitik* than from devotees of other approaches to U.S. foreign policy. Our ensuing discussion emphasizes that the concept of national interest has always suffered heavily from subjectivism. Routinely, every individual and group advocating a course of action in foreign affairs equates its prescriptions with the national interest, while contrary proposals are viewed as being adverse to it.

Let us attempt to analyze the concept of the national interest of the United States further by reference to three broad categories of ideas: the preservation of national security, ideological principles with which the United States is identified, and the domestic implications of the concept.

According to many students of U.S. foreign relations, the core meaning of the concept of national interest is the protection and maintenance of national security. Thus one former U.S. official has cited William Pitt's assertion that safeguarding national security was "the first law of nature" (that is, the law of "self-preservation") governing the conduct of sovereign states.[17]

The next obvious question is: what is meant by national security, and what are the steps required to achieve it? In recent years, a number of well-informed students of international relations have devoted attention to this question; and it must be said that their deliberations still leave several fundamental questions about the national security of the United States unresolved. Most commentators are aware of the existence of the paradoxical nature of the concept of U.S. national security in the nuclear age: the continuing expansion in U.S. military power, for example, has been accompanied by a growing sense of insecurity by people inside and outside the United States. In the contemporary era, there appears to be an inverse correlation between the nation's possession of the tangible ingredients of national power (such as military force and economic strength) and a pervasive sense of security among citizens.

Expressed differently, the concept of national security appears increasingly to possess a highly subjective dimension. It is above all a feeling that individuals and groups exhibit about how they relate to the world, about their ability to control events, and about their capacity to produce beneficial vis-à-vis deleterious results. Construed in that sense, what might be called the security index of many Americans seems unquestionably lower today than in the 1950s or early 1960s. One impetus for the election of Ronald Reagan to the White House in 1980, and for his overwhelming reelection in 1984, was a widespread popular belief (justified or not) that he could restore to Americans a sense of security and well-being that had been lacking for many years.[18]

After recognizing these intangible and subjective aspects of the concept of national security, political realists would insist it remains true that security ranks at the top of the list of U.S. foreign policy objectives, today no less than in the past. Difficult as national security may be to define adequately, three statements about the concept must be accepted as axiomatic. One is that, its New World ethos to the contrary, the United States resembles all other nations, in that it ranks the preservation of national security as its paramount foreign policy objective. The second is that, if it is to achieve that objective, it must possess a varied arsenal of power, containing adequate military force, along with other instruments needed to accomplish its diplomatic objectives. The third is that the United States must be prepared to use its power when necessary to preserve and strengthen its national security. Both the people of the United States and societies abroad must understand that when the security of the United States is endangered, military force and other forms of power will be employed to protect it. As already emphasized, this means specifically that the United States will defend its military allies, that it will assist other countries (such as Israel) to maintain their security, and that it will engage in a variety of other activities — under the rubric of what might be called preventive diplomacy — to prevent threats to national security from developing or from becoming critical. In brief, the preservation of national security requires the United States to practice selective interventionism on a continuing basis beyond its own borders. Moreover, the political realist believes that informed citizens must accept, and base the nation's foreign policy upon, such realities without apology and without the kind of emotional trauma and sense of national guilt that gripped the United States during much of the 1970s.

If the devotees of *Realpolitik* insist that the United States has, and must always be prepared to defend, its interests, they also caution against an inflated conception of the national interest. Most especially in the light of the Vietnam War experience, the United States must not universalize its interests. The nation's security is not involved in the outcome of every war, political conflict, or controversy that erupts in the contemporary world; whether one political faction or another gains control of country X is not necessarily a question affecting U.S. security and well-being. In some instances, however, the outcome of wars, conflicts, and political rivalries abroad may directly involve the security interests of the United States. To be specific: the outcome of a political struggle in Upper Volta or Sri Lanka may not impinge directly upon U.S. security interests; by contrast, the future of the government of Saudi Arabia or Thailand would have major security implications for the United States.[19]

The political realist also recognizes that in the post-World War II era, as a rule the United States must seek to preserve and promote its security interests in collaboration with other nations. This was another graphic lesson of the Vietnam War episode: except for the government of South Vietnam, the United States largely endeavored to defend Southeast Asia from communism alone, often in the face of sustained criticism of its efforts by other countries. Many of the NATO allies, for example, criticized prolonged U.S. involvement in the Vietnam conflict because it weakened the ability of the United States to defend Western Europe. Realists are aware that military alliances and informal security arrangements (such as those existing between the United States and Israel) are essential in enabling the nation to achieve its diplomatic objectives. As the Vietnam experience underscored, powerful as it is the United States is not Atlas: it cannot carry the political universe on its own shoulders, and the chances are that attempts to do so will prove unsuccessful.

In this sense of course, political realism implicitly concedes a principle that has long been identified with an idealistic approach to international politics. As in the allied effort that brought about the Axis defeat in World War II, the United States must seek to create and maintain a coalition or coalitions of nations that share common interests and that are prepared also to share the responsibilities implicit in promoting them in an unstable and often hostile external environment. U.S. power and influence abroad, in other words, are enhanced to the degree that they are concerted with the power of other nations to achieve shared diplomatic goals.[20]

While concerting U.S. power with other nations may be the general rule of diplomacy in the contemporary period, it must also be noted that political realists are prepared when necessary to act unilaterally to preserve and defend the nation's vital diplomatic interests. Ideally, most realists recognize, the United States' involvement in the Vietnam War would have been more successful if it had been broadly supported by the nation's allies and friends abroad. Yet few realists regard this as the primary reason for the failure of the Vietnam intervention. Several years later, realists usually supported the Reagan administration's intervention in Grenada and Central America, although in both cases these moves elicited considerable criticism from the nation's allies and friends overseas. The realist, in other words, is not reluctant to act unilaterally when necessary to safeguard the security interests of the United States. Devotees of *Realpolitik* are seldom prepared to allow the security interests of the United States to be defined by majority vote in the U.N. General Assembly or by world public opinion.

Realistic thought rejects a number of ideas and assumptions associated with classical isolationist thought and with an idealistic approach to international politics. Realists, for instance, do not believe that the U.S. example can be a substitute for adequate power in defending the nation's security interests. What evidence exists, realists would ask, that the behavior of the U.S. society internally has any significant effect upon the domestic or foreign policies of the Soviet Union, upon the behavior of Qadaffi's regime in Libya, or upon internal and external conduct of Castro's government in Cuba?

A related idea is that Americans must choose between guns and butter in formulating national policy. To the minds of realists, this is another set of false alternatives or specious idea. Both guns and butter — or domestic and external needs — must be met if the United States is to remain a secure, prosperous, and powerful nation. Realists are aware that the nation's internal well-being is a vital element in its power and influence abroad. A powerful military establishment requires, among other things, a strong and vibrant economic system for its foundation; high levels of industrial and agricultural productivity are essential in sustaining military power. Nor are realists indifferent to the need to keep military spending within acceptable bounds, to reduce waste in the Pentagon's spending, and to curb the impulse toward military adventurism abroad. Yet after allowing for these caveats and qualifications, realists still insist that there is no substitute for a strong and modern military arsenal, available for use by policy-makers in Washington when the security and diplomatic interests of the nation require it. More so than liberals and left-wing groups, realists are convinced that a large defense budget is essential in fact for preserving conditions under which domestic prosperity may continue to flourish within an environment of democratic freedoms.[21]

Nor do realists believe that the use of U.S. military power abroad is inherently immoral, destructive of the values of foreign societies, and always diplomatically self-defeating. The democratization of German and Japanese society in the post-World War II era was possible only because the United States and its allies overwhelmingly defeated the Axis Powers. In almost all respects, the results of the ensuing military occupation of defeated Germany and Japan were beneficial for these countries and for the international system. Far from exhibiting lasting enmity toward the United States, the Germans and Japanese in time became strong allies and defenders of U.S. diplomacy in the postwar period. Ironically, proponents of *Realpolitik* would emphasize, the most far-reaching and beneficial revolutions witnessed in recent history were those carried out by the U.S. military authorities in occupied Germany and Japan after World War II. On balance, the radical changes made in German and Japanese society proved more positive and durable than most of those carried out by Communists and other self-styled revolutionary regimes in other countries.

Realists also believe that the United States cannot become immobilized or otherwise inhibited diplomatically because of widespread apprehensions about U.S. interventionism. Advocates of *Realpolitik* are aware of Prince Metternich's observation that, for a powerful nation, there is really no such thing as a foreign policy of nonintervention; there are only various forms of intervention. This means that, for a superpower like the United States, whatever it does diplomatically — including ostensibly doing nothing — affects the well-being and destiny of other nations. Fully as much as a policy of overt interventionism, U.S. failure or unwillingness to act abroad can be a decisive force in determining the future of democracy in Latin America, the economic well-being of millions of Africans, or the resolution of the question of war and peace in the Middle East. Realists, in other words, reject the premise that isolationism and nonaction by the United States are equivalent to peace, while interventionism is equivalent to war.

In somewhat different terms, realists believe that in most cases the argument over U.S. interventionism versus noninterventionism is misplaced and misleading. The real issues, in the vast majority of cases, are the nature and form of U.S. interventionism abroad or the question of how the United States should use its vast power to influence the course of events overseas. One reason the debate is irrelevant is that, as often as not, when Latin Americans complain about "Yankee interventionism," what they really mean is that Washington is supporting their political opponents. Conversely, when the influence and power of the United States is used to support their cause, this is equated with being responsive to Latin America's needs, or strengthening democracy, or protecting human rights, or showing concern with the problems of needy societies abroad. Realists also understand that in Latin America, and in other foreign settings as well, vocal opposition to U.S. interventionism is part of the ritual of domestic politics; such denunciations are often required by successful candidates for political office.

The reader who has followed our analysis is aware that national interest is a highly variegated and multidimensional concept. On the basis of lengthy service in the State Department, Charles B. Marshall concluded that the overall utility of the concept is severely limited. The term national interest "begs more questions than it answers."[22] Philip Quigg has criticized the concept because it suggests a greater orderliness to the U.S. foreign policy process than is in fact the case.[23] Thomas L. Hughes views the concept of national interest as little more than a label to describe "uninspired policies pursued by uninspired men." It is inherently an approach to foreign affairs reflecting little interest in, or concern for, the problems of other nations and is, therefore, incapable of winning their enthusiastic support for U.S. diplomatic efforts.[24]

As our treatment thus far has suggested, no consensus exists — or perhaps has ever existed throughout U.S. history — concerning a definition of the national interest, not even among officials involved in the process of trying to achieve it. Given the U.S. tradition of pragmatism, along with the pluralistic nature of the society, the United States finds it perhaps even more difficult than other nations to formulate an acceptable definition of the concept.[25] Seabury is but one among many commentators who believe that ambiguity and confusion are inherent in the doctrine of the national interest. He identifies three distinct connotations of the concept: (1) it may refer to a set of normative or prescriptive principles specifying what the United States ought to achieve in foreign affairs; (2) it may serve as a purely descriptive term referring to what the United States has sought to achieve throughout its diplomatic history (or during selected eras of it); and (3) it may designate the end result of the resolution of diverse intergroup competition within the U.S. society, with the most influential group (or coalition of groups) having its views accepted by policy-makers as being in the national interest.[26] To Seabury's list, we may add another major connotation: the term national interest is frequently invoked to legitimate whatever policy is finally decided upon by foreign policy decision makers.

Moreover, reliance upon the doctrine of national interest as a guide to policy making is likely to obscure the challenge of policy making in a democracy. As Senator Fulbright complained, the effect of designating certain policies as dictated by the national interest sometimes is to close debate on their merits, suggesting that they are no longer properly in the realm of public discussion and that all doubts about their contribution to the welfare of the United States have been resolved.[27] Or, as Quigg has emphasized, in reality "deciding upon the national interest is what politics is all about. And deciding how to promote that interest is what policy-making is all about."[28]

As used by proponents of *Realpolitik,* the concept of national interest also suggests a degree of permanence about the diplomatic goals of the United States, which can be misleading and difficult to reconcile with the kind of rapidly changing global milieu existing since World War II. Lord Palmerston, it will be recalled, defined England's interests as "eternal and perpetual." U.S. commentators like Charles A. Beard and Hans J. Morgenthau have tended to attribute a kind of immutability and inevitability to the national interest, which makes little allowance for contingencies and for the impact of changing circumstances upon the external behavior of the United States.

Yet whatever the national interest of the United States may be precisely, it seems clear that the concept must always be construed dynamically, not statically. It is evident, for example, that U.S. national interest during the 1930s was (or was widely viewed as being) very different from its national interest during the 1950s. Even in the era of U.S. internationalism after World War II, fundamental changes have occurred — and continue to occur — in the conception of the nation's diplomatic interests. One period of significant change in this regard, for example, was the post-Vietnam War era. The prevalent lack of consensus about the proper role of the United States in global affairs could be interpreted to mean that the U.S. people and their leaders were in the process of redefining the national interest, particularly as it related to the use of military force abroad to achieve diplomatic objectives.[29] To cite but one example of this phenomenon: the Kennedy and Johnson administrations believed that it was essential to U.S. interests to contain the spread of communism in Southeast Asia; the Nixon and later administrations concluded that it was not. An interesting question for the future is how the United States would once more redefine its national interest if expansionism by North Vietnam seriously threatened the security of Thailand or Malaysia.

Other fundamental questions relate to the concept of national interest. Who determines it? And whose definition of the national interest is accepted as authoritative for the purpose of formulating and administering U.S. foreign policy? Answering these questions in detail would require more space than is available here because doing so would involve an examination of the foreign policy process of the United States.[30] A long list of major and minor actors — from the president and the secretary of state, to Congress, to general public opinion and interest groups — plays a role in that process and influences its outcome. Since the Vietnam War, an increasingly assertive Congress, for example, injected itself into foreign policy decision making to an extent unprecedented in recent experience.[31] Most students of the U.S. system of government are also agreed that pressure group activities have never been more intense, competitive, and costly, as lobbies seek to influence the decisions of executive and legislative officials in both domestic and foreign affairs. As a matter of course, each participant in the foreign policy process assumes that its viewpoints are equivalent to the national interest of the United States.[32]

As a general rule, ultimately the president arrives at an authoritative determination of U.S. diplomatic interests, and his decision becomes the basis of U.S. foreign policy. Forces like Congressional activism and increased lobbying activity have not fundamentally altered the fact that, as

President Harry S. Truman was prone to say, "I make American foreign policy." Naturally, presidential decisions are influenced by numerous major and minor variables, such as the nation's diplomatic traditions, the recommendations of advisers, Congressional attitudes, and other forces. Exactly how an incumbent president makes key foreign policy decisions remains a process that is imperfectly understood. In the end, however, the president's role is normally decisive in determining whose conception of the national interest shall prevail. In the U.S. democratic system, the chief executive's decisions are in turn subject to the approval or disapproval of the people as expressed, for example, in the outcome of national elections.[33]

In practice, therefore, the term national interest denotes the foreign policy decisions of the president. The national interest may thus be thought of as the end product of the U.S. foreign policy process with the realization that that process is dynamic and that the nation's diplomatic interests change in the light of time and circumstances. Although the dynamic quality of the national interest must never be forgotten, at the same time it must be noted that since World War II U.S. foreign policy has been characterized by a remarkable continuity. Despite differences in the ideological viewpoints and styles of incumbent administrations, from Presidents Truman to Reagan — for a period approaching a half-century — in its fundamentals, the foreign policy of the United States has in fact changed relatively little. For example, the Reagan administration remains committed to the containment policy, enunciated by the Truman administration in 1947. Although the foreign aid program has undergone several administrative reorganizations and changes, providing assistance to Third World nations (as originally proposed by the Truman administration) continues to be a major component of U.S. foreign policy. In the case of the containment policy, it must be admitted of course that official and public conceptions of what that policy means, and the specific steps required to implement it, have changed significantly since the late 1940s — most recently, in the post-Vietnam War era.

We conclude our discussion of the concept of national interest by reiterating a point made earlier. The term national interest is elusive, ambiguous, and in many respects unsatisfactory. It perhaps raises more questions than it answers about the formulation and administration of U.S. foreign policy. Yet it is difficult to think of a satisfactory substitute for it. Terms like "the public interest" or "national well-being" or "the general welfare" have fully as many defects. Accordingly, the term national interest continues to be widely used by statesmen and informed students of contemporary global politics.

THE BALANCE OF POWER

A second concept associated with a *Realpolitik* approach to U.S. foreign policy is the strategy of balance of power. Any informed understanding of the principle of balance of power must be based upon an understanding of the key role of power in the political process. In the *Realpolitik* approach, it is accepted as axiomatic that nation-states inherently seek to acquire and pursue power. Thomas Hobbes (1588–1679), one of the philosophical progenitors of *Realpolitik,* discerned a "generall inclination of all mankind" toward a "perpetuall and restlesse desire of Power after power, that ceaseth onely in Death."[34]

Many commentators believe that power conflicts are characteristic of all political relationships — more so perhaps among nation-states than on any other level of political interaction.[35] Some political scientists assert that the concept of power is to the realm of political experience what the concept of wealth is to the economic realm: both ideas serve as the principal integrating concept of the discipline.[36]

When it is asserted that nations pursue power or are engaged in a perennial power struggle, what precisely is meant by such statements? The concept of power possesses a number of significant (and sometimes contradictory) connotations. According to some interpretations, the struggle for power is synonymous with life itself; as Hobbes said, the pursuit of power "ceaseth onely in Death." A nation that did not pursue power would be (or soon would become) extinct.[37] Other commentators, however, believe that the concept of national power is intrinsically issue oriented; it can be meaningfully understood and discussed only by reference to specific issues or controversies arising among nations. In this formulation, the power of State A vis-à-vis State B varies, depending upon the issues between them. State A might be more powerful in military matters but less powerful in the attraction of its ideology, and so forth.[38]

The possession of power is of course crucial to the achievement of the goal that many commentators regard as the paramount objective of external policy: the maintenance of national security or self-preservation. Nearly every other goal to which a nation might be committed — peace, justice, a rising standard of living, a sense of global community, regional cooperation — presupposes the continued existence of the state as an independent political entity.

Nations also seek to acquire and use power to promote a variety of other goals. Here, it may be useful to think in terms of two broad categories of cases involving the utilization of power: those entailing cooperative and harmonious relationships among nations, involving the sharing or pooling of power for common purposes; and those involving conflict and tension among nations, generating power struggles and wars among them. In the judgment of some commentators, the former category of cases does not properly belong in the study of politics at all, because in their conception the political process inherently requires conflict, produced by some degree of opposition and disagreement, among the nations (or other political units) engaged in it.

This view, however, seems unduly restrictive. There is no inherent or logical reason why the concept of power must always imply conflict among nations. In reality, even ideological and diplomatic rivals like the United States and the Soviet Union engage in a range of relationships, some admittedly hostile and some reasonably harmonious, perhaps leading to a détente in spheres like nuclear proliferation, trade, and cultural agreements.

Some commentators are inclined to construe the concept of national power quite narrowly, equating it essentially with the capacity to wage (or to threaten) war successfully and, after victory, to impose the national will upon adversaries. The core meaning of the doctrine of national power, Alan James has observed, is the realization that "at the back of diplomatic interchanges is the threat of armed force, the possibility that policies will be supported by the use of violence."[39] In Kenneth Waltz's succinct expression: "In international politics power has appeared primarily as the power to do harm."[40]

Again, however, to confine the concept of power to the application of military force and the capacity to impose harm seems unnecessarily and misleadingly restrictive. National power expressed as violence (or threatened violence) is, as a matter of fact, infrequently relied upon by nations to realize their goals. Normally, nations employ a wide variety of techniques, ranging from reliance upon friendship and mutual interests, to persuasion and diplomacy, to nonviolent forms of coercion and sanctions (like propaganda and boycotts), to threatened hostilities, to war, for accomplishing their purposes. Thus, Stephen Wasby defines national power broadly as the ability of one nation "to induce, by *whatever means,* specified behavior by another [italics added]."[41] Still other students of the phenomenon view power mainly in psychological terms. Assuming a relationship between two or more nations, power is "the sense of satisfaction felt with the relationship" by the parties to it.[42]

Defining the concept of power quite broadly — equating it, for example, with influence or a feeling of satisfaction with the nation's external relationships — has one fundamental drawback, which is particularly troublesome in evaluating the strategy of balance of power. Such a definition of national power tends to make it almost impossible to measure (or sometimes even accurately estimate) the power of one nation vis-à-vis another in the international system. When power is construed as denoting mainly military force, this approach has the merit of enabling decision makers to arrive at reasonably accurate estimates of the power of their own and of other nations and to base national policies upon these calculations. It is possible to determine with fair accuracy the size and destructive capability of the Soviet and U.S. nuclear arsenals or, more broadly, the overall military strengths of the two superpowers and other countries. Admittedly, such determinations usually leave unanswered certain key questions, such as the relevance of nuclear power to problems like alliance cohesion or ideological contests, or the credibility of each side's nuclear deterrent. Yet, regardless of their limitations, measurements of national military power are almost always more reliable than trying to gauge the relative influence of the United States or the Soviet Union throughout the Third World or the degree of satisfaction that U.S. or Soviet citizens may exhibit toward the performance of their respective governments.

It may as well be conceded frankly that, when power is defined in such broad terms, attempts to measure or estimate it are, and will remain, highly subjective and impressionistic. Now this qualification does not mean that a broad definition of national power completely lacks utility or ought to be categorically rejected. To the contrary, the notion that power is tantamount to influence is in some respects more in conformity with what modern nations actually seek to accomplish externally, than is restricting the concept of national power merely to the capacity to inflict harm. More than in any other historical era, today nations, especially superpowers, are pervasively and routinely engaged in endeavoring to influence others outside their own borders, to inculcate a favorable image for their nation abroad, and to engender a feeling of goodwill and respect in other nations. In the process, national policy-makers are almost daily reminded of what several commentators have identified as the "paradox of power": the greater a nation's power militarily — and the more it is inclined to rely upon it for achieving its external objectives — often the less it is able to exert positive influence upon governments and masses abroad. Indeed, in the nuclear age, a superpower's ability to affect the course of events may sometimes be in inverse ratio to its armed strength. As John Herz has phrased the paradox, in the contemporary global system often "absolute power equals absolute impotence."[43] Or to state the question differently, as it confronted Americans in the mid 1980s: what is the United States going to do with the most potent and modern military arsenal witnessed in the history of the world? By many criteria, at no other time had the United States been so ostensibly powerful. At the same time, in no era in recent memory had it had such difficulty achieving its foreign policy objectives.

If national power is a pivotal concept in the *Realpolitik* perspective, a logical corollary is the idea that the maintenance of a balance or an equilibrium of power among the nations of the world ought to be a dominant objective of statecraft. Discussing the strategic implications of World War II, Nicholas Spykman concluded that "a Russian state from the Urals to the North Sea can be no great improvement over a German state from the North Sea to the Urals" insofar as the security of the United States was concerned. After the war, as in the past, U.S. policy-makers had to endeavor to preserve "a balance in Europe and Asia."[44] Some 25 years later, one reason why many critics deplored massive U.S. involvement in the Vietnam War was because it ignored and, in many respects, jeopardized the preservation of the true basis of national security: creating and maintaining a viable balance of power throughout the global system.[45] Hans J. Morgenthau remained convinced that the security of the United States must be preserved by reliance upon "the traditional methods of the balance of power."[46]

What precisely do these calls for U.S. policy-makers to create and preserve a balance of power abroad mean? How do officials in the United States (and all other nations) know when an equilibrium of power exists, and, if it does not, what ought to be done to restore it? An attempt to answer such questions must take account initially of the manifold connotations and emendations of the concept of balance of power. In one rather simplistic sense, the principle appears to be an eminently sensible and perhaps irrefutable axiom of diplomacy — amounting in fact to little more than a truism. In a much deeper sense, however, the meaning and implications of balance of power are more complex, flexible, confusing, and often contradictory — to such a degree as nearly to preclude its adoption as a functional foreign policy strategy.

The goal of balance of power, a recognized authority on World War I has written, envisages such a "'just equilibrium' in power among the members of the family of nations as will prevent any one of them from becoming sufficiently strong to enforce its will upon the others."[47]

In its classical eighteenth- and nineteenth-century model, the principle of balance of power favored by Europe's diplomats, in Arnold Zurcher's words, was aimed at preventing "any state on the Continent from acquiring a hegemony or from achieving such a position of power and influence as to become a potential menace to the integrity of the remaining states."[48] Such conceptions of the balance of power underscore the idea that, for the sake of the continued independence of the members of the international system, global power must always remain decentralized. No single state or coalition of states must be allowed to dominate the system or impose its hegemony upon it.

In the pre-World War I period, European statesmen pursued a balance of power strategy within a context of unique conditions, permitting this principle to have a well understood meaning; adherence to it preserved global peace reasonably well for a century after 1815. The requisite conditions conducive to the effective operation of a balance of power strategy in that period were (1) the number of great powers was limited to five or six or so, which were relatively equal in power; (2) as members of Christendom, the European powers shared common cultural and ideological values, producing an underlying consensus concerning the rules of the game to be followed in political conflicts and war; (3) the universe of international politics was geographically limited, with the world's most influential states being located on the European continent, while societies in Africa, the Middle East, and Asia were subject to decisions made by the great powers in Europe (the United States, of course, was attached to isolationism, while the Western Hemisphere seldom figured directly in the controversies involving the European nations); (4) as a rule, diplomatic and political issues involved limited territorial and dynastic disputes — that is, these controversies were relatively limited in scope and duration, and they lent themselves to resolution by reliance upon armed force vis-à-vis conflicts in the modern era, entailing competition for "the minds of men" or efforts by one superpower to counteract another's political or psychological influence in the Third World; (5) most crucially perhaps, during the earlier era, the conduct of foreign affairs was the province of an aristocratic elite, which could engage in the kind of diplomatic maneuvering required by adherence to the balance of power principle without undue concern about the reaction of public opinion, the need to consider ideological values, attention to the nation's image in the minds of foreigners, or the domestic cost, in the form of higher taxation or citizen service in the armed forces, exacted by balance of power diplomacy.

Traditionally, in this milieu, Great Britain played a singular role in the balance of power system. Britain served as the balancer, casting its weight now on one side, now on the other, to preserve equilibrium on the Continent, in order to prevent a hostile combination from gaining hegemony over Europe and possibly the world. As Lord Palmerston said, this strategy meant that Britain had no permanent friends or enemies, only "permanent interests" — a paramount one being to see that European equilibrium was maintained. Britain coupled this continental strategy with the principle of maintaining naval supremacy on the high seas, to enforce the *Pax Britannica*. Imperial Germany's challenge to British naval power at the end of the nineteenth century was a leading cause of the collapse of the balance of power system, producing World War I.[49]

Although the meaning and requirements of balance of power were reasonably clear in this earlier age, certain problems were encountered with the principle even then, and many of these have become more difficult and complex with the passage of time. After World War I — and unquestionably by the post-World War II period — the concept of balance of power came to possess several important, and often contradictory and ambiguous, connotations. Since antiquity, balance of power has always had at least two primary meanings, and modern political commentators have identified a host of subordinate connotations as well. It can denote a more or less equal balance, or equilibrium, of power among the more influential nations of the world. A balance of power policy would, therefore, be directed at preserving equilibrium, at maintaining a decentralized distribution of power, at preventing a single state, or coalition of states, from achieving hegemony.

Yet balance of power also has a second, and completely opposite, meaning. It can designate a preponderance of power, such as Great Britain sought to preserve on the seas before World War I and as Morgenthau asserts that, very early in its history (beginning even before the Monroe Doctrine in 1823), the United States has endeavored to maintain in the Western Hemisphere. In this latter connotation, commentators routinely refer to a favorable or unfavorable balance of power, which the United States desires to continue within the hemisphere.

Semantically confusing as the idea may be, it is nonetheless correct to say that during the heyday of U.S. isolationism the United States (while publicly eschewing the principle of balance of power) utilized the concept in both senses concurrently. U.S. officials recognized that national security depended heavily upon maintaining a power equilibrium on the European continent, while the Monroe Doctrine stated in effect that the United States was committed to preserving a preponderance (more accurately perhaps, a hoped for preponderance) in the Western Hemisphere.

The dichotomy between these two conflicting conceptions of the balance of power may of course be partially resolved by differentiating between the public assertions of national leaders and their actual operational goals. Ostensibly, officials in nearly all nations endorse the idea of balance of power construed as equilibrium. They desire a stable international system, in which threats to national security are minimized and the prospects for peace enhanced. Yet, on the level of operating policies, where goals are often unpublicized and left implicit, in actuality most states desire a preponderance of power. In the process of planning their military strategies and defense budgets, national officials routinely desire insurance or allow for a margin for safety in estimating the defense requirements of the country. Despite their verbal endorsement of the balance of power construed as equilibrium, Spykman has pointed out, "there are not many instances in history which show great and powerful states creating alliances and organizations to limit their own strength." In practice, nations nearly always seek "a balance which is in their favor."[50]

Along with the two primary meanings associated with the idea of balance of power, the concept also has numerous subordinate and collateral connotations. A leading student of the concept has identified as many as eight more or less distinct meanings.[51] While our purpose does not require an exhaustive analysis of these diverse facets of the concept, let us at least briefly identify some of the more prominent collateral connotations of the term.

Balance of power may refer to a wide dispersion or diffusion of power throughout the international system, a condition that is sometimes viewed as a sine qua non of global peace and stability. In this conception of balance of power, states ought to encourage the widest diffusion of power possible; in contemporary phraseology, they ought to prefer a "multipolar" over a "bipolar" (and even more, over what might be termed a "unipolar") structure of global power, in contrast to the goal of establishing and perpetuating a hierarchy of power, limited perhaps to the nuclear giants.[52]

Other dissimilar and conflicting conceptions of balance of power are the notion that it is equivalent to, and demands the maintenance of, the status quo versus the notion that the balance of power must always be assessed dynamically, never statically. In its classical model, balance of power was more often than not synonymous with the idea of preserving the political status quo. After the Congress of Vienna in 1815, one commentator has observed, Europe's leaders assumed the existence of a "static world, based upon the sacred principle of legitimacy."[53] In the early postwar period, Adlai Stevenson noted, the United States successfully established a balance of power in Western Europe, based upon a "recognition on all sides that revision of the status quo in Europe by threat of force is not possible and that revision by force would provoke world war."[54] Needless to say, static versions of the balance of power have never appealed to groups or states that were dissatisfied with the status quo. Whether it was advocates of constitutionalism and of self-determination by subordinated nationalities in the nineteenth century, or newly independent Afro-Asian states that after World War II contested the dominant position of the superpowers in global decision making, opponents of the prevailing order are seldom enthusiastic about balance of power diplomacy.

Over against the idea that balance of power requires preservation of the status quo is the contrary notion that the concept must always be interpreted dynamically and that proponents of the principle must take account of changes within the global system. Even nineteenth-century disciples of the concept admitted this necessity. Thus, Lord Canning declared in 1826 that the balance of power could not be regarded as "a fixed and unalterable" guide to national policy; rather, it was a "standard perpetually varying, as civilization advances, and as new nations spring up."[55] Almost a century and a half later, advocates of *Realpolitik* like Henry A. Kissinger also emphasized the necessity for interpreting the balance of power dynamically and with due regard for significant changes in the global environment. For example, Kissinger believed that, in contrast with the era of classical diplomacy, today territorial conquests could well diminish the power or influence of a nation abroad.[56] Prolonged and costly U.S. involvement in the Vietnam War unquestionably impaired the nation's diplomatic effectiveness. The Soviet Union's effort to subdue Afghanistan, and its continuing efforts to suppress political dissent in Poland, detracted from its influence throughout the Third World and among leftist groups within Western Europe.

Given the nature of the contemporary global environment, it is tempting for the student of international politics to arrive at the paradoxical conclusion that, if a nation desires to promote true stability, then it ought to support change throughout the international system. Thus, an experienced observer of Middle Eastern affairs has asserted that the United States has a clear interest in preserving the stability of this crucial region. But such an approach does not dictate upholding the status quo throughout the Middle East, since this "is often both impossible and undesirable" because "the forces of change are ubiquitous and pressing." The United States must accept the idea that "true stability in some cases is only possible if change takes place."[57]

Expressed differently, the paradox we have identified may possibly be resolved by saying that in the contemporary world nearly all nations and political groups accept the idea that change is desirable, if not inevitable. The Cold War contest between the United States and the Soviet Union may be interpreted as a fundamental disagreement over the mode or method of change. The pragmatically oriented U.S. society is identified with the principle of gradual, orderly, and evolutionary change within its own borders and outside them.[58] The Soviet Union, its satellites, and other Marxist nations support the concept of radical, often violent, and revolutionary change. To the U.S. mind, Soviet-sponsored efforts to foment revolutionary change abroad are nearly always viewed as threats to the stability of the balance of power. For Communist officials in Moscow and other capitals, U.S. insistence upon gradual and evolutionary change is equated with an effort to maintain the status quo.

Special mention must be made of the Soviet Communist conception of balance of power. The Kremlin has demonstrated its familiarity with classical diplomatic precepts and has repeatedly shown a readiness to utilize them in advancing the ends of the Soviet state. One of the most experienced U.S. diplomatic officials has given this account of an interview with Soviet Premier Khrushchev, regarding the preservation of stability in the Far East:

> While he insisted that the Soviet Union only wanted to preserve the status quo, he made it very clear that his idea of the status quo was not the preservation of existing boundaries and balances. An essential element of the world's status quo, as Khrushchev saw it, is the Communist march toward world domination. Anything that opposes Communism on the march he considers is altering the status quo and is therefore an act of aggression [or a threat to the balance of power].[59]

In the Soviet Marxist worldview, international stability is assured by the ongoing revolutionary struggle to achieve Communist goals and by sponsoring "wars of national liberation" throughout the Third World. As emphasized earlier, U.S.-led efforts to resist these developments are destabilizing and are threats to the balance of power. On a different level — the plane of nuclear deterrence or military power — the Soviet conception of balance of power has substantially different connotations. There, it seems to imply approximate equilibrium between the super-powers. In the Soviet view, for example, the Reagan administration's proposed Star Wars defense system is viewed as highly inimical to the existing military balance.

One final connotation of balance of power remains to be identified and discussed. This aspect of the concept, while perhaps deriving from classical formulations, has become especially prominent in the recent period among students who focus upon the nature and the dynamics of the international system as furnishing the most influential forces shaping national policy. In this formulation, analogies are frequently drawn from physics: just as the behavior of matter is determined and regulated by the laws of mechanics, so in the international political system states must behave in conformity with its laws and requirements. (Implicit in most system-oriented conceptions of the balance of power is the idea that it is synonymous with equilibrium of power.) The distinctive idea here perhaps is the assumption that this system-derived impulse toward stability arises automatically and without conscious design by policy-makers. The balance of power thus becomes a kind of self-regulating principle or law of political mechanics designed to guarantee systems maintenance. In effect, as regards issues arising among its members affecting the system's survival, national policy-makers have very little to decide: once they perceive a threat to global equilibrium, their responses are dictated by an impulse toward systems maintenance, just as automatically as molecules obey the dictates of the law of gravitation. On this premise, other possible determinants of national policy, like ideological compulsions or the demands of domestic interest groups, influence national behavior only so long as no threat to the balance of power exists.[60]

Aside from the fact that this systems-derived formulation of the balance of power idea tacitly assumes that the balance sought is equilibrium, several fundamental questions may be raised about it. The usefulness of the concept depends heavily upon the validity of the underlying premise: that an international political system, more or less analogous to that describing the relationship existing among particles of matter, actually exists and, on that presupposition, that the behavior of components of the system is governed by laws designed to guarantee its continuation. In turn, this conception of the balance of power requires that we accept an extraordinarily passive, not to say atomistic, conception of the foreign policy-making process and the influence of individuals and groups upon it. Without officials themselves being aware of it, perhaps, their response to external events is presumably determined for them by forces extrinsic to the nation itself; human will plays a part in such decision making only to the degree that it decides how best to engage in systems maintenance under a given set of circumstances. If this system-based connotation of balance of power is accepted, discussion about whether the United States or any other nation ought to follow a balance of power strategy abroad becomes meaningless. One might as well inquire whether the planets in the solar system ought to obey the laws holding them in their orbits.

Yet very few modern-day realists and advocates of systems theory are prepared to carry the implications of their theories that far. Being familiar with history, most proponents of *Realpolitik* are amply mindful of two salient facts. First, throughout modern history national policy-makers not infrequently have preferred other principles and strategies to the balance of power; they have exercised a choice between balance of power and other possible diplomatic strategies. Second, even when national leaders followed (or thought they were following) balance of power precepts, global and regional instability have nevertheless sometimes resulted, leading to wars of greater or lesser magnitude. Thus, one student has said concerning a leading practitioner of balance of power politics: "What Bismarck bequeathed to Europe was not balance but extreme tension." Sidney B. Fay identifies attachment to the balance of power principle as a leading cause of World War I.[61]

How applicable are the principles of balance of power to the nuclear age? Can balance of power precepts successfully guide U.S. foreign policy in the modern era? Not surprisingly, well-informed commentators are divided over such questions. Some believe that the *Realpolitik* approach to international politics incorporates timeless principles, as valid in the late twentieth as in the late eighteenth century. These authorities are still convinced that the creation and maintenance of a stable balance of power is or should be the paramount goal of U.S. foreign policy. Thus, a prominent student of Soviet-U.S. relations regards the postwar strategy of deterrence as in reality "the nuclear age version of the balance of power."[62] Critical as he often was of *Realpolitik* doctrines, even Senator Fulbright was persuaded that U.S. security depends ultimately upon a "world balance of power"; in the contemporary period this means "a nuclear balance, involving Russia, China, Western Europe, Japan and the United States."[63]

In a variation on this basic idea, other commentators believe that the concept of balance of power continues to possess validity on the level of military competition between the superpowers, if its applicability to other dimensions of contemporary international politics is more doubtful. Perhaps even more in the nuclear age than in earlier eras of history, maintaining a balance or equilibrium between the Soviet and U.S. military arsenals is an indispensable precondition for global peace and stability. As experience has shown, that fact does not necessarily guarantee the absence of regional and local conflicts. Indeed, the strong interests of Washington and Moscow in preserving a nuclear balance, in fact, may encourage less powerful nations and political movements to believe that they can engage in violence with impunity, with minimum risk that a local conflict will escalate into a global war. Nor does the existence of a Soviet-U.S. military balance dictate the lack of competition between the superpowers in other dimensions of their relationship, like economic rivalry, efforts to influence the behavior of the Third World, and ongoing ideological conflict. During some periods, Cold War tensions have been at a high level, although approximate military parity existed between Washington and Moscow. The concept of balance of power, in other words, may operate selectively in contemporary international relations.

Other commentators, however, reject the idea that *Realpolitik* supplies eternal principles of statecraft, as applicable to the conditions of the modern world as to the era of Metternich. To their minds, regardless of its utility before World War II, the balance of power concept has now become outmoded — if not positively dangerous for the U.S. society and for humanity at large — as a guide to foreign policy. In general terms, the balance of power idea has lost its utility because of one overriding consideration: fundamental differences exist between the nature of the international system today and in the classical period of diplomacy, when balance of power supposedly preserved international equilibrium with nearly perfect efficacy.[64]

A number of salient criticisms can be made of efforts to pursue a balance of power strategy in the postwar global environment. Initially, and perhaps most crucially, there are the implications of the nuclear stalemate, risking nothing less than the future of civilization itself. In the nuclear era, the stakes of the international political process have become too momentous to permit the kind of diplomatic and military maneuvering and interventionism integral to the classical balance of power pattern.

Then, the wide dispersion of power throughout the contemporary global system since World War II militates strongly against any return to classical balance of power diplomacy. Currently, the world contains more than 160 nations or "national actors," ranging from two superpowers to a host of ministates, with certain nations — like Red China, Japan, and the countries of Western Europe — obviously influential in some spheres of international politics, while being relatively impotent in others. The "existence, problems, and interactions" of most of these nations, Stanley Hoffmann has asserted, "simply cannot be treated as a mere by-product of, or factor in, the central balance" between the nuclear giants.[65] In Needler's view, the old balance of power system has disintegrated into a "field of power," in which "all kinds of influences are exerted in every direction by a variety of states differing widely in size and wealth."[66] The global tendency toward political multipolarity, coupled with nuclear bipolarity, makes for a highly decentralized and unstable international system, rendering it all but impossible for the United States or any other nation to preserve a balance of power, or any other configuration of power, upon the world.

Another deterrent to a balance of power strategy in the contemporary period is the imprecision surrounding the concept. "International political life," George F. Kennan has observed after a lifetime of diplomatic experience, "is something organic, not something mechanical."[67] Even more than in earlier eras of history, national policy-makers are extremely hard pressed to determine objectively whether a global power equilibrium exists or whether to control influential forces — ongoing scientific and military technology, local and regional political upheavals — likely to affect it. Consequently, a strategy of balance of power, demanding a reasonably accurate estimate of power capabilities and potentialities of at least the more influential nations, becomes a highly uncertain, risky, and unsatisfactory undertaking.

The problem is highlighted by contemplating a dilemma that has confronted — and often frustrated — Americans in their recent diplomatic experience. On the one hand, by many of the traditional criteria used to measure national power, the power of the United States is vast, perhaps surpassing the power of any other nation in recorded history. Certainly from the perspective of military and economic strength, as compared with the power of other countries, the power of the United States is almost incalculable. On the other hand, however, since the 1960s Americans have experienced growing difficulty achieving their foreign policy goals. At no time in recent history perhaps have they encountered more problems in producing diplomatic outcomes favorable to the United States. In gaining respect for human rights abroad, in resolving the Arab-Israeli conflict, in maintaining democracy and stability in Central America — in these and other major policy areas, the enormous power possessed by the United States often seems irrelevant to the specific challenge facing policy-makers in Washington. Indeed, in some respects the United States' vast power may serve as a source of resentment and suspicion by less powerful nations abroad, making them less receptive than ever to U.S. influence. In the contemporary world, as the above example illustrates, there is a paradoxical quality to the concept of national power. For both the United States and the Soviet Union, the more ostensibly powerful they have become, the more they have encountered obstacles to their influence throughout the Third World.

Another obstacle to maintaining a durable balance of power in the modern world was highlighted by our earlier allusions to Soviet attitudes toward the balance of power. After 1815 balance of power successfully preserved global equilibrium for a century for several reasons, a central one being that the great powers of the age were agreed upon the desirability of preserving the existing distribution of global power. Today, Soviet Communists have publicly equated the achievement of global equilibrium with the pursuit of worldwide Marxist revolutionary goals. Despite the changes that have occurred within the Soviet system since the death of Stalin in 1953, from the evidence available the Communist hierarchy has not changed its conviction that true international peace and stability will only be achieved with the worldwide victory of communism. Communist ideology does not really accept the idea of equilibrium between Marxist and non-Marxist nations. It views the international environment as inherently dynamic or unstable, until the final victory of communism over capitalism. To the Marxist mind, the maintenance of a balance of power with the United States would be equivalent to abandoning the Communist revolutionary struggle.[68]

There remain two other major difficulties with the balance of power principle in the contemporary world, which relate specifically to the nature of the United States as a democratic society. As we have emphasized, in modern history the concept of balance of power was identified with the age of European autocracy, in which elitist control over foreign policy decision making was commonplace. But is an open, pluralistic, and democratic society like the United States capable of engaging in balance of power diplomacy successfully? Along with a number of other commentators, Ernst Haas is very skeptical. In his view, pursuing a balance of power strategy effectively would require the kind of governmental behavior — rapid adjustments and shifts in external policy dictated by balance of power calculations; a capacity for rapid decision making (presumably by the president and a limited number of advisers, with little participation by Congress or the public) in order to counter threats to the existing equilibrium; secret policy formulation designed to keep the enemy (and perhaps even the U.S. population) in ignorance of the nation's intended moves; disregard of moral and ideological considerations, with policy being formulated solely according to balance of power calculations; national defense policies (for example, the need to maintain a large standing army) geared to the possibility of external interventionism whenever a threat to global equilibrium was perceived — in contravention of the canons of democracy and severely inhibiting official accountability to the citizens for the conduct of the government.[69]

Finally, proponents of *Realpolitik* sometimes display a curious lack of realism of their own. As Walt W. Rostow has said, given its history and traditions as a nation, "it is unrealistic to expect American society . . . to perform in terms of pure power criteria."[70] Or, as Ernest Lefever has expressed the idea, "ethics is an inescapable factor in all foreign policy decisions"; ethical and ideological considerations unquestionably affect the power or influence of the United States abroad.[71] Senator Fulbright is but one among a number of recent commentators who have deplored the exercise of "power without philosophy or purpose" by the United States overseas. He believes, for example, that much of the alienation prevalent among U.S. youth can be accounted for as a reaction against U.S. reliance upon an "empty system of power," devoid of constructive purposes and results for the U.S. society itself.[72] Even the United States' modern-day equivalent to Metternich, Henry A. Kissinger, acknowledges that "there can be no stability without equilibrium," but it is also true that for the United States "equilibrium is not a purpose with which we can respond to the travail of our world." The kind of values and diplomatic tactics associated with the balance of power — for example, the management of power by the more influential nations to assure systems maintenance and preserve order in global affairs — are not those likely to attract U.S. youth or societies generally throughout the world.[73] A dominant reality, which political realists and other Americans must accept, Stanley Hoffmann agrees, is that in the modern era citizens are unlikely to support, or willingly make, the kind of sacrifices required to operate a balance of power approach to foreign relations.[74]

In a word, as the Vietnam War experience amply demonstrated, Americans expect that the application of national power abroad will possess legitimacy: it must be perceived as promoting some worthwhile human purpose. Lacking such legitimacy, the nation's foreign policy is unlikely to retain public support. (Practitioners of balance of power during the eighteenth and nineteenth century, for example, were largely indifferent to the public reaction to their diplomatic machinations.) It is difficult to envision a time when the people of the United States will be prepared to give enthusiastic and lasting support to a foreign policy that is explained and justified primarily on the basis of *Realpolitik* principles.

CONTAINMENT AS AN EXERCISE IN *REALPOLITIK*

According to several criteria, U.S. foreign policy toward the Soviet Union since early 1947 — known as the containment policy — provides a graphic illustration of the impact of *Realpolitik* principles upon the diplomacy of the United States.[75] Although Americans have never been congenial to the tenets of *Realpolitik* — and their political leaders seldom justify external policy in the language of political realism — in actuality, containment was based upon a number of realistic political ideas. In regions like Eastern Europe, for example, the imposition of Soviet hegemony was widely viewed by informed commentators in the West as a threat to the balance of power. Moscow had acquired a formidable power base from which, at some future date, it might decide to extend its hegemony into Western Europe. By contrast, a debilitated and defenseless Western Europe constituted a power vacuum that invited Soviet expansionism. Well-informed students of Soviet affairs, like George F. Kennan, were convinced that, as in the past, the Soviet state would be tempted to fill this and any other power vacuum along its borders. Despite the Roosevelt administration's efforts to do so, the United States could not count upon gentlemen's agreements between U.S. and Soviet leaders, upon treaties and other written documents, upon moral-ethical considerations, upon a sense of self-restraint by the Communist hierarchy, or upon other factors to inhibit Soviet expansionist tendencies.

In his widely circulated and influential article (written under the pseudonym of "X") analyzing the Soviet challenge in the early postwar period, George F. Kennan repeatedly emphasized the role of *Realpolitik* calculations in Soviet diplomacy.[76] Moscow's expansionist tendencies, he was convinced, could be successfully inhibited by only one U.S. response: the application of what Kennan called counterforce by the United States wherever Soviet power threatened the peace and security of nations outside the existing Communist bloc. As explained by George Kennan and other proponents of the policy, containment was a de facto exercise in classical balance of power politics. The goal of containment was preservation of the existing balance or distribution of power between the superpowers (with the understanding that in 1947, the outcome of the contest between the Soviet-supported Communist forces and the U.S.-supported Nationalist Government of China was still in doubt). By adopting the containment strategy, officials in Washington declared in effect that they would not actively and directly contest Moscow's hold over Eastern Europe. They would, however, attempt to contain any new efforts by the Kremlin to extend its hegemony beyond its existing orbit. The opposite side of the coin of accepting Soviet control over Eastern Europe, however, was that U.S. and other Western officials expected Moscow to accept Western Europe, the Mediterranean area, and Latin America as zones in which the power of the United States and its allies would be dominant. In the U.S. view, Soviet failure to respect this understanding led to the issuance of the Truman Doctrine early in 1947 — the first formal expression of the new containment strategy.[77]

Another aspect of the containment policy requires brief explanation at the outset. Our designation of U.S. policy as the containment strategy is admittedly misleading, in the sense that the precise meaning of containment was determined in the light of experience in the years after 1947. It would be accurate perhaps to say that containment became a strategy in the years ahead, as the United States confronted widely differing challenges in Europe and the Mediterranean area, in the Middle East, in East Asia, and in Latin America. What was the geographical compass of the containment policy? What role were other countries expected to play in its implementation? To what extent did its successful application depend upon military force, military and economic assistance, propaganda, covert and overt interventionism, and other steps by the United States? How would it apply to expansionist and interventionist efforts by the Soviet Union's proxies and clients, like Castro's Cuba, North Vietnam, and North Korea? What was its relevance for U.S. relations with other states — such as Syria, Iraq, and Libya — that had large stocks of Soviet-supplied weapons, maintained close ties with Moscow, and were sometimes actively opposed to U.S. diplomatic interests? Few of these questions could be answered authoritatively when the Truman Doctrine was issued in 1947. As with the other major doctrines of U.S. foreign policy, its meaning and implications would be spelled out in the light of future circumstances.[78] Containment of course remains an organic diplomatic strategy. The post-Vietnam War era, for example, has witnessed a number of changes in the way containment is envisioned by the U.S. people and their leaders.

THE TRUMAN DOCTRINE: CONTEXT AND RATIONALE

Appearing before a joint session of Congress on March 12, 1947, President Harry S. Truman delivered one of the momentous speeches in the annals of U.S. diplomacy.* On that occasion, he enunciated what came to be called the Truman Doctrine, the key principle of which was his statement: "I believe that it must be the policy of the United States to support free peoples who are resisting attempted subjugation by armed minorities or by outside pressures."

The promulgation of the Truman Doctrine decisively altered the course of U.S. foreign relations. Within a few weeks after Truman's speech, Congress enacted the Greek-Turkish Aid Program. The following year, it passed the European Recovery Program (or Marshall Plan), providing more than $12 billion for the rehabilitation of Western Europe. On July 21, 1949, the United States ratified the North Atlantic Treaty — the first peacetime defense alliance in its history. Soon thereafter followed the Mutual Defense Assistance Program (MDAP), providing arms-aid to the NATO countries. In the years that followed, as the United States acquired new military allies under treaties like ANZUS (Australia, New Zealand, the United States) created in 1952, the Southeast Asia Treaty (SEATO) and the U.S.-Philippine defense agreement in 1954, and the alliance with the Republic of China (Formosa) in 1955, massive quantities of U.S. arms-aid began to flow to the Afro-Asian world. All of these measures after 1947 were manifestations of the Truman Doctrine or containment policy.

If the Truman Doctrine may legitimately be interpreted as the United States' formal declaration of the existence of Cold War, it resembled a declaration of active warfare among nations in that its issuance was the result of both short-term, proximate and long-term, more remote causes. The immediate occasion for President Truman's speech was the violent and continuing crisis in the ancient homeland of Western democracy, Greece. In addition, at intervals in the early postwar period, Turkey had also experienced Soviet pressures, which aroused apprehensions in the West about its continued independence. As the European war drew to a close, violence erupted between two main forces vying for power in Greece. One consisted of rightist and promonarchial elements; the other faction consisted of leftist, antimonarchial, anti-British forces, of which

---

*The text of President Truman's message to Congress on this date is included as Appendix 3.

the most influential group was the National Liberation Front (EAM), whose military arm was the National People's Liberation Army (ELAS). Marxists constituted the dominant element in EAM's organization. As the defeat of the Axis Powers became imminent, these rival Greek political groups jockeyed for power in the hope of dominating whatever political system emerged from the war.

As a result of wartime agreements between Great Britain and Soviet Russia (which the United States either refused to support or openly opposed), Greece was allocated to the British sphere of influence. Accordingly, in the closing stage of hostilities, London reverted to its customary policy of supporting the Greek monarchy. The Greek insurgents were receiving supplies and encouragement and were making effective use of sanctuaries provided them by the neighboring Communist satellite states of Yugoslavia, Bulgaria, and Albania. For more than two years, British forces attempted to stabilize Greece internally, with no evident success. Finally, with its resources and prestige heavily depleted by World War II, Great Britain decided to relinquish its commitments in Greece.[79] Early in February 1947 Britain officially informed the United States of its decision to withdraw from Greece by April 1.

London's decision precipitated intensive studies and discussions by President Truman and his advisers, climaxed by Truman's historic address to Congress on March 12. In his speech Truman asked Congress to enact the Greek-Turkish Aid Program, entailing a total of $400 million ($250 million for Greece and $150 million for Turkey), as the initial step in implementing the new containment strategy his administration had devised to check Communist expansionism. As critics of later instances in which the containment policy was followed often pointed out, in the first case of its application toward Greece and Turkey, the bulk of the funds called for was allocated for nonmilitary assistance to these two countries; the United States' direct role in averting the Communist threat to them was extremely limited. Congress's subsequent enactment of the Greek-Turkish Aid Program by substantial majorities in the House and Senate set the course of U.S. foreign policy in the years ahead. Commitment to the containment policy has been a constant element in U.S. diplomacy from the Truman through the Reagan administrations.

The promulgation of the Truman Doctrine derived from a number of key determinations by officials in Washington regarding the nature and implications of the crisis in Greece and, more broadly, of the kind of regional and global political environment confronting the United States in the early postwar period. President Truman and his advisers concluded that the situation in Greece presented an urgent challenge to U.S. policy-makers, requiring a prompt and decisive U.S. response.[80] A significant determination in this decision also was the pervasive conviction that Greek independence was threatened by a Communist-instigated — more specifically, a Soviet-sponsored — threat.

In his speech to Congress, President Truman did not employ the term "international communism"; nor did Truman specifically mention the Soviet Union by name. Nevertheless, references to "terrorist activities . . . led by Communists" and to the dangerous consequences stemming from "totalitarian regimes imposed upon free peoples, by direct or indirect aggression," left little doubt about the Truman administration's identification of the ultimate source of political turmoil in Greece.[81]

Officials of the Truman administration were not alone in discerning a Soviet-instigated threat to the independence of Greece and Turkey in the period immediately following World War II. In view of the criticisms leveled against the Truman Doctrine at the time and in the years that followed, centering upon the doctrine's overtly anti-Communist coloration and the tendency of U.S. policy-makers to discover Moscow's guiding hand in nearly all revolutionary activities throughout the world, it should be noted that a significant number of leading Kremlinologists and students of international affairs in the late 1940s and afterward concurred in the Truman administration's verdict.[82]

Convinced that the Greek civil war was being utilized by Stalinist Russia to promote its global diplomatic objectives, policy-makers of the Truman administration also concluded that Moscow's expansionist tendencies endangered the security of the West generally and of the United States directly. The Communist threats to Greece and Turkey could not be evaluated in vacuo. Their meaning and implications had to be assessed within a broad context of relations among the great powers since World War II. By early 1947 Western policy-makers had concluded that their hopes for One World, a new postwar system based upon collaboration among the great powers within a functioning United Nations, and other idealistic wartime goals were rapidly being rendered unattainable, chiefly because of Soviet intransigence, hostility, and aggressiveness. In Robert C. Tucker's words, since World War II Western officials "encountered multiplying signs of Soviet aggressiveness and intransigence. Only gradually and reluctantly did the leaders of Western policy come to the conclusion that the Kremlin's policies were forcing upon the democracies a new struggle of deadly ernestness and consequences."[83]

Both before and after the promulgation of the Truman Doctrine in 1947, U.S. policy-makers could choose among a wide variety of theories and explanations advanced to account for Soviet Russia's expansionist conduct in the postwar period. Some students of Soviet affairs, for example, believe that while World War II was still in progress Stalin had already decided upon a course of noncooperation and conflict with the West. During the last few months of his life, even President Franklin D. Roosevelt — who made numerous wartime concessions to maintain harmonious relations with Stalin's government and who attempted to conciliate "Uncle Joe" Stalin in many instances — expressed serious doubts about Soviet objectives and the possibility of achieving lasting accords between Russia and the United States.[84]

In accounting for Soviet hegemonial impulses, which the Truman Doctrine sought to contain, one group of commentators has emphasized Russia's age-old preoccupation with security. Russia's deep concern for security, particularly along its vulnerable western frontier, was a conspicuous motif in the writings and reports of one of the ablest and most widely respected U.S. Kremlinologists after World War II, George F. Kennan. Kennan observed: "Behind Russia's stubborn expansion lies only the age-old sense of insecurity of a sedentary people reared on an exposed plain in the neighborhood of fierce nomadic peoples." Kennan wondered whether the expansionist urge stemming from the Russian feeling of insecurity would "know where to stop." He asked: "Will it not be inexorably carried forward . . . in a struggle . . . to attain complete mastery of the shores of the Atlantic and the Pacific?"[85] Yet Kennan and most other commentators who emphasized the role of security in shaping Moscow's worldview also acknowledged that other nations also had, and were entitled to have, an interest in preserving their security — which Moscow's actions often threatened. Throughout history, for example, the Kremlin has evinced little comparable interest in the security of Poland.

Another group of commentators (sometimes including Kennan and others who emphasized Russia's desire for security) became convinced that, as the end of World War II approached, Moscow began to exhibit certain behavior traits in its external relations that had long been characteristic of Czarist diplomacy. In accounting for the emergence of the Cold War, Philip W. Quigg quotes a remark once made by Karl Marx about Czarist Russia's external policies: "Its methods, its tactics, its maneuvers may change, but the guiding star of this policy — world hegemony — will never change."[86] In his account of Soviet-U.S. relations at the end of World War II and in the early postwar era, former

Secretary of State James F. Byrnes placed considerable stress on the historic and traditional goals of Russian foreign policy. In seeking to answer the question, "What are the Russians after?" he also cited statements by Karl Marx on the subject of the Russian state's expansionist tendencies, aimed at the ultimate creation (in Marx's words) of a "Slavonic Empire."[87] For many of the propensities that the West came to associate with the Stalinist regime — despotism, brutality, and periodic purges at home; violations of the terms of agreements with other countries; interventionism; reliance upon military force to achieve its objective; and disregard for the rights of smaller nations abroad — abundant evidence could be found in Russia's pre-Communist tradition.

In the view of other authorities and U.S. policy-makers, ideological compulsions supplied another important motivation accounting for Soviet hostility and aggressiveness after World War II. For some commentators, the tenets of Marxist ideology served as the single most influential force affecting Moscow's behavior and producing a condition of Cold War with the West. That Western liberal democracy and Soviet communism are in many crucial respects antithetical philosophies requires no detailed documentation. Indeed, by the mid 1940s many Western observers had become so repulsed by Bolshevism (and we should never forget that there were several varieties of Marxism even then, not to mention the schisms that disrupted the unity of the Communist bloc in later years) that they regarded it as in some respects a more ominous threat than Nazism. After successfully defeating the Axis Powers, the West soon found itself confronted with a new, aggressive, millenarian movement that endangered the peace of the world.[88]

From the perspective of U.S. policy-makers, ideological motivations influenced Soviet foreign policy in several ways. First, they produced a tendency in Stalin and his advisers to believe that genuine security for the Soviet Union — recognized by Marxist ideology as the bastion of the international Communist movement — could be achieved only by "communizing" neighboring countries.[89] Second, Marxist ideology persuaded Soviet leaders that the United States and other Western (or, for that matter, any non-Communist) nations were unfriendly, hostile, and ultimately devoted to the destruction of the Soviet Communist system. According to Marxist canons, genuine peace and cooperation between Communist and non-Communist states were impossible; at best, peace and coexistence were tactical phases engaged in expedientially to promote Moscow's interests and to separate eras of hostility and conflict.[90]

Third, Western leaders, and in time countless Western citizens, were disturbed by Soviet Marxism's avowedly millennial goals — the ultimate one being intensified revolutionary upheavals leading to a worldwide Communist system. Events by the end of the war provided compelling evidence that Moscow had not abandoned this dominant ideological compulsion.[91] Even such an outspoken critic of the U.S. postwar diplomatic record as Michael Harrington concedes that Soviet-instigated threats to Western Europe at the end of the war presented an intolerable situation to the West and that the contending powers in the ensuing Cold War "represented alternate ways of organizing the globe."[92]

Fourth, ideological considerations caused Stalinist Russia to view Communist parties outside the Soviet Union merely as instruments of Soviet foreign policy. Irrespective of whether indigenous Communist movements desired to play such a role (and Yugoslavia's ultimate defection from the Soviet bloc indicated that often they were reluctant), Communist parties outside the Soviet Union were expected to take their directive from the Kremlin and to promote its interests. The concept of national communism, or Communist parties independent of Soviet (and later Chinese) control, we must remember, did not gain currency or acceptance by the Soviet Union until the 1960s.[93]

Fifth, Soviet Russia's ideological guidelines might well have induced the Kremlin to judge the late wartime and postwar situation as providing a highly favorable setting for an intensified Communist ideological offensive in the expectation of achieving real advances. Toward the end of the war and for a prolonged period thereafter, the Kremlin's ideologists convinced themselves that the U.S. economy would soon collapse and, in the process, would precipitate massive economic dislocations in other Western nations as it proved unable to cope with the strains of transition from a wartime to a peacetime basis. Such economic adversities could be expected to produce a retreat by the United States into its traditional isolationist shell after the war. In addition, conditions in other Western countries — Great Britain's power was rapidly declining throughout the world, and its domestic problems were mounting; countries like France and Italy were demoralized and debilitated, with Communist Party influence growing; Germany was defeated and divided — appeared to offer favorable opportunities for Communist gains.[94]

A related explanation of Soviet foreign policy at the end of World War II is the idea that essentially expediential and pragmatic calculations induced Stalin's government to abandon collaboration with the West in favor of a policy of interventionism and expansionism abroad. A decisive factor perhaps inducing an opportunistically motivated Soviet hierarchy to expand its hegemony was what Paul Seabury has called the great military "asymmetry" existing between the Soviet Union and the United States after the Axis surrender. "Demobilization" would be too mild a term to describe what happened to U.S. armed forces once the war was over. It would be more accurate to refer to the disintegration of its military establishment. For example, at the close of the war with Germany the United States had an army of some 3.5 million troops in Western Europe, supported by 149 air groups. A year or so later the United States had just over one-tenth as many forces on the European continent. And by 1948 Soviet Russia (with some 3 million men still under arms) had some 300,000 troops in East Germany alone, versus two U.S. divisions (or some 30,000 men) in the whole of Europe.[95]

For several years the United States possessed one weapon — the atomic bomb — that the Soviet Union lacked. In the opinion of Winston Churchill and other observers, the U.S. nuclear arsenal was the only deterrent preventing the crushing power of the Red Army from sweeping across Western Europe to the English Channel. Yet, from the Kremlin's perspective, the U.S. nuclear monopoly could logically be regarded as at best only a partial, temporary, and not always effective deterrent to the realization of its external goals. After more than four years of total war, the U.S. society was war weary and determined to concentrate once again upon its domestic problems. After World War II, the United States might once again largely withdraw from active participation in the affairs of the world, confidently expecting that the newly created United Nations could deal with problems of peace and security.

Moreover, after 1945 there was — and there always remained — a substantial question about the credibility of the United States' nuclear deterrent. Would a U.S. president order the destruction of Moscow to save Western Europe from Soviet military aggrandizement? Even if the U.S. response to that form of overt Soviet expansionism were never in doubt, policy-makers in Washington faced the much more probable and ambiguous challenge of responding to various kinds of Soviet interventionism, such as extension of Moscow's influence by relying upon war by proxy, direct and indirect support for local insurgent movements against established governments, encouragement and assistance to the Communist parties of Western Europe, psychological warfare and ideological offensives, and other varieties of hegemonial impulses toward which U.S. nuclear superiority seemed marginally relevant. Nuclear strength was simply not adaptable for effective use against the wide range of Soviet moves that Western policy-makers believed threatened their security and enabled the Soviet Union to extend its power. In addition, to the surprise of many Westerners, the U.S. nuclear monopoly proved relatively short-lived. The U.S. monopoly was broken when the Soviet Union exploded its first nuclear device in 1949. Thereafter, the military asymmetry in the United States' favor is replaced by a nuclear balance of terror or nuclear duopoly, in which the two superpowers possessed atomic stockpiles powerful enough to jeopardize the future of civilization on the planet.

In the light of the differing theories offered by knowledgeable students of Russian affairs to explain Soviet behavior during and after World War II, it is not suprising or remarkable that spokesmen for the Truman administration described the emerging Soviet-U.S. conflict in various terms or that there was little apparent unanimity among U.S. officials concerning the precise nature of the threat that jeopardized Western security. As we have noted, George F. Kennan tended to emphasize two major motivating forces actuating Soviet foreign policy: traditional traits, like Czarist expansionism and Russian nationalism, and Marxist ideology — with the primary role being assigned to the former. Joseph M. Jones and other presidential advisers underscored the global objectives of a Communist ideology that instilled in the Kremlin's policy-makers a "drive toward world domination."[96] Undersecretary of State Acheson referred to the danger as entailing "a highly possible Soviet breakthrough" in the Balkans, which "might open three continents to Soviet penetration," imperiling the security of Europe, Africa, and Asia.[97] In Congress Senator Vandenberg related the dangers facing Greece and Turkey to "today's worldwide cleavage between democracy and communism" which he likened to the earlier struggle between democracy and Nazism.[98] President Truman feared the "extension of the Iron Curtain" (a Cold War frontier established mainly by Soviet military power) unless the United States maintained the integrity of Greece and Turkey. But to Truman's mind, the conflict was also an ideological contest involving a challenge to U.S. "ideals . . . and traditions."[99]

In comprehending the factors inducing the Truman administration to adopt the containment strategy, one other important consideration remains to be emphasized. This was the significant shift in U.S. public opinion regarding relations with the Soviet Union, and regarding collateral issues like the prospects for peace and global stability, that occurred after World War II. During the war U.S. opinion was generally favorable toward the

Soviet Union — a phenomenon no doubt aided by measures, often taken at President Roosevelt's suggestion, like Stalin's abolition of the Comintern (communism's agency for coordinating world revolutionary activities) and his liberalization of restrictions against religious organizations and practices within the Soviet Union. As the war drew to a close, however, the people of the United States began to exhibit genuine apprehension about Russia's intentions. Thus, at the end of the war about 40 percent of the respondents to one poll classified Russia as a "peace-loving" state, while an equal number described its policies as "aggressive." As time passed, U.S. suspicion and disillusionment with Soviet behavior became even more pronounced. By August 1946 some 70 percent of the respondents disapproved of Soviet Russia's conduct, while only 7 percent approved. Over half of the respondents polled believed that the Soviet Union was seeking a position of global domination.[100]

John L. Gaddis is persuaded that most Americans did not really want the United States to play an active or interventionist role in world affairs after World War II. But U.S. opinion was no less determined to avoid the mistakes of the recent past (like the near-disastrous "appeasement" of the Axis dictators in the 1930s); in time Soviet behavior induced Americans to demand that their officials take a firm stance in resisting Soviet encroachments. By the time of Truman's historic address to Congress early in 1947, a clear majority of the U.S. people endorsed the new policy of getting tough with Moscow. To a not inconsiderable extent, the Truman administration was compelled by stiffening U.S. opinion — vocally expressed in the Republican-controlled 80th Congress — to adopt the containment strategy.[101] Another characteristic of U.S. opinion in this period, which perhaps had some influence upon the form the Truman Doctrine ultimately took, has been identified by Seabury. He wrote that, whereas officials of the Truman administration were prone to think in terms of a more geographically limited "Soviet problem," the U.S. populace tended to view the threat in more generalized terms — as a worldwide Communist challenge to the U.S. way of life.[102]

ELEMENTS IN THE CONTAINMENT STRATEGY

The new diplomatic strategy announced by the Truman administration for dealing with the Communist threat to Greece and Turkey, and inferentially other countries facing a comparable challenge, was predicated on three central premises. First, it assumed that postwar Soviet foreign policy was hegemonial and expansionist. It accepted the view of George Kennan and other students of Soviet affairs in this period that Moscow could not be dissuaded from pursuing its goals by Western protests, gestures of friendship, offers to negotiate outstanding issues, or other steps, many of which would merely be interpreted by the Kremlin as signs of Western irresolution and weakness.[103]

Second, the Truman Doctrine rested on the presupposition that Soviet foreign policy after World War II threatened U.S. and, more broadly, Western security. Less than two years after the defeat of the Axis Powers, President Truman and others referred to the potential danger of a new global conflict, a prospect also alluded to by Senator Vandenberg in Congress.[104] Mindful that in the isolationist era the United States had done little or nothing to stop Axis expansionism until the nation had experienced a military debacle at Pearl Harbor, the Truman administration was determined to avoid a repetition of this nearly disastrous course in dealing with the Communist menace.

Third, in the light of these convictions, the United States had to devise a new counterstrategy designed to contain Soviet expansionist pressures. The heart of this new U.S. response was George Kennan's belief that the United States must match Soviet expansionist moves by adopting "long-range policies . . . no less steady in their purposes, no less variegated and resourceful in their application, than those of the Soviet Union itself." The United States must engage in "a long-term, patient but firm and vigilant containment of Russian expansive tendencies." The pivotal idea in this new strategy was "the adroit and vigilant application of counterforce at a series of constantly shifting geographical and political points, corresponding to the shifts and maneuvers of Soviet policy."[105]

It is useful perhaps to evaluate the main elements of the containment strategy by reference initially to its more immediate and limited application to the cases of Greece and Turkey, and then to its more generalized and doctrinal aspects. The Truman administration requested, and Congress ultimately appropriated, a total of $400 million for the Greek-Turkish Aid Program. As envisioned by executive and legislative officials, the funds were to be used mainly for economic and financial assistance to those countries. Military aid was to be limited to advice and consultation. Yet movements by U.S. naval units in the northern Mediterranean area during this period — "showing the flag" to possible adversaries — suggested the administration's readiness to invoke military measures in responding to the challenges faced by Greece and Turkey.[106]

Moreover, President Truman and his advisers repeatedly emphasized that aid to Greece and Turkey had been requested by their respective governments — a fact that Congress also highlighted in the enactment providing such assistance. This precondition for U.S. aid was stressed perhaps in the interests of achieving a twofold objective: to avoid (or at least to minimize) the appearance of unsolicited and unwanted U.S. intervention in the affairs of these two countries, and to reduce the risk that the United States would be expected to supply aid to other countries (possibly even to Communist countries) indiscriminately. Yet Joseph M. Jones acknowledges a fact that undoubtedly became known only at a much later stage: Athens' "request" to Washington for aid was "drafted in the State Department and suggested to the Greek government."[107]

The purposes to be achieved with U.S. aid to Greece and Turkey were viewed by U.S. policy-makers as multiple. In the case of Turkey, it was to preserve that country's independence and to accelerate its development in the direction of a more democratic political system. As for the more complicated case of Greece, in his address to Congress President Truman listed four main objectives of U.S. assistance: (1) to enable the Greeks to "make progress in solving their problems of reconstruction"; (2) to create "a stable and self-sustaining economy"; (3) to preserve Greece as an independent nation; and (4) to enable the country to become "a self-supporting and self-respecting democracy." By the end of 1949 — and Yugoslavia's expulsion from the Soviet orbit in 1948 was a turning point — the Greek insurgency had largely collapsed. Nor was there a resumption of Soviet pressures against Turkey in the years following.[108]

Critics of the containment policy at the time and in later years devoted considerable attention to the fact that, in providing aid to Greece and Turkey, the Truman administration was bypassing the United Nations, which had been established to deal with problems of global peace and security. In part, perhaps, because the United States had sponsored the U.N. enthusiastically, the administration was sensitive to his criticism. Yet it also believed that the newly created U.N. was in no position to furnish needed assistance to these countries; and even at this early stage, the problem of the Soviet veto in the Security Council made the likelihood of any effective U.N. action extremely remote.[109]

While Greece and Turkey provided the immediate occasion for the adoption of the United States' new containment strategy, events soon made clear that its implications were global in scope and would vitally affect the conduct of U.S. foreign relations for years to come. President Truman believed that his speech to Congress was as epochal as the issuance of the Monroe Doctrine, and developments after 1947 confirmed this assessment. What were the more doctrinal and universally applicable aspects of the containment policy? Initially, we may note that the president and his advisers were aware that the containment principle would be interpreted as having application beyond the limited scope of Greece and Turkey. In his defense of the containment idea, George Kennan urged the United States to counter "Russian expansive tendencies" — presumably wherever they occurred; he advocated the application of U.S. counterforce "at a series of constantly shifting geographical and political points"; and he proposed that the United States resist Soviet encroachments "at every point" where they threatened the security of non-Communist states. If Kennan intended his containment strategy to be geographically or otherwise limited (as he implied in later years), his defense of the strategy at the time conveyed a contrary impression.[110] In committing the United States to the Greek-Turkish Aid Program, President Truman later acknowledged, he was fully mindful "that this would be only the beginning" in terms of the assumption of new U.S. commitments abroad.[111] Even before Congress had completed action on the bill, Undersecretary of State Acheson had initiated a study within the State Department of other vulnerable countries that might require U.S. assistance.[112] While Congress was still deliberating on the Greek-Turkish Aid Program, for example, State Department officials had already undertaken the preliminary studies that led to passage of the Marshall Plan for European reconstruction the following year.[113]

With regard to the long-range implications of the Truman Doctrine, spokesmen for the Truman administration were clearly in a dilemma. They were unquestionably aware at the time that the president had enunciated a major diplomatic doctrine, potentially applicable to a long list of countries besides Greece and Turkey and capable of radically changing the direction of U.S. foreign policy. For obvious reasons, they did not want to deny the possibility of U.S. aid to other countries whose security might be jeopardized (several years later, right-wing critics denounced Secretary of State Acheson because he had seemed to suggest that the United States would not help defend South Korea, thereby perhaps inviting Communist encroachments against it). In his testimony to Congress urging support of the Greek-Turkish aid, Undersecretary of State Dean Acheson (as even Jones concedes) engaged in hedging with respect to the future implications of the Truman Doctrine. On the one hand, he repeatedly reassured Congress that aid would not be provided automatically or indiscriminately to other countries; he emphasized the fact that the circumstances in Greece and Turkey were in many respects unique and assured legislators that future requests for U.S. aid would be evaluated on their merits. On the other hand, Acheson acknowledged publicly that the United States was clearly interested in any international situation in which "a free people is being coerced to give up its free institutions."[114]

One of the more controversial aspects of the Truman Doctrine as time passed was the president's use of the enigmatic phrase "free peoples" as the object of proposed U.S. assistance. What did the Truman administration mean by this concept? In view of the fact, for example, that the Greek government was an authoritarian monarchy, and Greece continued in the pattern of absolutist rule in the years that followed, in what sense could U.S. aid be construed as defending "free peoples"? The same question was raised even more cogently years later, when the United States became committed to massive assistance to the government of South Vietnam.

Executive policy-makers were aware of this anomalous and troublesome aspect of the containment strategy. In his address to Congress, President Truman frankly conceded that Greece was not currently a democracy. He condemned excesses by both rightist and leftist groups within the country; nor did the United States necessarily sanction the behavior of the Greek government in all respects. Yet Truman also believed that a Marxist victory would foreclose any prospect for the development of a democratic political system in Greece. Truman anticipated that with the successful promotion of Greek economic rehabilitation and recovery, stability would gradually return to the country, and in time it would develop into "a self-supporting and self-respecting democracy." Once U.S. aid had begun, Truman later asserted, U.S. officials endeavored "to induce the government to broaden its base and to seek the widest possible popular support." As for Turkey, executive policy-makers believed that within recent years it had made progress in the direction of greater democracy and economic advancement, and that U.S. aid would provide momentum in that direction.[115]

Theoretically, the term "free peoples" (and the variant, "free world," which came to be widely used by U.S. policy-makers as time went on) might mean one of three things. It could be synonymous with democratic governments, which the Truman Doctrine pledged the United States to support in the future. Because neither Greece nor Turkey was a democracy in 1947, this obviously was not the intended meaning of the term.

Alternatively, free peoples might suggest the possibility and likelihood of ultimate progress toward democracy. With U.S. assistance, Greece, Turkey and presumably other societies would be afforded an opportunity to evolve democratically — a chance they would be altogether unlikely to have if they passed into the Soviet orbit. No evidence exists to suggest that President Truman and his advisers believed such evolution would occur automatically or inevitably; but without U.S. aid, it had little prospect of occurring at all.

Another possibility — and it seems evident that this connotation of free peoples was uppermost in the minds of U.S. policy-makers in the late 1940s — is that the term was a synonym for national independence. Both Greece and Turkey were recognized by the members of the international community as sovereign states; they were founding members of the United Nations. Unlike the case of Vietnam later, there was no question about whether Greece and Turkey were in fact independent nations. Speaking to Congress and the nation, President Truman defined the goal of his new doctrine as supporting nations that were seeking "to work out a way of life free from coercion" and maintaining their "free institutions and their national integrity against aggressive movements that seek to impose upon them totalitarian regimes." The threat to both countries was envisioned primarily as an external one, in the form of direct or indirect aggression and coercion. Greece and Turkey constituted free peoples in the sense that thus far they had retained their national independence, in contrast to the Communist satellite states of Eastern Europe, which Washington believed were examples of what Greece and Turkey might become without U.S. aid.

What was the long-range goal of the containment strategy? Beyond Kennan's projection of "a duel of infinite duration" between the superpowers, what did containment anticipate by way of changes in the nature of the Cold War? The Truman administration's response to the pressures faced by Greece and Turkey might be construed perhaps as a typical exercise in U.S. pragmatism. Statements by the president and most of his advisers show little or no expressed concern for the long-range future of Soviet-U.S. relations or the effect of the Truman Doctrine on the ultimate course of the Cold War. Except for George Kennan, U.S. policy-makers seemed largely immersed in the exigencies of the problems facing Greece and Turkey.

Yet implicitly the containment strategy appeared to contemplate several intermediate and long-term results. Successful containment of the Communist threats to Greece and Turkey would preserve the independence of these nations, enabling them to achieve political stability, to advance economically, and to make progress toward greater democracy. This result would in turn communicate a needed object lesson to the Kremlin: Moscow should abandon its operating premise that vulnerable societies would easily succumb to Communist pressures. Instead, the United States was prepared to assume a leadership role in preserving them as members of the non-Communist world. Once the Soviet hierarchy finally accepted this reality, successful containment would promote frustrations among Russian policy-makers, gradually inducing them to reexamine those foreign policy goals that imperiled the security of other nations. Thwarted in its hegemonial impulses abroad, Soviet officialdom would sooner or later decide to devote the nation's energies and resources to domestic concerns, which were likely to remain critical for years to come. As a long-range prospect, George F. Kennan believed, successful containment would lead to the eventual mellowing of Soviet policy and, in the final stage, to benign changes in the nature of the Communist system. Indeed, to Kennan's mind, containment would accelerate the process of "inner decay" already destroying Russia's Communist system; the sprouting of the seeds of its downfall were well advanced. Proponents of containment could thus anticipate "either the break-up or the gradual mellowing of Soviet power."[116]

In the years ahead, the goals of containment were formulated differently. During the Korean War, for example, U.S. intervention in behalf of South Korean independence was designed to teach aggressors a lesson. In the Vietnam War, it was (among other goals) intended to avert Communist threats to other Asian states (viewed in Washington as possible falling dominoes). In Afghanistan, it was to demonstrate the determination of the United States and its Western partners to preserve the security of the Persian Gulf area and to underscore their apprehension about the security of the Indian subcontinent. In Grenada and Central America, it was to demonstrate U.S. diplomatic credibility, to support prodemocratic forces, and to assert traditional U.S. opposition to foreign influence (especially military influence) within the Western Hemisphere.

CONTAINMENT: GAINS AND ACCOMPLISHMENTS

If adoption by the United States of the containment policy in 1947 is almost universally acknowledged as a landmark in the nation's diplomatic experience, many informed students of foreign policy also regard it as among the outstanding achievements in the U.S. diplomatic record. Paul Hammond, for example, argues that "the standard of achievement in foreign relations that Truman set has not been surpassed by any other postwar President."[117] To Eugene Rostow's mind, for some 20 years after 1947 the U.S. commitment to containment served as "the cement of the world, and its hope of peace." Containment was the "cornerstone" of national security and foreign policy.[118]

From a different perspective, a number of recent problems and challenges in U.S. diplomacy — such as the unwillingness of the Western allies to follow Washington's diplomatic lead compliantly, or the inability of the United States to control the Third World — could be attributed in some measure to the success of the containment policy. The Western allies, for example, were increasingly inclined to deemphasize the danger of a direct Soviet invasion of the NATO area. Third World governments could defy both the superpowers with impunity, in part because they had little fear of either Soviet or U.S. hegemony. Or to cite another example: political dissidents within Poland could assert new demands upon Communist authorities because they knew that Moscow was extremely reluctant to abandon détente with the United States.

To a number of commentators, adoption of the containment policy signified U.S. awareness of its status as a superpower and its readiness to assume the overseas responsibilities attending that role. Ernest Lefever's judgment is that, when the United States adopted the containment strategy, it "fully accepted the leadership of the free world which had been thrust upon us and took appropriate steps to build a viable Western coalition."[119] Another commentator has said that in time even the Soviet Union benefited from the U.S. containment policy. Ultimately, the Truman Doctrine evolved into a kind of common law of contemporary international politics and served as a "prudent rule of reciprocal safety."[120] As with all general rules, this one is subject to exceptions. In the Western view, the Soviet invasion into Afghanistan in 1979 was a new and dangerous push by a still-expansionist Kremlin into a vulnerable zone; Moscow was not content with nominal Soviet control of the country and — in the face of fierce Afghan resistance — insisted upon overt and complete domination of it. The Soviet intrusion into Afghanistan both surprised the West and created genuine concern in Washington and other capitals about the security of the Persian Gulf area. Similarly, growing Soviet involvement in the Caribbean area and Central America became a matter of deep concern by officials of the Reagan administration. To President Reagan and his advisers, the principal (if not the only) cause of political instability in Central America was the ongoing Soviet effort (directly by Moscow and indirectly by the governments of Cuba and Nicaragua) to establish a new Soviet power base in the Western Hemisphere. By its recent diplomatic offensive in Latin America, the Kremlin was violating long-established ground rules governing the conduct of the Cold War. In *Realpolitik* terms, the Soviet hierarchy was endangering the stability of the balance of power, thereby aggravating international tensions.[121]

Favorable judgments have been expressed about the containment policy for another reason. Better than any other conceivable response to the challenge of Soviet expansionism, containment accorded most closely with certain traits of the U.S. character and ethos and was consonant with a number of deeply rooted elements in the U.S. tradition. This fact was crucial in producing a broad base of public support for the containment principle, enabling it to serve as the basis for a long-range approach to external problems. In Gaddis's words, the U.S. decision to resist further Soviet encroachments "evoked overwhelming public approval."[122] Containment appealed to what is often termed the vital center of U.S. politics, thereby enjoying a broad and durable foundation of public approval. Programs and policies undertaken to implement the containment principle — the defense of Greece and Turkey, the reconstruction of Western Europe, the rehabilitation of West Germany, the encouragement of self-help and economic advancement in countries outside the West — gave expression to several cherished U.S. principles, such as national independence and freedom, self-government and self-help, progress toward economic development, and a humanitarian concern for less fortunate societies.[123]

Still other students of postwar U.S. foreign relations have lauded the containment policy because it was a controlled, moderate, and reasonable U.S. response to Soviet aggressiveness. Frederick Barghoorn commends the Truman Doctrine for avoiding two overriding dangers: the threat of global nuclear war and the challenge of piecemeal expansion by the Soviet Union, which, if unanswered, would leave the United States once again isolated in global affairs.[124] As former isolationists were amply aware, the containment policy marked a sharp break in the nation's diplomatic tradition. Yet containment was also a restrained and limited response to the Soviet challenge. It posed no threat to Moscow directly. In Eugene Rostow's words, it was fundamentally a policy of "live-and-let-live" among the superpowers.[125]

Confronted with what they viewed as irrefutable evidence of Soviet interventionism and expansionism, President Truman and his advisers had basically four options for responding to this phenomenon. They might (as a vocal but always small minority of right-wing extremists demanded) rely chiefly upon nuclear weapons and other forms of armed force in a misguided attempt to rid the world of the Communist menace once and for all. This course — culminating, in its most extreme version, in a preventive war against the Soviet Union — would have risked World War III and the nuclear devastation of the planet, not excluding the United States itself. Furthermore, as former Secretary of War Henry Stimson recognized at the time, such a military response would have been totally out of character for Americans, conflicting with their own most cherished ethical and ideological convictions and miscasting them as conquerors in the eyes of the world.[126] These considerations aside, there was also a practical difficulty with this alternative as a method for removing the Communist danger. If, as undertakings like the Marshall Plan and the Point Four program of economic aid to developing countries assumed, communism thrives in conditions of chaos, social disorganization, and human misery, how would a nuclear-devastated world provide an environment that inhibited the spread of communism?

A second option available to U.S. policy-makers was continuing to rely upon diplomatic negotiations to resolve outstanding issues between the United States and the Soviet Union. Experience since the end of World War II, however, offered little prospect that this course would reduce Cold War tensions significantly. In fact, after 1945 continued deadlock among the former Allies over issues like the German peace treaty and German reparations proved highly productive of disagreements and suspicions among them.

A third possible course was for Western policy-makers to emulate their predecessors during the 1930s, engaging in appeasement to satisfy the demands of expansionist dictatorships. A twofold objection existed to this alternative: it had been tried in relations with Stalinist Russia, with no very conspicuous success, by the Roosevelt administration during the war (in the face of emphatic recommendations against it by Soviet experts like George Kennan); and the Western diplomatic record in dealing with German, Italian, and Japanese demands during the 1930s offered very little encouragement to those who believed that threats to the peace could be eliminated by accepting the demands of expansionist nations. After World War II, from the point of view of political realities in the United

States, any policy that might be construed as involving another Munich would encounter great difficulty in achieving and holding public support.

The fourth alternative available was containment, or some combination of resistance to Soviet encroachments involving reliance upon economic and financial assistance, military aid (and the implicit threat at least of military force), the promotion of the economic and political development of vulnerable countries to strengthen their capacity to resist communism or other external dangers, diplomatic pressure, and efforts to engender the maximum degree of collaboration among the nations of the non-Communist world.

Considering the possible responses U.S. officials might have made to the Soviet challenge in the late 1940s, Adam B. Ulam is persuaded that the containment policy struck and maintained "the right balance between the extremes of bellicosity toward the Soviet Union and supine acquiescence in the face of Communist encroachment."[127] Barbara Ward shares this judgment. By adopting containment as its guiding foreign policy principle, the United States rejected "panicky talk of war" between the superpowers, in preference for "the policy of meeting Russian demands and Russian maneuvers not with hasty advances and equally hasty retreats but with a steady, patient insistence that there should be no further Russian encroachments and no undermining of the non-Russian world." To Barbara Ward's mind, the containment policy deserves commendation because it accepted the underlying reality that there is really no solution to the basic problem of international politics — power conflicts among rival nations. The only feasible solution is "a series of adjustments which will demand the continuous attention of great states." Moreover, containment was essentially an optimistic doctrine, since its basic premise was that "the final clash can be avoided" between the Cold War rivals.[128]

Other observers have called attention to a different aspect of the Truman Doctrine's limited and essentially moderate reaction to the Soviet challenge. We may effectively highlight the point by taking note of what the U.S. containment policy did not require or contemplate. It did not threaten the Soviet Union (or later Communist China) directly with superior U.S. nuclear power or other forms of military force. It did not call for the dismantling of the Soviet Communist system or any other Marxist regimes (although admittedly it did attempt to prevent the imposition of such regimes upon societies not having them before 1947) before a reasonably secure international system could be achieved. As some critics of U.S. foreign policy in 1947 and afterward incorrectly charged, as envisaged by the Truman administration containment did not commit the United States to a worldwide anti-Communist crusade; still less did it align the United States unswervingly against Socialist or other left-wing political movements (many of which were flourishing and continued to gain adherents, for example, in Western Europe). Despite much political and official rhetoric on the subject in the Eisenhower-Dulles era, at no time did President Truman and his successors in the White House seriously consider the liberation of Eastern Europe from Soviet control as a requirement of the containment policy. Additionally, containment was not predicated on the idea that war between the United States and the Soviet Union was inevitable. To the contrary, the strategy's assumption was that, if containment could be successfully carried out, Cold War tensions would ease somewhat in time and perhaps ultimately disappear. As Zbigniew K. Brzezinski has observed, by pursuing containment the United States chose to rely "primarily on the erosive effects of time and the pressures of change within the Communist States themselves" to improve the prospects for peace and international stability.[129]

In view of the frequent criticisms later directed at U.S. overcommitment abroad, it is worthwhile to note the attitudes of several commentators who have commended the containment policy because it did not call for the automatic commitment of U.S. armed forces in other countries. No U.S. troops were sent to Greece and Turkey in the late 1940s; the Truman administration's inclination in those cases was to depend mainly upon economic and financial reconstruction, together with quite limited U.S. military aid and advice, to preserve their security. President Truman and his advisers, Ronald Steel has stated, did not "intend, at least at the time . . . unilateral military intervention in support of client states threatened from within by Communist-inspired insurgents." Insofar as that tendency may have been characteristic of U.S. foreign policy in later years, it could rather persuasively be argued that this propensity was a misapplication or perversion of the original containment idea.[130]

Other students of postwar U.S. diplomacy have applauded the containment policy because it was essentially a defensive diplomatic posture, threatening no nations except those bent upon aggression or intervention in the affairs of their neighbors. Avoiding such provocative objectives as challenging the legitimacy of the Soviet Communist regime itself or commiting the United States to undertake the liberation of areas already under Moscow's hegemony, containment was basically a policy of maintaining the status quo in terms of the existing orbit of Soviet power.[131] As a number of critics (particularly right-wing individuals and groups) vocally complained, under containment the diplomatic initiative remained with the Soviet Union; whether containment would lead to an intensification or relaxation of Cold War tensions was a decision that in the main would be made by policy-makers in the Kremlin. Thus, Charles Bohlen emphasized that containment emerged as the U.S. guiding diplomatic principle "in response to a Soviet action." However negative the policy might appear to some observers, actually its defensive character was one of its most attractive features, serving as proof that the United States "had no sinister design, no hidden purpose, certainly no imperialist ambitions in our policy, but simply moved in answer to a challenge that was presented by the Soviet Union."[132]

Containment has appealed to other commentators because, in Michael Armacost's words, as a policy it proved "immensely flexible as well as enormously resilient." Specific diplomatic moves and programs identified with the containment strategy after 1947 underwent "continuous evolution in response to the ebb and flow of international developments and to domestic reactions to those developments."[133]

Assertions by many critics of the U.S. role in the Vietnam War to the contrary, defenders of containment do not believe the policy committed the United States to a doctrinaire and indiscriminate anti-Communist crusade throughout the world. Herbert Tillema's study of postwar U.S. interventionism, for example, offers rather convincing contrary evidence. His conclusion is that policy-makers in Washington have not instinctively or automatically detected a Communist threat masterminded by the Kremlin whenever an established government found its authority or existence threatened. In time, U.S. officials demonstrated considerable sophistication in differentiating among several varieties of Communist threats (Tillema employs a sevenfold classification) and in tailoring their responses accordingly. Only in a very limited number of cases — a few instances in which a Communist threat posed an imminent peril to U.S. security — has the United States intervened militarily abroad to thwart it.[134] With a handful of exceptions (the Vietnam War and the Johnson administration's intervention in the Dominican Republic serve as two prominent examples), U.S. policy-makers ultimately made a distinction that perhaps was not sufficiently clear in the minds of some officials of the Truman administration: the difference between the threat of Soviet (or Chinese) expansionism and hegemony, on the one hand, and between Soviet and other varieties of communism, on the other hand.

The two phenomena were never identical, and they became increasingly distinct after the death of Stalin in 1953. Thus, very soon after Yugoslavia's break with the Kremlin in 1948 the United States supplied that country economic and military assistance, which continued for many years. In later years, Washington engaged in a policy of "building bridges" to other smaller Marxist nations, like Poland and Rumania. Ever since the Truman administration, the United States has provided economic assistance to Third World nations, most of which are governed by some kind of avowedly Socialist or left-wing regime, and a number of which also receive aid from the Soviet Union. India, for example, has been a major recipient of U.S. foreign assistance. Under the Carter administration, substantial U.S. aid was extended to Marxist-ruled Nicaragua (the aid was in time discontinued, as relations between Washington and Managua steadily deteriorated). By the 1980s, Egypt had become (next to Israel) the second largest recipient of U.S. assistance. The Carter administration endeavored to maintain cooperative relations with the left-wing government of Zimbabwe, while the Reagan administration was receptive to Mozambique's efforts to reduce its long-time dependency upon Moscow. The contention that the containment policy committed the United States to a position of inflexible and indiscriminate opposition to left-wing movements throughout the world is not supported by the evidence.

Another misplaced criticism of the containment policy is the idea that it identified the United States with the ancien régime and made it the defender of the status quo throughout the world. Again, this contention has little or no validity. Political developments within Greece since the late 1940s, for example, indicate that democratic evolution is possible in countries benefiting from U.S. aid; with the passage of time, the Greek government became an outspoken critic of U.S. diplomatic behavior. Under the Kennedy and successive administrations, the Alliance for Progress called for far-reaching changes in Latin American social, economic, and political systems — more radical changes, in fact, than many Latin Americans were prepared to make. We have already alluded to the drastic changes carried out in Germany and Japan during the military occupation of these countries. Philip Quigg also has pointed out that since World War II some 80 new nations, with a combined population of approximately one billion people, joined the international system. It would be difficult to imagine a more far-reaching change than this phenomenon. Far from opposing this tendency, the United States basically approved it and often used its influence to accelerate it. Meanwhile, its commitment to containment permitted these nations to gain their independence with minimum risk that their newly acquired freedoms would be jeopardized by Soviet (or Chinese) aggrandizement.[135]

The strategy of containment has also been justified according to another essentially different set of criteria. Several leading proponents of *Realpolitik* have commended the policy as promoting U.S. national interests in a number of key respects. Toward the end of World War II, from his post in Moscow George Kennan advised Washington that a stable postwar political system could be preserved among the Allies by "the preservation of a realistic balance of strength between them and a realistic understanding of the mutual zones of vital interest."[136] To Kennan's mind, U.S. adoption of the containment strategy would largely fulfill this requirement. Similarly, Hans J. Morgenthau has said that the Truman administration was fully justified in assuming that Moscow (often relying upon foreign Communist parties) was seeking to expand its hegemony and that this tendency had to be countered by the United States.[137]

From a *Realpolitik* perspective, containment was an advantageous policy for the United States for a number of reasons. It rested upon a clear conception of U.S. security interests and the crucial role of power in global political relations, which had been conspicuously lacking from U.S. foreign policy in earlier eras.[138] By adopting containment as its foreign policy strategy, the United States prevented Soviet hegemony from filling the power vacuum that existed in Western Europe and other areas in the early postwar period.[139] The United States' firm response to Soviet expansionism also enhanced the power position of other countries — tangibly, by providing economic and military aid to nations seeking to resist Communist encroachments, as well as intangibly and psychologically, by conveying the idea forcefully that communism was not inevitable and that it did not necessarily constitute "the wave of the future."[140]

Novel as it might be for the United States, to the minds of political realists there was really nothing very original or distinctive about the containment policy. Soviet Russia's postwar behavior and the U.S. response to it constituted a familiar exercise in classical balance-of-power politics among nations. Moscow was disturbing Western security by threatening the balance of power, and by adopting containment Washington was seeking to preserve it. As in the past, U.S. officials were reluctant to describe their policies in traditional balance-of-power terms; along with other tenets of *Realpolitik,* the idea was not congenial to the U.S. ethos. Even while U.S. policy-makers were applying *Realpolitik* principles, George Ball has said, they denied doing so.[141] This did not alter the fact that containment epitomized "the politics of alliances and spheres of influence and balance of power."

Finally, several students of postwar U.S. foreign policy believe that, as George Kennan had anticipated, successful implementation of the containment policy by the United States did induce significant changes in Soviet external behavior, leading the Kremlin in time to seek détente with the United States covering at least some issues previously engendering Cold War tensions.[142] If U.S. enunciation of the Truman Doctrine disturbed the Soviet Union, Ulam contends, it did so in the right way, by compelling Moscow in time to reexamine and modify its behavior.[143] Charles O. Lerche's judgment was that "the present state of Soviet-American relations in which major war has become literally unthinkable can in large measure be credited to the plus side of the containment account."[144] No less an authority on Soviet foreign policy than Nikita Khrushchev lent some credence to this conclusion about containment's accomplishments. In 1961, during one of the periods of intensified Soviet pressure on the Western position in Berlin, Khrushchev observed, "The experience of history teaches that, when an aggressor sees that he is not being opposed he grows more brazen. Contrariwise, when he meets opposition, he calms down. It is this historic experience that must guide us in our actions."[145]

The most outstanding accomplishment of the containment policy, in Wayne Cole's judgment, is that it was to a significant degree responsible for the fact that the superpowers have successfully avoided a nuclear conflagration since 1945. Given the possibilities for armed conflict between them during the late 1940s and the 1950s, he found this to be "no small accomplishment," a gain that in turn "enabled the world to survive long enough for younger and hopefully wiser people in America and abroad to try their hands at accomplishing that better and more peaceful world that mankind has sought over so many thousands of years."[146]

CONTAINMENT: CRITICISMS AND FAILURES

At the time of its promulgation in 1947 and throughout the years that followed, the Truman Doctrine faced a barrage of criticisms from widely diverse sources. Criticisms of the strategy tended to be extremely diversified and frequently characterized by internal inconsistencies and by a lack of clear alternatives to the containment idea.

The disparate nature of the criticisms leveled against the Truman Doctrine is graphically highlighted by the viewpoints of the individual who was often (and perhaps incorrectly) regarded as its best-known apologist, George F. Kennan. Even in 1947 Kennan viewed the Truman Doctrine as unduly belligerent toward the Soviet Union and generally anti-Communist. Rejecting the view that a worldwide contest for power and influence existed between the United States and the Soviet Union, Kennan believed that it was most unwise for the Truman administration to make or imply a blanket commitment to aid free peoples anywhere on the globe.[147] While Kennan did support the position that U.S. assistance ought to be extended to Greece in 1947 (but not to Turkey), he challenged the more general idea that the United States ought to enunciate a general policy of supporting democracy indiscriminately around the world. To Kennan's mind, the Communist challenge was primarily a political threat, to be countered by reliance chiefly upon political, economic, and other nonmilitary measures. Insofar as he favored containment, he was not proposing "the containment by military means of a military threat, but the political containment of a political threat." In Kennan's view, failure by President Truman and later chief executives to understand this distinction was the most serious defect of the containment strategy. As it came to be implemented in later years, the containment doctrine was also defective in that it ignored the geographical priorities that ought to underlie U.S. foreign policy. Along with Japan, the European continent was the center of the nation's paramount security interests; other regions, like Southeast Asia, were clearly secondary to it.[148]

Among all the critics of containment since 1947, however, one commentator merits special attention. This was perhaps the most widely respected U.S. political analyst, Walter Lippmann; his critique of the containment strategy remains in many respects even today the most cogent and penetrating appraisal available of the Truman Doctrine and its implications.[149]

The most serious defect of the containment policy, to Lippmann's mind, was its failure to identify the threat confronting the West clearly and unambiguously and to formulate a U.S. response addressed directly and effectively to it. Lippmann agreed that a threat to Western security did exist in the late 1940s, nor was he in any doubt about its precise nature. Lippmann was convinced that the force jeopardizing Western security was the threatened extension of Russian military power into the center of

Europe as a result of World War II. Insofar as communism menaced the West, it was only because Marxism might now be imposed upon unwilling societies by the Red Army. In brief, the United States faced a classical threat to the stability of the balance of power in the region of vital geopolitical importance to it — Western Europe. The Cold War was not basically a global contest between communism and capitalism or an apocalyptic struggle between totalitarianism and freedom or democracy. Russian power — and it did not really matter whether it was being extended by czars or commissars — jeopardized the security of the West. Because no other country was in a position to do so, the United States had to take the lead in restoring the balance of power. Ultimately, that could be done only in one effective way: by securing the withdrawal of Soviet military power back behind Russia's own borders. This in turn required an agreement among the former Allies on a German peace treaty and the ensuing neutralization of German power in the heart of Europe. This would permit the United States to reduce its own forces on the Continent, thereby lowering the threshold of possible conflict and preserving regional equilibrium. Without such an agreement, the Cold War would continue, and Moscow would likely be tempted in time to arrive at its own détente with Berlin, on terms posing an even graver threat to the security of Europe and the United States.

Several corollary ideas derived from Lippmann's analysis. The danger to Western security, Lippmann contended, was confined to Europe. It was not a global threat. Accordingly, there was no justification for extending the containment policy to countries like China and other Afro-Asian states, whose internal political struggles did not affect U.S. security interests directly. Nor was the United States obliged after World War II to defend democracy on a global basis (it had been a mistake to justify U.S. intervention in Greece on that basis). Similarly, no universally applicable doctrine or U.S.-sponsored crusade against communism was needed to counter the Soviet threat, nor did such steps contribute positively to eliminating that threat. What Lippmann viewed as perhaps the basic premise of the containment policy — the assumption that there could be no negotiated settlement or détente between the superpowers — was also faulty. Throughout history, rival nations with differing ideological systems had resolved their differences by relying upon diplomacy in an attempt to reach settlements reflecting their mutual interest. Ideological differences aside, agreements so reached were honored for the same reason: because adherence to them was in the national interest of the parties concerned. After World War II the only effective deterrent to aggression was the creation and maintenance of a stable balance of power, and this was possible despite Soviet and U.S. ideological differences.

Meanwhile, Lippmann anticipated innumerable problems for U.S. policy-makers if containment became their animating principle. Containment left the diplomatic initiative with the Kremlin, compelling the United States merely to react to its moves anywhere in the world. Anticipating an endless and inconclusive contest between the United States and the Soviet Union, the containment policy was ill suited to the character, propensities, and genius of the people of the United States. (Americans, as recently as World War II, had been conditioned by their experience to win wars in which they participated. Conversely, their diplomatic heritage and temperament left them ill equipped psychologically for the kind of prolonged and indecisive involvement in the affairs of other countries that containment envisioned.) Lippmann believed that containment would inevitably increase presidential power and lead to a decline in Congress's role in foreign relations. A policy of diplomatic shifts and maneuvers, such as containment anticipated, also demanded more centralized planning and allocation of national resources than U.S. free market economy permitted.

Militarily, for the United States Lippmann was persuaded that containment would prove a "strategic monstrosity." The policy was unsuitable for effective use of the strongest weapons in the U.S. military arsenal, sea and air power. Conversely, the policy permitted Moscow to employ its overwhelming superiority in ground forces to maximum advantage. In effect, containment contemplated a prolonged period of trench warfare between the United States and the Soviet Union, with geography giving most of the advantages to the Kremlin. In contrast to Kennan, Lippmann believed it would be the people of the United States, not Soviet policy-makers, who would become frustrated with the outcome of the containment strategy.

Lippmann also predicted innumerable difficulties in the attempt to apply the policy outside the West. The United States would soon discover that the Afro-Asian world was a "seething stew of civil strife" — an environment much more conducive to success for Communist intrigues than for countermeasures by the United States. In this milieu, the United States would be compelled to depend heavily upon allies of greater or less reliability, forcing the United States into "recruiting, subsidizing and supporting a heterogeneous array of satellites, clients, dependents, and puppets." In pursuit of containment, the United States would attempt to lead "a coalition of disorganized, disunited, feeble or disorderly nations, tribes and factions around the perimeter of the Soviet Union." But the containment strategy overlooked the fact that weak allies are not assets; they are liabilities for the United States. More likely they would have to be defended by the United States, and in the process of doing so, the United States would almost certainly lose the respect and diplomatic support of its natural allies in Europe and the Western Hemisphere. Instead of such a vain endeavor, the United States should concentrate its resources and diplomatic energies on organizing and strengthening the Atlantic Community. The United States' agonizing involvement in the Vietnam War, along with Washington's interventionist moves in Lebanon and Central America during the 1980s, provided ongoing evidence of the cogency of many of Lippmann's doubts about the containment policy. As Lippmann anticipated, Americans are still unclear about the relationship of military force to diplomacy; and as the Reagan administration discovered, Congress and the people remain apprehensive about interventionist policies abroad (even while they also remain opposed to Communist expansionism).

In "The Sources of Soviet Conduct," Kennan had anticipated the mellowing — and perhaps in time the ultimate collapse — of the Soviet Communist system. Lippmann was extremely doubtful about what he characterized as this "optimistic prediction." Kennan's projection was based on scanty evidence. But even if Kennan were right — if the Communist system within Russia did become more benign (as occurred in the period of de-Stalinization under Khrushchev and his successors) — Lippmann was skeptical that this fact would necessarily alter the Russian state's foreign policy objectives and behavior traits. Achieving the ultimate goal that Kennan postulated for containment also exceeded U.S. power and capabilities. Instead of seeking the mellowing of Soviet power, much less the disintegration of Russia's Communist system, the United States ought to concentrate upon a long-range objective that was both crucial for Western security and attainable: securing the evacuation of Russian power from the center of Europe, thereby creating a stable equilibrium of power.

Although his critique of containment ranked as perhaps the most thorough and penetrating ever made of the doctrine, Walter Lippmann was not alone in challenging its underlying assumptions or in calling attention to many of its deleterious consequences. Insofar as the criticisms and reservations expressed about containment lend themselves to being categorized (and in reality, of course, the thought of commentators like Kennan, Lippmann, and a number of other students of U.S. foreign policy qualifies them for inclusion in more than one such category), three more or less cohesive schools of thought about the doctrine can be identified. Let us concentrate initially on the viewpoints of what might be called a group of "moderate critics," most of whom basically accept the Truman administration's analysis of postwar events and whose verdict on the containment policy (as it was originally promulgated) often tends on balance to be favorable.

The common denominator of this viewpoint perhaps is the idea that, with the passage of time, the containment policy came to be distorted, broadened, and misapplied to areas and situations that were not envisioned by the authors of the strategy in 1947. The result was that, in Paul Seabury's words, evaluating the lasting consequences of containment is extremely difficult, in part "because containment's progeny include many illegitimate children."[150] Or, as Ronald Steel has expressed it, President Truman "probably did not envisage the extreme ends toward which this policy would eventually be applied."[151]

Four examples of such distortions and misapplications of the containment idea may be cited to illustrate this general criticism. First, as applied initially to Greece and Turkey, containment was viewed by the Truman administration as involving mainly economic and financial assistance, as the primary instrument enabling these countries to strengthen their positions against Communist encroachments. In both cases — and the idea was highlighted even more prominently in the Marshall Plan for European reconstruction the following year — it was expected that recipients of U.S. aid would engage in a maximum degree of self-help to promote their security and internal stability. Western Europe, for example, furnished 85 percent or more of the total funds available for the region's recovery.

Yet after 1947–48, especially in settings outside the West, this initial component of the containment policy tended increasingly to be ignored, leading to the opposite situation, as when by the late 1960s the United States had assumed almost the entire burden of providing for the defense, economic welfare, and other needs of South Vietnam.[152]

Second, along with George Kennan, this group of observers holds that it was always a mistake to envision containment as requiring primarily a military response to the Communist challenge. Steel notes that President Truman did not advocate unilateral U.S. military intervention in Greece, Turkey, or any other country endangered by communism in the late 1940s.[153] Although the creation of NATO in 1949 might have been justified (and many commentators of this school of thought agree that it was), the later syndrome of military alliances more or less patterned after the NATO model, military aid, and in some cases military interventionism by the United States outside Europe was a distortion and unjustified extension of the containment idea.

Third, the containment idea as enunciated in connection with the Greek problem was initially a limited strategy, designed to deal with a specific crisis or crises. Yet over the course of time it was universalized and applied to areas and situations beyond its original intention and scope. Unfortunately, Kennan observed several years after 1947, Americans have shown a penchant for such universal diplomatic norms; they like general principles in which to wrap their foreign policies, and they desire a uniform way of responding to external problems — possibly because of their preference for a "government of laws" applicable to a multitude of analogous cases.[154] Yet, as a study by Simon Serfaty concludes, when containment was extended to countries outside Europe, the three major ingredients enabling it to operate successfully in that region — effective U.S. foreign aid programs, progress in achieving regional unification, and a functioning Western alliance system — were usually lacking, causing the containment strategy to fail wholly or partially in other areas.[155]

This leads us to a fourth way in which the containment strategy was misapplied and misused in the years after 1947. With containment as its animating principle, Edmund Stillman and William Pfaff have said, U.S. foreign policy often involved little more than a "ritual invocation" of the strategy used in Europe, dealing with "circumstances where it could not and did not work."[156] Originally, as formulated by George Kennan, the containment strategy had anticipated the adroit application of U.S. countermeasures to halt Communist encroachments at a series of constantly shifting points around the globe. Undersecretary of State Acheson had assured Congress that future cases involving the application of the containment principle would be decided on their merits. As time passed such qualifications tended to be forgotten. For Americans, commitment to containment produced a kind of seige mentality or Maginot Line complex in dealing with the Communist world. For example, successive administrations in Washington, Arnold S. Kaufman asserts, "consistently underestimated the potentialities of Communist systems for change and diversification."[157] Containment led the United States to engage in a kind of static warfare against communism, with the approach used during the late 1940s becoming increasingly obsolete and irrelevant to contemporary conditions. The result, in the view of Stillman and Pfaff, was a widening "discrepancy between the real Soviet threat and the measures we undertook to contain it" — a gap that tended to widen with the passage of time.[158]

A second rather distinct school of critics with regard to the containment policy consists of certain right-wing individuals and groups. These critics indicted containment because, in general terms, it was a negative stance in dealing with the Soviet Union, leaving the diplomatic initiative with Moscow and committing the United States to an indefinite and wasteful global contest in which there was no hope of ultimate victory. Right-wing critics of containment often repeated the well-known dictum of General Douglas MacArthur, "In war there is no substitute for victory." According to this principle, the dominant purpose of U.S. diplomacy toward the Soviet Union ought to be to win the Cold War. (What winning the Cold War meant precisely was often left unclarified by critics of containment. Did it imply, for example, that the United States should seek the total elimination of the Soviet Communist system, perhaps as the result of a nuclear conflagration between the superpowers?) A related idea was that, instead of containment, the United States ought actively to seek the liberation of Eastern Europe and other zones under Communist domination.[159] In the right-wing assessment, containment ought to be abandoned in favor of a positive and winning strategy designed to remove the Communist danger once and for all as a threat to international peace and security.[160]

In the late 1940s and afterward, an increasingly vocal group of left-wing and revisionist commentators leveled a different set of indictments against the containment policy. In general terms, their position was that containment had produced U.S. overinvolvement in the affairs of other countries and had led the United States to adopt indiscriminate interventionism as the guiding impulse of its foreign policy. Ironically, promulgated to counter Soviet interventionism, containment had produced U.S. interventionism on a global scale. The titles of several studies advancing this thesis — Gar Alperowitz's *Atomic Diplomacy,* David Horowitz's *The Free World Colossus,* Claude Julien's *America's Empire,* James L. Payne's *The American Threat,* Ronald Steel's *Pax Americana,* John C. Donovan's *The Cold Warriors* — suggest the overall orientation of these criticisms.

Shortly after President Truman's historic speech to Congress, a widely circulated indictment of containment was delivered by his Secretary of Commerce, Henry A. Wallace. Wallace totally disagreed with the administration's decision to adopt a tough stance toward Soviet Russia. By embracing containment as its foreign policy credo, the United States was in effect allowing itself to be manipulated to serve the interests of British imperialism. Instead, he argued, national policy ought to be directed at resolving outstanding differences with the Soviet Union. Wallace predicted that the containment policy would provoke Moscow, thereby further inflaming Soviet-U.S. tensions and increasing the risks of World War III.[161]

As the years passed, other commentators echoed and amplified Wallace's criticisms of containment. The containment strategy, they said, was based upon an erroneous evaluation of the origins and nature of the Cold War. Growing tensions between the superpowers characterized the postwar political environment primarily because of U.S. (along with British) behavior and policy failures. Soviet intransigence and hostility were viewed as primarily a reaction against the interventionist and hegemonial tendencies of policy-makers in Washington. Thus, in Frederick L. Schuman's opinion, the Cold War began because of U.S. efforts to democratize Eastern Europe and to rob the Soviet Union of the fruits of victory in World War II. After adopting containment as its policy, the United States became committed to a campaign to "suppress Communism all over the world and to destroy the Soviet regime in the U.S.S.R. itself."[162] Having rejected the idea of a Soviet sphere of influence in Eastern Europe, Isaac Deutscher has argued, the United States adopted the containment policy, whose real goal was to achieve the rollback of Soviet power from this zone.[163]

To the minds of several commentators in this group, economic considerations served as the motive force leading the United States to espouse containment. The real goal of policy-makers in Washington was to restore a capitalist system in Europe and to maintain the prewar social structure in that region. In brief, they wanted to reduce Eastern Europe to an economic colony of the West.[164] But the impulse to U.S. economic expansionism was not limited merely to Eastern Europe. For the Truman administration, the Greek crisis was, in Stephen Ambrose's words, the opportunity that U.S. policy-makers had long sought, providing justification for abandoning isolationism and adopting an "active foreign policy," which would assure U.S. economic dominance regionally and globally. Officials of the Truman administration supported containment enthusiastically, thereby permitting the United States to take its place "with other imperialist powers" throughout history.[165] The Truman Doctrine's emphasis upon promoting freedom and democracy, Anatol

Rapoport has observed, in reality masked a desire for worldwide U.S. economic dominance and expansionism on the part of U.S. business interests. In effect, adoption of containment meant that the United States equated its national interest with "preserving and extending global capitalism."[166] Lloyd C. Gardner is similarly persuaded that the real objective of containment was to displace traditional British power in the Mediterranean and the Middle East, thereby giving the United States a dominant position in the Middle East oil industry.[167] Another study contends that in reality the Free World, which the Truman Doctrine sought to defend, was equivalent to "the world economic area in which the American businessman enjoys greatest freedom of commercial maneuver. . . . The Free World itself is the American Empire."[168]

A variation on this theme is the charge that the Truman administration's policy of toughness toward the Soviet Union reflected the larger U.S. purpose of imposing its own system of order on the world. U.S. leaders became convinced, Rapoport has stated, that "the world *needed* America, and America would see to it that the world was properly organized, in accordance with American precepts."[169] After 1947 the United States engaged in a massive anti-Communist crusade. Steel has said that the United States created its own "counter-empire of anti-Communism."[170] D. F. Fleming contends that President Truman, strongly influenced by U.S. military leaders, desired to promulgate a militantly anti-Communist doctrine. Once he did so early in 1947, the United States became "the world's anti-Communist, anti-Russian policeman."[171]

Another serious defect of the containment doctrine was its underlying apocalyptic or Manichean view of postwar global politics. A crucial miscalculation, a number of commentators believe, was its basic presupposition that the United States and the Soviet Union were engaged in a kind of political Battle of Armageddon — an epochal and worldwide struggle between the forces of Good and those of Evil, the outcome of which would determine the future of civilization itself. Conceiving of the Cold War within such a Manichean perspective, Americans found it nearly impossible to compromise with the adversary (the police, in the popular parlance, do not make compromises with bank robbers and rapists). After 1947 U.S. policy-makers lost the ability to make fine, but often crucial, distinctions among the actions of Communist states, to differentiate between those that actually posed a threat to regional and global security and those that did not. Once containment became national policy, it became extremely difficult for Americans to accept Tillema's judgment: "It is doubtful that every new Communist government, no matter what part of the world it is in, poses a significant long-term threat to the United States."[172] Gaddis has made substantially the same point:

> By presenting aid to Greece and Turkey in terms of an ideological conflict between two ways of life, Washington officials encouraged a simplistic view of the Cold War which was, in time, to imprison American diplomacy in an ideological straitjacket almost as confining as that which restricted Soviet foreign policy.

Among the other adverse consequences of this fact, because of their Manichean outlook toward the world, U.S. officials found it extraordinarily difficult to respond to conciliatory gestures by the Kremlin that might have ended (or at least ameliorated) the Cold War.[173]

When Congress debated the Greek-Turkish Aid Program, a number of liberal and left-wing critics denounced it on the ground that, by intervening in support of the Greek government, the United States would thereafter be committed to bailing out reactionary and oppressive regimes throughout the world. These early objections to containment foreshadowed what became in time a veritable crescendo of criticism expressed by liberal and left-wing commentators.[174]

According to this school of thought, after adopting the containment policy the United States consistently opposed revolutionary changes and radical (particularly left-wing) movements globally. President Truman and his successors in the White House operated on the basis of two erroneous assumptions about revolutionary movements in the modern period: that all revolutionary efforts seeking to transform primitive and backward societies were Communist- (that is, Soviet-) directed and that revolutionary changes in Greece and a succession of other countries conflicted with the United States' own vital diplomatic interests and must, therefore, be opposed. The overriding lesson of U.S. interventionism in Greece, one study concludes, was "the willingness of the United States to act severely and decisively to make certain that an independent Left willing to act on its own initiative would not survive to challenge larger American objectives in the region."[175]

For the United States, Todd Gitlin has stated, "Greece was the Vietnam of the 1940s." The real but undeclared purpose of the Truman Doctrine was to "contain . . . domestic revolution" and to thwart the emergence of genuine democracy, in Greece and elsewhere. The real losers in this encounter were the Greeks and Vietnamese people, not communism or the Soviet Union."[176] Containment, David Horowitz is certain, expressed Washington's open-ended commitment to suppress "*social revolution*" wherever it occurred and to assume the role of "guardian of the global *status quo.*"[177] The all-inclusive language of the Truman Doctrine, Fleming contends, in effect "forbade every kind of revolution, democratic or otherwise," since it would be difficult to discover any revolution that was not carried out by (in the doctrine's language) an armed minority. One of the more tragic aspects of this development was that the Truman Doctrine prohibited other countries from following the United States' own revolutionary example.[178] Owing to the antirevolutionary cast of the containment policy, Chester Bowles has declared, the policy proved much less successful in the Afro-Asian world than in Europe. In the former areas, U.S. policy-makers "largely ignored the strength of the new revolutionary pressures against the *status quo.*" Because containment identified the United States with the existing order, the Communists were able to seize the initiative and to emerge as the agents of change.[179]

Finally, the Truman Doctrine has been severely criticized by spokesmen for this school of thought because, in Horowitz's words, one of its major premises — the idea of a world divided into two hostile blocs — became a self-fulfilling prophecy after the United States adopted the containment strategy.[180] From the beginning, George Lukacs wrote, the containment policy was flawed by a monumental contradiction. Stemming from the Anglo-U.S. determination to prevent the future division of Europe and to promote the region's reunification and reconstruction, containment in fact produced the very result it had sought to avert: Europe's permanent partition into rival camps, as symbolized by the continued division of Germany. Even more crucially, the result of the containment policy was to divide the world into hostile blocs.[181] In brief, the containment policy itself either caused, or seriously escalated, the Cold War, gravely impairing the prospects for peace and leading after 1947 to a spiraling arms race between two hostile power blocs.[182]

The story (possibly apocryphal) is told that, during the Civil War, President Abraham Lincoln assigned a general to administer occupied territory in which both pro-Union and pro-Confederate sentiments were strong. In giving him this challenging responsibility, Lincoln advised the officer that the time for him to be concerned was when his policies were no longer criticized by both factions. By this criterion, in view of the great diversity of reactions and criticisms that containment has elicited since 1947, officials of the Truman and later administrations might be justified in concluding that the containment policy was an outstanding success.

NOTES

1. Lord Palmerston's views are quoted in James Chace, *A World Elsewhere: The New American Foreign Policy* (New York: Scribner's, 1973), p. 86.

2. De Gaulle's views are quoted in Charles E. Bohlen, *The Transformation of American Foreign Policy* (New York: Norton, 1969), p. 97.

3. See Prime Minister Nehru's speech to the Constituent Assembly on December 4, 1947, as cited in *Independence and After* (New Delhi: Government of India, Ministry of Information and Broadcasting, 1949), pp. 204–5.

4. See Hans J. Morgenthau, "The Mainspring of American Foreign Policy," *American Political Science Review* 44 (December 1950):833–54. For a more detailed exposition of his thesis, see *In Defense of the National Interest* (New York: Alfred A. Knopf, 1951). An informative overall view of the realistic approach to international politics is Ira S. Cohen, *Realpolitik: Theory and Practice* (Belmont, Calif.: Dickenson, 1975). A convenient summary of the ideas of a leading exponent of the *Realpolitik* school is Roger A. Leonard, ed., *Clausewitz on War* (New York: Capricorn Books, 1967). Another helpful analysis, sometimes highly critical of the realistic perspective, is Inis L. Claude, Jr., *Power and International Relations* (New York: Random House, 1962).

5. George F. Kennan, *Memoirs: 1925–1950* (New York: Bantam Books, 1969), p. 262. Here Kennan is quoting from one of his earlier papers dealing with the goals of Soviet foreign policy.

6. See Hans J. Morgenthau, *A New Foreign Policy for the United States* (New York: Praeger, 1969), pp. 241–44.

7. Hughes's views are quoted in Charles A. Beard, *The Idea of National Interest* (New York: Macmillan, 1934), p. 1; for Beard's views, see pp. 4, 21, 548.

8. George F. Kennan, *American Diplomacy: 1900–1950* (New York: New American Library, 1951), p. 94.

9. For commentary on this address, see Arthur M. Schlesinger, Jr., *A Thousand Days: John F. Kennedy in the White House* (Boston: Houghton Mifflin, 1965), pp. 900–2.

10. See the White House document, "U.S. Foreign Policy for the 1970s — Building for Peace: A Report to the Congress by Richard Nixon" (Washington, D.C., February 25, 1971), p. 13.

11. See Walter Lippmann, "The Rivalry of Nations," *Atlantic Monthly* 181 (February 1948): 19–20; and Stanley Hoffmann, *Gulliver's Troubles, or the Setting of American Foreign Policy* (New York: McGraw-Hill, 1968), p. 10.

12. See, for example, Robert O. Matthews et al., eds., *International Conflict and Conflict Management: Readings in World Politics* (Englewood Cliffs, N.J.: Prentice-Hall, 1984); Robert Johansen, *The National Interest and the Human Interest: An Analysis of U.S. Foreign Policy* (Princeton, N.J.: Princeton University Press, 1980); Robert W. Tucker, *The Purposes of American Power: An Essay on National Security*

(New York: Praeger, 1981); and see several of the essays in Don L. Mansfield and Gary J. Buckley, eds., *Conflict in American Foreign Policy: The Issues Debated* (Englewood Cliffs, N.J.: Prentice-Hall, 1985).

13.   Bohlen, *The Transformation of American Foreign Policy*, p. 97.

14.   Walter Lippmann, *U.S. Foreign Policy: Shield of the Republic* (Boston: Little, Brown, 1943), p. 167.

15.   See Henry A. Kissinger, *American Foreign Policy: Three Essays* (New York: Norton, 1969), p. 93.

16.   Ibid.

17.   Pitt's views are quoted in Lincoln P. Bloomfield, *The United Nations and U.S. Foreign Policy*, rev. ed. (Boston: Little, Brown, 1967), p. 27; and Leslie Lipson, "Where Do Our Vital Interests Lie?" in Paul Seabury and Aaron Wildavsky, eds., *U.S. Foreign Policy: Perspectives and Proposals for the 1970's* (New York: McGraw-Hill, 1969), p. 38.

18.   For diverse interpretations of U.S. national security, with emphasis upon the post-Vietnam War era, see *U.S. Defense Policy: Weapons, Strategy, and Commitments*, 2d ed. (Washington, D.C.: Congressional Quarterly, 1980) and later volumes in this series; James Fallows, *National Defense* (New York: Random House, 1981); (n. a.), *Defending America* (New York: Basic Books, 1977); Christopher Coker, *U.S. Military Power in the 1980s* (New York: Macmillan, 1983); William H. Becker, *Economics and World Power: An Assessment of American Diplomacy since 1789* (New York: Columbia University Press, 1984); Harold Brown, *Thinking about National Security* (Boulder, Colo.: Westview Press, 1983); Daniel J. Kaufman et al., *U.S. National Security: A Framework for Analysis* (Lexington, Mass.: D. C. Heath, 1985); Robert W. Poole, Jr., ed., *Defending a Free Society* (Lexington, Mass.: D. C. Heath, 1984); and Christoph Bertram, ed., *America's Security in the 1980s* (New York: St. Martin's Press, 1983).

19.   See George W. Ball, *The Discipline of Power: Essentials of a Modern World Structure* (Boston: Little, Brown, 1968); and the same author's *Diplomacy for a Crowded World: An American Foreign Policy* (Boston: Little, Brown, 1976).

20.   The necessity for allies, for example, is emphasized strongly in the Nixon Doctrine, President Richard M. Nixon's comprehensive reformulation of U.S. foreign policy in the post-Vietnam War period. More extended discussion of the doctrine is available in Cecil V. Crabb, Jr., *The Doctrines of American Foreign Policy: Their Meaning, Role, and Future* (Baton Rouge: Louisiana State University Press, 1982), pp. 278–325.

21.   See the discussion of the Reagan administration's diplomacy in Strobe Talbott, *The Russians and Reagan* (New York: Random House, 1984); in Rowland Evans and Robert Novak, *The Reagan Revolution* (New York: E. P. Dutton, 1981); and in Cecil V. Crabb, Jr., "'Standing Tall' as a Foreign Policy," in Ellis Sandiz and Cecil V. Crabb, Jr., eds., *Election '84: Landslide without a Mandate?* (New York: New American Library, 1985), pp. 179–204.

22.   Charles B. Marshall, "The National Interest," in Robert A. Goldwin and Harry M. Clor, eds., *Readings in American Foreign Policy*, 2d ed. (New York: Oxford University Press, 1971) p. 685.

23.   Philip W. Quigg, *America the Dutiful: An Assessment of U.S. Foreign Policy* (New York: Simon and Schuster, 1971), pp. 112, 114.

24.   Thomas L. Hughes, "On the Cause of Our Discontents," *Foreign Affairs* 47 (July 1969):666.

25.   Bohlen, *The Transformation of American Foreign Policy*, p. 96.

26.   Paul Seabury, *Power, Freedom, and Diplomacy* (New York: Random House, 1963), pp. 86–87.

27.   Fulbright, *The Crippled Giant*, p. 153.

28.   Quigg, *America the Dutiful*, p. 107.

29.   The lack of clear consensus in U.S. public opinion concerning the nation's diplomatic role after the Vietnam War is discussed more fully in Samuel P. Huntington, *American Politics: The Promise of Disharmony* (Cambridge, Mass.: Harvard University Press, 1981); George H. Quester, *American Foreign Policy: The Lost Consensus* (New York: Praeger, 1982); Schuyler Foster, *Activism Replaces Isolationism: U.S. Public Attitudes, 1940–1975* (Washington, D.C.: Foxhall Press, 1983), pp. 329–93; James Chace, "Is Foreign Policy Consensus Possible?" *Foreign Affairs* 57 (Fall 1978):1–17; and David W. Moore, "The Public Is Uncertain," *Foreign Policy* 35 (Summer 1979):68–74.

30.   A comprehensive analysis of the U.S. foreign policy process is Cecil V. Crabb, Jr., *American Foreign Policy in the Nuclear Age,* 4th ed. (New York: Harper and Row, 1983). Other useful studies are Lincoln P. Bloomfield, *The Foreign Policy Process: A Modern Primer* (Englewood Cliffs, N.J.: Prentice-Hall, 1982); I. M. Destler, *Presidents, Bureaucrats, and Foreign Policy: The Politics of Organizational Reform* (Princeton, N.J.: Princeton University Press, 1972); and Charles W. Kegley, Jr. and Eugene R. Wittkopf, *American Foreign Policy: Pattern and Process* (New York: St. Martin's Press, 1979).

31.   See, for example, Cecil V. Crabb, Jr. and Pat Holt, *Invitation to Struggle: Congress, the President, and Foreign Policy*, 2d ed. (Washington, D.C.: Congressional Quarterly Press, 1984); Philip Brenner, *The Limits and Possibilities of Congress* (New York: St. Martin's Press, 1983); Thomas Franck and Edward Weisband, *Foreign Policy by Congress* (New York: Oxford University Press, 1979); and John Spanier and Joseph Nogee, eds., *Congress, The Presidency, and American Foreign Policy* (New York: Pergamon Press, 1981).

32.   Detailed information on the nature and extent of lobbying activity in the contemporary period is available in *The Washington Lobby*, 4th ed. (Washington, D.C.: Congressional Quarterly, 1982) and in future volumes in this series; Norman J. Ornstein and Shirley Elder, *Interest Groups, Lobbying, and Policy-Making* (Washington, D.C.: Congressional Quarterly Press, 1978); Abdul A. Said, ed., *Ethnicity and U.S. Foreign Policy* (New York: Praeger, 1978); Jeffrey M. Berry, *Lobbying for the People: The Political Behavior of Public Interest Groups* (Princeton, N.J.: Princeton University Press, 1977); and Carol S. Greenwald, *Power, Lobbying, and Public Policy* (New York: Praeger, 1977).

33.   The problem of intraexecutive disunity in foreign affairs, and an assessment of mechanisms and techniques designed to solve the problem, is available in Cecil V. Crabb, Jr. and Kevin V. Mulcahy, *The President and the Administration of Foreign Policy: The Problem of "One Secretary of State at a Time"* (Baton Rouge: Louisiana State University Press, 1986). See also Destler, *President, Bureaucrats, and Foreign Policy.*

34.   Thomas Hobbes, *Leviathan* (London: E. P. Dutton, 1928), p. 49.

35. See Herman Miller, "Power, Political," *Encyclopaedia of the Social Sciences* 12 (New York: Macmillan, 1933):301.

36. Ernest Lefever, *Ethics and United States Foreign Policy* (New York: Meridian Books, 1959), pp. 5, 8.

37. Nicholas J. Spykman, *America's Strategy in World Politics* (New York: Harcourt, Brace, 1942), p. 12.

38. For an elaboration of this view, see Cyril Roseman, Charles Mayo, and F. B. Collinge, *Dimensions of Political Analysis: An Introduction to the Contemporary Study of Politics* (Englewood Cliffs, N.J.: Prentice-Hall, 1966), pp. 196–97.

39. Alan James, "Power Politics," *Political Studies* 12 (October 1964):315.

40. Kenneth N. Waltz, "International Structure, National Force, and the Balance of World Power," in Rosenau, *International Politics and Foreign Policy*, p. 305.

41. Stephen L. Wasby, *Political Science: The Discipline and Its Dimensions — An Introduction* (New York: Scribner's, 1970), p. 531.

42. Maurice A. Ash, "An Analysis of Power, with Special Reference to International Politics," *World Politics* 3 (January 1951):220.

43. Herz's views are quoted in Waltz, "International Structure, National Force, and the Balance of World Power," p. 307.

44. Spykman, *America's Strategy in World Politics*, p. 460.

45. This is the contention, for example, of Roger D. Masters, *The Nation is Burdened: American Foreign Policy in a Changing World* (New York: Alfred A. Knopf, 1967), esp. pp. 84–123.

46. Morgenthau, *A New Foreign Policy for the United States*, p. 242.

47. Sidney B. Fay, "Balance of Power," *Encyclopaedia of the Social Sciences* 2 (New York: Macmillan, 1933):395.

48. Arnold Zurcher, "Balance of Power," *Dictionary of American Politics* (New York: Barnes and Noble, 1944), p. 25.

49. For more detailed analysis of the preconditions for successful operation of the classical balance of power system, see Edward Vose Gulick, *Europe's Classical Balance of Power* (New York: Norton, 1967), esp. pp. 3–95.

50. Spykman, *America's Strategy in World Politics*, p. 21.

51. Ernst B. Haas, "The Balance of Power: Prescription, Concept, or Propaganda?" *World Politics* 5 (July 1953):447–58.

52. A number of different terms and concepts describing the nature of the contemporary international system is analyzed more fully in Joseph L. Nogee, "Polarity: An Ambiguous Concept," *Orbis* 18 (Winter 1975):1193–224. See also Richard Rosecrance, "Bipolarity, Multipolarity, and the Future," *Journal of Conflict Resolution* 10 (September 1966): 314–27; and Keith R. Legg and James F. Morrison, *Politics and the International System* (New York: Harper and Row, 1971).

53. Chace, *A World Elsewhere*, p. 28.

54. Adlai E. Stevenson, *Call to Greatness* (New York: Harper and Row, 1954), pp. 52–53.

55. Canning's views are quoted in Chace, *A World Elsewhere*, pp. 29–30.

56. Kissinger, *American Foreign Policy*, pp. 60–61.

57. Badeau, *The American Approach to the Arab World*, p. 19.

58. The impact of the United States' pragmatic tradition upon its diplomatic behavior is analyzed more fully in Cecil V. Crabb, Jr., *The American Approach to*

Foreign Policy: A Pragmatic Perspective (Lanham, Md.: University Press of America, 1985); and in the same author's *A Pragmatic World-View: American Diplomacy and the Pragmatic Tradition* (forthcoming).

59.   Averell Harriman, *Peace with Russia?* (New York: Simon and Schuster, 1959), p. 167.

60.   Inis L. Claude, Jr., *Power and International Relations* (New York: Random House, 1962), pp. 20–25, 42–93.

61.   See the views of L. C. B. Seaman, as quoted in Chace, *A World Elsewhere*, p. 34; and Fay, "Balance of Power," p. 398.

62.   Anatol Rapoport, *The Big Two: Soviet-American Perceptions of Foreign Policy* (New York: Bobbs-Merrill, 1971), p. 153.

63.   Fulbright, *The Crippled Giant*, p. 92.

64.   See Morton A. Kaplan, "Balance of Power, Bipolarity, and Other Models of the International System," *American Political Science Review* 51 (September 1957):687–89.

65.   Stanley Hoffmann, "Will the Balance Balance at Home?" in Robert W. Tucker and William Watts, eds., *Beyond Containment: U.S. Foreign Policy in Transition* (Washington, D.C.: Potomac Associates, 1973), p. 25.

66.   Needler, "Understanding Foreign Policy," p. 330.

67.   Kennan, *Memoirs*, p. 229; and Fay, "Balance of Power," p. 397.

68.   See, for example, the discussion of the Soviet concept of *mir* or "peace," in Paul Nitze, "Living with the Soviets," *Foreign Affairs* 63 (Winter 1984/85):360–75.

69.   Ernst B. Haas, "The Balance of Power as a Guide to Policy-Making," *Journal of Politics* 15 (August 1953): 373–75.

70.   Rostow, "Defining the National Interest," p. 23.

71.   Lefever, *Ethics and U.S. Foreign Policy*, p. 21.

72.   Fulbright, *The Crippled Giant*, pp. 275–76.

73.   Kissinger, *American Foreign Policy*, pp. 94–96.

74.   Hoffmann, "Will the Balance Balance at Home?" pp. 120–21.

75.   Our analysis of the containment policy in the context of *Realpolitik* principles should not be interpreted to mean that the policy was not influenced by alternative forces and perspectives. Unquestionably, for example, the architects of containment were aware of, and motivated by, fundamental ideological differences between the U.S. democratic and Soviet Communist systems. Officials of the Truman administration also were aware of certain economic and financial issues at stake in Soviet-U.S. rivalry. As always, domestic political factors played some part in the Truman administration's increasingly tough position toward the Soviet Union. The personalities of the president and his key advisers, especially their aversion to communism, also entered into the decision to adopt the containment policy. For diverse interpretations of the rationale and implications of the containment strategy, see John L. Gaddis, *Strategies of Containment* (New York: Oxford University Press, 1982); Aaron Wildavsky, *Beyond Containment: Alternative American Policies toward the Soviet Union* (San Francisco: Institute for Contemporary Studies, 1983); Richard A. Melanson, *Writing History and Making Policy: The Cold War, Vietnam, and Revisionism* (Lanham, Md.: University Press of America, 1983); Seyom Brown, *The Faces of Power: Constancy and Change in United States Foreign Policy from Truman to Reagan* (New York: Columbia University Press, 1983); Adam B. Ulam, *The*

Rivals: America and Russia since World War II (New York: Viking Press, 1971); Richard J. Barnet, *The Giants: Russia and America* (New York: Simon and Schuster, 1977); Anatol Rapoport, *The Big Two: Soviet-American Perceptions of Foreign Policy* (Indianapolis, Ind.: Bobbs-Merrill, 1971); and Thomas B. Larson, *Soviet-American Rivalry* (New York: W. W. Norton, 1978).

76. George F. Kennan, "The Sources of Soviet Conduct," *Foreign Affairs* 25 (July 1947):556–83. The celebrated "X" article is also included as an appendix in Kennan's *American Diplomacy: 1900–1950* (New York: New American Library, 1951) and in later editions of this work.

77. For the formulation and rationale of the Truman Doctrine, see Harry S. Truman, *Memoirs: Years of Trial and Hope, 1946–1952* (Garden City, N.Y.: Doubleday, 1956), pp. 96–109; Dean Acheson, *Present at the Creation: My Years in the State Department* (New York; W. W. Norton, 1969), pp. 220–26; Susan M. Hartmann, *Truman and the 80th Congress* (Columbia: University of Missouri Press, 1971); and Herbert Druks, *Harry S. Truman and the Russians: 1945–1953* (New York: Robert Speller, 1966).

78. More extended discussion of the manner in which the Truman Doctrine was interpreted and applied after 1947 may be found in Brown, *Constancy and Change,* and in Crabb, *The Doctrines of American Foreign Policy.*

79. For a detailed discussion of the late wartime and early postwar political situation in Greece, see Hugh Seton-Watson, *The East European Revolution* (New York: Praeger, 1956), pp. 318–38.

80. Joseph M. Jones, *The Fifteen Weeks* (New York: Viking Press, 1955), p. 148. The author was intimately involved in the formulation of the Truman Doctrine; his account is perhaps the most complete available of events leading to the formulation of the containment strategy.

81. See Harry S. Truman, *Memoirs,* 1:108–9; and Jones, *The Fifteen Weeks,* pp. 5-6, 219.

82. See Harry Schwartz, *The Red Phoenix: Russia since World War II* (New York: Praeger, 1961), p. 231; Philip E. Mosely, ed., *The Soviet Union: 1922–1962* (New York: Praeger, 1963), p. 186; his *The Kremlin and World Politics* (New York: Vintage Books, 1960), pp. 230–31; Jan Librach, *The Rise of the Soviet Empire: A Study of Soviet Foreign Policy* (New York: Praeger, 1964), pp. 186–87; Michael H. Armacost, *The Foreign Relations of the United States* (Belmont, Calif.: Dickenson, 1969), p. 59; Adam B. Ulam, *The Rivals: America and Russia since World War II* (New York: Viking Press, 1971), p. 278; and John W. Spanier, *American Foreign Policy since World War II,* 4th ed. (New York: Praeger, 1971), pp. 3, 21–22, 28.

83. Robert C. Tucker, "Stalinism and World Conflict," in Arthur E. Adams, ed., *Readings in Soviet Foreign Policy: Theory and Practice* (Boston: D. C. Heath, 1961), p. 287.

84. See William E. Griffith, *Cold War and Coexistence: Russia, China, and the United States* (Englewood Cliffs, N.J.: Prentice-Hall, 1971), pp. 35–36.

85. See the article entitled, "Russia — Seven Years Later" (September 1944), included as an Appendix in George F. Kennan, *Memoirs: 1925–1950,* p. 547; and his article "Russia's International Position at the Close of the War with Germany" (May 1945), included as an Appendix in ibid., p. 567.

86. Karl Marx's views are quoted in Philip W. Quigg, *America the Dutiful,* p. 58.

87. James F. Byrnes, *Speaking Frankly* (New York: Harper and Row, 1947), pp. 277–97.

88. For a detailed evaluation of the U.S. tendency after World War II to equate communism with Hitlerism, see Les K. Adler and Thomas G. Paterson, "'Red Fascism' and the Development of the Cold War," in Gary R. Hess, ed., *America and Russia: From Cold War Confrontation to Coexistence* (New York: Thomas Y. Crowell, 1973), pp. 62–74.

89. Alvin Z. Rubinstein, ed., *The Foreign Policy of the Soviet Union* (New York: Random House, 1960), p. 204.

90. See ibid., pp. 202–3; and Griffith, *The Cold War and Coexistence,* pp. 35–36.

91. John L. Gaddis, *The United States and the Origins of the Cold War: 1941–1947* (New York: Columbia University Press, 1972), pp. 353–55.

92. See Michael Harrington, "American Power in the Twentieth Century," in Irving Howe, ed., *A Dissenter's Guide to Foreign Policy* (Garden City, N.Y.: Doubleday, 1968), p. 34.

93. Herz, *Beginnings of the Cold War,* p. 192; Librach, *The Rise of the Soviet Empire,* pp. 186–87; and see the views of Hans J. Morgenthau, in Lloyd C. Gardner, Arthur Schlesinger, Jr., and Hans J. Morgenthau, *The Origins of the Cold War* (Waltham, Mass.: Ginn, 1970), pp. 96–97.

94. For the evolution in George Kennan's thought concerning the Soviet challenge and the proper U.S. response to it, see his *Memoirs: 1925–1950*; and the second volume of his *Memoirs: 1950–1963* (New York: Pantheon Books, 1972); and his *The Nuclear Delusion: Soviet-American Relations in the Atomic Age* (New York: Pantheon Books, 1982). See also Barton D. Gellman, *Contending with Kennan: Toward a Philosophy of American Power* (New York: Praeger, 1984).

95. See Paul Seabury, *The Rise and Decline of the Cold War* (New York: Basic Books, 1967), p. 34; and Spanier, *American Foreign Policy since World War II,* p. 31.

96. Jones, *The Fifteen Weeks,* p. 77.

97. Dean Acheson, *Present at the Creation,* p. 219.

98. Arthur H. Vandenberg, Jr., ed., *The Private Papers of Senator Vandenberg* (Boston: Houghton Mifflin, 1952), pp. 341–42.

99. Truman, *Memoirs,* 2:101–2.

100. See the surveys of U.S. opinion on the Soviet Union and related issues in Peter G. Filene, ed., *Americans' View of Soviet Russia* (Homewood, Ill.: Dorsey Press, 1968), p. 166; and Leonard S. Cottrell, Jr. and Sylvia Eberhart, *American Opinion on World Affairs* (Princeton, N.J.: Princeton University Press, 1948), pp. 48 ff.

101. Gaddis, *The United States and the Origins of the Cold War,* pp. 360–61; and Armacost, *The Foreign Relations of the United States,* p. 57.

102. Paul Seabury's views are quoted in Quigg, *America the Dutiful,* pp. 47–48.

103. This is one of the prominent themes of Kennan's analysis entitled "The United States and Russia," written in 1946, excerpts from which are included in his *Memoirs,* pp. 599–604.

104. Truman, *Memoirs*, 2:101; and Vandenberg, *The Private Papers of Senator Vandenberg*, pp. 342–43.

105. The reader should be aware that, as the years passed, George F. Kennan gave a different interpretation of what his containment strategy meant from its evident meaning in 1947. In his later view, by counterforce Kennan intended that the United States would engage in "political containment" of communism vis-à-vis reliance upon military interventionism. See Kennan's *Memoirs: 1925–1950*; the second volume of his *Memoirs: 1950–1963*; and the commentary on his thought by Barton Gellman, *Contending with Kennan.*

106. Former Secretary of Defense James Forrestal urged the creation of the American Mediterranean Task Force because (in Millis's words) he sought to "buttress Turkish resistance to the seeping advance of Soviet power." See Walter Millis, ed., *The Forrestal Diaries* (New York: Viking Press, 1951), p. 141.

107. Jones, *The Fifteen Weeks*, p. 77.

108. See Walter LaFeber, *America, Russia, and the Cold War, 1945–1966* (New York: Random House, 1968), pp. 42–46; and Ulam, *The Rivals*, pp. 126–33.

109. See Public Law 75, 80th Congress, 1st Session, 1947; and Vandenberg, *The Private Papers of Senator Vandenberg*, pp. 340–51.

110. Again, the reader is referred to Kennan, "The Sources of Soviet Conduct," passim.

111. Truman, *Memoirs*, p. 104.

112. LaFeber, *America, Russia, and the Cold War*, p. 47.

113. Acheson, *Present at the Creation*, p. 226.

114. Acheson's views are quoted in Jones, *The Fifteen Weeks*, pp. 190–93.

115. See President Truman's address to Congress on March 12, 1947, Appendix 3; and Jones, *The Fifteen Weeks*, p. 187.

116. The reader is referred once more to Kennan's views in "The Sources of Soviet Conduct," pp. 119–20.

117. Paul Y. Hammond, *The Cold War Years: American Foreign Policy since 1945* (New York: Harcourt, Brace, and World, 1969), p. 10.

118. Eugene V. Rostow, *Law, Power, and the Pursuit of Peace* (New York: Harper and Row, 1968), p. 42.

119. Ernest Lefever, *Ethics and United States Foreign Policy* (New York: Meridian Books, 1957), p. 42.

120. Hammond, *The Cold War Years*, p. 10.

121. See, for example, the findings of the Kissinger Commission, on Soviet diplomatic objectives in Central America, in *The Report of the President's National Bipartisan Commission on Central America* (New York: Macmillan, 1984); and the analysis of Soviet versus U.S. interests in Central America and other regions in George P. Shultz, "Shaping American Foreign Policy: New Realities and New Ways of Thinking." *Foreign Affairs* 63 (Spring 1985):705–22.

122. John L. Gaddis, "A Defense of American Policy," in Gary R. Hess, ed., *America and Russia: From Cold War Confrontation to Coexistence* (New York: Thomas Y. Crowell, 1973), p. 24.

123. Armacost, *The Foreign Relations of the United States*, pp. 58–60.

124. Frederick. C. Barghoorn, "Needed: A Counter to Moscow's New Line," in Robert A. Divine, ed., *American Foreign Policy since 1945* (Chicago: Quadrangle

Books, 1969), pp. 88–89.

125. Rostow, *Law, Power, and the Pursuit of Peace*, pp. 43–44.

126. See Stimson, "The Challenge to Americans," in Mosely, *The Soviet Union*, p. 191.

127. Ulam, *The Rivals*, p. 125.

128. Barbara Ward, "The New Year: The Decisive Year for Us," in Divine, *American Foreign Policy since 1945*, p. 51.

129. See the views of Zbigniew Brzezinski as quoted by Quigg in *America the Dutiful*, p. 49. For other commentators who believe that the Truman Doctrine represented essentially a restrained and moderate U.S. response to the Soviet Union, see Rostow, *Law, Power, and the Pursuit of Peace*, pp. 43–44; Ronald Steel, *Pax Americana* (New York: Viking Press, 1970), pp. 22–23; and Hammond, *The Cold War Years*, p. 23.

130. Steel, *Pax Americana*, p. 22.

131. David Rees, *The Age of Containment: The Cold War* (New York: St. Martin's Press, 1967), p. 8; and Sir William Hayter, "The Cold War and the Future," in Evan Luard, ed., *The Cold War: A Reappraisal* (New York: Praeger, 1965), pp. 318–19.

132. Charles E. Bohlen, *The Transformation of American Foreign Policy* (New York: Norton, 1969), pp. 115–16.

133. Armacost, *The Foreign Relations of the United States*, p. 59.

134. Herbert K. Tillema, *Appeal to Force: American Military Intervention in the Era of Containment* (New York: Thomas Y. Crowell, 1973), pp. 25, 196.

135. Quigg, *America the Dutiful*, p. 51.

136. Kennan, *Memoirs*, p. 262.

137. See the views of Hans J. Morgenthau in Gardner, Schlesinger, and Morgenthau, *The Origins of the Cold War*, pp. 96–97.

138. Kennan, *Memoirs*, pp. 384–85; and John Lukacs, *A New History of the Cold War* (Garden City, N.Y.: Doubleday, 1966), p. 71.

139. Griffith, *Cold War and Coexistence*, pp. 38–39; and Chester Bowles, "The Crisis That Faces Us Will Not Wait," in Divine, *American Foreign Policy since 1945*, p. 119.

140. Spanier, *American Foreign Policy since World War II*, pp. 39-40; Kennan, *Memoirs*, p. 335; Armacost, *The Foreign Relations of the United States*, p. 59.

141. George W. Ball, *The Discipline of Power: Essentials of a Modern World Structure* (Boston: Little, Brown, 1968), pp. 299–301.

142. Kennan, *Memoirs*, p. 385.

143. Ulam, *The Rivals*, p. 126.

144. Charles O. Lerche, *The Cold War . . . and After* (Englewood Cliffs, N.J.: Prentice-Hall, 1965), p. 72.

145. Khrushchev's views are quoted in Rees, *The Age of Containment*, p. 8.

146. Wayne S. Cole, *An Interpretative History of American Foreign Relations*, rev. ed. (Homewood, Ill.: Dorsey Press, 1974), p. 432.

147. Kennan's objections to President Truman's speech are presented in Jones, *The Fifteen Weeks*, p. 155.

148. See Kennan, *Memoirs*, pp. 378–79. Yet, in the "X" article, Kennan himself had proposed that the United States respond to what he argued was Russia's innately

expansionist tendencies by "the adroit and vigilant application of *counterforce* at a series of constantly shifting geographical and political points, corresponding to the shifts and maneuvers of Soviet policy." "The Sources of Soviet Conduct," in *American Diplomacy*, p. 113, italics added. In later years, Kennan acknowledged his use of this phraseology and conceded that his meaning was "at best ambiguous." *Memoirs*, p. 378.

149.   Walter Lippmann's analysis of containment originally appeared as a series of newspaper articles, which were published collectively in his book, *The Cold War: A Study in U.S. Foreign Policy* (New York: Harper and Row, 1947).

150.   Seabury, *The Rise and Decline of the Cold War*, p. 77.

151.   Steel, *Pax Americana*, p. 22.

152.   Ibid.; Armacost, *The Foreign Relations of the United States*, pp. 58–59; and Seton-Watson, *The East European Revolution*, p. 336.

153.   Steel, *Pax Americana*, p. 22.

154.   Kennan, *Memoirs*, pp. 340–41.

155.   Simon Serfaty, *The Elusive Enemy: American Foreign Policy since World War II* (Boston: Little, Brown, 1972), pp. 76–77.

156.   Edmund Stillman and William Pfaff, "Cold War and Containment," in M. Donald Hancock and Dankwart A. Rostow, eds., *American Foreign Policy in International Perspective* (Englewood Cliffs, N.J.: Prentice-Hall, 1971), p. 134.

157.   Arnold S. Kaufman, "The Cold War in Retrospect," in Howe, *A Dissenter's Guide to Foreign Policy*, p. 70.

158.   Stillman and Pfaff, "Cold War and Containment," p. 136.

159.   Courtney Whitney, *MacArthur: His Rendezvous with History* (New York: Alfred A. Knopf, 1956), p. 497; Robert A. Taft, *A Foreign Policy for Americans* (Garden City, N.Y.: Doubleday, 1951), p. 7; Barry Goldwater, *The Conscience of a Conservative* (New York: Macfadden Books, 1963), p. 91; Seabury, *The Rise and Decline of the Cold War*, p. 72; and the excerpts from the GOP Platform of 1952, as quoted in ibid., pp. 72–73.

160.   Goldwater, *The Conscience of a Conservative*, pp. 123–25; and his *The Conscience of a Majority* (Englewood Cliffs, N.J.: Prentice-Hall, 1970), pp. 90–94.

161.   For Henry A. Wallace's early criticisms of the containment policy, see Edward L. Schapsmeier and Frederick H. Schapsmeier, *Prophet in Politics: Henry A. Wallace and the War Years, 1940–1965* (Ames: Iowa State University Press, 1970), pp. 142–79.

162.   Frederick L. Schuman, "The U.S.S.R. in World Affairs: An Historic Survey of Soviet Foreign Policy," in Samuel Hendel and Randolph L. Braham, eds., *The U.S.S.R. after Fifty Years: Promise and Reality* (New York: Alfred A. Knopf, 1967), pp. 217–18.

163.   John Bagguley, "The World War and the Cold War," in David Horowitz, ed., *Containment and Revolution* (Boston: Beacon Press, 1967), pp. 103–4, 119; and Isaac Deutscher, "Myths of the Cold War," in Horowitz, *Containment and Revolution*, p. 17.

164.   Stephen E. Ambrose, *Rise to Globalism: American Foreign Policy, 1938–1970* (Baltimore: Penguin Books, 1971), pp. 103–4.

165.   Ibid., pp. 145–46.

166.   Anatol Rapoport, *The Big Two*, pp. 138–39.

167. Gardner, "Dean Acheson and 'Situations of Strength,'" in Hess, *America and Russia*, pp. 49–50.

168. Carl Oglesby and Richard Shaull, *Containment and Change* (New York: Macmillan, 1967), p. 73.

169. Rapoport, *The Big Two*, p. 91, italics in the original.

170. Steel, *Pax Americana*, p. 16.

171. D. F. Fleming, *The Cold War and Its Origins* (Garden City, N.Y.: Doubleday, 1961), 1:440–42, 446.

172. Tillema, *Appeal to Force*, p. 190. For a discussion of Manicheism, see Lee Cameron McDonald, *Western Political Theory: From Its Origins to the Present* (New York: Harcourt, Brace, and World, 1968), pp. 106–7.

173. Gaddis, *The United States and the Origins of the Cold War*, p. 352.

174. Richard J. Barnet, *Intervention and Revolution: America's Confrontation with Insurgent Movements around the World* (New York: World, 1968), pp. 127–28.

175. Joyce and Gabriel Kolko, *The Limits of Power: The World and United States Foreign Policy, 1945–1954* (New York: Harper and Row, 1972), p. 219.

176. Todd Gitlin, "Counter-Insurgency: Myth and Reality in Greece," in Horowitz, *Containment and Revolution*, pp. 141, 178–80.

177. Horowitz, *Containment and Revolution*, pp. 10–11, italics in the original.

178. Fleming, *The Cold War and Its Origins*, 1:446–47.

179. Chester Bowles, "The Crisis That Faces Us Will Not Wait," in Divine, *American Foreign Policy since 1945*, p. 120.

180. David Horowitz, *The Free World Colossus: A Critique of American Foreign Policy in the Cold War*, rev. ed. (New York: Hill and Wang, 1971), p. 90.

181. Fuller discussion of the Carter Doctrine and its implications may be found in Crabb, *The Doctrines of American Foreign Policy*, pp. 325–71; and in Hamilton Jordan, *Crisis: The Last Years of the Carter Presidency* (New York: G. P. Putnam's Sons, 1982).

182. For commentators expressing this viewpoint, see Blair Bolles, "The Fallacy of Containment," in Edwin C. Rozwenc and Kenneth Lindfors, eds., *Containment and the Origins of the Cold War* (Boston: D. C. Heath, 1967), p. 54; Fleming, *The Cold War and Its Origins*, 1:474–75; Horowitz, *The Free World Colossus*, p. 85; and Kenneth Ingram, *History of the Cold War* (London: D. Finlayson, 1955), p. 228.

5

Liberal and Humanitarian Interventionism

THE UNITED STATES' "MISSION" AND THE INTERVENTIONIST IMPULSE

On the eve of the American Revolution, Thomas Paine wrote that "the cause of America is in a great measure the cause of all mankind." More than a half-century later, Abraham Lincoln observed that the Declaration of Independence gave "liberty, not alone to the people of this country, but hope for the world for all future time. It was that which gave promise that in due time the weights should be lifted from the shoulders of all men."[1]

During World War I, President Woodrow Wilson stated that the nation's "flag is the flag not only of America, but of humanity." In time, other nations would "turn to America for those moral inspirations which lie at the basis of all freedom."[2] Then, in the early months of World War II, during Great Britain's darkest hour following the evacuation of its forces from Europe (in June 1940), Prime Minister Winston Churchill told Parliament that Britain would fight on "until in God's good time the New World with all its power and might, sets forth to the liberty and rescue of the Old."[3]

Spanning more than one and a half centuries of U.S. experience, these statements have a unifying theme, which is the focus of this chapter. It is the concept of the U.S. "mission," which is succinctly conveyed by the motto engraved upon the Great Seal of the United States (reproduced on the back of every one dollar bill): *Novus Ordo Seclorum* — the U.S. Republic was "a new order of the ages." Internally, Americans were convinced that in nearly every important sphere of human relations they had created a novel order, a new and superior social, economic, and political system. Externally, Americans believed that their new order of the ages would in time have a profound and revolutionary impact upon the conduct of global affairs and upon the nature of the international system. As Edmund Stillman and William Pfaff have expressed it, Americans regarded themselves as members of a "redeemed" society, with "a mission of redemption to others."[4]

As was emphasized in Chapter 1, from the founding of the U.S. Republic until the promulgation of the Truman Doctrine early in 1947 the preferred foreign policy posture of the United States was isolationism. For a century and a half after 1789, departures from the isolationist norm — such as U.S. participation in two world wars — were exceptional. Although we must continually bear in mind the deeply entrenched isolationist tradition, it is also necessary to emphasize the phenomenon with which this chapter is centrally concerned: the essentially paradoxical or dual nature of the U.S. outlook toward foreign affairs that has existed from the beginning of the Republic. The long era of isolationist behavior was interspersed with avowedly interventionist episodes, the impulse toward which often arose from the deeply embedded sense of the United States' mission to other countries. While admittedly exceptional and usually episodic, these tendencies foreshadowed the kind of activist, internationalist, or avowedly interventionist foreign policy role the United States assumed after World War II.

It should also be observed that the conflict between the traditional U.S. policy of isolationism and what we are calling in this chapter "liberal and humanitarian interventionism" was in many respects more apparent than real. Logically, and according to many criteria, isolationism and interventionism are opposite and apparently irreconcilable diplomatic impulses. On a deeper philosophical and ideological level, however, the isolationist and liberal interventionist urges have much in common. To the minds of many Americans, their ultimate goals were substantially identical, however much their methods for reaching them might differ. Max Lerner has pointed out that, for the U.S. society, isolationist and liberal interventionist tendencies often had the same basic purpose: to create conditions in the outside world conducive to the enhancement of U.S. liberty, democracy, and welfare; and to the degree that this goal was achieved, the condition of the human race generally would be uplifted and improved. Isolationism relied upon noninvolvement in Europe's rivalries, neutrality, a go-it-alone approach to foreign policy issues, and the attraction of the U.S. example to produce conditions of stability and peace abroad. The liberal interventionist has been prepared to go even farther. At intervals, advocates of this course have urged the United States government to take an active and avowedly interventionist role in producing those conditions abroad requisite for the survival of democracy at home and its extension throughout the world. The underlying premise of this approach was that an organic relationship exists between the maintenance and perfection of a democratic system within the United States, coupled with efforts to promote democracy on a worldwide basis, and the preservation of global peace and stability. It was but a logical step from believing that the expansion of democracy was vital for the creation of a peaceful global system to acting on that belief in U.S. relations with other countries.

For the sake of clarity, we need to reiterate briefly a point made at length in Chapter 1. Most of the ideas and values associated with the U.S. way of life — belief in democracy, freedom, equality, progress, the perfectability of human institutions, faith in rational processes and modern science — are predominantly tenets of the liberal political faith. By liberal interventionism then, in this chapter we mean those diplomatic behavior patterns exhibited by the United States in its foreign relations that have been calculated to safeguard or promote the goals and values integral to the U.S. way of life, as embraced specifically by the mission of projecting democracy abroad and uplifting the condition of the human race.

PATTERNS OF INTERVENTIONIST BEHAVIOR BEFORE WORLD WAR II

Before World War II, innumerable opportunities arose for the U.S. society to display its propensity toward liberal interventionism in foreign affairs. The overall rationale for such interventionist conduct was succinctly expressed by Secretary of State William H. Seward, in referring to Czarist Russia's repression of Polish nationalism in 1863. Concerning the U.S. reaction to that event, Seward stated:

> Founding our institutions upon the basis of the rights of man, the builders of our Republic came all at once to be regarded as political reformers, and it soon became manifest that revolutionists in every country hailed them in that character, and looked to the United States for effective sympathy, if not for active support and patronage.[5]

Hardly had the battles of Lexington and Concord ended when the effects of the American Revolution began to be felt in the Old World. The "shots heard round the world," for example, had a profound impact upon France. The American Revolution served as a major contributing factor triggering the French Revolution in 1789.

It will be recalled from Chapter 1 that formulating a response to the challenge posed by revolutionary France and the ensuing European wars posed an unusually difficult decision for the Washington administration. Public sentiment was unquestionably on the side of Paris. Following prolonged discussion, however, in 1794 Congress enacted a Neutrality Act, effectively nullifying the Franco-American treaty. Jeffersonians and other friends of French liberty were incensed. This internal debate was no doubt fresh in President Washington's mind when, in his Farewell Address (September 19, 1796), he cautioned his fellow citizens against "permanent, inveterate antipathies against particular nations" (for example, Great Britain) and "passionate attachment for others" (for example, Republican France) — a warning issued to counteract a strong national impulse toward interventionism in behalf of freedom and democracy.

Liberal interventionist sentiments also in some measure accounted for issuance of the Monroe Doctrine in 1823. The Monroe Doctrine, a leading diplomatic historian has said, was unquestionably "an ideological tract, praising the democratic principle and exalting democratic forms in contrast to the monarchies of Europe." Monroe's message reflected a powerful U.S. aversion to Old World political values and systems. While it pledged U.S. noninvolvement in the political quarrels of Europe, tacitly at least the doctrine also committed the United States to an interventionist position in several senses. Preventing the Holy Alliance from intervening in Latin America and preventing Czarist Russia from expanding to the northwest would contribute to the maintenance and extension of democratic systems throughout the New World; it would in some measure frustrate, and perhaps in time defeat, attempts by the European powers to impose the nineteenth-century aristocratic concept of legitimacy upon unwilling subjects, in the face of a rising popular demand throughout Europe for political liberty; and a pledge of noninvolvement in European political rivalries by the United States would contribute significantly to the democratic experiment at home, thereby, many Americans believed, assuring its ultimate adoption by other societies.

The century from 1815 to World War I witnessed numerous episodes in which the U.S. society manifested liberal interventionist proclivities.

President Monroe and other Americans, for example, had been keenly interested in the Greek struggle for independence from Turkish rule, which erupted actively early in the 1820s. In the years that followed, at intervals Americans exhibited their sympathy for ongoing struggle for Greek independence and democracy. Not untypically, in cases involving political developments in the old country, this was a cause in which Greek-Americans were especially interested, although they usually had no difficulty finding support among likeminded Americans. In the early 1900s, for example, volunteer units were formed in New England to fight for the cause of Greek liberty. Then, during World War I, Greek-Americans believed that service in the U.S. armed forces was tantamount to enlistment in the Greek independence movement. As was not unusual in revolutionary situations abroad, political leaders within Greece urged the United States to inject itself into the political life of their country to assure the success of freedom and democracy.[6]

The years 1830 and 1848 were times of great political turbulence in Europe. Whenever revolutionary upheavals erupted against established European political systems, Americans could nearly always be counted on to identify with them and to support them, almost always verbally and sometimes materially. The novelist James Fenimore Cooper called upon Americans to remember that their "great example is silently wearing away the foundations of despotism" and to conduct themselves as "the true repositories of the persecuted right of human nature."[7] During the early 1830s, U.S. opinion was overwhelmingly sympathetic to the effort by the Poles and other peoples of East-Central Europe to win freedom from Russian or Austrian oppression. Many Americans did contribute their money — and many more, their evident enthusiasm and moral support — to the cause of Polish freedom. Throughout the United States, Czarist tyranny was frequently denounced, while the U.S. debt to the Polish heroes of the American Revolution (like Tadeusz Kosciuszko and Kasimierz Pulaski) was publicly acknowledged. So strongly did Americans identify with Poland's struggle that Congress took the extraordinary step of granting public lands to Polish exiles for the creation of a "Little Poland" in the Midwest. For reasons that need not detain us, the Little Poland plan proved a failure, but it marked the zenith of U.S. support for Polish independence.[8]

Sympathy of the United States for the European revolutionary movements of 1848 was even more widespread and intense, as epitomzied by Henry Wadsworth Longfellow's conviction: "So long as a King is left upon his throne there will be no justice on the earth."[9]

German-Americans called upon the United States to sponsor a great army of the spirit to liberate Europe from despotism; one advocate of German liberation looked forward to the time when the German flag "flutters proudly beside the Star Spangled Banner, and the spirit of George Washington watches over them both."[10] When a new (but short-lived) revolutionary regime seized power in Paris, the U.S. Minister said that his country "naturally feels gratified at seeing another nation, under similar institutions, assuring to themselves the benefits of social order and public liberty." Taking note of this new French regime in an address to Congress (April 3, 1848), President Polk declared that, although the United States remained devoted to the principle of noninterventionism, "all our sympathies are naturally enlisted on the side of a great people, who, imitating our example, have resolved to be free."[11]

Yet no event in this period — and perhaps no other comparable development in the diplomatic history of the United States — stirred the sympathies of Americans, and tested the firmness of their attachment to isolationism, so much as Hungary's fight for freedom against Austrian domination. One historian refers to the U.S. "popular detestation of Austria" and to the popular belief that, if Hungary could acquire its freedom, this would "give a powerful impetus to liberalism in France and Germany." President Zachary Taylor stated publicly that, if a new regime appeared in Hungary, it would be quickly recognized by the United States.[12]

The crushing of the Hungarian revolution by Austrian authorities incensed U.S. opinion. In due time, as so many foreign revolutionary figures have done, the Hungarian revolutionary leader, Lajos Kossuth, visited the United States, where he sought to continue the struggle for Hungarian independence. Following his arrival in New York City on December 5, 1851, "Kossuth fever" gripped the U.S. society. In one city after another, "the George Washington of Hungary" was lionized; hundreds of thousands of Americans pledged their support to his cause. Secretary of State Daniel Webster informed the distinguished Hungarian: "We shall rejoice to see our American model upon the Lower Danube and on the mountains of Hungary."[13]

Yet, like others before and after his time, Kossuth left the United States a dejected man. Kossuth's purpose had been to enlist "money, arms, men and the diplomatic or military intervention of the government of the United States" in the cause of Hungarian freedom. Most crucially, he sought to persuade the United States government to abandon its isolationist posture.[14] The Filmore administration was distinctly negative about his call for direct U.S. intervention in the political affairs of the Austro-Hungarian Empire; U.S. officials in Vienna informed the Austrian government that no such intervention would occur.

Despite episodes like the ill-fated Kossuth mission, supporters of political freedom in the Old World continued to solicit U.S. involvement in behalf of their struggles. One of the most moving and eloquent appeals addressed to the U.S. people, summoning them to face squarely the foreign policy implications of their own revolutionary and democratic political principles, came from the Italian patriot Giuseppe Mazzini (1805–72), who led the campaign for Italian unification and republicanism. In 1865 Mazzini informed Americans that the United States had become the representative of democratic forces in Europe and around the world; the United States was "a Nation-Guide, and you must act as such." Condemning their isolationist stance, Mazzini informed Americans that "standing aloof is a crime. . . . You must manfully aid morally and, if necessary, materially your republican brethren everywhere the sacred battle is fought."

Another sphere in which U.S. liberal interventionist tendencies were manifested — and have continued down to the present day — was in Russian-U.S. relations. One commentator has said that from the end of the eighteenth century onward Russian-U.S. relations were characterized by "a strange mixture of mistrust and hope for friendship" — and it was mistrust, and in time deep suspicion and hostility, which finally prevailed. Openly hostile toward the new U.S. democracy, Empress Catherine II did not recognize the United States until 1809; in the eyes of Russia's rulers, the new Republic was a "dangerous revolutionary upstart."[15] U.S. opinion was highly critical of Russia for crushing the Polish Revolt of 1830. The adverse U.S. reaction in time induced Russia to protest U.S. departure from the avowed principles of the Monroe Doctrine. During this same period, James Buchanan, who served as U.S. Minister to Russia during this period, referred to the "calm of despotism" that pervaded Russian society; he accused the Czarist regime of being "afraid of the contagion of liberty."[16] Active Czarist opposition to democracy was also held in large part responsible for the failures of many European revolutionary movements in 1848.

Despite contrary tendencies (like cordiality between Czarist Russia and the United States during the U.S. Civil War), as time passed relations between the two countries deteriorated. An influential contributing factor was the speeches, writings, and activities of George Kennan (1845–1924), a distant relative of George F. Kennan, sometimes regarded as the author of U.S. post-World War II containment policy. After an extensive tour of Russia, Kennan wrote *Siberia and the Exile System* (1882), a widely publicized exposé of Czarist oppression. In his well-attended public lectures, Kennan aroused U.S. "indignation against Russian despotism and the persecution of the political opposition."[17] Kennan was a founder of an organization (based in London) dedicated to the overthrow of Czarist tyranny. Referring to the activities of the Russian Nihilists, individuals who submit to no political authority, Kennan endorsed their reliance upon assassination and violence to achieve their political goals. After hearing Kennan describe the Czarist autocracy, Mark Twain remarked: "If such a government cannot be overthrown otherwise than by dynamite, then, thank God for dynamite!"[18]

That Kennan's activities had a potent influence both upon U.S.-Russian relations and upon the course of political developments within Russia itself seems undeniable. His book has been described as the *Uncle Tom's Cabin* of the Russian revolutionary movement, which brought about moderate reforms in the Czarist system in 1905 and finally resulted in its overthrow in 1917.[19] Meanwhile, Russian authorities were fully cognizant of Kennan's activities and influence. They repeatedly protested to Washington about his activities (in common with other nondemocratic systems, the Czarist government had great difficulty distinguishing between the activities of private U.S. citizens or groups and the official behavior of the United States government).[20]

Another source of mounting tension between the two countries — and an issue that has evoked liberal interventionist impulses in the United States down to the present day — was the treatment of the Jews by the Russian government and other states (in which Americans believed Russian influence was often dominant) in Eastern Europe. During the 1880s, pogroms and anti-Semitic campaigns erupted in Russia and Eastern Europe, leading many Jews to emigrate to the United States (ultimately giving the United States approximately half the Jewish population of the world). These events, in Bailey's words, elicited a "spontaneous outcry" from Americans against Russia's anti-Semitic practices. In response to public pressure, the State Department conveyed its displeasure to the Russian government. Adverse U.S. opinion was largely responsible for Congress's refusal to approve food shipments to Russia for the relief of famine conditions in 1891–92.[21]

For a generation or so before World War I, Russian treatment of the Jews elicited a strong and highly critical reaction by Americans. For example, in 1903 a new Russian-instigated pogrom triggered mass protest meetings throughout the United States, where Czarist barbarities were denounced. Although as usual Washington was reluctant to intervene officially in Russia's internal affairs (in part out of fear that Moscow might in turn protest U.S. treatment of the Indian, Negro, or other minorities in the United States), the State Department did communicate the highly adverse public reaction to Russian authorities. In 1906 Congress passed a resolution expressing its strong disapproval of Russia's conduct. Then, in 1911, the House of Representatives expressed its displeasure by voting (301 to 1) to abrogate the 1832 commercial treaty with Russia.[22]

Thomas Bailey has underscored another reason why U.S. opinion reacted so sharply on this issue. As Czarist officials harassed Jewish citizens and political opposition groups, leading many of them to emigrate to the United States, Americans believed this contributed to the growth of political radicalism in their own society, as typified by the Haymarket Riot of 1886. Russian anti-Semitism might in time even pose a threat to the stability of the U.S. democratic system.[23]

In view of the long-standing and increasingly acrimonious record of suspicion and tension between the democratic United States and Czarist Russia, it is not surprising that Americans greeted the overthrow of the Czarist regime in 1917 with widespread rejoicing. President Wilson did not conceal his enthusiasm for what he publicly described as "the wonderful and heartening things that have been happening" in Russia. To his mind the Czarist institution was never Russian in origin, character, or purpose; and the new democratic Russian government was now a fit partner for a league of honour."[24] On these premises, the United States was the first nation to extend official recognition to the Russian Provisional Government.

The triumph of democracy within Russian society, however, proved short-lived. Following the overthrow of the Provisional Government by the Bolsheviks under Lenin late in 1917, U.S. attitudes toward the Russian government changed abruptly. The Bolshevik government was determined to take Russia out of World War I, a step that it completed early in 1918. Much of the enthusiasm that Wilson and other Americans had displayed toward the Provisional Government earlier stemmed from an expectation that it would keep Russia on the Allied side and would wage war with renewed vigor and success. Yet U.S. opinion tended to be oblivious to the toll that continued participation in World War I was exacting from the Russian society.

United States relations with China provide another chapter from the annals of pre-World War II diplomacy illustrating liberal interventionist tendencies by the U.S. society. Beginning with the establishment of trade relations between the two countries after the American Revolution, Sino-U.S. relations entailed a long and complex saga, impossible to summarize adequately in a brief space.[25] Our purpose is served by concentrating on several aspects of it, highlighting the U.S. interventionist impulse.

After the U.S. Civil War, one of the most influential developments affecting Sino-U.S. relations was the growth of Christian missionary enterprises on the Chinese mainland. By the late 1800s church organizations in the United States and Europe viewed China as a fertile field for Christian proselytizing activities. In time, these activities were sanctioned and actively encouraged by the United States government, which relied upon methods like gunboat diplomacy, the concept of extraterritoriality, and the Open Door policy to preserve missionary access to China in the face of official — and sometimes violent public — Chinese opposition to missionaries, along with other foreign devils. So intertwined were the activities of American missionary groups in China and the behavior of the United States government that a British observer declared: "The foreign policy of the United States is foreign missions."[26]

In China, as well as in certain other countries, the impact of missionary activities upon the indigenous society was profound and in many respects beneficial.[27] Among their positive accomplishments, missionaries often provided the Chinese masses with the only access to education, access to modern medical and sanitation services, and exposure to foreign ideas and cultural values available to them. Missionary influence played a part in launching the modernization process for one of the most primitive and isolated societies on the globe. Nevertheless, on balance the Chinese people increasingly resented this Western intrusion into their affairs, particularly as the entire missionary enterprise appeared to rest upon a premise of overall Western cultural superiority vis-à-vis Chinese cultural and religious backwardness. Because of the close association between the missionary cause and the policies of the United States government in China, the missionaries came to be perceived by the Chinese as an integral part of the Western imperialistic penetration and subordination of their country.

As the main purveyors of Western ideas and culture, missionaries also inevitably contributed to mounting political instability within China; and in some instances, they directly fomented and encouraged political change. Thus, many missionaries welcomed Japan's victory over China in 1895 because it discredited and weakened the Manchu Dynasty. The overthrow of the imperial dynasty by the Chinese revolutionary movement in 1911 met with almost universal missionary (and, more broadly, U.S.) approbation. It was assumed (as matters turned out, with little justification) that the new Chinese regime under Dr. Sun Yat-sen and his successor, Chiang Kai-shek, would be more receptive to Christian missionary operations in China and that (as missionaries and other "old China hands" had long predicted), under U.S. tutelage, China would soon evolve into a Western-style democracy. Before and after World War I, prominent Americans served as advisers to the new Chinese government.

According to one liberal critic of the U.S. diplomatic record in China, the United States missed two key opportunities after 1911 to influence decisively the political development of modern China. The first occurred in the early years of Dr. Sun's regime, when China sought and expected aid, loans, and other forms of assistance from the United States to make his regime viable. Meeting with apparent indifference to China's needs in Washington, Dr. Sun in time turned to the new Communist government of Russia for assistance and ideological guidance, which Moscow was not reluctant to supply. Again after 1927 (when Chiang Kai-shek's Kuomintang Party had apparently achieved political dominance over its opponent, the Chinese Communist movement), the United States had a comparable opportunity. Once more Washington refused to translate its verbal and moral support for Chinese democracy into tangible assistance.[28]

No reference to modern Sino-U.S. relations would be complete without at least a brief discussion of one of the landmarks of U.S. diplomacy — the Open Door policy. Proclaimed by Secretary of State John Hay at the turn of the nineteenth century, the Open Door concept quickly became the hinge of U.S. diplomacy in the Far East. A full discussion of this diplomatic milestone would carry us far afield.[29] Again, it must suffice to emphasize those aspects of it most directly relevant for an understanding of U.S. liberal interventionist tendencies.

In its original form, the Open Door policy was quite limited, entailing little more than a pledge for the principle of equal commercial and financial opportunities for foreign powers having concessions in China. The key concept was that if the Chinese government (becoming progressively weaker and subject to foreign influence) granted new concessions to one foreign country, the same concessions must be made available to all others. Thus, no foreign nation (for example, Czarist Russia, which was currently establishing a strong position in northern China) could gain a preferential position vis-à-vis other countries.

Despite its initially limited objectives, within a few years the Open Door policy became equated in the U.S. mind with a guarantee by the United States of China's political and territorial integrity, as symbolized by President Wilson's opposition to Japan's Twenty-one Demands during World War I.[30] Protected by the United States' Open Door policy from such foreign encroachments, after 1911 China was expected to emerge from its traditional backwardness and make rapid social, economic, and political progress.

Yet this romanticized conception of the Open Door policy overlooked two critical considerations. One was the Chinese reaction to the policy. For the Chinese, the Open Door principle had few of the idealized or humanitarian connotations attributed to it by Americans. The policy's original and continuing purpose appeared to be preserving the U.S. competitive position in the midst of an impending colonial race at China's expense. The policy actually did nothing really to dismantle or impede foreign colonial systems in China: it merely guaranteed that the United States would receive the same concessions granted to other foreign powers.

The other notable weakness of the Open Door policy — vocally criticized by liberal commentators during the 1930s and afterward — was the repeated unwillingness of the United States to enforce its provisions against determined and well-armed violators, primarily an expansionist Japan. Effective enforcement required two prerequisites: a willingness by the United States to depart from its isolationist stance, which perhaps was never stronger than during the interwar period and the possession of sufficient power by the United States to deter Japanese or other violations of the Open Door principle. With occasional exceptions, from 1900 to 1941 neither the U.S. people nor their leaders were prepared to supply either of these preconditions. Thus, after Japan embarked upon the path of aggression against China's Manchurian territories in the early 1930s, the main U.S. weapon for defending the Open Door principle was the Stimson Doctrine, according to which the United States refused to recognize any change in the political status quo produced by Japanese expansionism in violation of existing international agreements.[31] The Stimson Doctrine not only predictably failed to deter future Japanese aggression in Asia; it may have facilitated and encouraged further expansionism by Japan and other Axis Powers by implying that in a crisis the United States would do nothing to defend its avowed foreign policy principles or diplomatic interests.[32]

Another development illustrating liberal interventionism by the United States before World War II — and one of the most instructive chapters in the saga of U.S. diplomacy — involved President Wilson's relations with Mexico. For Wilson the idealist, this proved an extraordinarily frustrating experience. Perhaps more than any other occupant of the White House, President Wilson was a passionate believer in democracy as a universally applicable ideology and system of government.

With this frame of mind, Wilson was understandably dismayed by the course of events in Mexico. For a generation after 1877, the Mexican dictator Porfirio Díaz had misgoverned the country. During the era of "Díazpotism," U.S. investments in Mexico (totaling some $1 billion by 1913) grew substantially. Opposition to the Díaz regime mounted, and the dictator was finally ousted in May 1911, when a new government headed by President Francisco Madero took office. As with the Chinese and Russian revolutions, Wilsonians believed that the era of Mexican democracy had dawned. But this euphoria was short-lived. Early in 1913 the Madero administration was deposed, and President Madero was later murdered. A new regime under Victoriano Huerta seized power, inaugurating one of the most repressive and corrupt dictatorships in Latin American history. In the words of one commentator, liberal opinion in the United States "clamored for immediate intervention to redress the crime" of Huerta's subversion of the Mexican revolution. Wilson characterized Huerta's regime as "a government of butchers"; and he seriously considered enlisting European support for a joint foreign intervention to depose the dictator (a plan he abandoned after little interest was shown for it among the European powers). Yet Wilson became compulsively determined to depose Huerta and, in his words, to teach the Latin Americans "to elect good men."[33]

To achieve his purposes, Wilson relied mainly upon two methods: armed military intervention in Mexico's affairs and a new recognition policy. Relations between the United States and Mexico became increasingly strained, and Wilson was frustrated in his attempt to oust Huerta. On April 20, 1914, the president asked Congress for authority to employ armed force; the next day the Vera Cruz crisis erupted, as U.S. warships shelled the Mexican seaport. War between the two countries was imminent, and it was only through the mediation of the ABC powers (Argentina, Brazil, and Chile) that armed conflict was averted. The Vera

Cruz incident left a deep reservoir of ill will toward the United States in Mexico and throughout Latin America generally.

Concurrently, Wilson formulated and relied upon a new recognition policy against the Huerta regime. Previously, the United States (along with nearly all other governments) had followed the principle of recognizing a new regime as the de facto government of the country, irrespective of its ideological character, if it proved capable of exercising its authority and discharging its international responsibilities effectively. Wilson replaced this traditional recognition test by a new standard of constitutional legitimacy. As was true with many other Latin American states before and after the Wilsonian period, ostensibly Mexico was a democracy, with many of the appurtenances of a democratic system. Yet, according to Wilson's principle, the United States would evaluate and decide whether Mexico (or, by extension, any other government) was actually a democracy — that is, whether the incumbent regime had the support of the people and whether it governed in their best interests. Insofar as Wilson's appraisal of the Huerta regime was concerned, the answer was of course never in doubt (the United States did not recognize the government of Mexico until October 1915, several months after a new government under General Carranza had taken office). A related Wilsonian principle — differentiating between the Huerta (or any incumbent) government, which the United States opposed, and the Mexican people, whose interests Washington was trying to promote — was a distinction that was not grasped by the Mexican people, was not meaningful to them, nor did it in any evident way promote cordial Mexican-U.S. relations.

As we emphasized in Chapter 1, the interwar period was in many respects the heyday of U.S. isolationism. Never in their history, perhaps, did the people of the United States appear so firmly attached to their isolationist credo and so determined to remain uninvolved in the affairs of the oustide world, regardless of developments abroad. As the Axis menace grew more ominous, certain prominent U.S. citizens and groups in time began to advocate an interventionist course for the United States. President Roosevelt, Secretary of State Cordell Hull, and other high officials favored at least limited interventionist measures against the Axis danger long before the U.S. public was prepared to tolerate them. In addition, as Axis expansionism continued apace, several public groups demanded that the United States join with the other democracies in resisting Axis encroachments and taking steps (like enhancing military preparedness) essential to Western security. As was also true of isolationist thought, such interventionist opinion was not monolithic. Some spokesmen (like Walter Lippmann) favoring intervention based their arguments chiefly on *Realpolitik* considerations, believing that Axis hegemony must be opposed because it jeopardized the balance of power and hence the peace of the world and the security of the United States.

Other groups urging abandonment of isolationism during the 1930s, however, based their case on many of the same principles invoked by President Wilson when he intervened in Mexico. The liberal interventionist condemned the Axis Powers on several counts. Germany, Italy, and Japan engaged in naked aggression against other countries; they violated treaties and other international agreements with impunity; repeatedly, they infringed upon neutral rights; they were contemptuous of world opinion; their regimes were internally oppressive; and their overall conduct was at variance with the laws of humanity and the canons of civilized behavior. The record of Axis behavior in these respects gradually alienated U.S. opinion, making it in time heavily pro-Allied in its sympathies.[34] By the 1940–41 period, Dexter Perkins has observed, the United States' sense of outrage at Nazi conduct had produced a general feeling of "real antagonism" toward the Axis Powers in the United States.[35]

Many interventionist groups also believed that unopposed Axis expansionism posed a threat to the future of U.S. democracy and of democratic principles throughout the world generally. Organizations that called for the abandonment (or at least the substantial modification) of the isolationist stance — like the Council on Foreign Relations and the Foreign Policy Association — "urged their fellow countrymen to reaffirm the Wilsonian belief that rule of law, principles of democratic government, and American conceptions of fair play and morality were universally applicable."[36] Another interventionist organization, known as the Century Group, sought to reverse the United States' long-standing isolationist posture becaue "democracy in North America could not long survive if the totalitarians dominated the rest of the world."[37]

Religious organizations and leaders were also often at the forefront of those calling for interventionist policies toward the Axis Powers. In 1941 the theologian Reinhold Niebuhr began to advocate a course of interventionism and became one of the founders of the Union for Democratic Action to achieve that purpose. Formerly a pacifist, by the late 1930s Niebuhr came to believe that "one must continue to defend and to extend if possible whatever decency, justice and freedom still exist in this day when the lights are going out one by one."[38] (Militantly opposed to Nazism, after the war Neibuhr was no less opposed to communism and urged U.S. resistance to its expansion.)

Two general observations may be made about the U.S. diplomatic record during the 1930s as it relates to our subject. The first is that it highlighted a deep bifurcation in the U.S. mind regarding the proper response to such dangerous tendencies abroad as Axis expansionism. Isolationism was unquestionably the preferred and cherished stance of the U.S. society toward the Axis dictatorships. Yet by the late 1930s, the sentiment of both the U.S. people and their leaders was distinctly unneutral in favor of the democracies vis-à-vis the dictatorships. The existing neutrality legislation did not reflect their underlying sentiments.

The second observation concerns the profound conviction of many spokesmen for U.S. liberalism during and after the 1930s that the U.S. policy of noninterventionism had been a disaster — for the United States, for its friends in the international community, and for the cause of democracy generally. The U.S. democracy's record of too little and too late had made the most destructive war in the history of the world possible and had guaranteed that it would be prolonged, devastating, and extremely costly in both human and material terms.

LIBERAL INTERVENTIONISM AFTER WORLD WAR II

With the defeat of the Axis nations in 1945, the United States emerged as one of the world's superpowers. U.S. initiative in planning and creating the United Nations, along with active U.S. support for the organization since 1945; the assumption of long-range commitments like the Greek-Turkish Aid Program, the Marshall Plan, and the Point Four program of aid to the developing countries; sponsorship of, and active membership in, the North Atlantic Treaty Organization (NATO), as well as other regional and bilateral security agreements; the maintenance of a high level of defense spending and a condition of military readiness — these developments supplied tangible evidence that the United States had finally abandoned isolationism. The new policy was variously described as internationalism, globalism, or interventionism. Such labels were frequently employed by critics of postwar U.S. foreign policy. By contrast, defenders of the nation's new foreign policy orientation referred to the necessity for the United States to meet its international responsibilities, to recognize its obligations as the wealthiest and (in some respects at least) most powerful nation on the globe, to remember the lessons taught by the failure of U.S. (and, more generally, Western) diplomacy during the 1930s, and to exercise the leadership in solving global problems expected of the world's oldest and most successful democracy.

As in the period of Wilsonian idealism during and after World War I, liberal expectations about the nation's proper role in global affairs were expansive and exceedingly ambitious, tending to acknowledge few bounds. According to one early and widely publicized formulation, the goal of postwar U.S. foreign policy was nothing less than the creation of a new world order, based upon the Four Freedoms enunciated by President Roosevelt in his message to Congress on January 6, 1941:

> In the future days, which we seek to make secure, we look forward to a world founded upon four essential human freedoms.
>
> The first is freedom of speech and expression — everywhere in the world.
>
> The second is freedom of every person to worship God in his way — everywhere in the world.
>
> The third is freedom from want — which, translated into world terms, means economic understandings which will secure to every nation a healthy peacetime life for its inhabitants — everywhere in the world.
>
> The fourth is freedom from fear — which, translated into world terms, means a worldwide reduction of armaments to such a point and in such a thorough fashion that no nation will be in a position to commit an act of physical aggression against any neighbor — anywhere in the world.[39]

To the extent that statements like the Four Freedoms represented serious enunciations of U.S. foreign policy goals, they conflicted directly with the provisions of the Monroe Doctrine and other expressions of the isolationist position. Such policy pronouncements served an evident propaganda purpose during World War II; they were designed to weaken Axis morale and to provide a stimulus for the Allied war effort. After recognizing their wartime utility, how authoritative were such statements as guides to wartime and postwar U.S. diplomatic aims? Were they intended as serious formulations of the foreign policy goals of the United States? Considerable evidence exists that they were so intended. President Roosevelt's closest adviser, for example, believed at the time, that FDR intended the Four Freedoms as something other than catch phrases: "He believes they can be practically attained." Roosevelt intended to act upon that premise.[40] Then there was Roosevelt's keen interest in promoting objectives like greater religious freedom within Soviet Russia — an issue that arose on several occasions in

Russian-U.S. relations during World War II, and toward which the Roosevelt administration could claim some degree of success.[41]

Also consonant with the liberal-humanitarian urges of the U.S. society were the strong anticolonial propensities of the Roosevelt, Truman, and later administrations. President Wilson's concept of self-determination had furnished a powerful stimulus to nationalist aspirations throughout the world. During World War II, President Roosevelt often appeared to be more interested in dismantling the British Empire than he was concerned about other problems (like Communist expansionism) endangering postwar peace and stability. According to one historian, FDR believed "that a refusal by the imperial powers to grant independence to colonial peoples was far more likely to produce a third world war than anything that Russia might do."[42]

The United States' grant of independence to the Philippines in 1946 provided tangible evidence of the nation's opposition to colonialism. Owing in no small measure to Washington's influence, the Netherlands was finally induced to grant independence to Indonesia in 1949.[43] Although, in the years that followed, its position and diplomatic conduct on specific colonial issues often did not satisfy critics (particularly after 1960, when an Afro-Asian majority began to control the U.N. General Assembly), U.S. spokesmen reiterated their opposition to colonialism and their belief that decolonization was an essential step for the maintenance of world peace.

During and after World War II, another idea long prominent in liberal viewpoints toward foreign affairs — the conviction that the United States should use its influence to promote democracy in other countries — infused the U.S. approach to a host of global issues. Traditionally, Americans have believed that an organic connection exists between the extension of democracy and the maintenance of global peace and stability. One purpose of the Greek-Turkish Aid Program in 1947 was to enable Greece "to become a self-supporting and self-respecting democracy."[44] In the months that followed, the encouragement of democracy was also a paramount goal of the European Reconstruction Program (ERP or Marshall Plan) for Western Europe. The importance of the goal was underscored by two facts: although Russia and its European satellites were invited to participate in it (an invitation that Moscow refused), in the end U.S. aid was furnished only to governments sharing its commitment to Western liberal democracy, and strengthening democratic institutions and processes in Western Europe was cited by U.S. officials as one of the program's most fundamental aims.[45]

If active encouragement of democracy overseas ought to be a dominant principle actuating U.S. diplomacy, a logical corollary is that the United States should discourage — and in certain cases, actively oppose — antidemocratic political movements and regimes abroad. A test case arising in the early postwar period involved the Franco regime in Spain. For some 20 years, liberal groups in the West had outspokenly opposed Franco's right-wing Falangist movement ever since he led a long and bloody revolt against the Spanish Republic in 1936. Franco's victory in the Spanish civil war was made possible only with massive German and Italian assistance. To the consternation of liberal critics, during the struggle Western governments followed a policy of nonintervention, thereby virtually guaranteeing the Republic's defeat.

After the inauguration of the containment policy in 1947, U.S. officials became convinced that Spain played a pivotal role in Western defense; in the face of vocal objections by its European partners and opposition by liberal groups in the United States, Washington sought Spain's inclusion in NATO.

Close association with Franco's regime in Spain, critics charged, seriously tarnished the image of the United States as the bastion of global democracy and perhaps encouraged Communist and other extremist opposition to the Franco dictatorship. Accordingly, Washington was urged to place principle ahead of military and diplomatic expediency and to express forcefully its opposition to the Spanish government's political ideology and behavior. Thus, a leading authority on Spanish-U.S. relations asserted that, as a condition for extending economic aid to Madrid, the United States should endeavor "to help the Spanish government put its economic house in order"; it should put Madrid on notice that "it will not indefinitely bail out or coddle a regime that does not mend its ways"; and it should express its "disappointment" at "the failure of the Spanish government to give effect to the princples of 'individual liberty and free institutions,'" as Madrid pledged to do in the agreement providing for U.S. foreign assistance. Such steps were not viewed as involving direct intervention in Spain's internal affairs. But even if they did, they were a less objectionable form of interventionism than supporting the Franco dictatorship by furnishing it with aid that enabled it to solve its internal problems and by failing to express U.S. disapproval with its ideology and conduct.[46]

A similar case involving U.S. relations with a fascist-type dictatorship in the Western Hemisphere occurred in the early postwar period. In March 1944 Colonel Juan D. Perón led a successful *putsch* in Argentina;

his position as president was confirmed in the elections of 1946. Expressing a pervasive reaction in the United States, Dean Acheson described Perón as "a fascist and a dictator detested by all good men — except Argentines." As the Perónist regime increasingly relied upon oppressive methods to enforce its authority, U.S.-Argentine relations became extremely tense. Early in 1946, on the eve of Argentina's national elections, U.S. Ambassador Spruille Braden publicly circulated a Blue Book (prepared by the State Department) documenting Argentina's pro-Axis orientation during World War II. Washington's evident intention was to discredit Colonel Perón and bring about his defeat. But the effort badly miscarried. Colonel Perón — presenting the issue to the Argentina electorate as a matter of *Perón o Braden* (Perón or Braden) exploited his opportunity and was elected to the presidency decisively. Argentines were not only deeply offended by Washington's overt intrusion into their political affairs; the adverse reaction against the United States was hardly less intense among other Latin American nations. When the results of the election became known, Dean Acheson later commented, in the State Department "we licked our wounds."[47]

A comprehensive and truly adequate analysis of liberal interventionist tendencies after World War II would entail nothing less than an overall review of the course of postwar U.S. foreign policy. Here we shall confine our attention to two major diplomatic challenges that illustrate some of the problems and complexities encountered in following the liberal interventionist impulse.

One important dimension of postwar foreign relations graphically illustrating the liberal-humanitarian interventionist urge involves the recrudescence of an old theme in the drama of U.S. diplomacy: the long-standing interest of the U.S. citizens and their leaders in the welfare of the Jewish peoples, especially those in Russia and Eastern Europe. Since World War II, active U.S. involvement in the Palestine controversy has exemplified this tendency.[48]

Beginning with the publication of Theodor Herzl's book *Judenstaat* (*The Jewish State*) in 1896 — prompted in no small part by ongoing anti-Semitic campaigns in Europe — the Zionist movement was founded. Initially, its goal was establishment of a Jewish homeland in Palestine. This goal received British endorsement in the Balfour Declaration (November 2, 1917), which was incorporated in the terms of the League of Nations mandate, under which Britain administered Palestine until termination of the mandate on August 1, 1948.[49] By the 1930s, the Zionist movement had expanded the limited objective of a Jewish homeland in Palestine to the aim of creating a Jewish commonwealth or Jewish national state (Israel) in the country. This was achieved when the State of Israel came into existence on May 14, 1948, following a decision by the U.N. General Assembly to partition Palestine into separate Jewish and Arab states.

After World War I, U.S. opinion became highly receptive to Zionist aspirations in the Middle East. President Wilson, for example, endorsed Zionist aims, as did President Franklin D. Roosevelt.[50] (FDR also assured King Ibn Saud of Saudi Arabia that nothing would be done to change the status of Palestine without full consultation between the Arabs and Jews and that no changes would be made in the country that might prove "hostile to the Arab people.")[51] For some 30 years after 1917, Congressional resolutions — along with others passed by several state legislatures — expressed U.S. support for Zionist aspirations.

Increasingly disturbed by mounting Arab opposition to Jewish settlement in Palestine and mindful of the crucial role of the Middle East in the emerging struggle against the Axis Powers, by the late 1930s Great Britain had begun to resist Zionist demands (like unlimited Jewish immigration to Palestine to escape Nazi persecutions). In time, therefore, Zionist groups shifted their base of operations to the United States. During and after World War II, official U.S. support for Zionist goals intensified — all the more so when, at the end of the war, the emigration of Jews to Palestine seemed an ideal solution to the European Jewish refugee problem. By his own admission, President Truman distrusted the Arabists in the State Department (whose views were believed to be unduly influenced by British colonial and economic interests in the Middle East). Accordingly, in the early postwar period Truman demanded that British-imposed barriers to large-scale Jewish emigration to Palestine be immediately lifted.[52] In the words of his former Secretary of State, President Truman was motivated by two dominant considerations: to secure Jewish freedom of emigration to Palestine and "to assume no political or military responsibility for this decision."[53]

After the war, a debilitated Great Britain decided to relinquish its mandate over Palestine and to entrust the future of the troubled country to the United Nations. During the ensuing U.N. debate, the United States campaigned actively in favor of partitioning Palestine into separate Jewish and Arab states — a solution that Zionists accepted reluctantly and that Arabs vowed to resist by force, as they have down to the present day. Vigorous U.S. support for the partition plan was clearly a crucial factor in the decision by the United Nations to adopt the proposal.[54]

After its creation in 1948, the State of Israel remained heavily dependent upon the United States to maintain its security, in an environment of continuing Arab hostility toward it. By the Reagan administration, the United States had provided over $20 billion in military and economic aid to Israel, not counting several additional billions in private assistance (such as donations and Government of Israel bond sales) by Americans. For fiscal year 1984, for example, the United States government extended $2.6 billion in military and economic aid to Israel. As had been the case for several years, Israel ranked as the largest single recipient of U.S. foreign aid.[55] Although no formal treaty of alliance exists between the two nations, successive presidents have pledged the United States to preserve the security of Israel in the face of ongoing Arab animosity. During the 1973 war in the Middle East, for example, Washington airlifted modern U.S. tanks to Israel, at a time when Israeli forces were in danger of being defeated by Egyptian military units. The U.S. action was crucial in enabling Israel to reverse the military tide and finally to emerge as the victor in this contest.[56] To the minds of many Americans and Israelis, the United States had a strong moral commitment to maintain the security of Israel, in part because of Western failure to defend Jewish rights against Hitler's almost successful efforts to exterminate Europe's Jewish population before and during World War II.[57]

According to many of the usual criteria employed to define an important national (or vital) diplomatic interest, U.S. support for Zionist goals vis-à-vis Arab viewpoints was difficult to justify. The pro-Israeli stance of the United States, for example, alienated Arabs; because of that fact, it greatly enhanced Soviet influence throughout the Middle East; and by the 1970s it had subjected the United States and other industrialized nations to the threat of an Arab oil boycott entailing grave economic consequences. Nevertheless, many liberal commentators (not excluding a number who expressed deep concern about the overextension of U.S. power in other regions) believed that continued U.S. support for Israel ranked as a vital interest of the United States. Lincoln P. Bloomfield believed that the American nation had a clear moral obligation to assist the State of Israel, growing out of the fact that both the United States and Israel were democracies.[58]

As Arabs are well aware, for many years the Israeli case with regard to Palestine has been more effectively and persuasively presented to the U.S. people than has the Arab viewpoint. Yet, as propagandists have also long known, the most influential propaganda reinforces pre-existing belief inclinations and persuades people to accept ideas (perhaps tentatively held) toward which they are already favorably predisposed. After World War II, a number of significant influences inclined U.S. opinion in a pro-Israeli direction. Undeniably, for officials of the Truman and later administrations, domestic political considerations often played a major role in their pro-Israeli orientation. In key states like New York, Massachusetts, Illinois, and California, the Jewish vote (unmatched by a comparably influential Arab vote) unquestionably influenced the attitudes of executive and legislative officials. Moreover, among minority groups, Jewish citizens have long enjoyed the reputation for being informed about, and interested in, global affairs. The intensity of their viewpoints about Israel — coupled with the relative absence of an equally effective and energetic Arab lobby in the United States — has given advocates of Zionism an extraordinarily strong position from which to influence U.S. foreign policy decision making.[59] Support for Israel appeared to be merely a continuation of long-standing U.S. concern for Jewish welfare and rights. In addition, most Americans were themselves products of the Judeo-Christian tradition, a fact accounting in no small measure for the active involvement of church leaders and organizations in behalf of Zionist goals. By contrast, going back to the period of the Crusades, the Islamic faith has frequently suffered denigration and severe criticism in Western thought (with Muhammad the Prophet often viewed as a kind of anti-Christ or false prophet by Christian thinkers).[60] For many years also, to the U.S. mind, Israel was the underdog — an image that the Israelis have had difficulty making credible after its victories in four wars against Arab forces. In several key respects the establishment and development of the State of Israel was a reenactment of U.S. experience. As a result of their dedication and hard work, Israel's pioneers were developing and opening up new territories for settlement, dramatically raising the productivity of a formerly backward region.

No less influential in shaping U.S. opinion was the fact that Israel was a stable, Western-style democracy — the only one in a region characterized by political upheaval and revolutionary ferment, by authoritarian patterns of government, and during some periods by growing Communist influence. The experience of Israel seemed to prove that rapid national development was possible within a democratic political system. Moreover, for many of its supporters in the United States, Israel stood as an effective barrier against Communist inroads in the Middle East. Israel's ties with the United States were firm and unswerving, while in other Middle Eastern states anti-Americanism (abetted by Moscow and its clients) was endemic.

For these reasons, and even after they had begun to criticize the U.S. role in Vietnam and the overcommitment of the United States in global affairs, routinely liberal interventionists viewed the preservation of Israeli security as an essential U.S. diplomatic commitment; and they called upon officials in Washington to provide the economic and military assistance, along with the diplomatic support, needed to defend Israel in a still-dangerous Middle Eastern environment. It was not unusual also for spokesmen for this viewpoint, however, to condemn U.S. interventionism in the Persian Gulf area, the Caribbean region, or Central America.

The second concrete case illustrating liberal interventionist tendencies in U.S. foreign policy since World War II involves the problem of racial discrimination in southern Africa. Many liberals believe that international respect for basic human rights forms (or should form) an essential element in an emerging sense of global community — a concern that should serve as the cornerstone of U.S. foreign policy. From the time the U.N. began considering the problem of racial conflict in Africa (starting with the first session of the General Assembly in 1946), few issues have elicited more severe indictments of U.S. foreign policy by liberal opinion than this question. Among all the major regions, Africa has enjoyed the lowest priority in U.S. foreign policy since World War II (in part, because of Western Europe's continuing ties with, and programs of economic assistance for, the area). In President Nixon's phrase, the United States' overall stance in Africa has been one of low profile; or, as one student of African affairs has expressed it, throughout most of the postwar period the United States has followed a course of "benign neglect" in dealing with African problems.[61]

Until the Kennedy administration in the early 1960s, U.S. officials periodically endorsed the principle of racial equality in Africa and elsewhere. Washington was unwilling, however, to participate in coercive measures designated to eliminate racial injustice in particular societies, like South Africa and southern Rhodesia. Aware that this passive stance won very little goodwill and admiration for the United States among the Afro-Asian nations, and believing that concern for international human rights was coming increasingly to the forefront of global concern, the Kennedy administration toughened the U.S. position on racial questions and took other steps designed to enhance U.S. influence in black Africa.[62] Yet neither under Kennedy nor under his successors in the White House was the United States willing to engage in (much less to lead) the kind of confrontation against South Africa that militant opponents of apartheid demanded. Fairly consistently, the official U.S. view has been that use of instruments like economic boycotts and blockades, nonrecognition of white-dominated governments, withdrawal of U.S. investments, and the threat of reliance upon military force were counterproductive. American officials were dubious about using such techniques against the South African government for two reasons. In many cases (such as boycotts), on the basis of experience the effectiveness of such methods seemed highly questionable. And it was also doubtful that in the end, such methods would produce the desired result: greater racial justice within South African society. Indeed, conditions of economic stringency within the country might in fact lead to exactly the opposite conditions, with blacks and other nonwhite elements of the society suffering a disproportionate hardship as a result of such sanctions. As in the earlier case of southern Rhodesia (Zimbabwe), U.S. officials believed that ultimately the white South African elite had to be persuaded to relinquish power and had to be given firm assurances that its interests would be safeguarded in any new political order existing in the country.[63]

On several grounds, liberal critics of U.S. policy found the nation's diplomatic record of caution, passivity, and ambiguity on African racial issues indefensible. From an ideological perspective, it contravened the avowed belief of the United States in principles like democracy, freedom, and equality, making a mockery of the nation's claim to lead the free world.

The United States' stake in the maintenance of world peace is often cited as another compelling justification for actively opposing racial injustice abroad. As one study expresses the idea: "The United States has a direct concern lest racial tensions in Africa flare into open conflict and threaten the internal stability of a country or region." The possibility that mounting racial tensions will lead to regional, and perhaps global, violence — in the process hindering U.S. access to vital African raw materials — ought to pose "large and realistic worries" for the United States.[64]

Advocates of a more forceful U.S. stand on racial questions also invoke an argument used by critics of isolationism during the 1930s. As Waldemar Nielsen asks rhetorically, "Does nonintervention by the United States on behalf of blacks under present circumstances not in effect amount to intervention on the side of the existing regimes [in South Africa and Southern Rhodesia]?" A policy of nonintervention in effect places "the United States on the side of the present white regimes in the coming struggle for power" in Africa — a struggle that, such assertions nearly always assume, the white regimes and their supporters will eventually lose. Therefore, considerations of U.S. "self-interest, political principles, and moral responsibility" coalesce to dictate a fundamental change in the foreign policy of the United States in behalf of racial justice and equality.[65]

By the mid 1980s, racial conflict in southern Africa had reached a new level of intensity, and the future of South Africa's apartheid system was being severely challenged by opponents inside and outside the country. Hardly a day passed without one or more violent incidents between the South African governments and groups that were determined to bring an end to white political rule. Within the United States, critics of apartheid staged frequent demonstrations and protests against the government of South Africa; and they were convinced that the Reagan administration's policy of constructive engagement with South African political authorities had reached a dead end. By contrast, although they called for major reforms by South African authorities, officials of the Reagan administration continued to believe that coercive measures, violent confrontations between supporters and critics of apartheid, and revolutionary programs for changing the country's political system would in the end create more problems than they solved. Experience with other African political systems in recent years, for example, offered very little assurance that violent confrontational tactics and revolutionary methods of political change ultimately promoted the cause of human rights or strengthened the future of democracy on the African continent. For these reasons, the Reagan administration continued to believe that some kind of negotiated settlement or compromise solution was essential for a stable and just political order within South Africa. Yet to the minds of many of apartheid's critics, it was too late for a compromise solution of the country's political crisis; nothing less than acceptance of the principle of majority rule by the entrenched white elite would bring an end to the recurrent pattern of violence and upheaval. Unless U.S. officials accepted that idea, the influence of the United States on the African continent would continue to decline, while Soviet influence would almost certainly increase.[66]

The ongoing crisis in South Africa called attention to one of the problems related to liberal-humanitarian interventionism that we shall discuss at a later stage. Here, it suffices merely to allude to it in the South African context. This is the question of the degree or kind of responsibility that interventionist groups were willing to assume for the consequences of their policies. In the instance of South Africa, what responsibility were critics of apartheid willing and able to bear for the enforcement of any agreement reached among the principal ethnic groups within South African society? Would they, for example, be as outspoken, active, and diligent in protecting the future rights of the white minority as they were in calling for rule by the country's black majority? In more general terms, would they be as ready to advocate interventionist steps by the United States to enforce compliance with the provisions of a new constitutional system as they were to dismantle the old white-ruled regime?[67]

LIBERAL INTERVENTIONISM: AN ASSESSMENT

How has liberal interventionism contributed to the realization of U.S. foreign policy goals? Conversely, what problems arise for U.S. relations with other countries as a result of this diplomatic impulse? Taking its positive features first, we may begin by noting that liberal diplomatic interventionism is a logical, natural, and perhaps inevitable outgrowth of the U.S. ethos and ideological tradition. It is an authentically U.S. diplomatic behavior trait — and perhaps the remarkable fact is that, until World War II, in most cases the impulse was checked or severely limited by the U.S. society's very strong underlying commitment to the isolationist position.

Advocates of liberal interventionism have also served a useful (perhaps increasingly essential) purpose in diplomacy. Prince Metternich of Austria once said that for a great power there was really no such thing as a policy of nonintervention; there were only various forms of intervention. This is an idea that proponents of liberal interventionism in the United States have periodically emphasized. In responding to many crises and developments abroad, whatever the United States does — including ostensibly doing nothing or officially remaining noninvolved — sometimes constitutes a de facto form of interventionism in the affairs of other countries, with results often highly inimical to the interests of the United States and its friends abroad.[68]

This conclusion has been emphasized many times by students of the U.S. diplomatic record — no more frequently and vocally perhaps than in reference to the 1930s. For example, during the Ethiopian crisis of 1936, the United States and other Western nations proclaimed an ineffectual moral embargo against both Italy and Ethiopia. The result of this official noninterventionism was to guarantee an Italian victory in the conflict (Mussolini's government could readily acquire arms and supplies from its Axis partners and other sources, while Ethiopia could not). Again, during the Spanish civil war the United States and the European Allies proclaimed their official neutrality toward this conflict, with identical results: General Franco's movement easily obtained weapons and other forms of aid from Germany and Italy, while comparable outside support was denied to pro-Republican forces, thereby assuring the ultimate victory of the Franco regime.[69]

But the outstanding example illustrating Metternich's dictum from the pre-World War II era was perhaps U.S. policy toward the Holocaust — Hitler's systematic efforts to eliminate the Jewish population of Europe. On countless occasions since the war, pro-Israeli groups at home and abroad have condemned the moral failure of the United States and other Western nations because they did not intervene decisively to prevent the Holocaust in which some 6 million Jews died. In theological terms, U.S. inaction was a crucial sin of omission, amounting to acquiescence in Nazi Germany's genocidal conduct. Time and again, supporters of the State of Israel have cited this diplomatic failure as a major reason why the United States should support the creation and continued security of Israel in the postwar period.[70]

Despite a number of setbacks and failures in the national diplomatic record, it is also clear that the liberal interventionist urge has sometimes had a significant impact upon developments in other countries. For example, insofar as the Monroe Doctrine represented interventionism in Latin American affairs in behalf of that region's freedom from foreign domination and perhaps the ultimate emergence of democratic systems, it did in some measure dissuade the Holy Alliance from extending the principle of legitimacy to the New World, especially after Great Britain endorsed the doctrine. A student of German history has said that U.S. support for the democratic movement in that country "uncovered a propensity, lying dormant in Germany, to challenge governmental authority"; U.S. sympathy contributed to the emergence of "organs of public opinion" in Germany that "defended freely and aggressively what they considered to be the rights of the people."[71] Another commentator has said concerning the U.S. missionary effort in Africa that, in no small measure because of it, Africans acquired the faith and aspirations leading them to make demands like decolonization, democracy, and racial justice.[72]

Over against the advantages and gains realized by following the liberal interventionist impulse must be set a long list of disadvantages, problems, and anomalies accompanying that foreign policy orientation. Many of these adverse consequences are serious enough to raise a fundamental question about whether, under all but the most exceptional circumstances, the liberal interventionist approach actually promotes the diplomatic interests of the United States.

It must be recognized initially that the liberal interventionist urge is an ethnocentric and, in many respects, sometimes remarkably provincial approach to foreign affairs, growing out of and expressing the United States' unique sense of mission in the world. Most of the principal and correlative assumptions underlying the mentality — the idea that democracy is a universally applicable ideology or system of government, or the notion that the extension of democracy is tantamount to the preservation of global peace and security, or the assumption that primitive societies are destined to evolve politically in a democratic direction — are ideas and presuppositions long identified with U.S. liberal thought. Yet it is by no means evident that such assumptions are widely shared or cherished by societies outside the West. U.S. society, Stillman and Pfaff have observed, was "the creation of men who did not truly like it elsewhere." For that reason, Americans "are not well suited to be the world's mentor." Even if they were, Americans have seldom demonstrated any very deep interest in, or appreciation of, foreign cultures.[73] Communist China's Hate America campaign during the 1950s — and Iran's deep-seated animosity toward the United States in the more recent period — in some measure derived from foreign reaction to this traditional U.S. conviction. More generally, throughout the Third World, indigenous governments and political movements seek to define and apply their own conceptions of democracy, which will often differ fundamentally from the U.S. or Western versions.

The ethnocentric origins of the liberal interventionist tendency give rise to a host of collateral problems and dilemmas. U.S. insistence upon the adoption of democratic principles and institutions by other societies, for example, frequently strikes outsiders as deriving from little more than ignorance and naiveté about the conditions required to sustain democracy and the absence of these conditions throughout much of the modern world. Unflattering as it may be to Americans, from the evidence available it can persuasively be argued that many societies prefer some form of nondemocratic government over democratic models. At a minimum (and the distinction may be more apparent than real), they prefer their own versions of democracy, which often bear little resemblance to Western models.[74]

A closely related defect is the danger that, in the postwar world, U.S. insistence upon the emergence of democracy in other states risks making the diplomacy of the United States largely irrelevant to the true challenges facing it abroad. As the liberal interventionist mentality often mistakenly implies, in the modern world the choice confronting U.S. policy-makers is almost never one of supporting democratic versus nondemocratic governments and political movements abroad. Rather, it is of defining democracy in terms meaningful to modern (particularly newly independent) societies; of calculating whether the long-term prospects for democracy are more or less favorable under one political movement or another; and of distinguishing meaningfully among rival political groups, all of whose conceptions of democracy usually fall short of Western standards. Referring to postwar Asia, one commentator has remarked upon the recurrent U.S. tendency to overestimate the prospects for democracy in that region. For an indefinite period in the future, the United States will have to "accept the existence in Southeast Asia of authoritarian governments of one kind or another. . . . The best we can hope for in this area is authoritarianism without totalitarianism."[75] During the 1980s, the Reagan administration and its supporters frequently differentiated between authoritarian and totalitarian regimes abroad. For example, a crucial distinction between them was that, as a rule, totalitarian governments were expansionist, while authoritarian regimes were not. Yet liberal interventionists were usually not inclined to accept this distinction.[76]

The liberal interventionist compulsion to promote democracy overseas may also lead to the kind of diplomatic crusade (as during World War I) on which Americans have periodically embarked — usually with more negative than positive results. The liberally oriented Kennedy administration, for example, was convinced that it could successfully promote the process of modernization and nation building throughout the Third World. (The assumption always was, of course, that the result would be democratic nations, oriented toward the United States.) During such crusades, the danger is that the specific and limited diplomatic interests of the United States become obscured in a larger campaign to reform the world politically — to make the world safe for democracy or to guarantee the Four Freedoms, which will presumably in turn usher in a more peaceful and stable global order. Aside from the fact that these crusades have almost invariably failed, Perkins has observed that they nearly always bear "some family resemblance to imperialism," particularly for societies that do not want to be saved politically according to U.S. standards through interventionism by the United States.[77] In the contemporary phrase, as illustrated by the Vietnam War experience, they have led to the overextension of U.S. power abroad and often in time to profound public disillusionment with the nation's diplomatic efforts.

Another troublesome problem with liberal interventionism is underscored by Bernard Crick's observation that traditionally liberals have exhibited an attitude of "prudery" toward the political process and revealed "a dangerous incapacity for action — a refusal to use force ... in the defence of political values." Liberals are "often unwilling to will the means" necessary to achieve their desired goals.[78] U.S. diplomatic experience provides innumerable examples of this tendency. The cases of Israel and South Africa in the postwar period, for example, are merely two illustrating an inability or unwillingness of the liberal interventionist to face the consequences in terms of a commitment of national power required to achieve liberal objectives overseas. Similarly, discussing the Stimson Doctrine of the early 1930s, Julius W. Pratt concluded that it was not only an ineffectual diplomatic instrument for deterring Japanese aggression. Generalizing upon the basis of this example, he observed that "to oppose international aggression with weapons that are irritating but ineffectual is worse than not to oppose it at all."[79] Critics of liberal interventionism have often called attention to a fundamental contradiction in its approach to U.S. diplomacy. On the one hand, liberals often call for interventionist behavior by the United States in behalf of ideologically approved causes. On the other hand, advocates of this viewpoint also frequently condemn the buildup and modernization of U.S. military power, the provision of arms-aid to other countries and other steps required to make such interventionism effective. The net result is that in many cases, the liberal-humanitarian approach amounts to little more than verbal intervention in the affairs of other countries. Or as a British official said several years ago about U.S. diplomacy, all London could count upon from the United States was words. In turn, this diplomatic behavior pattern created a serious problem about the nation's diplomatic credibility.

A student of African affairs has made much the same point about proposed U.S. intervention against South Africa. Interventionist rhetoric on African racial questions aside, the cry for greater U.S. involvement in such issues is often "more symbolic than substantive." Neither a majority of Americans nor, for that matter, Africans is really "psychologically prepared for full American engagement, with all its social, cultural, political, and economic implications" in Africa's problems.[80] Verbal interventionism against South Africa by U.S. policy-makers, coupled with an official unwillingness to bring U.S. power to bear upon African racial disputes, has caused blacks to "doubt the genuineness of foreign sympathy" for their cause and to create the impression that the whole issue is "an international nightmare."[81]

The liberal interventionist mentality also often fails to come to grips with the limits of U.S. power. Implicit in the philosophy of political liberalism are such ideas as belief in progress, in the perfectability of human institutions, in the rational nature of man, and faith in the results to be obtained by reliance upon the scientific method and modern technology. Some of these presuppositions (like belief in the desirability, perhaps the inevitability, of progress and in human society's ability to solve problems) are especially prominent tenets of U.S. liberal thought. Yet by the late twentieth century, many Americans had begun to question whether certain domestic problems (like poverty, racial conflicts, political corruption, misuse of power and economic instability) can ever be definitively solved, even by the wealthiest and most politically stable society on the globe.

Outside the United States, particularly throughout the Third World, even less ground for optimism existed that many of the goals long identified with U.S. liberal thought were susceptible of realization. Long-standing U.S. foreign policy aspirations — like making the world safe for democracy or guaranteeing the Four Freedoms to hundreds of millions of people throughout the world, or eliminating global poverty — more and more exceeded the capabilities of a superpower to achieve. For example, almost 40 years after the Truman administration launched the Point Four program of aid to the developing nations, many Third World societies were retrogressing economically, and their efforts to achieve modernization had encountered formidable obstacles. To cite but one example of this phenomenon: throughout the world, one Third World nation after another was experiencing difficulty in feeding itself, and a growing number were faced with chronic food shortages.

Nearly always, the tendency of liberal interventionist policies has been for the goals of U.S. diplomacy to outstrip the capacity of the nation to achieve them. This fact has been in large part responsible for a familiar cycle in U.S. diplomatic history, and it is a pattern that shows no sign of disappearing in the contemporary era. As in the period of Wilsonian idealism, liberal opinion in the United States postulated many ambitious goals for U.S. foreign relations, most of which were perhaps inherently incapable of realization. After that fact became apparent, widespread disillusionment gripped the U.S. mind. The hope of making the world safe for democracy was quickly superseded by the mentality of letting Europe stew in its own juice and other forms of narrow isolationism and provincialism. This cycle was also discernible with regard to several problems in U.S. foreign relations after World War II. The interventionist impulse that led to U.S. involvement in the Vietnam War was followed during the 1970s by a period of profound doubt and disillusionment about the U.S. role in global affairs. The Carter administration's efforts to promote human rights abroad was followed a few years later by relative indifference toward that goal under the Reagan administration.

Still another problem engendered by liberal interventionist tendencies relates to the manner in which U.S. foreign policy has sometimes been formulated and to the forces that have been decisive in influencing national decision making in particular cases. Liberal interventionist behavior by the United States has often been a product of two influences that, although perhaps always operative in the decision-making process, assumed a disproportionate role in shaping national policy decisions: internal pressure group activities and demands for interventionist conduct by the United States expressed by governments and political movements overseas, which sought to utilize U.S. power in behalf of their own goals.

The classic example of U.S. policy-formulation in response to pressure group activity is Washington's support for the Zionist cause after World War II. It seems clear that the U.S. decision to take an almost unqualifiedly pro-Israeli stance stemmed largely from factors like humanitarian sympathy for Europe's Jewish refugees, from intensive Zionist lobbying efforts, from awareness of the influential role of the Jewish vote in key states, and from overall public ignorance about the issues involved in the Palestine dispute and about the Middle East generally. By contrast, at no stage was there sober, comprehensive, and objective evaluation of U.S. diplomatic interests in the Middle East or of the numerous and adverse consequences for U.S.-Arab relations and regional stability that could be expected from an unqualified endorsement of Zionist demands. After 1948, Israel could usually count upon the automatic support of the United States, regardless of the consequences of that fact for Arab-U.S. relations or the opportunities this created for enhanced Soviet influence throughout the Middle East.

While in some ways admittedly exceptional, this example of interventionist decision making has by no means been uncommon in U.S. diplomatic experience. Much of the impetus in favor of U.S.

involvement in Europe's political struggles during the nineteenth century came from ethnic minorities in the United States, who called for departure form the isolationist norm in behalf of independence movements or democratic causes in the old country. Within the kind of free and pluralistic political system existing in the United States, there is, of course, nothing wrong with the fact that pressure groups seek to express their viewpoints and to urge their adoption by decision makers. For both internal and external issues, such groups supply important information in the policy-making process. But if the concept of the national interest (or, alternatively, the public interest) as a basis for foreign policy possesses any validity, it surely denotes decisions in external affairs reflecting the welfare of the nation as a whole, as distinct from the interests merely of vocal minorities and skillful lobbies. Yet in many instances, liberal interventionist behavior by the United States has appeared to be the result mainly of successful lobbying campaigns and of domestic political pressures.

A different source of the liberal interventionist propensity has been foreign-based demands that the United States immerse itself actively in the political processes of other countries. One of the more interesting aspects of the interventionist episodes in U.S. diplomatic experience is that foreigners have often been outspoken in objecting to U.S. policy of noninvolvement in their political affairs. Time after time, policy-makers in Washington have been subjected to impassioned entreaties, urging them to abandon the nonintervention principle and calling upon the United States to recognize its responsibilities as the champion of political freedom and democracy throughout the world. The reader will recall, for example, the Italian leader Mazzini's moving appeal to Americans in this vein.

Foreign demands for interventionist conduct by the United States in behalf of particular political causes did not come to an end after World War II. Since then nationalist groups throughout the Afro-Asian world have looked to the United States to champion and back their anticolonial struggles — and they have criticized U.S. policy severely when Washington failed to do so or when the level of U.S. assistance for anticolonialist causes was less than expected. Similarly, an undisclosed number of citizens of Hungary and perhaps other Eastern European states no doubt anticipated U.S. assistance when the Hungarians revolted against Soviet rule in 1956. In more recent years, the people of Poland, and organizations like Solidarity, have looked to the United States for support in their efforts to achieve a greater degree of political freedom.[82]

Impassioned requests for U.S. interventionist moves often are expressed by political exile groups seeking to gain power in their homeland. For example, a leading spokesman for the Free Philippines movement, a former Philippine foreign secretary, in 1973 called upon the United States to fulfill its long-standing commitment to democracy in that country.[83] During the following years, Washington was repeatedly urged to use its influence with the government of President Marcos in an effort to expand freedom and human rights within the Philippines. Inside and outside South Korea, critics of the established government have similarly called for U.S. support in their attempts to gain a greater degree of political freedom.[84] We have already taken note of the mounting pressure exerted upon the Reagan administration to exert its influence with the white-ruled government of South Africa in behalf of a democratic political system within that country.

There is the further problem of what might be called the selectivity of the liberal interventionist urge. Very few advocates of this approach urge the United States to inject itself actively in all cases involving impediments to democracy or the deprivation of human rights in over 160 nations throughout the world. From the earliest days of the Republic until the present time, the liberal interventionist impulse has been manifested episodically and selectively. Those advocating a U.S. confrontation with South Africa have been largely indifferent to other instances of racial and ethnic conflict on the African scene — like efforts by black-dominated governments in East Africa to expel or discriminate against Asians. Nor have liberal groups as a rule been overtly troubled by the oppressive policies of several regimes in black Africa in dealing with their own citizens. Perhaps inevitably, liberal groups are also nearly always more disturbed by political excesses carried out by right-wing, than by left-wing, governments. At any rate, the question of how and why liberal interventionists select certain causes for vocal U.S. attention, while ignoring others, can seldom be answered with assurance.

Critics have raised the same question about U.S. intervention in behalf of the Jews of Soviet Russia. Why is the United States not equally concerned about the right of Russia's Christians, or Moslems, or other religious minorities that experience persecution and discrimination at the hands of Soviet authorities? Or from a different perspective, if concern about the plight of Jewish refugees in Europe in the early postwar era led the United States to support the Zionist cause, why are not Americans equally troubled about the condition of the Arab refugees who have been made homeless since 1948? In these and other cases, the underlying problem is that the grounds or criteria for liberal-humanitarian interventionism are seldom identified explicitly or discussed objectively in terms of their relationship to overall U.S. foreign policy goals.

Finally, devotees of liberal interventionism have been largely indifferent to another problem intrinsic to their foreign policy orientation. If the United States is justified in intervening in the political affairs of other countries to promote democracy, to protect human rights, or in behalf of other liberally approved causes, then are not other governments equally entitled to intervene in the domestic affairs of the United States, to achieve goals central to their own ideology or ethos? The issue was highlighted by an ambiguity that lay at the heart of the U.S. Open Door policy toward China; it was one reason why the Chinese regarded the policy as something less than a symbol of U.S. humanitarianism and devotion to political freedom abroad. The expressed interest of the United States in the cause of Chinese independence and democracy was seriously compromised by the nation's prolonged exclusion of Chinese immigrants and by the discriminatory character of legislation enacted by several states against Chinese-Americans. Yet Americans always took the view that the status of Chinese-Americans was a domestic question. For Chinese-Americans and other minorities, Washington was nearly always unresponsive to foreign efforts designed to improve their condition.

A number of commentators have raised basically the same question about interventionism in the affairs of South Africa in the contemporary period. By what standard is it permissible for the United States to inject itself into the political affairs of South Africa without admitting a comparable right, perhaps of the Soviet Union or a United Nations majority, to become directly involved in racial disputes in Little Rock, Watts, or Boston? Inexact as the parallel between the United States and southern Africa may be, as many African diplomats can testify firsthand, racial discrimination does exist in the United States; it has to some extent become a matter of global concern, and there is no inherent reason why foreign countries theoretically might not mount a campaign to eliminate racial injustice or otherwise improve the condition of minorities in the United States. Or as one white South African commented during the mid 1980s: the main reason why the white-ruled government was encountering vocal criticism directed at its apartheid system was that the politically dominant white segment of the population had not treated blacks and other racial minorities like the U.S. society had treated the Indians, who had been reduced to a relatively small and uninfluential minority of the U.S. population.

Equally difficult questions may be raised about U.S. intervention in behalf of Russia's Jewish population before and after World War II. If the United States may legitimately so intervene, why is it not equally permissible for the Soviet Union to intervene in U.S. affairs on behalf of blacks, Mexican-Americans, or (more appropriately for a Communist regime) the oppressed proletariat, which, according to Communist ideology, constitutes a majority of the U.S. population, making this an even more flagrant and indefensible case of human rights deprivation than persecution of a minority? Yet before it extended official recognition to the Soviet government in 1933, the Roosevelt administration insisted that the Kremlin agree to abandon its revolutionary and interventionist activities in the affairs of other nations (a pledge that Moscow more often violated than honored in the years after).

Still another problem associated with liberal-humanitarian interventionism became evident in the post-Vietnam War era. Ironically, advocates of U.S. interventionism in behalf of liberally approved causes — individuals and groups who drew their ideological inspiration from champions of democracy like Thomas Jefferson and Woodrow Wilson — were often indifferent to the attitudes and desires of the U.S. people concerning the diplomatic behavior of the United States. After Vietnam, for example, only negligible public support existed for a policy of active confrontation with the government of South Africa — and even less for a confrontational approach to Pakistan, the Philippines, South Korea, and other governments whose records on human rights issues elicited vocal criticism abroad. On the basis of evidence supplied by public opinion polls, for example, majority opinion in the United States nearly always opposed such interventionist conduct by the United States; and the level of such opposition was higher in the post-Vietnam War period than before that conflict. (Typically, Americans approved the abstract goal of racial justice in Africa, or respect for human rights by foreign governments generally, but they were seldom willing to support positive or interventionist measures by Washington to make these goals a reality. In this sense, liberal and humanitarian interventionism could not be called a policy most Americans were prepared to accept.)[85]

Finally, advocates of liberal interventionism must confront this question: on the basis of experience, to what extent are U.S.-sponsored efforts to plant the seeds of democracy and freedom in foreign societies likely to succeed? In most cases — as in the lifting of restrictions against emigration by Soviet Jews or the recent announcement by the government of South Africa of minor revisions in its apartheid regulations, in part as a response to foreign criticisms — liberal interventionists can claim no more than limited success. One of the most distinguished U.S. diplomatic historians has observed, with regard to Washington's interventionist behavior in the Caribbean area, that "it is extremely doubtful whether the United States strengthens democracy ... by active participation in the affairs of other states."[86] Insofar as the Carter administration's human rights policies abroad contributed to the collapse of the Iranian monarchy and the emergence of the Shi'ite-based revolutionary government, it is highly debatable whether this transition was a net gain for freedom and democracy in Iran. Similarly, the overthrow of the authoritarian and corrupt Somoza regime in Nicaragua in 1979 was followed by the Communist-ruled Sandinista government that threatened the security of neighboring states in Central America. Similarly, the overthrow of the Ethiopian monarchy in 1974 led to the establishment of a Marxist-oriented military dictatorship in that key East African nation.[87]

Except in rare instances, liberal interventionists would be hard pressed to demonstrate that their efforts have actually enhanced the prospects for democracy and expanded political freedom in other societies. By the late twentieth century, the prospects that Western-type democratic regimes will emerge in regions like black Africa, the Arab world, or Asia seem more remote today than in the early postcolonial period (when nearly all the former British colonies, for example, had parliamentary regimes, most of which have since been abandoned).

Yet other results of the liberal interventionist impulse seem much less debatable. As in the case of the Iranian monarchy, the effort to implant democracy in foreign soil has left a residue of anti-Americanism and resentment against the United States. Its effect in many cases has been to discredit political movements associated with a foreign power. In the United States and the foreign country concerned, it has aroused hopes and expectations that were not subsequently fulfilled, soon engendering an attitude of disillusionment and frustration in both countries. When the cost of U.S. involvement in the political affairs of other societies to encourage democracy and human rights becomes apparent — and when Americans customarily shrink from paying it — the United States is denounced for being hypocritical and for not being "sincerely" devoted to the cause of political freedom abroad. And, in the last analysis, liberal interventionism inescapably implies the presence of a strong ethnocentric bias at the center of U.S. foreign policy, the gist of which is that the United States is as conscious of its "mission" as ever and believes no less today than in the past that its political system and ideology are normative for the human race.

NOTES

1. See the edition of Thomas Paine's *Common Sense* (1776) edited by Nelson F. Adkins (Indianapolis: Bobbs-Merrill, 1953), pp. 3, 19, 23. Lincoln's views are cited in John Foster Dulles, *War or Peace* (New York: Macmillan, 1950), p. 254.

2. Wilson's views are cited in William Pfaff, "A Case Against Interventionism," in William Taubman, ed., *Globalism and Its Critics: The American Foreign Policy Debate of the 1960s* (Lexington, Mass.: D. C. Heath, 1973), p. 97.

3. Churchill's views are cited in Walter Johnson, *The Battle against Isolation* (Chicago: University of Chicago Press, 1944), p. 5,.

4. Edmund Stillman and William Pfaff, *Power and Impotence: The Failure of America's Foreign Policy* (New York: Random House, 1966), p. 9.

5. For excerpts from Seward's statement on May 11, 1863, and commentary on the Polish crisis, see Norman A. Graebner, *Ideas and Diplomacy: Readings in the Intellectual Tradition of American Foreign Policy* (New York: Oxford University Press, 1964), pp. 309–10.

6. Our discussion of the U.S. response to the Greek independence movement is largely based upon Theodore Saloutos, *The Greeks in the United States* (Cambridge, Mass.: Harvard University Press, 1964), pp. 162, 170–76, 209, 256–57, and passim.

7. The text of Cooper's appeal is included in Jerzy Jan Lerski, *A Polish Chapter in Jacksonian America: The United States and the Polish Exiles of 1831* (Madison: University of Wisconsin Press, 1958), pp. 167–71.

8. For further discussion of the Little Poland scheme and the reasons for its failure, consult ibid., pp. 126–55.

9. The views of Buchanan and Longfellow are cited in Carl Wittke, *Refugees of Revolution: The German Forty-Eighters in America* (Philadelphia: University of Pennsylvania Press, 1952), p. 39.

10. Quoted in ibid., p. 33.

11. The views of the U.S. Minister to France and of President Polk are cited in Graebner, *Ideas and Diplomacy*, pp. 263–64.

12. John G. Gazley, *American Opinion of German Unification, 1848–1871* (New York: Columbia University Press, 1926), pp. 51–61.

13. These and other U.S. tributes to Kossuth are cited in Emil Lengyel, *Americans from Hungary* (Philadelphia: Lippincott, 1948), pp. 37–43.

14. Gazley, *American Opinion of German Unification*, p. 62.

15. See the views of Vera M. Dean, in Lerski, *A Polish Chapter in American Democracy*, p. 16.

16. Buchanan's views are cited in Thomas A. Bailey, *America Faces Russia: Russian-American Relations from Early Times to Our Day* (Ithaca, N.Y.: Cornell University Press, 1950), p. 47.

17. Max M. Laserson, *The American Impact on Russia — Diplomatic and Ideological: 1784–1917* (New York: Macmillan, 1950), p. 311.

18. Mark Twain's views are cited in ibid., p. 306.

19. Bailey, *America Faces Russia*, p. 133.

20. Laserson, *The American Impact on Russia*, pp. 314–17.

21. Bailey, *America Faces Russia*, pp. 123–24; and William Appleman Williams, *Russian-American Relations, 1781–1947* (New York: Rinehart, 1952), p. 27.

22. Bailey, *America Faces Russia*, pp. 179–83.

23. Ibid., pp. 125–26.

24. For Wilson's views on the new Provisional Government of Russia under Alexander Kerensky, see "Address of the President of the United States" (April 2, 1917), 65th Congress, 1st Session, House of Representatives, Document No. 1 (Washington, D.C.: Government Printing Office, 1917), pp. 6–7.

25. Useful treatments of Sino-U.S. relations are Foster Rhea Dulles, *China and America: The Story of Their Relations since 1784* (Princeton, N.J.: Princeton University Press, 1946); John K. Fairbank, *The United States and China*, rev. ed. (New York: Viking Press, 1958); and Warren I. Cohen, *America's Response to China: An Interpretive History of Sino-American Relations* (New York: Wiley, 1971).

26. See the views of Dr. George Smith, as cited in Warren F. Ilchman, *Professional Diplomacy in the United States, 1779–1939: A Study in Administrative History* (Chicago: University of Chicago Press, 1961), pp. 58–59. For discussions of U.S. missionary influence in China, see the discussion in Tyler Dennett, *Americans in Eastern Asia: A Critical Study of the Policy of the United States with Reference to China, Japan, and Korea in the 19th Century* (New York: Barnes and Noble, 1941), pp. 555–76; and Cohen, *America's Response to China*, pp. 52–65.

27. See, for example, the discussion of U.S. missionary activities and their effect upon modern Turkey, in Lewis V. Thomas and Richard N. Frye, *The United States and Turkey and Iran* (Cambridge, Mass.: Harvard University Press, 1951), pp. 140–43.

28. This is the judgment expressed by Chester Bowles on U.S. foreign policy toward China during the early 1900s, in Chester Bowles, *The Conscience of a Liberal: Selected Writings and Speeches* (New York: Harper and Row, 1962), p. 50.

29. For more detailed explanation of the origins and meaning of the Open Door policy, see Julius W. Pratt, *A History of United States Foreign Policy* (Englewood Cliffs, N.J.: Prentice-Hall, 1955), pp. 434–41; and Tyler Dennett, *John Hay: From Poetry to Politics* (New York: Dodd, Mead, 1933).

30. See Edwin O. Reischauer, *The United States and Japan* (Cambridge, Mass.: Harvard University Press, 1950), p. 23.

31. For the text of what came to be called the Stimson Doctrine, see the message from Secretary of State Stimson to the U.S. ambassador to Japan on January 7, 1932, in *Foreign Relations of the United States — Japan: 1931–1941* (Washington, D.C.: Government Printing Office, 1943), 1:76; and for commentary on the doctrine, see Pratt, *A History of United States Foreign Policy*, pp. 582–83.

32. For a trenchant criticism of U.S. behavior with regard to the Open Door policy, see George F. Kennan, *American Diplomacy: 1900–1950* (New York: Mentor Books, 1952), pp. 41–56.

33. Our discussion of Wilson's Mexican diplomacy relies upon Howard F. Cline, *The United States and Mexico,* rev. ed., (Cambridge, Mass.: Harvard University Press, 1963), pp. 139–62; and upon Thomas A. Bailey, *A Diplomatic History of the American People,* 8th ed. (New York: Appleton-Century-Crofts, 1968), pp. 553–62.

34. Bailey, *A Diplomatic History of the American People,* pp. 711–25; and Sumner Welles, *The Time for Decision* (New York: Harper and Row, 1944), p. 71.

35. See Dexter Perkins, *Foreign Policy and the American Spirit* (Ithaca, N.Y.: Cornell University Press, 1957), p. 30.

36. Mark L. Chadwin, *The Hawks of World War II* (Chapel Hill: University of North Carolina Press, 1968), p. 17.

37. The views of the Century Group are quoted in ibid., p. 33; for a detailed discussion of its activities, see pp. 32–42.

38. Quoted in D. R. Davis, *Reinhold Niebuhr: Prophet from America* (Freeport, N.Y.: Books for Libraries Press, 1945), p. 75.

39. Text in Senate Foreign Relations Committee, *A Decade of American Foreign Policy: Basic Documents, 1941–49,* 81st Congress, 1st Session (Washington, D.C.: Government Printing Office, 1950), p. 1.

40. See the views of Harry Hopkins in Robert E. Sherwood, *Roosevelt and Hopkins* (New York: Bantam Books, 1950), 1:324–25.

41. See ibid., 2:13; and Vera M. Dean, *The United States and Russia* (Cambridge, Mass.: Harvard University Press, 1947), pp. 73–74.

42. Gaddis Smith, *American Diplomacy during the Second World War: 1941–45* (New York: John Wiley and Sons, 1966), p. 81; for details illustrating FDR's anticolonialist crusade, see pp. 81–98. During the 1920s and 1930s, liberal opinion in the United States had been extremely sympathetic to the Indian nationalist movement led by Mohandas K. Gandhi. See Pramod Vyas, *Dawning on Capitol Hill: U.S. Congress and India* (Calcutta, India: Mascot Publications, 1966), pp. 17–18.

43. See Malcolm Caldwell, *Indonesia* (London: Oxford University Press, 1968), pp. 80–81.

44. See the text of President Truman's message to Congress on March 12, 1947, in Senate Foreign Relations Committee, *Decade of American Foreign Policy — Basic Documents, 1941–1949,* pp. 1253–57.

45. See the speech by Secretary of State George C. Marshall on June 5, 1947, and statement to Congress on the ERP on November 10, 1947, as reproduced in ibid., pp. 1268–77.

46. See the views of Arthur P. Whitaker, *Spain and the Defense of the West: Ally and Liability* (New York: Harper and Row, 1961), pp. 380–90.

47. U.S. intervention in Argentina after World War II is discussed in Dean Acheson, *Present at the Creation: My Years in the State Department* (New York: W. W. Norton, 1969), pp. 187–90; and in Federico G. Gil, *Latin American-United States Relations* (New York: Harcourt Brace Jovanovich, 1971), pp. 194–96. A much more detailed account may be found in Harold F. Peterson, *Argentina and the United States: 1810–1960* (New York: University Publishers, 1964), pp. 427–525.

48. A comprehensive and objective analysis of this controversy, highlighting the role of the United States in it, is Fred J. Khouri, *The Arab-Israeli Dilemma* (Syracuse, N.Y.: Syracuse University Press, 1968); and for a study focusing upon U.S. foreign

policy toward the problem, see Nadav Safran, *The United States and Israel* (Cambridge, Mass.: Harvard University Press, 1963).

49. For the text of the Balfour Declaration and a discussion of its provisions, see George Lenczowski, *The Middle East in World Affairs,* rev. ed. (Ithaca, N.Y.: Cornell University Press, 1956), pp. 77–81.

50. See William R. Polk, *The United States and the Arab World* (Cambridge, Mass.: Harvard University Press, 1965), pp. 110–12. For statements by U.S. presidents after World War I endorsing Zionist aims, see the excerpts in Frank Gervasi, *The Case for Israel* (New York: Viking Press, 1967), pp. 199–201.

51. See President Roosevelt's letter to King Ibn Saud (April 5, 1945), as reproduced in Lenczowski, *The Middle East in World Affairs,* p. 433; and the account of the wartime meeting between FDR and King Saud in Sherwood, *Roosevelt and Hopkins,* 2:516–18.

52. For President Truman's views on the Palestine question, see Harry S. Truman, *Years of Trial and Hope: 1946–1952* (Garden City, N.Y.: Doubleday, 1956), pp. 132–69.

53. Acheson, *Present at the Creation,* p. 170.

54. See, for example, the analysis of Washington's efforts to secure Latin American support for a Jewish state in Palestine in Edward B. Glick, "Latin America and the Establishment of Israel," *Middle Eastern Affairs* 9 (January 1958):11–16.

55. See the speech by Secretary of State George Shultz, "Promoting Peace in the Middle East," in the Department of State, Current Policy No. 528 (November 19, 1983), p. 3.

56. The 1973 war in the Middle East is discussed more fully in Trevor N. Dupuy, *Elusive Victory: The Arab-Israeli Wars, 1947–1974* (New York: Harper and Row, 1978), pp. 387–584; and see several of the essays in Robert O. Freedman, ed., *World Politics and the Arab-Israeli Conflict* (New York: Pergamon, 1979).

57. See John S. Badeau, *The American Approach to the Arab World* (New York: Harper and Row, 1968), pp. 15–34. U.S. ties with, and support for, the State of Israel since its establishment in 1948 are analyzed in considerable detail in Steven L. Spiegel, *The Other Arab-Israeli Conflict: Making America's Middle East Policy, from Truman to Reagan* (Chicago: University of Chicago Press, 1985).

58. See Lincoln P. Bloomfield's analysis of the principles which ought to motivate U.S. foreign policy in his *In Search of American Foreign Policy: The Humane Use of Power* (New York: Oxford University Press, 1974).

59. The importance of the Jewish vote in affecting the attitudes of officials during the 1940s, for example, is emphasized in John Snetsinger, *Truman, the Jewish Vote, and the Question of Israel* (Stanford, Calif.: Hoover Institution Press, 1974), esp. pp. 115–41. The nature and activities of the Zionist lobby in the United States are analyzed in *The Middle East,* 5th ed. (Washington, D.C.: Congressional Quarterly, 1981), pp. 63–68 and in subsequent editions of this work.

60. Factors predisposing the U.S. mind away from the Arab, and toward the Jewish, point of view on the Palestine question are identified in detail in Mohammad T. Mehdi, *An Arab Looks at America: A Nation of Lions . . . Chained* (San Francisco: New World Press, 1962); Hisham Sharabi, *Palestine and Israel: The Lethal Dilemma* (New York: Pegasus Press, 1969), pp. 13–29; Raphael Patai, *The Arab Mind* (New York: Scribner's, 1973), pp. 290–301; Edward W. Said, *The Question of*

Palestine (New York: Random House, 1979); and William B. Quandt, *Decade of Decisions: American Policy toward the Arab-Israeli Conflict, 1967–1976* (Berkeley, Calif.: University of California Press, 1977).

61. Donald Rothchild, "Engagement versus Disengagement in Africa: The Choices for America," in Alan M. Jones, Jr., ed., *U.S. Foreign Policy in a Changing World* (New York: David McKay, 1973), p. 215. For more recent discussions of the U.S. policy toward Africa, see René Lemarchand, ed., *American Policy in Southern Africa: The Stakes and the Stance,* 2d ed. (Lanham, Md.: University Press of America, 1981); Desaix Myers III et al., *Business in South Africa: The Economic, Political, and Moral Issues* (Bloomington, Ind.: Indiana University Press, 1980); Michael A. Samuels, ed., *Africa and the West* (Boulder, Colo.: Westview Press, 1980); and Julian W. Witherell, comp., *The United States and Africa: 1785–1975* (Washington, D.C.: Library of Congress, 1978).

62. See the discussion of this aspect of the Kennedy administration's diplomacy in Arthur Schlesinger, Jr., *A Thousand Days* (Boston: Houghton Mifflin, 1965), pp. 551–84.

63. See, for example, the analysis of the problem of apartheid in South Africa and of U.S. response to it by former Undersecretary of State George W. Ball in *The Discipline of Power: Essentials of a Modern World Structure* (Boston: Little, Brown, 1968), pp. 241–59.

64. William O. Brown and Hyland Lewis, "Racial Situations and Issues in Africa," in Walter Goldschmidt, ed., *The United States and Africa* (Arden House, N.Y.: The American Asssembly, 1958), p. 160.

65. Waldemar A. Nielsen, *The Great Powers and Africa* (New York: Praeger, 1969), pp. 358–59.

66. American foreign policy toward South Africa under the Reagan administration is analyzed more fully in J. Gus Liebenow, "American Policy in Africa: The Reagan Years," *Current History* 82 (March 1983):97–102; Michael Clough, "United States Policy in Southern Africa," ibid. 83 (March 1984):97–101; Lloyd N. Cutler, "The Right to Intervene," *Foreign Affairs* 64 (Fall 1985):96–113; Ernest van den Haag, "The Busyness of American Policy," ibid. 64 (Fall 1985):113–30; and Henry F. Jackson, "The African Crisis," ibid. 63 (Summer 1985):1081–95.

67. See again the critique of recent exercises in U.S. interventionism by van den Haag, "The Busyness of American Policy," pp. 113–30; and the earlier criticism of U.S. interventionist moves in South Africa by George W. Ball in *The Discipline of Power: Essentials of a Modern World Structure* (Boston: Atlantic-Little Brown, 1968), pp. 221–60.

68. Marshall Cohen quotes John Stuart Mill to the effect that unless the concept of nonintervention becomes universally accepted and acted upon by all states, then the profession of nonintervention "by free countries comes but to this miserable issue, that the wrong side may help the wrong, but the right must not help the right." See Marshall Cohen, "Toward a Liberal Foreign Policy," in Douglas MacLean and Claudia Mills, eds., *Liberalism Reconsidered* (Totowa, N.J.: Rowman and Allanheld, 1983), p. 83.

69. For a detailed indictment of Western nonintervention policy toward the Spanish civil war, assuring Franco's victory, see D. F. Fleming, *The Cold War and Its Origins: 1917–1950* (Garden City, N.Y.: Doubleday, 1961), 1:62–67.

70. See, for example, the indictment of the inaction by the United States and other Western nations in responding to the Holocaust in Soloman Grayzel, *A History of the Jews*, rev. ed. (New York: New American Library, 1968), pp. 670–78.

71. Peter von Zahn, "From Germany," in Franz M. Joseph, ed., *As Others See Us: The United States through Foreign Eyes* (Princeton, N.J.: Princeton University Press, 1959), p. 98.

72. Bowles, *The Conscience of a Liberal*, p. 166.

73. Stillman and Pfaff, *Power and Impotence*, pp. 44–45.

74. For a recent and illuminating study of the prospects for democracy and overall political stability in the developing nations, see Gerald A. Heeger, *The Politics of Underdevelopment* (New York: St. Martin's Press, 1974), pp. 1–12 and passim.

75. Vera M. Dean, "Southeast Asia and Japan," in James Roosevelt, ed., *The Liberal Papers* (Chicago: Quadrangle Books, 1962), p. 255.

76. The distinction between authoritarian and totalitarian regimes was a conspicuous theme in the diplomacy of the Reagan administration; it was especially prominent in the views of U.N. Ambassador Jeane Kirkpatrick. See, for example, Seymour M. Finger, "Jeane Kirkpatrick at the United Nations," *Foreign Affairs* 62 (Winter 1983/84):436–58. In the view of the Reagan White House, Soviet communism was sui genris: it had no rivals in the contemporary world in terms of the danger it posed both to freedom within Communist-ruled nations and to the independence and security of non-Communist nations. See, for example, Strobe Talbott, *The Russians and Reagan* (New York: Random House, 1984); and Seweryn Bialer and Joan Afferica, "Reagan and Russia," *Foreign Affairs* 61 (Winter 1982/83):249–72.

77. See Perkins, *Foreign Policy and the American Spirit*, p. 26.

78. See the discussion of the "apolitical liberal," in Bernard Crick, *In Defence of Politics* (Baltimore: Penguin Books, 1964), pp. 123–30.

79. Pratt, *A History of United States Foreign Policy*, p. 585.

80. Donald Rothchild, "Engagement versus Disengagement in Africa: The Choices for America," in Jones, *U.S. Foreign Policy in Changing World*, pp. 238–40.

81. Douglas Brown, *Against the World: Attitudes of White South Africa* (Garden City, N.Y.: Doubleday, 1969), p. 238.

82. More detailed discussion of the continuing crisis in Poland and U.S. response to it is available in Charles Gati, "Polish Futures, Western Options," *Foreign Affairs* 61 (Winter 1982/83):292–309; Arthur R. Rachwald, "Poland's Socialism," *Current History* 83 (November 1984):357–61; and Piotr S. Wandycz, *The United States and Poland* (Cambridge, Mass.: Harvard University Press, 1980).

83. See the views of Raul S. Manglapus, in the New York *Times*, October 4, 1973.

84. See Robert A. Manning, "The Philippines in Crisis," *Foreign Affairs* 63 (Winter 1984/85):392–411; Belina A. Aquino, "The Philippines under Marcos," *Current History* 81 (April 1982):160–64; Edward J. Baker, "Politics in South Korea," ibid. 81 (April 1982):173–77; and Ross H. Munro, "Dateline Manila: Moscow's Next Win?" *Foreign Policy* 56 (Fall 1984):173–90.

85. For more detailed examination of the U.S. public attitudes toward interventionism by the United States in the post-Vietnam War era, see Ralph B. Levering, *The Public and American Foreign Policy, 1918–1978* (New York: William

Morrow, 1978); David W. Moore, "The Public Is Uncertain," *Foreign Policy* 35 (Summer 1979):68–74; and Daniel Yankelovich and John Doble, "The Public Mood," *Foreign Affairs* 63 (Fall 1984):47–62.

86.   See Dexter Perkins, *The United States and the Caribbean* (Cambridge, Mass.: Harvard University Press, 1947), p. 165.

87.   For discussions of recent U.S. diplomacy toward Iran, see Yonah Alexander and Allan Nanes, eds., *The United States and Iran: A Documentary History* (Lanham, Md.: University Press of America, 1980); Michael M. J. Fischer, *Iran: From Religious Dispute to Revolution* (Cambridge, Mass.: Harvard University Press, 1980); William H. Forbis, *Fall of the Peacock Throne* (New York: Harper and Row, 1980); and Harry Rubin, *Paved with Good Intentions: The American Experience and Iran* (New York: Penguin Books, 1980). U.S. relations with Nicaragua in recent years are discussed in Jimmy Carter, *Keeping Faith: Memoirs of a President* (New York: Bantam Books, 1982), pp. 178–83, 585; Alexander M. Haig, Jr., *Caveat: Realism, Reagan, and Foreign Policy* (New York: Macmillan, 1984), pp. 117–41; Eldon Kenworthy, "United States Policy in Central America: A Choice Denied," *Current History* 84 (March 1985):97–101; and Forrest D. Colburn, "Nicaragua under Seige," ibid.:105–9.

6

U.S. Interventionism after Vietnam: The Search for a Rationale

INTRODUCTION

From a number of perspectives, the Vietnam War was perhaps the most traumatic episode in U.S. diplomatic experience. Here, our interest in the conflict is confined to taking note of its momentous effect upon the diplomatic behavior of the United States in the years that followed. The impact of the conflict in Southeast Asia was especially far-reaching for efforts by the U.S. people and their leaders to arrive at a new national consensus concerning the use of military force in behalf of diplomatic objectives in the post-Vietnam War era.[1]

Our analysis begins, therefore, with a brief examination of the leading lessons of Vietnam for future U.S. diplomacy. As will become apparent, these lessons do not comprise a fully coherent and logically consistent package of diplomatic guidelines. Collectively, they are contradictory and incongruous — a key to explaining why it was so difficult for a new foreign policy consensus to emerge within the U.S. society after the Vietnam War.

On the basis of a reasonably extensive review of the literature, we have identified approximately 30 separate lessons to be derived from prolonged and agonizing U.S. involvement in the Vietnam conflict. For our purposes, however, these have been grouped into ten broad categories of diplomatic guidelines applicable to U.S. diplomatic behavior in the future.

Cognitive Failures and Deficiencies

If one conclusion about what can be learned from the Vietnam experience would command nearly universal support, it would be the idea that the outcome of the war in Southeast Asia stemmed from a pervasive cognitive failure by the U.S. people and their leaders in foreign policy.[2] Toward Vietnam, as toward countless other diplomatic challenges since World War II, the evidence indicated beyond doubt that Americans are poorly informed about and, for the most part, uninterested in, foreign policy issues. For more than 200 years, domestic concerns have been uppermost in the U.S. mind, and that focus did not change significantly after the United States became a superpower.[3]

In the case of the Vietnam War, this cognitive gap had three primary dimensions. First, a number of commentators have emphasized the failure of the United States to understand, and to relate to the needs of, the Third World. Factors contributing to the U.S. defeat in Vietnam were an inability by the United States to comprehend such potent forces as nationalism, anticolonialism, anti-Westernism, and the desire for radical change within most Third World societies today.[4]

A second dimension of this failure was the U.S. lack of expertise on Southeast Asia. The United States had relatively few experts on the region; and in many instances their views and recommendations were ignored by policy-makers.[5]

A third aspect of this cognitive failure relates to the role of the news media — especially television — in their coverage of the Vietnam War. As the first U.S. "television" war, the conflict in Southeast Asia was depicted vividly in the homes of millions of citizens. Yet in the nature of the case, media coverage of events in Southeast Asia was inherently one-sided: the military and other activities of Americans and South Vietnamese were fully presented, but equal coverage could not be given to Communist activities. Even the most objective reporter faced insurmountable difficulties in presenting a balanced and fair account of the Vietnam War. And this fact unquestionably contributed to the emergence and steady growth of antiwar sentiment within the United States and other countries.[6]

Faulty National Goals and Objectives

Another widely drawn lesson from the Vietnam experience is that, in order to achieve its diplomatic purposes, the United States must possess a clear and unambiguous set of foreign policy objectives. Their absence contributed significantly to the nation's diplomatic setback in Southeast Asia.

What precisely was Washington seeking to accomplish by its massive intervention in Vietnam? For over a decade, beginning in the early 1960s, policy-makers and informed students of U.S. diplomacy gave varying answers to this question — sometimes, concurrently. The containment of communism in Asia and on a global basis; teaching the Communists and other aggressors a lesson that they would not forget and that would deter expansionist tendencies elsewhere; politically unifying Indochina (which had been artificially divided into North and South Vietnam at the end of World War II); creating a democratic and modern political system within the country; demonstrating ability of the United States to stay the course diplomatically — these were among the leading objectives that, from time to time, were associated with U.S. interventionism in Southeast Asia.[7]

As is apparent, these goals are conflicting and, in some respects, incompatible. Moreover, as during the Korean War, U.S. objectives in the Vietnam conflict changed in response to new circumstances. The crucial point about them perhaps was the fact that, as the Vietnam conflict escalated, widespread confusion existed in the U.S. mind concerning what the United States was seeking to accomplish by its massive expenditure of lives, resources, and psychological enervation in Southeast Asia. In brief, during the Vietnam conflict the United States lacked a clear sense of its diplomatic vital interests, and this deficiency played a key role in its defeat in Vietnam.

The Relationship between Power and Diplomacy

The Vietnam conflict also underscored another lesson for Americans in their foreign relations: an integral relationship exists between national power and diplomatic results.

As several commentators have assessed it, a fundamental error made by the Johnson administration was that it sought to fight a painless war against the Communist adversary in Southeast Asia. The Johnson White House believed, erroneously, that the U.S. society could have both guns and butter during the 1960s. In the end, however, most of the objectives of the Great Society had to be abandoned; and the United States failed to accomplish its goals in Southeast Asia.[8]

Another way of expressing this relationship is to say, as several students of the Vietnam conflict have observed, that the United States was unable to create and maintain a reliable power base in Vietnam. The government of South Vietnam was so corrupt, ineffectual, and lacking in popular support that its weakness continually undermined the U.S. military effort against communism in the country. The general lesson from the Vietnam experience is that, before it intervenes in other Third World settings, Washington must make every effort to assure that the indigenous power base is firm and reliable. As many commentators view it, this requirement dictates that the indigenous regime be stable, reasonably efficient, have the support of its own people, and offer an attractive alternative to communism or other revolutionary programs.[9]

The Failure to Understand Limited War

With the Korean War earlier, the Vietnam conflict provided new evidence supporting the conclusion that Americans do not understand the nature and rationale of limited war. Because of their unique history, ethos, historic attachment to peace, the isolationist tradition, and other factors, Americans find it difficult to participate in limited war and to engage in it successfully; and little evidence exists that this phenomenon has changed significantly since the Vietnam War episode.

In his still cogent critique of the containment policy in the late 1940s, Walter Lippmann questioned whether Americans were tempermentally able to apply the containment strategy for an indefinite period in the future.[10] Similarly, during the Korean War, Secretary of State Dean Acheson, and other officials and commentators, raised basically the same question. Was it even possible for Americans to wage limited war successfully? To critics who asserted that the United States could not afford another Korea, Acheson replied that, to the contrary, in the nuclear age, a Korean-type conflict was the only one that the U.S. society — and the international system as a whole — could afford. For Dean Acheson, the principal alternatives to limited war — such as U.S. acquiescence in Communist expansionism or reliance upon nuclear weapons in dealing with diplomatic adversaries — were infinitely worse than the consequences of limited war.[11]

As the Vietnam experience confirmed, the problem of limited war continues to perplex and frustrate Americans, whose attitudes were perhaps crucially affected by concepts like total war and the unconditional surrender of the enemy, which governed the military effort of the United States during World War II. The Reagan administration's diplomacy in Lebanon and Central America encountered many of these same obstacles during the 1980s.

Critics of U.S. involvement in the Vietnam conflict continue to confront two questions that Dean Acheson posed during the 1950s. If limited war is ruled out as a diplomatic option available to the U.S. government, what alternatives are then left for the nation in responding to the moves of determined, resourceful, and expansionist diplomatic adversaries? And will the U.S. society really prefer the consequences of these alternatives to the limited use of military force to achieve its foreign policy goals?[12]

The Limits of U.S. Power

Another widely perceived lesson of the Vietnam War is that the conflict called attention to the limits of U.S. power. According to this view, the United States became embroiled in a no-win contest in Southeast Asia primarily because its behavior was motivated by what D. W. Brogan earlier called, "the illusion of American omnipotence" or the naive notion that every problem existing within the global system has a U.S. solution.[13]

As with other conclusions derived from the Vietnam episode, a considerable diversity of opinion is encountered concerning how and why the people of the United States and their leaders exhibited what was sometimes called "the arrogance of power" in dealing with Southeast Asia and other regions. Some students of U.S. foreign policy attribute it to a deliberate and conscious hegemonial impulse in the nation's foreign policy, created by such factors as the inherent nature of the capitalistic economic system, the influence of the military-industrial complex upon national decision making, and the indiscriminate anticommunism exhibited by the nation's political elite. In these interpretations, the urge to impose its power upon weaker countries is viewed as an ingrained tendency of the U.S. society.[14]

As other commentators have assessed it, however, the hegemonial impulses in the nation's diplomacy since World War II have been less conscious than unconscious, less calculated than unintentional. As exemplified by the diplomacy of President Franklin D. Roosevelt, Americans have traditionally been opposed to imperialism; and neither in

Southeast Asia nor in other settings since World War II have they intentionally sought to impose a *Pax Americana* upon weaker societies. Yet in Southeast Asia, Americans lost sight of the crucial distinction between possessing great power and possessing infinite power. Although it may be a superpower, the United States cannot single-handedly engage in successful nation building, modernization, and democratization throughout the Third World. Nor can it save Vietnam and other vulnerable societies from communism and other forms of radical political change largely by its own efforts.[15]

From the Vietnam experience, it seems clear that in the future the United States must ration or apportion its power, using it in behalf of diplomatic objectives that are centrally related to promoting its security and diplomatic interests.

The Reappraisal of Containment

For a number of observers, the dominant conclusion to be drawn from the Vietnam War was that the containment policy required reexamination and sweeping modification. As explained more fully in Chapter 4, containment has served as perhaps the United States' most consistent foreign policy strategy since World War II.

To the minds of many critics, the United States was led astray in Southeast Asia mainly because of an obsession with anti-communism. This pervasive frame of mind blinded Americans to such decisive developments abroad as the increasingly polycentric and schismatic nature of the international Communist movement, the true origins of revolutionary political currents within the Third World, and the effects of Washington's own interventionism in fostering support abroad for anti-U.S. attitudes in other countries. In this view, since 1947 containment had become perverted into a universal policy, leading the United States to oppose all forms of communism, political radicalism, and other movements advocating sweeping political change. In the process, the U.S. society forgot its own revolutionary heritage and too often became identified in the minds of foreigners with support for the status quo.[16]

After Vietnam the application of the containment policy needed to be governed by a clearer sense of geographical priorities: some regions were clearly more vital to the security and diplomatic interests of the United States than other regions. Moreover, as George F. Kennan and other commentators repeatedly insisted after 1947, the successful containment of communism must be envisioned as involving fully as much a political and economic, as it entailed a military, challenge.[17] In addition, in an increasingly multipolar global environment, U.S. foreign policy had to reflect a clearer sense of what ought to be contained abroad and how the United States could successfully do so, under widely varying local and regional conditions.

Failures in the Foreign Policy Process

Other assessments of the Vietnam War experience have highlighted a number of defects in the U.S. foreign policy process as basic causes of the nation's defeat in Southeast Asia. These also cover a wide diversity of viewpoints — ranging from assertions that the system failed (there was a general collapse in the decision-making process as a whole), to the machinations of the imperial presidency, to failures by Congress and U.S. public opinion.

According to some commentators, a broad leadership failure in Washington accounts for the U.S. defeat in Southeast Asia. Some commentators believe this is an endemic condition within the U.S. system of government; others attribute it primarily to the particular leadership (or lack of it) provided by the Johnson and Nixon administrations.[18]

Other commentators, however, believe that the defects in the diplomatic decision-making process can be more specifically identified. In some interpretations, they lie chiefly in the concept of the imperial presidency, as exemplified by the administrations of Lyndon B. Johnson and later of Richard M. Nixon. The wall of secrecy that surrounded presidential decision making, the premium placed upon conformity with the known views of the chief executive, and White House manipulation of Congress and public opinion in behalf of diplomatic goals — these were leading features of the imperial presidency.[19]

According to other assessments, among executive agencies, the State Department failed to provide forceful leadership during the Vietnam conflict, especially when it was confronted with vigorous and confident efforts by the Pentagon to gain the president's support for its views. An alternative interpretation is that, both in Washington and in Vietnam, the military leaders imposed their (usually erroneous) views upon civilian authorities. Other critics have contended, however, that the Vietnam disaster stemmed from a civilian failure to listen to and follow the recommendations of the nation's military leaders.[20] A still different viewpoint is that during the Vietnam conflict, there was a notable absence of Congressional initiative in foreign affairs. This conviction underlay the case for forceful legislative initiative in foreign policy after the Vietnam War.[21] And a totally contrary interpretation of what went wrong in Vietnam was that the system worked: the diplomatic failure must be attributed to factors other than defects in the decision-making process itself.[22]

The Evils of Incrementalism

A fundamentally different judgment about the nation's setback in Southeast Asia — and a recurrent lament about U.S. foreign policy generally since World War II — is that the United States lacks an overall theory of foreign policy, relating its separate actions in Southeast Asia, to those in Western Europe, the Middle East, and other regions. Diplomatic decisions are made in Washington, this complaint asserts, incrementally, on an ad hoc basis, and frequently in an atmosphere of crisis diplomacy. In Vietnam, incrementalism meant that, without quite realizing it, U.S. officials assumed a growing burden of commitments to South Vietnam; even while they denied doing so, they gradually "Americanized" the war in Southeast Asia without understanding the costs and implications of their actions.[23]

The lesson to be drawn from the Vietnam episode is, therefore, clear. If the United States seeks to avoid another Vietnam, it must adopt a set of guiding principles — or a reasonably clear rationale — for employing its armed forces in behalf of diplomatic objectives. Predictably perhaps, considerable attention was devoted in the post-Vietnam era to discussions of which principles should govern U.S. diplomatic behavior.

The Costs of Diplomatic Commitments

A related lesson of Vietnam is that, in Southeast Asia and other recent settings, Americans have consistently failed to calculate the costs of assuming overseas obligations. As in Vietnam, when the costs become sometimes painfully evident, the United States decides it cannot afford them; and it abandons or reduces its diplomatic commitments.[24]

In the Vietnam conflict, Americans forgot General William T. Sherman's dictum, that "War is Hell!" By definition, war entails military and civilian casualties, wholesale property damage, emotional and psychological anguish, and other consequences. When, owing in substantial measure to extensive television coverage of the Vietnam conflict, the rising cost became obvious to national leaders and the people of the United States alike, the Johnson administration's policy in Southeast Asia began to lose legitimacy. A growing body of citizens in time concluded that, whatever the United States was achieving in Southeast Asia, it was not worth the price exacted — the same conclusion they drew during the early 1980s about the Reagan administration's intervention in Lebanon.

Throughout their diplomatic history, Americans have devoted insufficient attention to the actual and anticipated consequences of their foreign policy behavior. Informed and objective diplomatic cost accounting is an essential ingredient in any successful policy abroad. The Vietnam experience reinforces the belief that such calculations ought to be made before the United States assumes major overseas commitments.[25]

The United States Must Stay the Course Diplomatically

The final lesson of the Vietnam War to be considered is in some opposition to the one examined above. (The lessons of Vietnam, it is worth reiterating, comprise a highly variable, and not totally consistent, list of diplomatic precepts for the United States.) Several observers believe that above all, it is essential for the United States to stay the course diplomatically or to honor its existing diplomatic commitments. If it does not, as in Southeast Asia, the United States' diplomatic credibility will be seriously impaired; and this development might in turn have crucial consequences for global peace and stability.[26]

This view is, of course, identified primarily with conservative officials and commentators, such as the supporters of President Ronald Reagan. In this assessment, as predicted the "dominoes fell" in Southeast Asia: defeat of the United States did embolden North Vietnam to embark upon an aggressive course. Moreover, during the 1970s it encouraged the Soviet hierarchy to believe that the Kremlin could become more diplomatically adventurous, without fear of effective opposition by the United States. It was not by coincidence, therefore, that Moscow intensified its interventionist activities in several Third World societies after the United States' dramatic defeat in Southeast Asia.[27]

If (as even many conservative spokesmen have conceded) the United States must become more discriminating and selective in assuming new global commitments, it must concurrently be resolute in fulfilling the diplomatic obligations it has assumed. Americans must not become war weary, confused and internally divided, psychologically exhausted, or otherwise prone to abandon their international obligations under adverse conditions. In this perspective, failure to be guided by such lessons of the Vietnam experience is a certain recipe for future diplomatic failure.

This brief analysis of the leading lessons of the Vietnam War provides a needed background against which to examine alternative approaches to U.S. foreign policy after the war. Collectively, these diverse assessments of the changes needed in the nation's diplomacy in the post-Vietnam era may be thought of as constituting the search for a new rationale for U.S. interventionism in the light of the Vietnam War experience. As the reader will discover, like the lessons of Vietnam, these diplomatic orientations are extremely diverse; their proponents often start from dissimilar underlying assumptions; and they naturally arrive at fundamentally different conclusions about what is wrong with U.S. foreign policy and how it ought to be corrected. From the various approaches available, we have chosen six for detailed examination.

THE ISOLATIONIST RESURGENCE

Not unexpectedly perhaps, the United States' defeat in the Vietnam War led to a resurgence of isolationist sentiment among the U.S. people. The conclusion drawn by some citizens from that traumatic experience was that the United States should carefully refrain from all intervention, especially reliance upon military force to influence the course of global events.

This sentiment was especially pronounced in the United States during most of the 1970s. Reflecting awareness of this frame of mind, President Richard M. Nixon wondered whether the United States had become "a pitiful, helpless giant" on the global scene. Congressional enactment of the War Powers Resolution (1973) — followed by Congressionally imposed restrictions upon U.S. military involvement in Africa during the Ford administration — provided additional evidence of the isolationist resurgence.[28] Indicative of the strength of isolationist thinking also was the fact that, until the Soviet invasion of Afghanistan late in 1979, defense spending was accorded a relatively low priority by national leaders and the U.S. people. During the 1980s, obvious public and Congressional anxiety about the Reagan administration's interventions in Lebanon and Latin America afforded additional evidence of the isolationist mentality.

Studies of public opinion during the 1970s revealed that the U.S. people were either totally opposed to, or extremely dubious about, the possible use of military force abroad — even to defend the United States' friends and allies, like Western Europe, Japan, and Israel. (All studies of public sentiment, we need to be reminded, provide only approximations of prevailing attitudes at the time the study is undertaken. Experience has amply confirmed the reality that U.S. public sentiment is crucially affected by internal and external developments and by the leadership exerted by the incumbent president.)[29]

A resurgence of isolationist attitudes following the Vietnam War was predictable for another reason. Some students of U.S. diplomatic history are convinced that a pattern of cycles can be identified in the nation's diplomatic experience. For some two centuries, periods of interventionism abroad have frequently been followed by eras of withdrawal and strong isolationist currents within the U.S. society.[30] A noteworthy example was provided by the period of Wilsonian interventionism during World War I, followed by one of the most profoundly isolationist eras in U.S. history during the 1920s and 1930s. Within a few years, U.S. opinion had swung from Wilson's vision of a Brave New World created under his leadership, to rejection of the League of Nations and (in the phrase popular during the 1920s) a willingness to "let Europe stew in its own juice."

A comparable reaction occurred after the Vietnam War. From believing during the 1960s that there were few global problems that defied solution by the United States, by the 1970s many Americans were exhibiting the Vietnam War syndrome of disillusionment and self-doubt about whether U.S. power was capable of accomplishing any worthwhile purpose abroad. Indeed, some Americans were convinced that the power of the United States was per se the major cause of international instability and conflict.

Without drawing the distinction too finely, two broad isolationist currents could be identified in U.S. attitudes toward foreign affairs after the Vietnam War. One was exemplified by what we have already described as the Vietnam War syndrome. This frame of mind in turn comprised a cluster of highly diverse U.S. opinions, reactions, and emotional responses engendered by the traumatic Vietnam experience.

The syndrome was primarily an emotional and psychological reaction by citizens, most of whom possessed limited knowledge of, and interest in, foreign policy problems. In this approach, preventing another Vietnam became almost a ritualistic slogan or incantation, applied indiscriminately to U.S. diplomatic efforts in the Middle East, Latin America, and other regions. Precisely how the United States could successfully avoid another Vietnam — or how U.S. interests in the Persian Gulf area and Central America differed from its interests in Southeast Asia — were not questions to which a majority of the citizens of the United States devoted serious attention.[31]

The other species of isolationist thought emerging from the Vietnam War was more rational, more carefully calculated, and based upon a more informed understanding of global events. This version — and it also was characterized by considerable diversity of viewpoints — was advocated by influential commentators and was expressed sometimes even by public officials and political leaders. The common denominator of this opinion — reflecting a frequently cited lesson of the Vietnam War — perhaps was that international ideological, political, social, and economic problems cannot be resolved by military means. For some observers, the United States' principal mistake in Southeast Asia had been the failure to comprehend this reality.

Among his prescriptions for *A New Foreign Policy for the United States*, Hans J. Morgenthau contended that "The ideological contests between hostile philosophies, social and political systems, and ways of life will ultimately not be decided by the political, military, propagandist, and economic interventions of the contestants in the affairs of other nations. . . ." Instead, they will be determined by "the visible virtues and vices of their respective political, economic, and social systems." Morgenthau identified this precept (which, from Chapter 1, the reader will recognize as an axiom of classical U.S. isolationist thought) as "the source of America's ideological strength and attractiveness." (As we shall see, despite this assertion Hans J. Morgenthau also remained a tireless champion of diplomacy based on *Realpolitik* precepts, including the United States' preservation of the global balance of power.)[32]

A variant view was presented by Paul Nitze. In the aftermath of the Vietnam conflict, according to Nitze the United States had to "learn to conduct strategy from relative weakness" — a reality that had also long characterized Soviet foreign policy. Nitze questioned whether "there are any circumstances under which it would be wise for the United States actually to commit military forces in combat with Soviet forces on the periphery of the European landmass." Referring specifically to the Persian Gulf area, Nitze did not hesitate to assert that, as between the United States' relying upon force to protect the region and relinquishing Western access to Persian Gulf oil, the latter alternative was preferable to the former.[33]

By the 1970s, the thought of George F. Kennan, whose views had undergone a significant evolution since the 1940s, also reflected isolationist tenets. After the Vietnam War, Kennan urged Americans to avoid interventionist tendencies abroad, such as efforts to assure foreign societies democratic and racially just political systems. In his view, such efforts almost invariably failed to accomplish their purposes, in large part because they lacked ethical and legal legitimacy. Such goals exceeded the power of the United States to achieve them; the U.S. society bore no direct responsibility or mandate to solve the internal problems of other countries; and more often than not the net result of efforts by the United States to do so was a reduction in U.S. influence abroad. The United States, therefore, ought to concentrate upon how to avoid interventionist behavior beyond its own borders, rather than upon how to engage in it more successfully. Kennan reiterated the well-known isolationist contention, that the United States' own example was perhaps the most crucial factor determining its ability to influence events abroad.[34]

Yet with most other commentators on post-Vietnam U.S. diplomacy, Kennan also acknowledged that occasionally the United States was required to intervene to protect its vital interests overseas. Kennan insisted, however, that these interests be construed narrowly; to his mind, most developments abroad do not affect the well-being of the U.S. society directly. Typically perhaps for most commentators whose thought is examined in this chapter, Kennan's ideas were usually clearer about what the United States should avoid in foreign affairs than about the underlying principles that ought to motivate U.S. diplomatic conduct.

In the judgment of Earl Ravenal, a transcendent lesson of the Vietnam conflict is that (with extremely rare exceptions), intervention by the United States beyond its own borders "is likely to be expensive, risky, and fruitless. . . ." With that predictable result, interventionist enterprises "should not be undertaken" by Washington in the future. The Vietnam experience created "a strategic presumption against intervention" by the United States. Rather than seeking to extricate itself from Vietnam-type conflicts in the future, the United States should learn "how not to fight them at all."[35]

Three concluding observations may be made about post-Vietnam isolationism, as advocated by well-informed students of U.S. foreign policy. First, the isolationist mentality is deeply embedded in the U.S. ethos; even in the late twentieth century it has a powerful hold upon the U.S. mind. Although convincing proof might be lacking, it is not unreasonable to believe that (from an emotional and psychological, if not a rational, perspective) isolationism remains the preferred diplomatic orientation of a majority of the U.S. people.

Second, among qualified commentators on U.S. diplomacy, however, the isolationist approach to global issues is a minority viewpoint. At its peak during the early and mid 1970s, the isolationist resurgence proved relatively short-lived. As a result of the collapse of the Iranian monarchy, the U.S. hostage crisis in Iran that followed, the Soviet incursion into Afghanistan, and other developments, Americans again became concerned about the decline of the nation's power, the loss of diplomatic credibility, and the relative military weakness of the United States vis-à-vis the Soviet Union. From the national election returns, it was evident that a substantial majority of the people approved President Ronald Reagan's determination to stand tall diplomatically and to protect the nation's vital interests abroad. As always, U.S. public opinion proved responsive to external events.

Third, even those commentators who advocated a return to isolationist principles as the basis for U.S. diplomacy almost never called for a total ban on military interventionism in other countries. With George Kennan, most isolationist oriented observers conceded that as a superpower, the United States has vital diplomatic interests that it is required from time to time to protect by reliance upon military force. Yet they were seldom agreed about how these interests could or should be defined. Taking Kennan's thought as illustrative, the reader of his essays gains the impression that the United States' vital diplomatic and security interests should in most cases be defined pragmatically.

CONTAINMENT AFTER VIETNAM

Inevitably, the Vietnam War episode had a profound impact upon the United States' policy of containment — perhaps the most consistent guiding principle of the nation's diplomacy since World War II. Regardless of their particular ideological orientations, most commentators on U.S. foreign affairs would agree that Soviet-U.S. relations are the key axis of contemporary international politics, a reality that is unlikely to change. The widely publicized Reagan-Gorbachev summit conference in Geneva in 1985 underscored the continuing centrality of relations between Washington and Moscow for the maintenance of global peace and security.[36]

Two diametrically opposite conclusions have been drawn by informed interpreters of U.S. diplomacy concerning the implications of the Vietnam experience for the containment strategy. One viewpoint — exemplified by many political liberals and revisionist students of the Cold War — is that the United States' defeat in Southeast Asia signified the end of the road for the containment policy. In this assessment, obsessive and indiscriminate anti-communism led the U.S. society into the morass of Vietnam; and in order to avoid another Vietnam, the United States must abandon — or substantially modify — the policy of containment. For several years after the war, a number of commentators believed that détente had replaced containment as the basis of Soviet-U.S. relations. In turn, détente was expected to lead to new arms control agreements between the superpowers, expanded Soviet-U.S. trade and cultural relations, and an overall lowering of international tensions.[37]

A contrary verdict was reached by other commentators about containment in the post-Vietnam War era, notably by political conservatives. As exemplified by the views of President Ronald Reagan and his supporters, in this appraisal the United States' primary failure in Vietnam consisted of its unwillingness or inability to implement the containment strategy successfully against determined Communist adversaries. As a result of this failure, the Soviet Union and its proxies (like North Vietnam, Cuba, and Nicaragua) had been emboldened to engage in diplomatic adventurism after U.S. power was withdrawn from Southeast Asia. By 1980, perhaps a majority of the U.S. people agreed with President Reagan that the Soviet Union was the locus of evil in the contemporary world. The Reagan administration was overtly skeptical about the benefits of détente for the United States, especially when under its guise, Moscow continued to sponsor "wars of national liberation" throughout the Third World. In brief, the overriding lesson of the Vietnam War was that the containment policy must be retained and revitalized. The United States could avoid another Vietnam only to the extent that it discovered a means of containing communism more effectively.[38]

In point of fact, as several studies of U.S. public opinion indicated clearly, the attitudes of most citizens toward Soviet-U.S. relations combined elements of both viewpoints toward containment. On the one hand, by the late 1970s, Americans were once again exhibiting distrust and suspicion of Soviet intentions abroad; they had little faith in Moscow's avowals of peaceful coexistence; and they approved of efforts by the Carter and Reagan administrations to strengthen the United States' military arsenal.

On the other hand, the U.S. people also viewed the Soviet Union as weak, vulnerable, and insecure. Under its Communist regime, the Soviet Union was steadily falling behind the United States, Japan, Western Europe, and other advanced regions economically. Americans were also clearly apprehensive about the continuing arms race and the danger of nuclear war. The people supported new efforts by the superpowers to reduce the level of global armaments and to resolve other outstanding issues engendering Cold War tensions. As always, public opinion was favorably disposed toward a new Soviet-U.S. summit conference and other steps that held promise (however remote) of reducing tensions between the superpowers.[39]

Among the more moderate critics of the containment policy, a basic consensus existed that it needed to be modified and adapted to the requirements of the post-Vietnam era in U.S. diplomacy. Robert Osgood, for example, called for the "revitalization of containment."[40] John L. Gaddis observed that, since the policy was promulgated in 1947, containment, in fact, had evolved; and it must be tailored to new circumstances confronting the United States after the Vietnam War. In his view, the U.S. people and their leaders had to devote more careful thought to what the United States seeks to contain abroad, to how it proposes to do so, and to the costs involved in implementing the containment strategy successfully.[41]

Reference has already been made to George F. Kennan's thought regarding the containment policy of which he is widely regarded as the leading architect. With the passage of time, Kennan expressed the view that his original conception of containment had been widely misconstrued and misinterpreted. From the beginning, the policy was designed to be applied selectively; it was never intended as a universal principle of U.S. diplomacy. Moreover, to Kennan's mind the containment strategy should be regarded as entailing mainly a political — rather than a military — response by the United States to Soviet expansionism and interventionism. (Kennan's ideas, however, were seldom explicit in spelling out the differences between political and military containment.)[42]

Aaron Wildavsky believed that, after the Vietnam conflict as before, no feasible alternative to the containment policy existed. At the same time, he was convinced that the old containment strategy needed refinement. After examining several possibilities for doing so, Wildavsky advocated what he called "containment plus." While continuing to resist Soviet expansionist tendencies, the United States should also concurrently seek "to change the Soviet Union or reduce the Soviet empire." Ultimately, this twofold approach to the Communist challenge would both counter Moscow's diplomatic adventurism and reduce the danger of a Soviet-U.S. nuclear conflict.[43] In the post-Vietnam era, Robert Tucker proposed that the United States adapt a policy of "moderate containment" of the Soviet Union. The revised containment strategy would give greater attention than before to the costs of opposing communism abroad. Its implicit premise was recognition that sometimes Communist policies jeopardize U.S. diplomatic and security interests, and sometimes they do not.[44] Or, in Ernest B. Haas's phrase, U.S. policy toward the Soviet Union ought to be one of "selective containment." This approach would not assume that the Soviet threat is ubiquitous and unalterable; it would recognize the fact that almost everywhere outside the West, the future of democracy is precarious; and it would acknowledge that some sources of contention between the superpowers may be resolved (or substantially mitigated), whereas other issues are likely to engender continuing tensions between Washington and Moscow.[45]

By contrast, Max Singer proposed that after Vietnam the United States follow a policy of "dynamic containment" toward communism. Key features of this approach are the idea that some Soviet policies and diplomatic activities threaten U.S. interests whereas others do not; that the United States must continue to oppose Soviet expansionism abroad; that U.S. power must, however, be used with restraint and in awareness of the twofold danger of nuclear war and of the nation's overcommitment abroad; and that the instruments of dynamic containment must be highly varied, to include (but not limited to) military force, political action, and economic, social, cultural, and other implements of diplomacy. Perhaps the policy's most innovative feature is the idea that dynamic containment would entail intensive efforts by the United States to reduce the dependency of North Vietnam, North Korea, Cuba, Nicaragua, and other client states upon Moscow.[46]

These examples suffice to illustrate the efforts made by informed students of U.S. diplomacy to reevaluate the containment strategy. As is evident, while substantial unanimity exists upon the need to rethink and reformulate the containment policy, a significant area of disagreement exists upon the basic components of a modified containment strategy.

Nevertheless, among knowledgeable observers and public officials in the post-Vietnam War era, a reasonably high degree of consensus exists upon the following propositions that must serve as the foundation of a more effective containment strategy:

Soviet-U.S. relations still serve as the central axis of contemporary global politics and the most decisive issue determining global peace and security.

Serious and continuing constraints (such as economic backwardness and ongoing domestic problems) inhibit the ability of the Kremlin to achieve its external goals; limited opportunity exists for the United States to reinforce these constraints upon Soviet activism abroad.

According to most criteria, the Soviet Union is weaker than the United States and, in some categories of national power, is becoming progressively more so; this fact does not, however, necessarily translate into more peaceful and benign Soviet diplomatic behavior.

Since the death of Stalin in 1953, some liberalization has occurred in the Soviet system; the United States ought to take advantage of available opportunities to encourage such tendencies; yet from recent evidence, a confrontational approach may well have the opposite results from those actually intended.

The tendency toward polycentricity within the Communist world continues; relying upon a wide variety of diplomatic devices, Washington should encourage this phenomenon, while recognizing that all varieties of national communism are not equally compatible with U.S. interests.

Despite the U.S. setback in Vietnam, from several perspectives, Moscow is losing (or may already have lost) the Cold War; with rare exceptions, the Kremlin is having little success in dominating the Third World; nor is there any reasonable prospect that its diplomatic fortunes will improve in the near future.

No feasible alternative exists to U.S. efforts to contain Soviet expansionism and adventurism in the post-Vietnam era; two possible alternatives — global nuclear war and U.S. acquiescence in Soviet adventurism — could be even more costly for the United States and its allies than the consequences of implementing the containment policy.

Successful containment requires U.S. reliance upon a highly diversified diplomatic arsenal, including military power, political and economic instruments, and other instruments; effective containment also demands the flexible use and skillful coordination of these policy techniques to achieve the desired goal.

A new sense of geographical priorities must govern the application of the containment policy after the Vietnam War; Americans must recognize that their national power is limited and that some regions (for example, Western Europe and Latin America) are more vital to the security and diplomatic interests of the United States than other regions.

In spite of the continuing gravity of the Soviet challenge, opportunities also exist for the resolution of some issues engendering tensions and misunderstanding between the superpowers; renewed efforts should be made to reach new arms control agreements, expand trade relations, engage in cultural exchanges, and widen contacts between the U.S. and Soviet societies.

THE REVIVAL OF *REALPOLITIK*

A fundamentally different approach is *Realpolitik* or political realism. This diplomatic orientation also enjoyed a revival in the post-Vietnam era of U.S. foreign policy.[47]

To the minds of several commentators and critics, U.S. diplomacy had miscarried in Southeast Asia because the people and their leaders had forgotten *Realpolitik* principles; and avoiding another Vietnam in the future demanded a rediscovery of these realistic political precepts. For realists, the Vietnam War symbolized the kind of ideological crusade upon which Americans are prone to embark from time to time; in the process, they lose sight of their essential diplomatic interests. As events after the Vietnam conflict indicated convincingly, the diplomatic and security interests of the United States were not directly affected by developments in Southeast Asia.

Predictably, during the last years of his life, Hans J. Morgenthau was outspoken in summoning Americans to return to the diplomatic verities of *Realpolitik*. In Morgenthau's view, these must become the foundation of the United States' new and more successful foreign policy after Vietnam.[48]

Other commentators echoed this idea. According to George Ball, the "East-West balance [of power] . . . remains the central element in the prevention of world disaster."[49] John C. Campbell viewed the maintenance of the balance of power — and reliance upon U.S. military power when necessary to preserve it — as the key to peace and security in the Persian Gulf area.[50] Similarly, on the European continent peace and stability were held to be dependent upon Western recognition of "the gradual shift of the overall military balance . . . in favor of the U.S.S.R. . . ." The NATO allies were compelled to take steps rapidly to counteract this tendency. Again, in the words of a leading conservative thinker, the beginning of wisdom was recognition that the overriding objective of U.S. diplomacy must be "to prevent the balance of military power, and the 'correlation of forces' [as Marxist thought describes it] generally, from tilting irreversibly toward the Soviet Union."[51] In this view, neglect of this *Realpolitik* axiom had been the cardinal diplomatic error of the Nixon, Ford, and Carter administrations. Since the Vietnam War, the "strategic balance" had tilted dangerously in Moscow's favor; and this fact had induced Soviet officials to embark upon a new stage of diplomatic adventurism. The restoration of a new and more stable balance of power, therefore, must now become the foremost goal of U.S. foreign policy.[52]

Political realists also emphasized another *Realpolitik* principle after the Vietnam War: the concept of the United States' national interest. To avoid another Vietnam, it was imperative that the national interest of the United States be defined more precisely and narrowly.[53] As already indicated, preserving the global balance of power remained the leading U.S. objective. During the early 1970s, the Nixon administration's diplomacy was strongly influenced by *Realpolitik* tenets, as epitomized by the ideas of Henry Kissinger. In the Nixon-Kissinger view, a high-ranking U.S. objective was to create a new global structure in what appeared to be an increasingly anarchistic and disorderly global environment.[54] This meant, as Kissinger assessed it, grounding U.S. foreign policy after Vietnam "in a realistic sense of national interest and the requirements of the balance of power." In turn, taking this overdue step would impart to U.S. diplomacy; the staying power required to accomplish the nation's external goals.[55]

The principles of political realism also infused the most comprehensive reformulation of U.S. foreign policy witnessed in recent years: the Nixon Doctrine, issued initially in July 1969 and amplified throughout the following months. Although considerable uncertainty always surrounded the core meaning of the Nixon Doctrine — in part, because it covered the entire range of U.S. foreign policy — three observations can be made about it. One is that the Nixon Doctrine represented a systematic and concerted effort by the Nixon-Kissinger team to redirect U.S. diplomatic activity in the light of the Vietnam experience. Another feature of the doctrine was that it typified the resurgence of *Realpolitik* concepts in the post-Vietnam War period. For example, the Nixon Doctrine emphasized the necessity for the United States to be guided diplomatically by its national interests; and it envisioned a clearer formulation of these interests in the years ahead.[56] Finally, in whatever degree the Nixon Doctrine was discredited by Richard Nixon's political demise, the doctrine did substantially chart a new course for U.S. diplomacy after Vietnam. The Carter administration and, still later, the Reagan administration accepted the Nixon Doctrine's contention that the United States must exercise greater discrimination in assuming commitments, and in applying its power, abroad.

Yet on the crucial level of U.S. public and Congressional opinion, the attempt to base the nation's foreign policy more overtly upon *Realpolitik* concepts was on balance a failure. The U.S. ethos has never been congenial to the Old World concept of political realism. Neither in the post-Vietnam War era nor before did Americans respond positively to diplomatic moves justified by concepts like balance of power and national interest. The U.S. mind remains skeptical that the nation's power — especially its military power — may legitimately be employed overseas whenever policy-makers determine that the balance of power is jeopardized or the national interest is endangered. (The Johnson administration, it must be recalled, ultimately failed to maintain public support for its policies in Southeast Asia by making such appeals during the 1960s.) After Vietnam, continuing public and Congressional anxiety about the covert activities of the Central Intelligence Agency (CIA) and other federal agencies abroad served as a vivid reminder of the traditional U.S. aversion for *Realpolitik*. Even more after the Vietnam War than before, the U.S. people and their spokesmen in Congress demanded that Washington's foreign policy moves possess legitimacy or be related in some demonstrable way to the promotion of U.S. and more broadly, human well-being.

THE IDEALIST REAPPRAISAL

This leads to a consideration of a fundamentally different orientation toward U.S. diplomacy in the aftermath of the Vietnam War. As a number of commentators assessed the matter, the major error made by the

United States in Southeast Asia lay in the fact that the steadily escalating U.S. presence in the region lacked ethical and ideological legitimacy. In brief, the United States lost the Vietnam War primarily because it was on the wrong side of a political contest whose nature it neither understood correctly nor learned how to wage successfully.

On this premise, it follows that to prevent new Vietnams in the future, U.S. policy-makers must devote greater attention to the ethical and ideological dimensions of the nation's behavior abroad. More specifically, Americans must remember at all times their own revolutionary heritage; they must comprehend more clearly that their own history provided impetus for individuals and groups throughout the world seeking a more just political, economic, and social order; they must exhibit greater sympathy for submerged peoples and disadvantaged societies who are endeavoring to engage in modernization; and they must not permit communism to serve by default as the agent of change throughout the world.[57]

For idealists, a dominant fact about the external political setting is that it is a revolutionary environment. In most Third World societies, for example, revolutionary ferment is a major cause of political instability. The Kremlin and other Communist centers did not create this revolutionary incentive, although, of course, Communist policy-makers and movements often seek to exploit and control it. More often than not, revolutionary upheaval within the Third World unquestionably has a strong anti-Western dimension, which interventionist conduct by the United States usually exacerbates. Moreover, Washington's efforts to prop up unpopular regimes in other countries, and to maintain them in power after they have lost the support of their own people, add fuel to the fires of anti-Americanism sentiment overseas.[58]

These ideas strongly influenced the diplomacy of the Carter administration, with its unprecedented emphasis upon the promotion of human rights in foreign societies. Throughout most of his tenure in the White House, President Carter agreed with critics who believed that in the past, U.S. diplomacy had reflected an almost compulsive anitcommunism and an ingrained opposition to radical political movements overseas. Accordingly, the Carter administration gave the promotion of human rights in the Soviet Union, in Iran, in South Africa, and in other settings the highest priority this goal received in the post-World War II period. Time and again, President Carter and his advisers demanded that foreign governments respect and expand the rights of their own citizens. With White House encouragement, Congress insisted upon evidence of progress respecting human rights as a condition for continued U.S. aid and trade concessions. The establishment in the State Department of a new bureau concerned with international human rights testified to the priority that the Carter White House attached to this goal.[59]

Although by no means totally abandoned, after 1980 the goal of actively promoting human rights in other countries was considerably deemphasized by the Reagan administration, which gave new priority to other objectives like restoring the military balance between the superpowers and preventing Communist gains in the Middle East and Central America. Moreover, in part on the basis of the experience of the Carter administration, President Reagan and his advisers believed that quiet diplomacy — the key element of which was the United States' effort to persuade foreign governments to modify their behavior — in the end was more productive than confrontational tactics. In the Reagan administration's view, the most ominous threat to human rights globally was posed by Communist tyranny and other totalitarian orders. During the early 1980s, U.N. Ambassador Jeane Kirkpatrick differentiated between totalitarian and authoritarian political systems. In the conservative view, the former — exemplified by the Soviet Union and other Marxist regimes — nearly always posed a more critical danger to human rights and global security than the latter. Dedication to the goal of human rights, in other words, demanded above all firm U.S. opposition to Communist domination of vulnerable societies.[60]

Now it must be admitted frankly that neither the Carter nor the Reagan administration's approach to the problem of human rights and revolutionary political change abroad resulted in any dramatic improvement in the global environment. By the mid 1980s, upheaval, conflict, and mounting terrorism were perhaps even more prominent features of the external milieu than earlier. International terrorism, for example, appeared to have become institutionalized, and no government had formulated an effective counterstrategy against it. Despite certain essentially minor changes, South Africa's apartheid system of rigid racial segregation has remained largely intact; and opposition to it by the country's black majority and critics is becoming more and more militant. In other nations with close ties to the United States — like the Philippines, South Korea, and Pakistan — political authorities continued to infringe upon the human rights of their own citizens. Yet it must also be noted that in some instances (such as El Salvador, Brazil, and Argentina), limited progress had been made during the 1980s in gaining official respect for the rights of the people and political dissenters.

The dilemma confronting national leaders in responding to the challenge of racial injustice in South Africa and other human rights' violations throughout the world illustrated a number of deep-seated problems with an idealistic approach to the challenge. In the first place, relatively few groups demanding that Washington do something about threats to human rights overseas usually also placed severe restrictions upon policy-makers' diplomatic freedom of action. Frequently, for example, groups calling for decisive U.S. leadership against the government of South Africa — the strongest military power on the African continent — were also among those demanding that policy-makers avoid another Vietnam abroad. Now as in the past, idealists had difficulty comprehending the relationship between possession and use of national power, on the one hand, and diplomatic results, on the other hand. Not infrequently, the campaign to democratize South Africa — or to establish a functioning democratic system in the Philippines, South Korea, and other countries — had many of the earmarks of efforts to save South Vietnam from communism earlier. In effect, they were a diplomatic form of painless dentistry; their advocates exhibited little or no thought to the costs or consequences to the United States of achieving the goal successfully. Minimum attention was directed also to the question of what happens (as in Vietnam) when, after the United States adopts a particular foreign policy objective, it becomes apparent that the costs and consequences of achieving it exceed those that the U.S. people are willing to bear.

The idealistic approach to U.S. diplomacy illustrated another aspect of foreign policy: the importance of geographical criteria in defining the United States' vital diplomatic and security interests. In the case of South Africa, for example, since World War II the African continent per se has enjoyed lower priority on the U.S. scale of diplomatic values than regions like Western Europe or Latin America. In no small measure, this reality accounted for the limited impact of U.S.-led efforts to democratize South Africa in recent years.

Finally, proponents of an idealistic approach to post-Vietnam U.S. diplomacy often overlooked a major lesson that could be drawn from the experience of the Iranian Revolution and its aftermath. The Carter administration's emphasis upon human rights had played a role in the collapse of the Iranian monarchy and the emergence of the religiously based Islamic Republic led by the Ayatollah Khomeini. Under the revolutionary regime, a reign of terror ensued; the Shi'ite clergy was ruthless in eliminating all actual or suspected political opposition movements. Consequently, it was at least debatable whether the U.S. emphasis upon promoting human rights in Iran had really contributed to enhancing freedom for the Iranians or whether generally it had benefited the United States, the Middle East, or the international system as a whole.[61]

GEOGRAPHICAL CRITERIA AND THE "REGIONALISTS"

A frequently drawn lesson of the Vietnam War was that the United States suffered a major reverse in that encounter primarily because Americans lacked a sense of geographical priority in assuming major commitments abroad. Southeast Asia, in other words, was — and remains — a zone of relatively low priority for the United States; developments there do not directly affect the security and well-being of Americans.

Nearly all formulations of the nation's diplomatic vital interests implicitly or explicitly rest upon some underlying sense of geographical priority. Perhaps the most celebrated pronouncement in U.S. diplomatic history — the Monroe Doctrine (1823) — quite clearly conveyed this idea. Its basic premise was that political developments in the Western Hemisphere impinged upon the security of the United States, while those in the Old World did not.[62] Similarly, after World War II most informed students of the containment policy believed that it was never intended to be applied universally and indiscriminately. From the beginning, for example, Washington largely conceded Soviet control over Eastern Europe. By contrast, a Soviet threat to Western Europe was viewed as highly inimical to U.S. security.[63]

The post-Vietnam War era witnessed a number of efforts to rely upon geographical criteria in the redefinition of the United States' interests and commitments abroad. As with the other schools of thought examined here, considerable diversity of opinion is encountered concerning which regions are highest on the U.S. scale of diplomatic values. Three broad viewpoints may be identified: the Northern Hemispherists; the Western Hemispherists; and the Southern Hemispherists.

Consider initially the Northern Hemispherists.[64] Within this orientation, there exists what may be called a narrow and a broad conception of U.S. diplomatic interests, construed in geographical terms. Starting with the former, for many years before and after World War II, State Department thinking was massively influenced by the views of the

Europeanists. Among this group, it was routinely assumed that the North Atlantic region was the zone of highest diplomatic priority for the United States. The New World had largely been colonized by Europeans; Americans drew most of their traditions, values, and heritage from European sources; and the United States had been compelled to participate in two global wars, primarily because of developments on the European continent. Advocates of *Realpolitik* believed that, after World War II, it was mainly the Soviet threat to the European balance of power that had triggered, and that perpetuated, the Cold War. It was not coincidental, therefore, that since 1949 the North Atlantic Treaty Organization (NATO) had served as the United States' most important alliance system. A frequent criticism of the nation's massive involvement in the Vietnam War was that it seriously weakened U.S. ability to defend the West.[65]

The Europeanist mentality in U.S. foreign policy was exemplified by the special relationship that had existed for many years between the United States and Great Britain. According to some interpretations, this relationship was as old as the Monroe Doctrine (which London had initially proposed be issued as a joint Anglo-U.S. declaration). Until 1900 (when the United States began to acquire formidable naval power), enforcement of the doctrine was heavily dependent upon the British fleet. Great Britain had also cooperated with Washington in the acquisition of the Panama Canal site. During the First and Second World Wars, Anglo-U.S. collaboration had been a major key to the Allied victory. During World War II, British scientists worked closely with U.S. scientists in the development of the atomic bomb. And in the postwar era, the United States' containment policy could be viewed as an effort by the United States to assume many of the historic global commitments that a now debilitated Great Britain had once accepted and protected.[66] In the narrow view, Anglo-U.S. relations are the keystone of Western solidarity; both symbolically and actually, NATO is the most essential defense network to which the United States belongs.

The broader conception among the Northern Hemispherists takes a more comprehensive view of U.S. security interests. In this perspective, the Europeanist orientation must be extended to include at least three other regions located in the Northern Hemisphere, which are also closely linked to U.S. security and well-being.

With a population exceeding 120 million people — and one of the most productive economic systems in the contemporary world — Japan has become an economic and financial giant. Beginning with Commodore Matthew Perry's celebrated opening of Japan to outside influence in

1853, Japanese-U.S. relations have been close. They were, of course, seriously impaired by Pearl Harbor and World War II. But in the postwar era, this historic pattern of collaborative relationships was restored and strengthened. In recent years, successive administrations have viewed Japan as perhaps the United States' closest Asian ally; cooperative Japanese-U.S. relations are regarded essential for a strong U.S. position in Asia after the Vietnam War.[67]

Since the oil boycott imposed by the producing states of the Middle East during the 1973 war, Americans have been graphically reminded of the importance of the Persian Gulf area for Western security and economic prosperity. If the United States has significantly reduced its reliance upon Persian Gulf oil in the interim, the NATO allies and Japan remain heavily dependent upon it. Another prolonged interruption of petroleum supplies from the Middle East could have devastating consequences for Western — and ultimately, U.S. — security.

Two developments in 1979 — the Iranian Revolution and the Soviet invasion of Afghanistan — provided added new sources of concern about the stability and security of the Persian Gulf area. Early in 1980, President Jimmy Carter issued the Carter Doctrine, which defined continued access to the Persian Gulf as a diplomatic vital interest of the United States. A new Rapid Deployment Force (RDF) was created to enforce the Carter Doctrine against a possible Soviet threat or other threats to Persian Gulf security. After 1980, the Reagan administration accepted the Carter Doctrine; the large and continuing U.S. naval presence in the area left no doubt that U.S. officials still accorded a high priority to preserving access to Persian Gulf oil.[68]

The Northern Hemispherist view of U.S. foreign policy (along with most other approaches) also includes close U.S. ties with the State of Israel. Since the World War II period (when Zionist organizations shifted their base of operations from Great Britain to the United States), U.S. power and influence have been used to create the State of Israel in 1948 and to defend and strengthen it against its Arab adversaries. Untold billions of dollars in official and private U.S. aid have been extended to Israel since its establishment; by the mid 1980s, Israeli dependence upon the United States showed no sign of diminishing.

The United States' strong ties with Israel since World War II are an example of what might be called an emotional or ethical national interest. The United States' overtly pro-Israeli position had unquestionably impaired its relations with most Arab states and had provided them with a strong incentive to develop closer links with Moscow. Yet a combination of policy influences created and perpetuated this strong Israeli-U.S. bond. These included the domestic political influence of the U.S. Jewish community; the acknowledged skill of the Zionist lobby in presenting Israel's case forcefully to Americans (coupled with the lack of an equally effective Arab lobby); the U.S. society's sympathetic understanding of, and participation in, the Judeo-Christian tradition; the fact that millions of Americans were personally acquainted with advocates of the Zionist position and many thousands of Americans had visited Israel since its creation; and the sense of guilt that many Americans felt — and which the State of Israel skillfully exploited — about the failure of the United States and other Western nations to prevent the Holocaust, in which Nazi Germany largely exterminated the Jewish population of Europe. For these reasons, for almost a half-century, support of the State of Israel has been, and remains a given of U.S. foreign policy.[69]

To summarize, the Northern Hemispherists believe that the United States' diplomatic vital interests are mainly confined to the zone north of the Equator. By implication at least, advocates of this approach attach minimum importance to U.S. relations with the Third World. Above all, the vital interests of the United States lie in preserving the security of North America and Western Europe. In the maximalist conception, the United States also has a vital security stake in the continued independence of Japan and Israel and in preserving future access to the Persian Gulf region. Diplomatic interests elsewhere are viewed as subordinate, meaning that they are seldom worth defending with military force.

A second regional orientation is provided by the Western Hemispherists. As we have already observed, the Monroe Doctrine reflected this approach: it declared (or strongly implied) that the United States would resort to armed force to counter any external threat to, or intrusion into, the Western Hemisphere. The doctrine presupposed the existence (or emergency) of a strong sense of community among the nations of the New World.

As all students of U.S. diplomatic history are aware, the original meaning of the Monroe Doctrine became amplified and extended over the years by a series of corollaries and interpretations.[70] For our purposes, an important stage in this process occurred in the early 1950s, when the Eisenhower administration persuaded the Latin American nations to declare Communist intrusion into the Western Hemisphere a threat to regional security (although it proved very difficult thereafter for the inter-American system to operate upon the idea). This concept was invoked by the Reagan administration in its effort to counteract Communist influence in Central America.[71]

Against this background, it was no coincidence that the most serious Soviet-U.S. confrontation since World War II — the Cuban missile crisis of 1962 — occurred in the Western Hemisphere. On the erroneous premise that the Monroe Doctrine had become obsolete, Soviet Premier Khruschev attempted to install offensive missiles in Cuba, less than 100 miles from U.S. shores. Moscow's move evoked a decisive reaction from the Kennedy administration; for a period of several days late in 1962, the world was brought to the brink of nuclear war. The Cuban crisis was resolved, but it played a key role in Premier Khrushchev's political retirement, in the growing schism between the Soviet Union and Communist China; and in Moscow's ongoing military buildup.[72]

Two decades later, the Reagan administration's intervention in Grenada and Central America again underscored the special place of the Western Hemisphere in U.S. foreign policy. The Reagan White House found the actual or possible existence of a Communist regime in the Carribean state of Grenada intolerable, and it acted decisively to neutralize that threat. The Reagan White House was no less determined to preserve the security of El Salvador from a Communist-supported insurgency, actively aided by the Soviet Union, Cuba, and Nicaragua. This effort involved military and economic assistance to the government of El Salvador; the buildup of military forces in Central American states; diplomatic and economic sanctions against Communist-ruled Nicaragua; and a variety of covert (but usually well-publicized) activities aimed at changing the nature and behavior of Nicaragua's Marxist regime. President Lyndon B. Johnson had said — and President Reagan and his advisers concurred — that the United States would not tolerate the existence of another Cuba in the Western Hemisphere.[73]

Under the Truman administration, the Western Hemispheric view was also illustrated by the "Fortress America" concept advocated by ex-President Herbert Hoover and Senator Robert A. Taft (Republican of Ohio). In this view, for the most part essential U.S. interests abroad were confined to preserving the stability and security of the Western Hemisphere. Yet as is true of most geographical formulations of the national interest, this idea could not be interpreted too literally. Ex-President Hoover, for example, believed that Great Britain and Japan were also vital to the security of the United States.[74] Despite such exceptions, the Western Hemispheric approach emphasizes the idea fundamental to the Monroe Doctrine. In the language of *Realpolitik,* since

1823 the security of the United States has rested upon the preservation of a favorable balance of power in the Western Hemisphere. Maintaining this balance may on occasion require that the United States use armed force for its successful accomplishment.

A third and more recent regional orientation is reflected in the views of the Southern Hemispherists. Advocates of this approach emphasize such lessons of the Vietnam War as the United States' failure to understand and identify with the aspirations of peoples throughout the Third World and Washington's alleged opposition to revolutionary political movements abroad. This approach calls attention to the fact that three-fourths of the human race — and the vast majority of independent nations today — are located in the Third World. With the principal exceptions of India and China (which are usually counted as Third World societies), the Third World is located in, or adjacent to, the Southern Hemisphere.

With the condition of nuclear equilibrium existing between the superpowers, the Southern Hemisphere has emerged as the principal zone of Cold War rivalry, where Washington and Moscow are engaged in a battle for the minds of men. Meanwhile, with its pervasive poverty and economic backwardness, the Third World is engaged in a cold war of its own: the struggle to achieve modernization and development. Nearly everywhere throughout the Southern Hemisphere, this quest includes political modernization or attempts to carry out rapid and sweeping political change. Frequently, the quest for political modernization involves a reaction against Western influence and political concepts. Modernization also nearly always includes the attempt to achieve economic equality, sometimes in the face of entrenched opposition by the United States and other industrialized nations. Avoiding another Vietnam requires above all that the U.S. people and their leader comprehend more objectively, and respond more sympathetically to, the political, economic, and social aspirations of societies throughout the Third World.[75]

The Southern Hemispherists believe that today, and for the indefinite future, the North-South conflict has replaced the East-West struggle as the dominant challenge of international politics. It follows that, if the United States seeks to enhance its global influence, Washington must accord higher priority than in the past to North-South relations. In turn, the most crucial problems existing within the Southern Hemisphere — pervasive (and in many cases, worsening) poverty, disease and malnutrition, inadequate educational facilities, and overpopulation — cannot be successfully solved by the growing military power of the

United States and the Soviet Union. Instead, U.S. military intervention in the Third World is likely to compound such problems and to create new animosities toward the United States. By contrast, increased U.S. economic assistance to Third World societies; more favorable terms of trade for the developing nations; U.S. respect for the determination of Third World nations to remain diplomatically nonaligned — these are the steps that will maximize U.S. influence throughout the Southern Hemisphere.[76]

Yet it must be observed that even toward the Southern Hemisphere, relatively few commentators on recent U.S. diplomacy believe that developments in more than 100 Third World nations are of equal importance to the United States. Most observers concede, for example, that U.S. ties with Mexico, or Nigeria, or Egypt are more crucial than those with Belize, or Mali, or Sri Lanka. Inevitably, the diplomatic priorities of the United States are conditioned by the size, location, raw materials supplies, volume of trade, regional influence and other factors affecting its relations with nations in the Southern Hemisphere. In some instances also, U.S. policy is determined by the nature or degree of Soviet involvement in other countries and regions. In practice, U.S. diplomatic activity within the Southern Hemisphere is likely to be influenced by pragmatic calculations, on a case-by-case basis. This fact leads us to consider the sixth and final approach to U.S. diplomacy in the aftermath of the Vietnam War.

THE PRAGMATIC APPROACH TO DIPLOMACY

The philosophy known as Pragmatism is the U.S. society's best-known and most original contribution to the philosophical heritage. Pragmatism's most influential spokesmen — Charles Peirce, William James, and John Dewey — were widely regarded as "quintessentially American," whose thought provided formal philosophical justification for ideas and modes of conduct long associated with the way of life in the United States.[77]

Without attempting a detailed analysis of pragmatic thought here — a task that is beyond our scope — it suffices to emphasize briefly a few basic characteristics of pragmatism.[78] As a mode of thought, it was philosophically omniverous: the pragmatist drew freely and heavily upon the existing philosophical tradition, taking ideas from the ancient Greeks and from more recent thinkers in the eighteenth and nineteenth centuries.

The pragmatists borrowed ideas widely and without apology from their philosophical predecessors.

The leading proponents of pragmatism were interested not so much in abstract philosophical speculation as in the twofold question of how truth is ultimately determined (or validated) and how it is used for human benefit. A fundamental pragmatic axiom was the belief that, among all possible methods for testing the truth of a proposition, ultimately experience provides the most reliable criterion. What does an idea mean in practice? What are the observable consequences of applying it to the realm of human experience? For the pragmatists, these were the decisive questions to pose about competing modes of thought and belief systems. As Charles Peirce time and again contended, for the pragmatists an idea has meaning only to the extent that it produces consequences for human experience. The idea has no real meaning apart from its results, and the latter must always be evaluated in terms of their positive and negative effects upon human society. To the pragmatic mind, therefore, the meaning of a statement and its proof by reference to human experience are inseparable phenomena.[79]

Pragmatic thinkers also emphasized the pluralistic nature of the universe. In their view, the universe (including the realm of political experience) is a mixed and dichotomous phenomenon: it contains order and disorder, symmetrical and asymmetrical forces, and rational and irrational elements. It was not possible, therefore, to explain nature satisfactorily by recourse to any unicausal, logically consistent, or completely unified theory of knowledge. Such monistic theories were always incomplete and distort the nature of reality. Moreover, the universe is envisioned by pragmatic thinkers as being dynamic and constantly in the process of becoming. Man's understanding of a dynamic universe continually evolves; time and again, old truths have been abandoned in favor of new truths. As has been true of the U.S. space program in recent years, the acquisition of new data often raised as many new questions about the nature of the universe as it provided answers to old questions.[80]

Another pragmatic tenet — clearly applicable to post World War II U.S. foreign policy — relates to the cognitive process. In cognition, the human mind functions primarily as a problem solver. The mind sorts out the multitude of impressions, images, perceptions, and the like impinging upon it; and it focuses the attention and energies of the organism upon those perceived as entailing a challenge or problem for human well-being. In turn, the faculty of intelligence enables humans to contemplate possible solutions for, or responses to, perceived problems, to consider the consequences of alternative responses, and ultimately to select the one that, on balance, appears to be most conducive to human welfare. The human response, pragmatists insisted, always occurs in a particular context of time and circumstances; and the existing milieu of decision making must be fully considered in evaluating both the nature of the challenge and possible responses to it.[81]

Upon reflection, few commentators would deny that these and other pragmatic tenets have momentously affected the diplomatic behavior of the United States since World War II. As a leading example, the crucial transition in U.S. foreign policy from isolationism to internationalism after World War II occurred primarily as a response by the United States to events, rather than from abstract speculation or theoretical reasoning about the ideal role of the United States in foreign affairs. Similarly, in 1947 U.S. officials promulgated the containment policy as a response to the perceived Soviet threat; the containment strategy clearly embodied what informed Americans had believed they had learned from recent experience about the nature and implications of Communist expansionism since World War II.[82] Similarly, by the early 1960s, Washington's growing commitment to the defense of South Vietnam was also a response to what U.S. officials perceived (correctly or not) as a Communist-sponsored effort to gain control of Southeast Asia.[83]

Paradoxically, in time the United States' misadventure in Vietnam was criticized in part because it was not sufficiently pragmatic: policy-makers in Washington consistently failed to identify and weigh the consequences of their actions. They failed to comprehend that the truth or meaning of the containment policy must always be determined within a specific context of circumstances; and experience in time demonstrated beyond reasonable doubt that containment was not a valid policy for the United States in Southeast Asia. The logical corollary of this idea, of course, was that, under a different set of conditions, containment might well be the best diplomatic alternative for the United States.

From the pragmatic perspective, therefore, the general lesson to be derived from the Vietnam experience about interventionism by the United States abroad is that each case must be decided on its merits. Ultimately, whether the United States resorts to armed force to protect its diplomatic interests depends upon a long list of factors and or variables present in any given context of events. In a particular case, the external challenge must be analyzed carefully; the possible responses available to the United States must be identified clearly; the likely consequences of each diplomatic option must be anticipated as objectively as possible; and a course of action selected that will have more positive, than negative, results. This mode of problem solving offers the best prospect of avoiding another Vietnam by the United States and, in more general terms, of enhancing its prospects for diplomatic success.

That pragmatic concepts have unquestionably influenced the attitudes of the U.S. people, and of a number of well-qualified commentators on the nation's diplomacy, in the recent period seems undeniable. Numerous studies of U.S. public opinion, for example, have emphasized the extent to which citizens are primarily interested in the results produced by the diplomatic activities of their leaders. The people are minimally concerned about the details of foreign policy or how these results are achieved. Rightly or wrongly, Americans routinely test their nation's foreign policy by reference to experience: on the basis of the evidence, is a particular policy working? In a given context of events at home and abroad, does the policy make sense? Is a specific diplomatic undertaking one that (in the language frequently employed by U.S. jurists) the reasonable man or reasonable person can defend? On the basis of such questions, Americans finally concluded that the United States' intervention in Vietnam — and several years later in Lebanon — was unjustified. In other cases, such as continued U.S. participation in NATO and the defense of South Korea and Japan, the people determined that these commitments were worth preserving.[84]

A dominant purpose of U.S. foreign policy, according to some interpretations, is to gain time. It is to keep diplomatic problems like Soviet-U.S. relations from deteriorating, to avoid nuclear war, to resolve as many outstanding controversies between the superpowers as possible, and to hope that — with the time gained — in a dynamic political universe changes will occur making the global milieu less turbulent and violence prone.[85]

Or as another student of U.S. diplomacy has expressed the idea that, with regard to the promotion of human rights abroad, the policy of the United States must take greater account of "what [is] possible and what [is] not" in dealing with foreign governments. When it does not take account, then U.S. diplomacy often amounts to little more than "hubris and finger-pointing" — conduct that is widely resented abroad.[86] In the same vein, President Reagan's U.N. Ambassador Jeane Kirkpatrick asserted that the United States must avoid the kind of "ideological globalism" that had been a hallmark of its diplomatic behavior in the past. Instead, it should act "on the concrete circumstances of each foreign policy case" and it must "assess alternative policies" in terms of their impact upon the security and well-being of the U.S. society and its allies. Still another commentator on U.S. policy toward the Middle East called upon Washington "to fashion more detached and flexible state-to-state relationships in keeping with local political predilections."[87]

Another observer described the diplomacy of the Reagan administration as "often reckless in rhetoric but cautious in action." On balance, he felt that the Reagan White House had "acted prudently and professionally" in foreign affairs; it had adopted "realistic and largely nonideological policies, but they did not fit into any unified concept." In Soviet-U.S. relations, for example, it was essential that the United States "be strong, but at the same time flexible." Washington must continue to resist new Soviet encroachments against the non-Communist world, and concurrently it must seek new ways for the two superpowers to coexist peacefully.[88] Or as another commentator explained, in the post-Vietnam War era the diplomacy of the United States must be based on the idea that peace is divisible. The Vietnam War and other recent experiences had demonstrated beyond doubt that many local and regional conflicts do not directly involve U.S. interests and do not, therefore, require an interventionist response by the United States.[89] Another study of U.S. diplomacy has formulated some eight different categories of nations — ranging from formal treaty allies, to friendly countries, to nonaligned states, to adversaries — with which Washington maintains relations. In this view, the pattern of relationships with nations in each category is — and should be — different; the U.S. response to external events, therefore, will vary widely according to circumstances.[90]

According to another analysis, in dealing with nations throughout the Third World, the United States must be governed by a greater sense of proportion in its diplomacy. In determining the nature and extent of U.S. involvement in the affairs of particular Third World nations, each case would be decided on its merits, with ample account taken of such diverse factors as the ability of the United States to defend the nation in question, the indigenous government's willingness and ability to defend itself, and its importance to U.S. interests.[91] As a general rule, Inis Claude is convinced that "the task of statesmanship is to judge whether American involvement *in a given situation* is more likely to produce consequences that weaken or strengthen the stability of the general international order [italics added]."[92]

Yet among the voices calling for a more pragmatically grounded U.S. diplomacy after the Vietnam War, the most articulate spokesman was

NOTES

1.   Numerous detailed accounts of the United States' involvement in the Vietnam War are available. See, for example, George C. Herring, *America's Longest War: The United States and Vietnam, 1950-1975* (New York: John Wiley and Sons, 1979); Stanley Karnow, *Vietnam: A History* (New York: Viking Press, 1983); Paul Kattenburg, *The Vietnam Trauma in American Foreign Policy, 1945-1975* (New Brunswick, N.J.: Transaction Books, 1980); Wesley R. Fischel, ed., *Vietnam: Anatomy of a Conflict* (Itasca, Ill.: F. E. Peacock, 1968); Larry Berman, *Planning a Tragedy: The Americanization of the War in Vietnam* (New York: W. W. Norton, 1982); and James P. Harrison, *The Endless War: Fifty Years of Struggle in Vietnam* (New York: Free Press, 1982).

2.   Stanley Hoffmann, *Primacy of World Order: American Foreign Policy since the Cold War* (New York: McGraw-Hill, 1978), pp. 231-32; and Henry T. Nash, *American Foreign Policy: A Search for Security*, 3d ed. (Homewood, Ill.: Dorsey Press, 1985), pp. 324-25.

3.   David Fromkin and James Chace, "What *Are* the Lessons of Vietnam?" *Foreign Affairs* 63 (Spring 1985): 724; and Zbigniew Brzezinski, *Power and Principle: Memoirs of the National Security Adviser, 1977-1981* (New York: Farrar, Straus, Giroux, 1983), pp. 543-44.

4.   Gerald Priestland, *America: The Changing Nation* (London: Eyre and Spotwoode, 1968), pp. 307-10; Hans J. Morgenthau, "The Lessons of Vietnam," in John H. Gilbert, ed., *The New Era in American Foreign Policy* (New York: St. Martin's Press, 1973), pp. 13-20; Jay Lifton, ed., *America and the Asian Revolutions* (New York: Transaction Books, 1970); and Melvin Gurtov, *The United States against the Third World* (New York: Praeger, 1974).

5.   See the views of Russell Weigley, in Peter Braestrup, ed., *Vietnam as History: Ten Years after the Paris Peace Accords* (Lanham, Md.: University Press of America, 1984), front matter, n. p.; W. Scott Thompson and Donaldson D. Frizzell, eds., *The Lessons of Vietnam* (New York: Crane, Russak, 1977), pp. 270-71; and Hans J. Morgenthau, *A New Foreign Policy for the United States* (New York: Praeger, 1969), p. 140.

6.   Peter Braestrup, *Big Story: How the American Press and Television Reported and Interpreted the Crisis of Tet 1968 in Vietnam and Washington* (Garden City, N.Y.: Doubleday, 1978); Fromkin and Chace, "What *Are* the Lessons of Vietnam?" p. 728; Robert M. Batscha, *Foreign Affairs News and the Broadcast Journalist* (New York: Praeger, 1975); and Dan Nimmo, *Political Communication and Public Opinion in America* (Santa Monica, Calif.: Goodyear, 1978).

7.   See the results of public opinion polls and other studies, indicating pervasive uncertainty and confusion in the foreign policy attitudes of Americans, in Fromkin and Chace, "What *Are* the Lessons of Vietnam?" pp. 737-38; James E. Veninga and Harry A. Wallace, eds., *Vietnam in Remission* (College Station, Texas: Texas A. & M. University Press, 1985), pp. 30-31; Norman Podhoretz, *The Present Danger* (New York: Simon and Schuster, 1980), pp. 29-30; the views of Earl Ravenal in Thompson and Frizzell, *The Lessons of Vietnam,* p. 264; and Townsend Hoopes, *The Limits of Intervention* (New York: David McKay, 1969), pp. 236-37.

8. Priestland, *America: The Changing Nation*, pp. 288-89; Hoffmann, *Primacy of World Order*, pp. 23-24; the views of Russell F. Weigley, in Braestrup, *Vietnam as History*, pp. 118-19; and the views of Harry G. Summers, in ibid., pp. 109-11.

9. In George Ball's view, after the Vietnam experience the United States "cannot effectively deploy [its] military power in an area where [as in South Vietnam] there is no adequate local power base to support it." George W. Ball, "Reflections on a Heavy Year," *Foreign Affairs* 59 (Special Issue 1980):488-89; and see the views of Robert Pfaltzgraff, in Thompson and Frizzell, *The Lessons of Vietnam*, pp. 275-76.

10. For Walter Lippmann's critique of the containment strategy and the U.S. society's ability to apply it successfully, see his *The Cold War: A Study of U.S. Foreign Policy* (New York: Harper and Row, 1947).

11. For Dean Acheson's views on the Korean War, see his memoirs, *Present at the Creation: My Years in the State Department* (New York: W. W. Norton, 1969). Other useful treatments are John W. Spanier, *The Truman-MacArthur Controversy and the Korean War* (Cambridge, Mass.: Belknap Press of Harvard University, 1959); and General Matthew B. Ridgway, *The Korean War* (New York: Popular Library, 1967).

12. Fuller discussion of U.S. attitudes toward limited war is available in Merlo J. Pusey, *The Way We Go to War* (Boston: Houghton Mifflin, 1969); Dexter Perkins, *The American Approach to Foreign Policy* (New York: Atheneum, 1968), pp. 98-116; Morton H. Halperin, *Limited War in the Nuclear Age* (New York: John Wiley, 1963); and Stephen D. Krassner, *Defending the National Interest* (Princeton, N.J.: Princeton University Press, 1978).

13. See D. W. Brogan, "The Illusion of American Omnipotence," *Harper's Magazine* 205 (December 1952): 21-28. See also the views of President John F. Kennedy on the limitations of U.S. power, in Theodore Sorensen, *Kennedy* (New York: Harper and Row, 1965), esp. pp. 509-17.

14. A representative view that attributes U.S. intervention to economic incentives is William A. Williams, *The Tragedy of American Diplomacy*, 2d ed. (New York: Dell, 1972). Other forces leading the United States to seek to dominate weaker countries are identified in Gar Alperovitz, *Cold War Essays* (Garden City, N.Y.: Doubleday, 1969); David Horowitz, *The Free World Colossus* (New York: Hill and Wang, 1971); Stephen E. Ambrose, *Rise to Globalism: American Foreign Policy since 1938*, 4th ed. (New York: Penquin Books, 1985); and Claude Julien, *America's Empire* (New York: Random House, 1973).

15. Senator J. William Fulbright, *The Arrogance of Power* (New York: Random House, 1966). A comparable view — that pervasive misperceptions have distorted the U.S. view of communism and other global movements — is expressed by John G. Stoessinger, *Nations in Darkness: China, Russia, and America*, 3d. ed. (New York: Random House, 1981).

16. Priestland, *America: The Changing Nation*, p. 308; and see the views of former Ambassador Robert Komer, in Thompson and Frizzell, *The Lessons of Vietnam*, p. 211; and the reflections by George F. Kennan on the containment policy, in Norman A. Graebner, ed. *The Cold War: A Conflict of Ideology and Power* (Lexington, Mass.: D. C. Heath, 1976), pp. 59-77, 180-87.

17. For a recent statement of George F. Kennan's ideas on the Soviet challenge and other contemporary issues in U.S. foreign policy, see his "Morality and Foreign Policy," *Foreign Affairs* 64 (Winter 1985/86): 205-18.

18. The view that the U.S. reverse in Southeast Asia resulted from the lack of overall coordination within the national government in diplomatic decision making is presented in Thompson and Frizzell, *The Lessons of Vietnam*, p. 271; see also Alexander Haig, *Caveat: Realism, Reagan, and Foreign Policy* (New York: Macmillan, 1984), pp. 121-22.

19. For more detailed discussion of the diplomatic decision-making process under the Johnson administration, see Eric F. Goldman, *The Tragedy of Lyndon B. Johnson* (New York: Dell Books, 1969); Doris Kearns, *Lyndon B. Johnson and the American Dream* (New York: New American Library, 1976); Irving L. Janis, *Groupthink*, 2d ed. (Boston: Houghton Mifflin, 1982); Richard E. Neustadt, *Presidential Power: The Politics of Leadership from FDR to Carter*, 3d ed. (Boulder, Colo.: Westview Press, 1978); and Herbert Y. Schandler, *The Unmaking of a President: Lyndon Johnson and Vietnam* (Princeton, N.J.: Princeton University Press, 1977).

20. For further discussion of the military role in decision making in the Vietnam conflict, see Jay K. Baral, *The Pentagon and the Making of U.S. Foreign Policy: A Case Study of Vietnam, 1960-1968* (Atlantic Highlands, N.J.: Humanities Press, 1978); Robert L. Galluci, *Neither Peace nor Honor: The Politics of American Military Policy in Vietnam* (Baltimore, Md.: Johns Hopkins University Press, 1975); Reginald Zelnik, *The Politics of Escalation in Vietnam* (Boston: Beacon Press, 1966); and Neil Sheehan et al., eds., *The Pentagon Papers* (New York: Bantam Books, 1971).

21. For case studies of Congressional diplomatic activism in the post-Vietnam era, see Cecil V. Crabb, Jr., and Pat Holt, *Invitation to Struggle: Congress, the President, and Foreign Policy*, 2d ed. (Washington, D.C.: Congressional Quarterly Press, 1984); John Spanier and Joseph Nogee, eds., *Congress, the Presidency, and American Foreign Policy* (New York: Pergamon Press, 1981); Thomas Franck and Edward Weisband, *Foreign Policy by Congress* (New York: Oxford University Press, 1979); and Pat M. Holt, *The War Powers Resolution: The Role of Congress in U.S. Armed Intervention* (Washington, D.C.: American Enterprise Institute, 1978).

22. See Leslie Gelb and Richard Betts, *The Irony of Vietnam: The System Worked* (Washington, D.C.: Bookings Institution, 1979).

23. The view that incremental decision making contributed significantly to the U.S. defeat in Vietnam is expressed by former Ambassador Robert Komer, in Thompson and Frizzell, *The Lessons of Vietnam*, p. 266; the same idea is a major theme in Hoopes, *The Limits of Intervention*. See also Haig, *Caveat*, p. 125; and Nixon, *No More Vietnams*, p. 46.

24. See the views of former Ambassador Robert Komer, in Thompson and Frizzell, *The Lessons of Vietnam*, pp. 265-66; Spanier, *American Foreign Policy since World War II*, pp. 150-51; Ravenal, *Never Again*, pp. 82-83; and the views of Robert Osgood, in Braestrup, *Vietnam as History*, p. 129.

25. Walter Lippmann, *U.S. Foreign Policy: Shield of the Republic* (Boston: Little, Brown, 1943), pp. 49-50; and his "The Rivalry of Nations," *Atlantic Monthly* 181 (February 1948): 17-20. See also the views of John L. Gaddis, that the United States must calculate the costs of overseas commitments and allocate its power to protect its truly vital diplomatic obligations, in his "The Rise, Fall, and Future of Détente," *Foreign Affairs* 62 (Winter 1983/84): 366-67.

26. See Senator Howard Baker, *No Margin for Error* (New York: Quadrangle Books, 1980), pp. 161-65; Brzezinski, *Power and Principle*, pp. 530-37; Henry

Kissinger, *White House Years* (Boston: Little, Brown, 1979), pp. 1252-57; and George Shultz, "Shaping American Foreign Policy: New Realities and New Ways of Thinking," *Foreign Affairs* 63 (Spring 1985): 705-22.

27. See the discussion of the implications of the U.S. defeat in Vietnam, in Haig, *Caveat*, p. 129; in Nixon, *No More Vietnams*, pp. 208-37; and in Strobe Talbott, *The Russians and Reagan* (New York: Random House, 1984).

28. See ex-President Nixon's views in his *No More Vietnams* and *The Memoirs of Richard Nixon* (New York: Warner Books, 1978), 2: 222-72. See also Gerald R. Ford, *A Time to Heal* (New York: Harper and Row and the Reader's Digest Association, 1979), pp. 249-52.

29. See the analysis of U.S. public opinion toward foreign affairs after the Vietnam War in Foster, *Activisim Replaces Isolationism*, pp. 329-93; in James Chace, "Is a Foreign Policy Consensus Possible?" *Foreign Affairs* 57 (Fall 1978): 1-17; and David W. Moore, "The Public Is Uncertain," *Foreign Policy* 35 (Summer 1979): 68-74.

30. A cyclical theory of U.S. diplomacy is proposed by F. L. Klingberg, "The Historical Alternation of Moods in American Foreign Policy," *World Politics* 4 (January 1952): 239-73.

31. For more detailed discussion of the Vietnam syndrome in U.S. foreign policy, see Michael Klare, "The Assault on the Vietnam Syndrome," in John Stack, *Policy Choices: Critical Issues in American Foreign Policy* (Guilford, Conn.: Dushkin 1983), pp. 122-24; John K. Galbraith, "Plain Lessons of a Bad Decade," *Foreign Policy* 1 (Winter 1970-71): 1-37; Thomas L. Hughes, "Liberals, Populists, and Foreign Policy," *Foreign Policy* 20 (Fall 1975): 98-137; and Lincoln P. Bloomfield, "Foreign Policy for Disillusioned Liberals," *Foreign Policy* 9 (Winter 1972-73): 55-69.

32. Morgenthau, *A New Foreign Policy for the United States*, p. 243; and Secretary of State George Shultz, "The Meaning of Vietnam," Department of State, Current Policy No. 694 (April 25, 1985), pp. 1-4.

33. Paul Nitze, "Policy and Strategy from Weakness," in W. Scott Thompson, ed., *National Security in the 1980s: From Weakness to Strength* (San Francisco: Institute for Contemporary Studies, 1980), pp. 443-56.

34. For the evolution in the thoughts of George F. Kennan about U.S. diplomacy in the post-World War II era, see his *Memoirs: 1925-1950* (New York: Bantam Books, 1969); *Memoirs: 1950-1963* (New York: Pantheon Books, 1972); and his "Morality and Foreign Policy." A useful commentary is Barton Gellman, *Contending with Kennan: Toward a Philosophy of American Power* (New York: Praeger, 1984).

35. Ravenal, *Never Again*, xii, 103.

36. For informative studies of recent Soviet-U.S. relations, see Adam B. Ulam, *Dangerous Relations: The Soviet Union in World Politics, 1970-1982* (New York: Oxford University Press, 1983); Richard J. Barnet, *The Giants: Russia and America* (New York: Simon and Schuster, 1977); Robin Edmonds, *Soviet Foreign Policy: The Brezhnev Years* (New York: Oxford University Press, 1983); and Coral Bell, *The Diplomacy of Détente: The Kissinger Era* (New York: St. Martin's Press, 1977).

37. The idea that the U.S. defeat in the Vietnam War derived mainly from the failure by Congress to support White House policies is a theme in Nixon, *No More Vietnams*. See also Richard Viguerie, *The New Right — We're Ready to Lead* (Falls

Church, Va.: Viguerie, 1980); and Norman Podhoretz, *The Present Danger* (New York: Simon and Schuster, 1980).

38. See Strobe Talbott, *The Russians and Reagan* (New York: Random House, 1984); Craig R. Whitney, "The View from the Kremlin," *New York Times Magazine,* April 20, 1980, pp. 31-33, 92; and Bernard A. Weisberger, *Cold War, Cold Peace: The United States and Russia since 1945* (New York: American Heritage, 1984).

39. Anomalies and contradictions in U.S. public opinion toward the Soviet Union are highlighted in Daniel Yankelovich and John Doble, "The Public Mood: Nuclear Weapons and the U.S.S.R.," *Foreign Affairs* 63 (Fall 1984): 33-46.

40. Robert E. Osgood, "The Revitalization of Containment," *Foreign Affairs* 60 (Special Issue 1981): 465-503.

41. John L. Gaddis, "The Rise, Fall, and Future of Détente," *Foreign Affairs* 62 (Winter 1983): 354-78.

42. See George F. Kennan's views as quoted in Nash, *American Foreign Policy,* pp. 250-51; and in James Chace, *A World Elsewhere: The New American Foreign Policy* (New York: Charles Scribner's Sons, 1973), pp. 12-14.

43. Aaron Wildavsky, "From Minimal to Maximal Containment," in Aaron Wildavsky, ed., *Beyond Containment: Alternative American Policies toward the Soviet Union* (San Francisco: Institute for Contemporary Studies, 1983), pp. 231-33.

44. Robert Tucker, *The Purposes of American Power: An Essay on National Security* (New York: Praeger, 1981), pp. 134-35.

45. Ernest B. Haas, "On Hedging Our Bets: Selective Engagement with the Soviet Union," in Wildavsky, *Beyond Containment,* pp. 93-124.

46. Max Singer, "Dynamic Containment," in Wildavsky, *Beyond Containment,* pp. 169-99.

47. In addition to the more detailed analysis of *Realpolitik* in Chapter 4, see Ira S. Cohen, *Realpolitik: Theory and Practice* (Encino, Calif.: Dickenson, 1975); Edward V. Gulick, *Europe's Classical Balance of Power* (Ithaca, N.Y.: Cornell University Press, 1955); and Paul Seabury, ed., *Balance of Power* (San Francisco: Chandler, 1965).

48. See Morgenthau, *A New Foreign Policy for the United States;* and Ronald Steel, "A Spheres of Influence Policy," *Foreign Policy* 5 (Winter 1971-72): 107-119.

49. Ball, "Reflections on a Heavy Year," p. 499.

50. John C. Campbell, "The Middle East: A House of Containment Built on Shifting Sands," *Foreign Affairs* 60 (Special Issue 1981): 624.

51. Peter Lellouche, "Europe and Her Defense," *Foreign Affairs* 59 (Spring 1981): 815.

52. Norman Podhoretz, "The Reagan Road to Détente," *Foreign Affairs* 63 (Special Issue 1984): 451; Seweryn Bialer and John Afferica, "Reagan and Russia," *Foreign Affairs* 61 (Winter 1982/83): 250-51; and the views of Stanley Hoffmann, as cited in James Chace, *A World Elsewhere: A Search for Security* (New York: Charles Scribners Sons, 1973), p. 106.

53. See the views of John L. Gaddis in "Containment: Its Past and Future," in Charles W. Kegley, Jr., and Eugene W. Wittkopf, eds., *Perspectives on American Foreign Policy: Selected Readings* (New York: St. Martin's Press, 1983). pp. 20-21; and Hans J. Morgenthau, "Defining the National Interest — Again Old Superstitions, New Realities," in Kegley and Wittkopf, *Perspectives on American Foreign Policy,* pp. 32-33.

54. See the two White House documents in which Henry Kissinger's ideas are evident, *U.S. Foreign Policy for the 1970's: Building for Peace* (Washington, D.C., 1971) and *U.S. Foreign Policy for the 1970's: The Emerging Structure of Peace* (Washington, D.C., 1972).

55. Henry Kissinger, *Years of Upheaval* (Boston: Little, Brown, 1982), p. 981. See also the first volume of Kissinger's memoirs, *White House Years* (Boston: Little, Brown, 1979), for additional evidence of *Realpolitik* concepts in his approach to foreign affairs.

56. The nature, main provisions, and primary implications of the Nixon Doctrine are examined more fully in Cecil V. Crabb, Jr., *The Doctrines of American Foreign Policy*, pp. 278-325.

57. The historic role of idealism in U.S. diplomacy is emphasized in Frank Tannenbaum, *The American Tradition in Foreign Policy* (Norman, Okla.: University of Oklahoma Press, 1955); Dexter Perkins, *The American Approach to Foreign Policy* (Cambridge, Mass.: Harvard University Press, 1952); Ambrose, *Rise to Globalism;* Michael Parenti, ed., *Trends and Tragedies in American Foreign Policy* (Boston: Little, Brown, 1971); and John Wheeler, "Coming to Grips with Vietnam" *Foreign Affairs* 63 (Spring 1985): 747-59.

58. See Barnet, *Intervention and Revolution;* Gurtov, *The United States against the Third World;* John C. Donovan, *The Cold Warriors: A Policy-Making Elite* (Lexington, Mass.: D.C. Heath, 1974); and Richard J. Walton, *Cold War and Counter-Revolution: The Foreign Policy of John F. Kennedy* (Baltimore: Penguin Books, 1972).

59. The Carter administration's strong emphasis upon promoting human rights abroad is highlighted in Jimmy Carter, *Keeping Faith: Memoirs of a President* (New York: Bantam Books, 1982), pp. 139-86, 433-597; and Cyrus Vance, *Hard Choices: Critical Years in American Foreign Policy* (New York: Simon and Schuster, 1983), pp. 256-349.

60. For the Reagan administration's views of global human rights problems and the United States' approach to them, see Paul E. Sigmund, "Latin America: Change or Continuity," *Foreign Affairs* 60 (Special Issue 1981): 58-61; Kenneth L. Adelman, "Speaking of America: Public Diplomacy in Our Time," *Foreign Affairs* 59 (Spring 1981): 913-37; Samuel P. Huntington, "Human Rights and American Power," in Stack, *Policy Choices*, pp. 153-61; President Ronald Reagan, "Safeguarding Human Rights," Department of State, Current Policy No. 775 (December 10, 1985), pp. 1-4; and Elliott Abrams, "An End to Tyranny in Latin America," Department of State, Current Policy No. 777 (December 9, 1985), pp. 1-4.

61. See the discussions of developments in Iran after the revolution of 1979 in Barry Rubin, *Paved with Good Intentions: The American Experience and Iran* (Baltimore: Penguin Books, 1981), pp. 217-327; in Shaul Bakhash, *The Reign of the Ayatollahs: Iran and the Islamic Revolution* (New York: Basic Books, 1984); and James A. Bill, "Resurgent Islam in the Persian Gulf," *Foreign Affairs* 63 (Fall 1984): 108-127.

62. For the text of the Monroe Doctrine, see President James Monroe's speech to Congress on December 2, 1823, in James D. Richardson, ed., *A Compilation of the Messages and Papers of the Presidents, 1789-1897* (Washington, D.C.: Government Printing Office, 1897), 2: 207-20.

63. See, for example, the view of Dean Acheson and other officials involved in the

formulation of the containment policy, as quoted in Crabb, *The Doctrines of American Foreign Policy,* pp. 137-39; and in Arthur H. Vandenberg, Jr., ed., *The Private Papers of Senator Vandenberg* (Boston: Houghton Mifflin, 1952), pp. 337-73. See also the symposium on the containment policy in *Foreign Policy* 7 (Summer 1972): 5-54.

64. The views of the Northern Hemispherists are exemplified by the ideas of George W. Ball. See his *The Discipline of Power: Essentials of a Modern World Structure* (Boston: Little, Brown, 1968) and *Diplomacy for a Crowded World: An American Foreign Policy* (Boston: Little, Brown, 1976). This viewpoint was also prominent in the ideas of Henry Kissinger. See, for example, his *White House Years* and *Years of Upheaval.* The same orientation is also evident in the views of Hans J. Morgenthau. See his "Defining the National Interest — Again: Old Superstitions and New Realities," in Kegley and Wittkopf, *Perspectives on American Foreign Policy,* pp. 38-39.

65. The Europeanist orientation among high-ranking officials involved in the foreign policy process has deep historical roots and was prominent in U.S. diplomacy until at least the Kennedy administration. In the view of several commentators, it was sustained by the upper socioeconomic backgrounds of these officials; they were often graduates of Ivy League institutions; and they came predominately from the eastern United States, which had a strong affinity for European culture and modes of thought. This outlook was typified, for example, by the New York-based Council on Foreign Relations and its influential (sometimes called, semiofficial) publication, *Foreign Affairs.* For a recent discussion of this viewpoint, see Robert Komer, "Maritime Strategy vs. Coalition Defense," *Foreign Affairs* 60 (Summer 1982): 1124-44.

66. More detailed discussion of the nature of the special relationship between Great Britain and the United States is available in H. C. Allen, *Great Britain and the United States* (New York: Macmillan, 1955); and in Crane Brinton, *The United States and Great Britain* (Cambridge, Mass.: Harvard University Press, 1948).

67. Historical background on Japanese-U.S. relations is provided in Edwin O. Reischauer, *The United States and Japan,* 3d ed. (Cambridge, Mass.: Harvard University Press, 1965). More recent discussions are Hans H. Baerwald, "The Foreign Policy of Japan," in James Rosenau et al., *World Politics: An Introduction* (New York: Macmillan, 1976), pp. 129-50; and the symposium on Japan in *Current History* 84 (December 1985): 401-31.

68. U.S. diplomatic and strategic interests in the Persian Gulf region are examined more fully in Emile A. Nakhleh, *Arab-American Relations in the Persian Gulf* (Washington, D.C.: American Enterprise Institute, 1975); in J. B. Kelly, *Arabia, The Gulf, and the West* (New York: Basic Books, 1980); and in Peter Mangold, *Superpower Intervention in the Middle East* (New York: St. Martin's Press, 1977).

69. The nature and evolution of U.S. ties with the Zionist Movement and the State of Israel are analyzed more fully in Fred J. Khouri, *The Arab-Israeli Dilemma* (New York: Syracuse University Press, 1968); in Samuel Halperin, *The Political World of American Zionism* (Detroit, Mich.: Wayne State University Press, 1961); and in Bernard Riech, *Quest for Peace: United States-Israeli Relations and the Arab-Israeli Conflict* (New Brunswick, N.J.: Transaction Books, 1977).

70. The evolution of the Monroe Doctrine is traced in Dexter Perkins, *A History of the Monroe Doctrine* (Boston: Little, Brown, 1955), 2 vols. Briefer treatments are Donald M. Dozer, ed., *The Monroe Doctrine: Its Modern Significance* (New York:

Alfred A. Knopf, 1965); Edward Lieuwen, *U.S. Policy in Latin America: A Short History* (New York: Praeger, 1965); and the "Monroe Doctrine," in Crabb, *The Doctrines of American Foreign Policy*, pp. 9-56.

71. See the discussion of the Communist challenge within the Western Hemisphere, in Dwight D. Eisenhower, *Waging Peace: 1956-1961* (Garden City, N.Y.: Doubleday, 1965), pp. 514-43; the New York *Times* edition of *The Rockefeller Report on the Americas* (New York: Quadrangle Books, 1969); and Herbert L. Matthews, *The United States and Latin America*, 2d ed. (Englewood Cliffs, N.J.: Prentice-Hall, 1963), pp.121-171.

72. The Cuban missile crisis of 1962 is discussed more fully in Theodore Sorensen, *Kennedy* (New York: Harper and Row, 1965), pp. 667-718; in Arthur Schlesinger, Jr., *A Thousand Days* (Boston: Houghton Mifflin, 1965), pp. 794-819; and in Robert Kennedy, *Thirteen Days: A Memoir of the Cuban Missile Crisis* (New York: New American Library, 1968).

73. On U.S. involvement in recent Communist activities in the Caribbean area and Central America, see George Shultz, "New Realities and New Ways of Thinking," pp. 712-14; the New York *Times*, August 20, 1984, dispatch by Robert Pear; the text of President Ronald Reagan's Second Inaugural Address, in the New York *Times*, January 22, 1985; and President Ronald Reagan, "U.S. Interests in Central America," Department of State, Current Policy No. 576 (May 9, 1984), pp. 1-4.

74. For a discussion of the Fortress America concept before World War II, as often advocated by isolationists, see Robert E. Sherwood, *Roosevelt and Hopkins* (New York: Bantam Books, 1950), 1: 161. Postwar versions of the concept are explained more fully in Robert A. Taft, *A Foreign Policy for Americans* (Garden City, N.Y.: Doubleday, 1951), pp. 66-79; and in ex-President Herbert Hoover's *Addresses upon the American Road, 1950-1955* (Stanford, Calif.: Stanford University Press, 1955), pp. 3-11, 23-45.

75. The Southern Hemispherist or Third World orientation in U.S. foreign policy is exemplified by John P. Lewis and Valeriana Kalleb, eds., *U.S. Foreign Policy and the Third World: Agenda 1983* (Washington, D.C.: Overseas Development Council, 1983); Richard E. Feinberg, *The Intemperate Zone: The Third World Challenge to U.S. Foreign Policy* (New York: W. W. Norton, 1983); Robert A. Packenham, *Liberal America and the Third World* (Princeton, N.J.: Princeton University Press, 1973); Harrison Brown, *The Human Future Revisited* (New York: W. W. Norton, 1978); Howard Wriggins and Gunnar Adler-Karlson, *Reducing Global Inequities* (New York: McGraw-Hill, 1978); and Commission on International Development Issues (Willy Brandt, Chairman), *North-South: A Programme for Survival* (Cambridge, Mass.: M.I.T. Press, 1980); and Seymom Brown, *On the Front Burner: Issues in U.S. Foreign Policy* (Boston: Little, Brown, 1984), pp. 128-32.

76. See, for example, the views of Hans J. Morgenthau on the consequences of U.S. intervention in the Third World, in his *A New Foreign Policy for the United States*, pp. 127-28; see also Fulbright, *The Arrogance of Powers*, pp. 67-157; and Gurtov, *The United States against the Third World*, pp. 201-17.

77. Useful introductions to the pragmatic mode of thought are Robert J. Mulvaney and Philip M. Zeltner, eds., *Pragmatism: Its Sources and Prospects* (Columbia, S.C.: University of South Carolina Press, 1981); David W. Marcell, *Progress and Pragmatism: James, Dewey, Beard, and the American Idea of Progress* (Westport,

Conn.: Greenwood Press, 1974); and Edward C. Moore, *American Pragmatism: Peirce, James, and Dewey* (New York: Columbia University Press, 1961).

78. The relevance of pragmatic thought for U.S. foreign policy is examined more fully in Cecil V. Crabb, Jr., *The American Approach to Foreign Policy: A Pragmatic Perspective* (Lanham, Md.: University Press of America, 1985); and in the author's *A Pragmatic World-View: American Diplomacy and the Pragmatic Tradition* (forthcoming).

79. The pragmatic idea that experience is the only reliable basis for determining or validating truth was a major concept in the views of the founder of the U.S. pragmatic movement, Charles S. Peirce. See C. Harshorne and P. Weiss, eds., *Collective Papers of Charles Sanders Peirce* (Cambridge, Mass.: Harvard University Press, 1931-35), 4 vols. Briefer discussion may be found in Moore, *American Pragmatism: Peirce, James, and Dewey*.

80. See William James, *A Pluralistic Universe* (New York: Longmans, Green, 1909); and Bernard Brennan, *William James* (New York: Twayne Publishers, 1968), pp. 131-33.

81. See William James, *Pragmatism* (New York: Longmans, Green, 1959), pp. 20-21, 45-58; his *The Meaning of Truth* (Cambridge, Mass.: Harvard University Press, 1975); and John Dewey, *Reconstruction in Philosophy* (New York: Henry Holt, 1920).

82. See, for example, President Harry Truman's views on the necessity for the containment policy in his *Memoirs: Years of Trial and Hope* (Garden City, N.Y.: Doubleday, 1956), pp. 100-9; in his widely-publicized defense of the containment strategy, George F. Kennan left no doubt that it was designed primarily as a response by the United States to the reality of Soviet expansionism and interventionism. See "X," "The Sources of Soviet Conduct," *Foreign Affairs* 25 (July 1947): 556-83; and for comparable views on Capitol Hill, see Vandenberg, *The Private Papers of Senator Vandenberg*, pp. 337-73.

83. See, for example, the growing anxiety by President John F. Kennedy and his advisers about growing Communist influence in Southeast Asia, in Roger Hilsman, *To Move a Nation: The Politics of Foreign Policy in the Administration of John F. Kennedy* (Garden City, N.Y.: Doubleday, 1967), pp. 97-159, 413-51; and in Sorensen, *Kennedy*, pp. 639-81.

84. The idea that U.S. public opinion is primarily influenced by the results of diplomatic efforts is emphasized in Daniel Yankelovich and Larry Kaagan, "Assertive America," *Foreign Affairs* 59 (Special Issue 1980): 703-4; in Ben J. Wattenberg, *The Real America: A Surprising Examination of the State of the Union* (Garden City, N.Y.: Doubleday, 1974), pp. 203-13, 283-300; and in the analysis of the concept of presidential popularity in John E. Mueller, *War, Presidents, and Public Opinion* (New York: John Wiley and Sons, 1973), pp. 196-241.

85. Paul Nitze, "Strategy for the Decade of the 1980s," *Foreign Affairs* 59 (Fall 1980): 100-1.

86. Viron P. Vaky, "Hemispheric Relations: 'Everything Is Part of Everything Else,'" *Foreign Affairs* 59 (Special Issue 1980): 643.

87. See former Ambassador Jeane Kirkpatrick's views, as quoted in Sigmund, "Latin America: Change or Continuity?" p. 631; and Christopher von Hollen, "Don't Engulf the Gulf," *Foreign Affairs* 59 (Summer 1981): 1071.

88. Henry Grunewald, "Foreign Policy under Reagan II," *Foreign Affairs* 63 (Winter 1984/85): 220-21.

89. Ernest van den Haag, "The Busyness of American Foreign Policy," *Foreign Affairs* 64 (Fall 1985): 116-17.

90. Terry L. Deibel, "Power Projection and U.S. Alliance Cohesion," in John H. Maurer and Richard H. Porth, eds., *Military Intervention in the Third World* (New York: Praeger, 1984), pp. 103-4.

91. Max Singer and Aaron Wildavsky, "A Third World Averaging Strategy," in Gregg and Kegley, *After Vietnam*, pp. 86-94.

92. Inis L. Claude, Jr., "The United Nations, the United States, and the Maintenance of Peace," in Gregg and Kegley, *After Vietnam*, pp. 255-56.

93. Secretary of Defense Caspar Weinberger's views are quoted in Fromkin and Chace, "What *Are* the Lessons of Vietnam?" pp. 729-730. See also the New York *Times*, July 23, 1985, dispatch by Bill Keller; the views of Senator Richard Lugar (Republican of Indiana), Chairman of the Senate Foreign Relations Committee, on the need for an acceptable rationale for U.S. interventionism, in the New York *Times*, January 24, 1985; and the views of former Secretary of State Cyrus Vance, that the United States should commit its armed forces abroad on a pragmatic basis, in his *Hard Choices*, pp. 91-92.

94. See the analysis of differing State and Defense Department viewpoints on the use of armed force in behalf of diplomatic goals by ex-Senator J. William Fulbright and Seth P. Tillman in the New York *Times*, December 9, 1984; and divergent viewpoints among President Reagan's advisers about the use of military force in responding to Libyan-based terroristic activities early in 1986, in the New York *Times*, January 12, 1986, dispatch by Bernard Weinraub.

95. Several studies have emphasized the crucial impact of presidential efforts to educate U.S. public opinion on foreign policy issues and the tendency of the people to follow White House guidance in dealing with external problems. See, for example, Bernard C. Cohen, *The Public's Impact on Foreign Policy* (Boston: Little, Brown, 1973); and the discussion of the Carter administration's successful effort to gain public support for the new Panama Canal Treaties, in Crabb and Holt, *Invitation to Struggle*, pp. 75-99.

96. See the retrospective analysis of the United States' role in the Vietnam conflict by Charles Mohr in the New York *Times*, April 30, 1985.

97. A different pragmatically based framework for determining the United States' vital interests in major regions of the world is offered in Donald E. Nuechterlein, *America Overcommitted: United States National Interests in the 1980s* (Lexington, Ky.: University of Kentucky Press, 1985), pp. 208-9; and see the discussion of changing public attitudes toward the government's response to international terrorism, in *Newsweek* 106 (July 15, 1985): 18-20.

APPENDIXES

Appendix 1

Washington's Farewell Address

The following excerpts from President George Washington's address on September 19, 1796, are taken from John C. Fitzpatrick, ed., *The Writings of George Washington from the Original Manuscript Sources, 1745–1799* (Washington, D.C.: Government Printing Office, 1940), 35:214–38.

Observe good faith and justice towds. all Nations. Cultivate peace and harmony with all. Religion and morality enjoin this conduct; and can it be that good policy does not equally enjoin it? It will be worthy of a free, enlightened, and, at no distant period, a great Nation, to give to mankind the magnanimous and too novel example of a People always guided by an exalted justice and benevolence. Who can doubt that in the course of time and things the fruits of such a plan would richly repay any temporary advantages wch. might be lost by a steady adherence to it? Can it be, that Providence has not connected the permanent felicity of a Nation with its virtue? The experiment, at least, is recommended by every sentiment which ennobles human Nature. Alas! is it rendered impossible by its vices?

In the execution of such a plan nothing is more essential than that permanent, inveterate antipathies against particular Nations and passionate attachments for others should be excluded; and that in place of them just and amicable feelings towards all should be cultivated. The Nation, which indulges towards another an habitual hatred, or an habitual fondness, is in some degree a slave. It is a slave to its animosity or to its affection, either of which is sufficient to lead it astray from its duty and its interest. Antipathy in one Nation against another, disposes each more readily to offer insult and injury, to lay hold of slight causes of umbrage, and to be haughty and intractable, when accidental or trifling occasions of dispute occur. Hence frequent collisions, obstinate envenomed and bloody contests. The Nation, prompted by illwill and resentment sometimes impels to War the Government, contrary to the best calculations of policy. The Government sometimes participates in the national propensity and adopts through passion what reason would reject; at other times, it makes the animosity of the Nation subservient to projects of hostility instigated by pride, ambition and other sinister and pernicious motives. The peace often, sometimes perhaps the Liberty, of Nations has been the victim.

So likewise, a passionate attachment of one Nation for another produces a variety of evils. Sympathy for the favourite nation, facilitating the illusion of an imaginary common interest, in cases where no real common interest exists, and infusing into one the enmities of the other, bertrays the former into a participation in the quarrels and Wars of the latter, without adequate inducement or justification: It leads also to concessions to the favourite Nation of priviledges denied to others, which is apt doubly to injure the Nation making the concessions; by unnecessarily parting with what ought to have been retained; and by exciting jealousy, ill will, and a disposition to retaliate, in the parties from whom eql. priviledges are withheld: And it gives to ambitious, corrupted, or deluded citizens (who devote themselves to the favourite Nation) facility to betray, or sacrifice the interests of their own country, without odium, sometimes even with popularity; gilding with the appearances of a virtuous sense of obligation a commendable deference for public opinion, or a laudable zeal for public good, the base or foolish compliances of ambition corruption or infatuation.

As avenues to foreign influence in innumerable ways, such attachments are particularly alarming to the truly enlightened and independent Patriot. How many opportunities do they afford to tamper with domestic factions, to practice the arts of seduction, to mislead public opinion, to influence or awe the public Councils! Such an attachment of a small or weak, towards a great and powerful Nation, dooms the former to be the satellite of the latter.

Against the insidious wiles of foreign influence, (I conjure you to believe me fellow citizens) the jealousy of a free people ought to be *constantly* awake; since history and experience prove that foreign influence is one of the most baneful foes of Republican Government. But that jealousy to be useful must be impartial else it becomes the instrument of the very influence to be avoided, instead of a defence against it. Excessive partiality for one foreign nation and excessive dislike of another, cause those whom they actuate to see danger only on one side, and serve to veil and even second the arts of influence on the other. Real Patriots, who may resist the intriegues of the favourite, are liable to become suspected and odious; while its tools and dupes usurp the applause and confidence of the people, to surrender their interests.

The Great rule of conduct for us, in regard to foreign Nations is in extending our commercial relations to have with them as little *political* connection as possible. So far as we have already formed engagements let them be fulfilled, with perfect good faith. Here let us stop.

Europe has a set of primary interests, which to us have none, or a very remote relation. Hence she must be engaged in frequent controversies, the causes of which are essentially foreign to our concerns. Hence therefore it must be unwise in us to implicate ourselves, by artificial ties, in the ordinary vicissitudes of her politics, or the ordinary combinations and collisions of her friendships, or enmities:

Our detached and distant situation invites and enables us to pursue a different course. If we remain one People, under an efficient government, the period is not far off, when we may defy material injury from external annoyance; when we may take such an attitude as will cause the neutrality we may at any time resolve upon to be scrupulously respected; when belligerent nations, under the impossibility of making acquisitions upon us, will not lightly hazard the giving us provocation; when we may choose peace or war, as our interest guided by our justice shall Counsel.

Why forego the advantages of so peculiar a situation? Why quit our own to stand upon foreign ground? Why, by interweaving our destiny with that of any part of Europe, entangle our peace and prosperity in the toils of European Ambition, Rivalship, Interest, Humour or Caprice?

'Tis our true policy to steer clear of permanent Alliances, with any portion of the foreign world. So far, I mean, as we are now at liberty to do it, for let me not be understood as capable of patronising infidility to existing engagements (I hold the maxim no less applicable to public than to private affairs, that honesty is always the best policy). I repeat it therefore, let those engagements be observed in their genuine sense. But in my opinion, it is unnecessary and would be unwise to extend them.

Taking care always to keep ourselves, by suitable establishments, on a respectably defensive posture, we may safely trust to temporary alliances for extraordinary emergencies.

Harmony, liberal intercourse with all Nations, are recommended by policy, humanity and interest. But even our Commercial policy should hold an equal and impartial hand: neither seeking nor granting exclusive favours or preferences; consulting the natural course of things; diffusing and deversifying by gentle means the streams of Commerce, but forcing nothing; establishing with Powers so disposed; in order to give to trade a stable course, to define the rights of our Merchants, and to enable the Government to support them; conventional rules of intercourse, the best that present circumstances and mutual opinion will permit, but temporary, and liable to be from time to time abandoned or varied, as experience and circumstances shall dictate; constantly keeping in view, that 'tis folly in one Nation to look for disinterested favors from another; that it must pay with a portion of its Independence for whatever it may accept under that character; that by such acceptance, it may place itself in the condition of having given equivalents for nominal favours and yet of being reproached with ingratitude for not giving more. There can be no greater error than to expect, or calculate upon real favors from Nation to Nation. 'Tis an illusion which experience must cure, which a just pride ought to discard.

Appendix 2

The Monroe Doctrine

The following excerpts from President James Monroe's Seventh Annual Message to Congress, December 2, 1823, are taken from James D. Richardson, ed., *A Compilation of the Messages and Papers of the Presidents, 1789–1897* (Washington, D.C.: Government Printing Office, 1896), 2:207–20.

At the proposal of the Russian Imperial Government, made through the minister of the Emperor residing here, a full power and instructions have been transmitted to the minister of the United States at St. Petersburg to arrange by amicable negotiation the respective rights and interests of the two nations on the northwest coast of this continent. A similar proposal had been made by His Imperial Majesty to the Government of Great Britain, which has likewise been acceded to. The Government of the United States has been desirous by this friendly proceeding of manifesting the great value which they have invariably attached to the friendship of the Emperor and their solicitude to cultivate the best understanding with his Government. In the discussions to which this interest has given rise and in the arrangements by which they may terminate the occasion has been judged proper for asserting, as a principle in which the rights and interests of the United States are involved, that the American continents, by the free and independent condition which they have assumed and maintain, are henceforth not to be considered as subjects for future colonization by any European powers.

. . . .

A strong hope has been long entertained, founded on the heroic struggle of the Greeks, that they would succeed in their contest and resume their equal station among the nations of the earth. It is believed that the whole civilized world take a deep interest in their welfare. Although no power has declared in their favor, yet none, according to our information, has taken part against them. Their cause and their name have protected them from dangers which might ere this have overwhelmed any other people.

The ordinary calculations of interest and of acquisition with a view to aggrandizement, which mingles so much in the transactions of nations, seem to have had no effect in regard to them. From the facts which have come to our knowledge there is good cause to believe that their enemy has lost forever all dominion over them; that Greece will become again an independent nation. That she may obtain that rank is the object of our most ardent wishes.

It was stated at the commencement of the last session that a great effort was then making in Spain and Portugal to improve the condition of the people of those countries, and that it appeared to be conducted with extraordinary moderation. It need scarcely be remarked that the result has been so far very different from what was then anticipated. Of events in that quarter of the globe, with which we have so much intercourse and from which we derive our origin, we have always been anxious and interested spectators. The citizens of the United States cherish sentiments the most friendly in favor of the liberty and happiness of their fellow-men on that side of the Atlantic. In the wars of the European powers in matters relating to themselves we have never taken any part, nor does it comport with our policy so to do. It is only when our rights are invaded or seriously menaced that we resent injuries or make preparation for our defense. With the movements in this hemisphere we are of necessity more immediately connected, and by causes which must be obvious to all enlightened and impartial observers. The political system of the allied powers is essentially different in this respect from that of America. This difference proceeds from that which exists in their respective Governments; and to the defense of our own, which has been achieved by the loss of so much blood and treasure, and matured by the wisdom of their most enlightened citizens, and under which we have enjoyed unexampled felicity, this whole nation is devoted. We owe it, therefore, to candor and to the amicable relations existing between the United States and those powers to declare that we should consider any attempt on their part to extend their system to any portion of this hemisphere as dangerous to our peace and safety. With the existing colonies or dependencies of any European power we have not interfered and shall not interfere. But with the Governments who have declared their independence and maintained it, and whose independence we have, on great consideration and on just principles, acknowledged, we could not view any interposition for the purpose of oppressing them, or controlling in any other manner their destiny, by any European power in any other light than as the manifestation of an unfriendly disposition toward the United States. In the war between those new Governments and Spain we declared our neutrality at the time of their recognition, and to this we have adhered, and shall continue to adhere, provided no change shall occur which, in the judgment of the competent authorities of this Government, shall make a corresponding change on the part of the United States indispensable to their security.

The late events in Spain and Portugal shew that Europe is still unsettled. Of this important fact no stronger proof can be adduced than that the allied powers should have thought it proper, on any principle satisfactory to themselves, to have interposed by force in the internal concerns of Spain. To what extent such interposition may be carried, on the same principle, is a question in which all independent powers whose governments differ from theirs are interested, even those most remote, and surely none more so than the United States. Our policy in regard to Europe, which was adopted at an early stage of the wars which have so long agitated that quarter of the globe, nevertheless remains the same, which is, not to interfere in the internal concerns of any of its powers; to consider the government *de facto* as the legitimate government for us; to cultivate friendly relations with it, and to preserve those relations by a frank, firm, and manly policy, meeting in all instances the just claims of every power, submitting to injuries from none. But in regard to those continents circumstances are eminently and conspicuously different. It is impossible that the allied powers should extend their political system to any portion of either continent without endangering our peace and happiness; nor can anyone believe that our southern brethren, if left to themselves, would adopt it of their own accord. It is equally impossible, therefore, that we should behold such interposition in any form with indifference. If we look to the comparative strength and resources of Spain and those new Governments, and their distance from each other, it must be obvious that she can never subdue them. It is still the true policy of the United States to leave the parties to themselves, in the hope that other powers will pursue the same course.

Appendix 3

The Truman Doctrine

The "Truman Doctrine" was contained in President Truman's message to Congress on March 12, 1947. Text in *Public Papers of the Presidents of the United States: Harry S. Truman,* 1947 (Washington, D.C.: Government Printing Office, 1963), pp. 176–80.

Mr. President, Mr. Speaker, Members of the Congress of the United States:
The gravity of the situation which confronts the world today necessitates my appearance before a joint session of the Congress.

The foreign policy and the national security of this country are involved.

One aspect of the present situation, which I present to you at this time for your consideration and decision, concerns Greece and Turkey.

The United States has received from the Greek Government an urgent appeal for financial and economic assistance. Preliminary reports from the American Economic Mission now in Greece and reports from the American Ambassador in Greece corroborate the statement of the Greek Government that assistance is imperative if Greece is to survive as a free nation.

I do not believe that the American people and the Congress wish to turn a deaf ear to the appeal of the Greek Government.

Greece is not a rich country. Lack of sufficient natural resources has always forced the Greek people to work hard to make both ends meet. Since 1940, this industrious, peace loving country has suffered invasion, four years of cruel enemy occupation, and bitter internal strife.

When forces of liberation entered Greece they found that the retreating Germans had destroyed virtually all the railways, roads, port facilities, communications, and merchant marine. More than a thousand villages had been burned. Eighty-five percent of the children were tubercular. Livestock, poultry, and draft animals had almost disappeared. Inflation had wiped out practically all savings.

As a result of these tragic conditions, a militant minority, exploiting human want and misery, was able to create political chaos which, until now, has made economic recovery impossible.

Greece is today without funds to finance the importation of those goods which are essential to bare subsistence. Under these circumstances the people of Greece cannot make progress in solving their problems of reconstruction. Greece is in desperate need of financial and economic assistance to enable it to resume purchases of food, clothing, fuel and seeds. These are indispensable for the subsistence of its people and are obtainable only from abroad. Greece must have help to import the goods necessary to restore internal order and security so essential for economic and political recovery.

The Greek Government has also asked for the assistance of experienced American administrators, economists and technicians to insure that the financial and other aid given to Greece shall be used effectively in creating a stable and self-sustaining economy and in improving its public administration.

The very existence of the Greek state is today threatened by the terrorist activities of several thousand armed men, led by Communists, who defy the government's authority at a number of points, particularly along the northern boundaries. A Commission appointed by the United Nations Security Council is at present investigating disturbed conditions in northern Greece and alleged border violations along the frontier between Greece on the one hand and Albania, Bulgaria, and Yugoslavia on the other.

Meanwhile, the Greek Government is unable to cope with the situation. The Greek army is small and poorly equipped. It needs supplies and equipment if it is to restore authority to the government throughout Greek territory.

Greece must have assistance if it is to become a self-supporting and self-respecting democracy.

The United States must supply this assistance. We have already extended to Greece certain types of relief and economic aid but these are inadequate.

There is no other country to which democratic Greece can turn.

No other nation is willing and able to provide the necessary support for a democratic Greek government.

The British Government, which has been helping Greece, can give no further financial or economic aid after March 31. Great Britain finds itself under the necessity of reducing or liquidating its commitments in several parts of the world, including Greece.

We have considered how the United Nations might assist in this crisis. But the situation is an urgent one requiring immediate action, and the United Nations and its related organizations are not in a position to extend help of the kind that is required.

It is important to note that the Greek Government has asked for our aid in utilizing effectively the financial and other assistance we may give to Greece, and in improving its public administration. It is of the utmost importance that we supervise the use of any funds made available to Greece, in such a manner that each dollar spent will count toward making Greece self-supporting, and will help to build an economy in which a healthy democracy can flourish.

No government is perfect. One of the chief virtues of a democracy, however, is that its defects are always visible and under democratic processes can be pointed out and corrected. The government of Greece is not perfect. Nevertheless it represents 85 percent of the members of the Greek Parliament who were chosen in an election last year. Foreign observers, including 692 Americans, considered this election to be a fair expression of the views of the Greek people.

The Greek Government has been operating in an atmosphere of chaos and extremism. It has made mistakes. The extension of aid by this country does not mean that the United States condones everything that the Greek Government has done or will do. We have condemned in the past, and we condemn now, extremist measures of the right or the left. We have in the past advised tolerance, and we advise tolerance now.

Greece's neighbor, Turkey, also deserves our attention.

The future of Turkey as an independent and economically sound state is clearly no less important to the freedom-loving peoples of the world than the future of Greece. The circumstances in which Turkey finds itself today are considerably different from those of Greece. Turkey has been spared the disasters that have beset Greece. And during the year, the United States and Great Britain furnished Turkey with material aid.

Nevertheless, Turkey now needs our support.

Since the war Turkey has sought additional financial assistance from Great Britain and the United States for the purpose of effecting that modernization necessary for the maintenance of its national integrity.

That integrity is essential to the preservation of order in the Middle East.

The British Government has informed us that, owing to its own difficulties, it can no longer extend financial or economic aid to Turkey.

As in the case of Greece, if Turkey is to have the assistance it needs, the United States must supply it. We are the only country able to provide that help.

I am fully aware of the broad implications involved if the United States extends assistance to Greece and Turkey, and I shall discuss these implications with you at this time.

One of the primary objectives of the foreign policy of the United States is the creation of conditions in which we and other nations will be able to work out a way of life free from coercion. This was a fundamental issue in the war with Germany and Japan. Our victory was won over countries which sought to impose their will, and their way of life, upon other nations.

To ensure the peaceful development of nations, free from coercion, the United States has taken a leading part in establishing the United Nations. The United Nations is designed to make possible lasting freedom and independence for all its members. We shall not realize our objectives, however, unless we are willing to help free peoples to maintain their free institutions and their national integrity against aggressive movements that seek to impose upon them totalitarian regimes. This is no more than a frank recognition that totalitarian regimes imposed upon free peoples, by direct or indirect aggression, undermine the foundations of international peace and hence the security of the United States.

The peoples of a number of countries of the world have recently had totalitarian regimes forced upon them against their will. The Government of the United States has made frequent protests against coercion and intimidation, in violation of the Yalta agreement, in Poland, Rumania, and Bulgaria. I must also state that in a number of other countries there have been similar developments.

At the present moment in world history nearly every nation must choose between alternative ways of life. The choice is too often not a free one.

One way of life is based upon the will of the majority, and is distinguished by free institutions, representative government, free elections, guarantees of individual liberty, freedom of speech and religion, and freedom from political oppression.

The second way of life is based upon the will of a minority forcibly imposed upon the majority. It relies upon terror and oppression, a controlled press and radio, fixed elections, and the suppression of personal freedoms.

I believe that it must be the policy of the United States to support free peoples who are resisting attempted subjugation by armed minorities or by outside pressures.

I believe that we must assist free peoples to work out their own destinies in their own way.

I believe that our help should be primarily through economic and financial aid which is essential to economic stability and orderly political processes.

The world is not static, and the *status quo* is not sacred. But we cannot allow changes in the *status quo* in violation of the Charter of the United Nations by such methods as coercion, or by such subterfuges as political infiltration. In helping free and independent nations to maintain their freedom, the United States will be giving effect to the principles of the Charter of the United Nations.

It is necessary only to glance at a map to realize that the survival and integrity of the Greek nation are of grave importance in a much wider situation. If Greece should fall under the control of an armed minority, the effect upon its neighbor, Turkey, would be immediate and serious. Confusion and disorder might well spread throughout the entire Middle East.

Moreover, the disappearance of Greece as an independent state would have a profound effect upon those countries in Europe whose peoples are struggling against great difficulties to maintain their freedoms and their independence while they repair the damages of war.

It would be an unspeakable tragedy if these countries, which have struggled so long against overwhelming odds, should lose that victory for which they sacrificed so much. Collapse of free institutions and loss of independence would be disastrous not only for them but for the world. Discouragement and possibly failure would quickly be the lot of neighboring peoples striving to maintain their freedom and independence.

Should we fail to aid Greece and Turkey in this fateful hour, the effect will be far reaching to the West as well as to the East.

We must take immediate and resolute action.

I therefore ask the Congress to provide authority for assistance to Greece and Turkey in the amount of $400,000,000 for the period ending June 30, 1948. In requesting these funds, I have taken into consideration the maximum amount of relief assistance which would be furnished to Greece out of the $350,000,000 which I recently requested that the Congress authorize for the prevention of starvation and suffering in countries devastated by the war.

In addition to funds, I ask the Congress to authorize the detail of American civilian and military personnel to Greece and Turkey, at the request of those countries, to assist in the tasks of reconstruction, and for the purpose of supervising the use of such financial and material assistance as may be furnished. I recommend that authority also be provided for the instruction and training of selected Greek and Turkish personnel.

Finally, I ask that the Congress provide authority which will permit the speediest and most effective use, in terms of needed commodities, supplies, and equipment, of such funds as may be authorized.

If further funds, or further authority, should be needed for the purposes indicated in this message, I shall not hesitate to bring the situation before the Congress. On this subject the Executive and Legislative branches of the Government must work together.

This is a serious course upon which we embark.

Index

About the Author

Cecil V. Crabb, Jr. was born in Clarksdale, Mississippi, July 18, 1924. He was awarded the A.B. by Centre College (1947); the M.A. by Vanderbilt University (1948); and the Ph.D. by Johns Hopkins University (1952). He served as a faculty member at Vassar College (1952–1968). Currently he is professor of political science at Louisiana State University (Baton Rouge), and he has been visiting professor at several other academic institutions.

He is the author of numerous articles and book reviews on U.S. foreign policy and international relations. His major books include: *American Foreign Policy in the Nuclear Age* (5th ed., 1986); *The Elephants and the Grass: A Study of Non-Alignment* (1965); (with Pat Holt) *Invitation to Struggle: Congress, the President and Foreign Policy* (2d ed., 1985); (with Ellis Sandoz) *A Tide of Discontent: The 1980 Elections and Their Meaning* (1981) and *Election '84: Landslide without a Mandate* (1985); *The Doctrines of American Foreign Policy: Their Meaning, Role and Future* (1982); and (with Kevin V. Mulcahy) *Presidents and Foreign Policy Making: FDR to Reagan* (1986).